THE HISTORY OF
Interior
Decoration

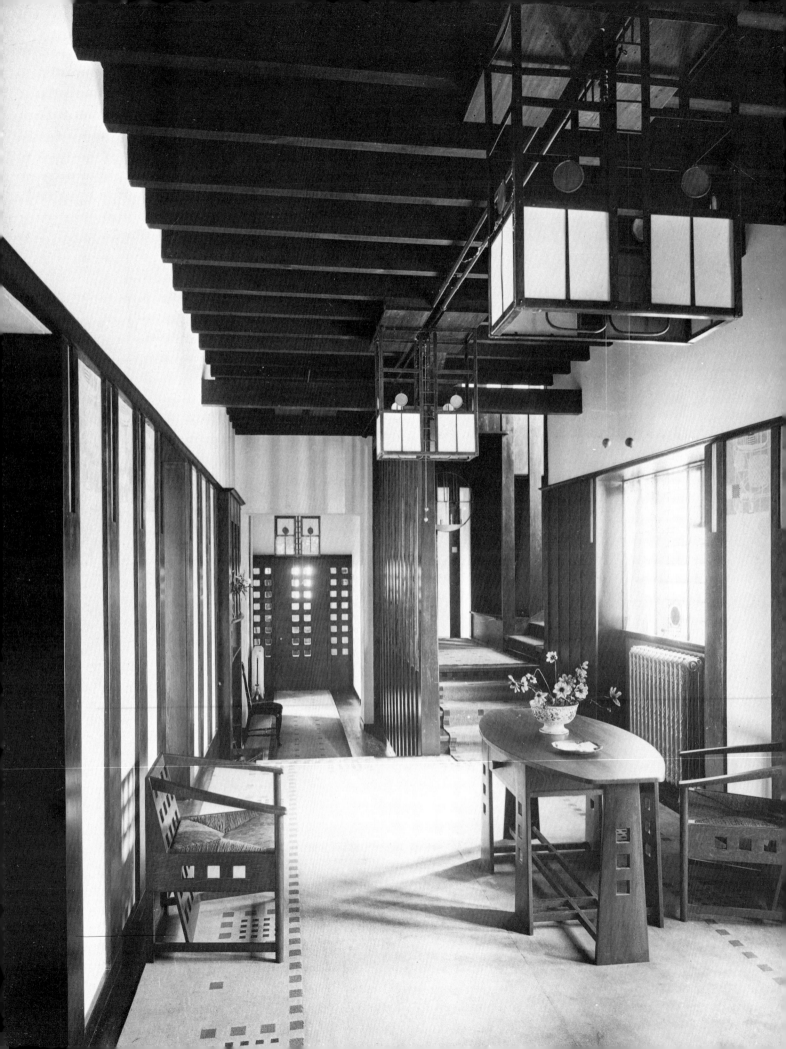

THE HISTORY OF
Interior
Decoration

Charles McCorquodale

Phaidon · Oxford

For Giorgiana and Filippo

First edition published in 1983 by
Phaidon Press Limited
Littlegate House, St Ebbe's Street, Oxford OX1 1SQ
Second edition (paperback) 1988

Published in the USA under the title *History of the Interior*

British Library Cataloguing in Publication Data
McCorquodale, Charles
    The history of interior decoration.
    1. Interior decoration—History
    I. Title
    645   NK2115
ISBN 0-7148-2560-3 (pbk)

This book was designed and produced by
John Calmann and King Ltd,
71 Great Russell Street, London WC1B 3BN

Designer: Gail Engert

Filmset in Great Britain by SX Composing Ltd, Rayleigh, Essex
Printed in Italy

1 *(frontispiece)* Hall of Hill House, Helensburgh,
by Charles Rennie Mackintosh, 1902

Contents

Foreword   6

1 The Classical World: Greece and Rome   9

2 Byzantium and the Middle Ages   29

3 Renaissance and Mannerism   55

4 The Age of the Baroque   85

5 Europe and the Rococo, 1700–1750   111

6 Neo-classicism   135

7 The Age of Revivals   165

8 Arts and Crafts   181

9 The Twentieth Century   199

Acknowledgements   220

Bibliography   221

Index   223

Foreword
to the second edition

When this book was first published in 1983 there was no other study of its kind, and to my astonishment this is still the case. In 1984, Peter Thornton's *Authentic Decor, the Domestic Interior 1620–1920* appeared, immediately becoming a classic and establishing itself as the *ne plus ultra* of reference books on furniture and fittings. However, it had never been my aim to write a study of the movable parts of the domestic interior, but to unite in one text all the elements from the disparate information available about what might be termed 'interior architecture'. Depressingly few interiors retain their original entity of interior architecture, attached fittings, movable furniture and other decorations such as pictures or tapestries. Thus the study of the shell and its former contents is too often of necessity carried out only through a painstaking reconstructive process – if either shell or contents survive. This is why Mario Praz's pioneering study, published in English as *An Illustrated History of Interior Decoration* in 1964, and Thornton's book both rely largely on contemporary illustrations to show what *was*, not what *is*. My book is largely concerned with what *is*.

Wherever possible, I selected illustrations which encapsulate a general point made in the text, and in some places this combination was well served by the inclusion of a painting, drawing or print of the period. Opposite a spectacular extant medieval chimneypiece in the House of Jacques Coeur the reader will see a reproduction of a Campin painting of *The Annunciation*, whose interior setting reproduces 'in little' the Bourges grandee's actual legacy (pages 36-7). Similarly, Sir John Soane's Breakfast Parlour in his London house is across the page from Clérisseau's Ruin Room design for the convent of the Trinità dei Monti (pages 156-7); at first sight this is a casual juxtaposition, but on reflexion it becomes clear that both are the product of nostalgia for the Antique and, more than that, they are both designed to cheat the eye and suggest infinite space where there is very little. This is also the reason for the inclusion, alongside well-known rooms, of others which are little-known or even unknown to many: into this category fall the Room of Apollo at Palazzo Grimani in Venice (Plate 55), Borromini's Palazzo Falconieri ceiling (Plate 75), de Wailly's breathtaking Palazzo Spinola interior (Plate 123), Boulanger's enchanting scene in the Pompeian

house of Napoléon III (Plate 140), the Hall of the Castello di Sammezano (Plate 143) and Gabriele d'Annunzio's study (Plate 162).

It is the aim of this book to outline, in as wide a context as possible given the limitations on space, the history of the delicate balance between 'architecture', 'design' and 'decoration' in the treatment of interiors. Dealing exclusively with domestic interiors, the survey covers, in all, twenty centuries. A certain amount of space is given to the discussion of important decorative schemes which are rarely, if ever, classified as interior decoration. This is particularly relevant in Italy, where, from the Renaissance onwards (although in a tradition going back to ancient Roman times), many of the major schemes of decoration are also the masterpieces of artists who by no stretch of the imagination could be classified as 'decorators'; Mantegna's Camera degli Sposi (Plate 44) and Pietro da Cortona's Pitti frescoes (Plate 73) in their astonishing stucco frames spring to mind. Not surprisingly, it was always in periods where the classical ideal retained its supremacy that internal architecture was the order of the day, while in periods where the antique became less significant, decorative elements gained the upper hand.

The concept of interior decoration as a creative entity within the visual arts is essentially a product of the present century; although the term 'interior decoration' makes its *début* with Percier and Fontaine's *Recueil de Décorations intérieures* in the Empire period, it is significant that its authors were, and remained, primarily architects. It is doubtful whether anyone without such an intensive training as theirs would have been considered able to tackle the decoration of an important room – the day of the decorator whose sole qualification was enthusiasm was still well in the future. The reason for this was that decoration only came to be regarded as divorced from architecture in the twentieth century. As was the case in each of the arts, an elaborate training was considered essential, which was why brilliant architects such as Robert Adam or Percier and Fontaine could not only design rooms of striking stylistic unity, but in doing so created major innovative works of art. In this age of mass production, can one name any architect capable of designing each facet of a room from the key-hole to the light-fittings and carpets in a wholly unified but forward-looking style? The sense of inventive exhaustion is never far away from that passion of the majority of today's decorators, the resuscitation of past styles.

The thorny question of the distinction between 'architecture', 'design' and 'decoration' is particularly difficult to resolve in the face of the attempt to integrate all three which is among the main aims of contemporary architecture, both external and internal. Whereas it was acceptable in the 1930s and 1940s to be a 'decorator', this term is shied away from by those at the top of the profession. They see themselves as 'designers', design being currently the most fashionable aspect of the visual arts. It is arguable that many of those who plan the adornment of pre-existing shells cannot by definition be anything other than decorators. The emphasis placed by many decorators on their training either as architects or designers is usually misplaced, since most of them have completely abandoned those disciplines. The designer of today shuns all the superficial echoes of past styles if he is committed to achieving genuine novelty; the decorator glosses over such difficulties with the superficial trappings of stylistic events from the past.

Many of the finest interiors of the past are the result of the closest collaboration between a major architect-designer and craftsmen whose manual skills have all but disappeared. It would be virtually impossible for architects of the calibre of Bramante, Le Vau or Adam to realize their designs now, which is one reason why conservation has become such a mania in our day. Since we cannot rival the skills of the past, we must preserve their products for posterity. The astonishing balance between inspiration, design and the craftsmanship necessary to create interiors such as those reproduced in Plates 91, 101, 119 and 122 finds no equals in the twentieth century, whose aims and needs are, after all, completely different.

The utilitarian aspect of so much twentieth-century interior decoration may, paradoxically, make it easier for the interior to aspire to the abstract condition of the 'major' arts than ever before; a fine Mies van der Rohe room (see Plates 180, 181) may not tell us as much about the concerns of twentieth-century life as Picasso's *Guernica*. Its formal relationship to, say, a Mondrian, on the other hand, shows that in many ways the formal language of this age extends more fluidly through all the arts than at any time since Classical antiquity. None the less, the important decorative schemes of the past often reveal as much about their period as do the fine arts. Louis XIV's interiors at Versailles are perhaps more revealing in historical terms than a painting by Poussin or a Racine tragedy, the rooms at the Hôtel de Beauharnais (Plate 137) more indicative of the First Empire's aspirations than a Canova sculpture and the Great Parlour at Wightwick Manor (Plate 155) more expressive of 'the Victorian dilemma' than a Pre-Raphaelite picture.

Robert de Montesquiou's claim, 'an apartment is a mood', encapsulates once and for all the superficiality of emotional experience which a room can convey. It is not surprising that such a statement, made at the end of the Romantic period, should have become the guiding theme of the writer J.-K. Huysmans in his book *À Rebours*, where his chief character is modelled on de Montesquiou, and in which he explores the emotive effects of colour in interior decoration. Contemporary Art Nouveau's deliberately *recherché* use of mauves, pinks and washed-out colours has no precedent in interiors. Colour-consciousness and the greatly increased variety of colours available to the twentieth century has played an important role in determining the direction of much contemporary decoration. A casual glance through any fashionable magazine on interior decoration reveals that one of the main concerns of today's decorators is to create particular 'moods' through colour, a preoccupation shared only marginally by the most subtle decorators of the past. The mind which conceived the *Studiolo* of Federico da Montefeltro in Urbino sought to create an environment conducive to intellectual activity. This was achieved not through colour but through the visually associative processes which form such an important part of so many decorative 'programmes' from the Renaissance onwards. Thus astrological and musical instruments figure in the decoration of the *Studiolo* because they were associated with the function of the room as a place for contemplation and study. Since we no longer use iconographical 'programmes' (other examples of such programmes illustrated in this book are the Room of the

Mysteries at Pompeii, the Salon de la Guerre at Versailles and the Camera degli Sposi in Mantua) to convey something about a room's occupants, we rely much more on colour and the amassing of interesting pieces to create individuality.

Apart from a few exceptions, I have deliberately refrained from discussing furniture in this book. I am the first to agree that in order to appreciate fully what rooms looked like during normal use one must be able to visualize their contents. Ideally one would like to know what pictures were hung against which fabric in conjunction with which *commode* or suite of chairs, what the carpets were like and where they were placed, what the curtains were made of and how they were tied back. But it is not possible in a book of this scope to pepper the text with such detail, and I hope the reader will find enough basic information to encourage him to make the necessary further investigations for himself. Every possible aspect of interior detail and furnishing is now receiving more serious attention than it had from what might have been termed the 'gimp and tassels' approach, and Peter Thornton's book, a deeply absorbing work of the highest academic quality, leads in this field. (Other titles of value to the scholar will be found in the bibliography, which has been expanded for the second edition.)

Even Thornton's study, thorough though it is, shows how wellnigh impossible it is to cover every aspect of the domestic interior in any detail. Until a vast amount of research into patronage, craftsmanship and the way in which interiors were assembled has been carried out, those illuminating generalizations which emerge only from vast knowledge of particulars cannot be made. Mario Praz's *Wunderkammer* of interiors in his history of decoration may never be rivalled for its sheer delight in the domestic interior as a social phenomenon; the original Italian title of his book – *La filosofia dell'arredamento* (The Philosophy of Furnishing) – tells us more accurately what his text is about. Perhaps by selecting that title, Praz, who knew more about the associative possibilities of inanimate objects than anyone, transcended the difficulties of interpreting domestic interiors as more than mere groupings of attractive components.

The late John Calmann first proposed the idea of my writing this history, and I hope that it will provide a general guide for those who wish to understand the evolution of the domestic interior from Classical times to the present day. While a very few plates show what might arguably be termed 'public' interiors, these are included only because they clarify aspects of private ones which are difficult to illustrate with better examples. For obvious reasons most of the examples chosen tend to be from the grander type of interior for it was here that the most important developments occurred.

Many friends and colleagues made countless valuable suggestions during the writing of this book. My very sincere thanks go to Dr I. Grafe, who at an early stage agreed to read and advise on my text as it emerged. At Calmann and King, a trio of ladies has staunchly supported me since the death of John Calmann: Elisabeth Ingles has alternately prodded and soothed me, demonstrating a patience surely unrivalled among publishers. Diana Davies has edited me with a sureness of touch and has throughout helped me to maintain an all-over view of the book which I believe has given it greater balance. Susan Bolsom-Morris has wrestled with what at times seemed insurmountable difficulties in obtaining the pictures I wanted, and has demonstrated a steely professional perseverance in her search for the best photographs. My profound debt to them is in effect posthumous thanks to John Calmann, who conceived the book and inspired me to write it. Finally, my thanks go to the staffs of the National Art Library and the Biblioteca Berenson at Villa I Tatti for their long-term help with source material at every stage of the book.

CHARLES MCCORQUODALE
London, January 1988

1

The Classical World: Greece and Rome

At last I can begin to live like a human being...

Emperor Nero on the completion of his Golden House
(from Suetonius, *The Twelve Caesars*)

The greatest artistic debt of the Western world has always been to the culture of ancient Greece and Rome. From the art of Imperial Rome evolved much of the imagery of early Christianity and Byzantium; even the medieval period owed many debts to the pagan past. The Renaissance, in reinstating the dignity of the individual, turned unashamedly to antiquity, seeking inspiration from many facets of classical life, moral, political and artistic. In the wake of the Renaissance, every artistic style until this century was more often than not judged by its degree of adherence to the supposedly absolute values of Classicism. In the eyes of post-medieval man, the arts of Greece and Rome had achieved perfection, from which any digression could only lead downwards. Even the wayward Baroque and Rococo styles continued to base their architecture on classical exemplars.

However, while architecture, painting and sculpture from the Renaissance aspired to the condition of antique art, interior decoration could not. The explanation for this is simple. Fresh examples of ancient architecture, sculpture and the decorative arts regularly came to light, either accidentally, or through systematic archaeological investigations, which became increasingly common in the wake of Renaissance curiosity. But many of the domestic interiors of the ancients, whether great or humble, remained concealed until the Renaissance had largely run its course, and it was only in the eighteenth century that the appearance of the Roman home could be seriously studied. It was also in the second half of the eighteenth century that Greek art *in situ* became better known, but again almost nothing survived of domestic interior decoration. Architects and designers in the Renaissance who prided themselves on their knowledge of ancient art probably knew almost nothing about the appearance of the fully evolved Roman interior, be it palace, house or country villa, and gave scarcely a thought to Greece. It was only a quirk of fate – the eruption in AD 79 of Mount

Vesuvius and the consequent preservation of the cities of Pompeii and Herculaneum under volcanic ash – which allowed posterity to see a virtually intact Roman interior at all.

Today, although we are better equipped to understand what ancient interiors were like in general, we still lack such precise evidence as exists for the medieval and subsequent periods. No pictorial record survives (if any ever existed) to show us a Greek or Roman interior of quality, complete with accoutrements of daily life, although furniture often appears in painting and sculpture as an adjunct to the principal concern of all Classical artists, the human body. For all their detachment from anecdotal detail, the great vase-painters and relief sculptors of Greece loved to depict furniture, but they never once show us a whole room. If only a great painter such as Zeuxis had left us a portrait of a Greek interior. Paintings which show the life of the gods, such as the *Courtship of Mars and Venus* from the House of Marcus Lucretius Fronto at Pompeii (Plate 10), tell us almost nothing of interior layout or decoration, although they reveal the Romans' bold use of colour.

The picture which we can build up of the evolution of domestic interior decoration from early Greek times to the end of the Roman Empire must of necessity be the result of a synthesis. Most of what survives *in situ* is found in Italy, although a little can still be seen in Greece. (No Greek domestic building of the Classical period of the fifth and fourth centuries survives above the lower wall-level.) These remains, together with fragments removed from their setting, and contemporary descriptions, can provide an adequate if not complete picture of the Classical interior. In certain instances, some important Roman interiors survived to be recorded in engravings or descriptions of the sixteenth to nineteenth centuries, such as Pietro Santi Bartoli's *Recueil de peintures antiques trouvées à Rome* of 1783. However, these were not always wholly reliable and many of the examples have subsequently perished; for example, in the five places where Giovanni Battista Piranesi indicated surviving stucco ceilings in the eighteenth century, only one remains intact today, plus a small part of another.

While ancient writers were naturally impressed by certain architectural monuments, they tended to describe an interior in detail only if it was of outstanding importance, as in the case of Suetonius's eulogy of Nero's Golden House (see below). One of the most meticulous of Roman authors, Pliny the Elder (AD 23–79), who compiled that breathtaking proto-encyclopedia, the *Natural History*, devotes disappointingly little space to describing the homes of even his most notable contemporaries. Although he considered the villa of Publius Clodius a worthy rival to the pyramids of Egypt, he declined to elaborate on this. He is nonetheless a prime source for information, more so perhaps than the more theoretical Marcus Vitruvius. Vitruvius was a practising architect who designed the Basilica at Fanum, and was roughly contemporary with the poet Virgil (70–19 BC). His chief claim to fame is his treatise on architecture, *De Architectura*, which encapsulates the thinking of many earlier theorists, mainly Greek. This treatise continued to be influential up to around AD 400, and was resurrected to become the principal manual of such Renaissance architects as Alberti and Palladio. Although Vitruvius regarded decoration as wholly subservient to function and fine proportion in architecture, he provides a considerable amount of information regarding the evolution of house types, and the techniques and materials used on interiors. Social and political historians in the ancient world refer to interiors only indirectly, when they expand the readers' consciousness of particular historical personalities. Surprisingly perhaps, in view of the dazzling luxury which prevailed in the homes of the rich from Hellenistic times on, many writers, including Pliny and Vitruvius, adopt a moralizing tone when speaking of conspicuous expenditure on decoration. This was often related to social stability in the Roman world. Pliny notes that Julius Caesar's chief engineer in Gaul, Mamurra, was 'the first man in Rome to cover with marble veneer whole walls of his house', and observes caustically: 'that such a man should have sponsored the invention is enough to make it utterly improper'.

There is a good reason for this apparent neglect of what might be termed the most complete of the luxury arts, and it stems from a positive rather than a negative aspect of Classical art. The term 'Classical' denotes a stylistic unity into which nothing extraneous intrudes and from which nothing can be removed without detriment to the whole. Such unity, and the absence from Greek and Roman thinking of our hierarchical division of the arts into 'major' and 'minor', precluded the recognition of a separate category for 'interior design'. Since the Classical elements of design and decoration pervaded every facet of the visual arts, no such divisions were feasible. The vocabulary of Classical ornament, while undeniably rich, was based on a few fundamental design concepts and extended from sculpted and painted ornament on architecture to decoration of every kind on walls, ceilings, floors, textiles, ceramics, metalwork and jewellery. This vocabulary was largely derived from natural forms. The human body, flora and fauna were either closely imitated (as in the case of caryatids) or abstracted. Many geometric patterns used throughout antiquity, such as the guilloche or wave motif, suggest natural origins. In the eighteenth century the French architectural theorist Abbé Laugier tried to account for the emergence of Classical architecture with his theory of 'the primitive hut' from whose tree members evolved columns, architraves and even the Orders – Doric, Ionic and Corinthian. It was the capitals on Corinthian columns which first featured the natural form of the acanthus leaf.

Every man-made form in the ancient world with any pretensions to design 'spoke' the same language. This gave a remarkable degree of unity to the visual arts, a unity which would seem monotonous to the twentieth century's diversified expectations. Such unity, however, produced principles of design and decoration which remained remarkably constant from the fifth century BC to the third and fourth centuries AD. The apparent simplicity of a fluted column (itself arguably based on the proportions of the ideal human body) was reflected in the fall of Classical garments. Both might bear the same decorative motifs – the so-called Greek key, palmettes, acanthus leaves and so on – which might also appear on wall-hangings, furniture and other artefacts. It was from this totality that the homogeneity of Classical interiors derived. Few later periods, with the possible exception of the Rococo and the twentieth century at its best, have aspired so unfailingly to such an ideal, although it was the constant dream of many designers. The nature of interior decoration as we too often conceive it today, separate and self-consciously 'stylish', is a reflection of our loss of such unity.

A further element which considerably enriched the domestic interior, especially in Roman times, was the very close connection between the principal elements in decorative schemes and aspects of everyday life, particularly religion. No subsequent Western civilization has allowed its religion to penetrate so pervasively into domestic life at every level, not only in the form of pictorial imagery, but also in the detail of furniture and other artefacts. Deities appear on lamps, toilet accessories, and eating utensils as much as on pavements, ceilings and walls. The lively murals of the Vesuvian cities abound in depictions of these deities whose role was much more domesticated for the Romans. Alongside images of the gods appear lifelike portraits of the owners of the houses in a conjunction so delightfully spontaneous that the elaborate iconographical programmes of the Renaissance and Baroque can appear leaden by comparison.

Although many features of the Roman domestic interior evolved from Greek prototypes, so eagerly sought out and copied by the Romans, the early Greek house would have seemed strikingly simple by comparison. The evidence for fixed mural, pavement or ceiling decoration in Greece is slight, but excavations in the ancient town of Olynthus near the Gulf of Toroni have revealed some surviving floors and the lower parts of walls.

The majority of pre-Hellenistic houses were boldly painted internally in one or more areas of colour, red being the favourite. Some idea of the effect of such interiors can be gained from the atrium of the House of the Bicentenary at Herculaneum, which has a simple black and white floor mosaic and red walls. In Greece, wall painting appears to have been executed in tempera on plaster using a binding medium. If the entire wall was painted, red would generally have been preferred, although there was often a dado area in white or yellow. Occasionally three equal horizontal bands of white, yellow and red ochre were used, and, increasingly later, the so-called 'structural' or 'Masonry' style appeared, as in the House of Dionysus at Delos. This style made use of plaster moulded in relief to imitate ashlar masonry and often painted in vivid colour; it finds its direct Roman echo in the First Pompeian Style of wall painting, and was described by Vitruvius as 'representing different kinds of marble slabs in different positions, and then cornices and blocks of yellow ochre arranged in various ways'. Pliny notes that even the greatest painters such as Apelles (court artist to Alexander the Great) used '... four colours only in their immortal works, white from Melos, Attic yellow, red from Sinope on the Black Sea, and the black called "atramentum"', and bemoans that 'now that even purple clothes our walls and India contributes the ooze of her rivers and the blood of dragons and of elephants, no famous picture is painted ... we are alive now only to the wealth of the material and not to the genius of the artist.' The fact that no other types of wall decoration in earlier Greek houses have been found does not prove that none existed, but we have no evidence to suggest that the kind of representational murals found in earlier civilizations like Crete were common later, in Greece.

Most of the houses found at Olynthus date from the fifth century BC, and bear out the descriptions of 'the Greek house' in Vitruvius. The floors of many Mediterranean houses consisted of nothing more than hard-packed earth on the ground floor with wooden flooring above if there was an upper storey. In poorer houses upper floors were made from clay spread over rushes laid across the joists, but in grander homes (such as the House of Hermes at Delos, where three of the original four storeys survive in part) wooden upper floors were occasionally found. Slate slabs were also used. Because the houses at Delos are Hellenistic, they represent the most mature architectural types in the pre-Roman world. Packed-earth floors, which we would regard as crude, were apparently not considered unfit settings for elegantly decorated walls and fine furniture, although it is probable that the Greeks evolved methods of disguising even the simplest materials. At Aegina, in what appears to have been a priests' house, the floor was painted or stained crimson, while the walls were painted a stark white with a red dado one metre in height. Such a dado, in red, white or yellow, seems to have been a constant of many interiors, and would have served as a perfect foil for furniture of exquisite delicacy. Allowing for artistic licence it is to the *Odyssey* and other Greek writings that we must turn for all-too-brief descriptions of what Homer termed 'lovely dwellings full of precious things'.

In the most ambitious houses at Olynthus are preserved what might be termed proto-mosaics. Mosaic, destined to become the essential feature of floors, walls and even vaults in rich Roman households, evolved with great rapidity in the Hellenistic period. The earliest mosaic examples consist of smooth pebbles, such as are found on river banks. Black and white predominate, with occasional examples in grey and red, and the most favoured pattern is a circle inscribed in a square, with the square outlined by waves or meanders and the circle enclosing a figure or decorative design. For the first time mythological themes appear in pavement decoration. Small fragments of broken quartz might be incorporated, with their flat surface uppermost to add sparkle, and minute pebbles could be added for greater detail. That such floor patterns echo carpet designs and placing seems undeniable, especially as they were often set within an undecorated border of concrete – an idea later evoked in Imperial Roman interiors, where such patterns occur on both floor and ceiling and may have a precise symbolism. By comparison with the sophisticated mosaics developed in Hellenistic times, the Olynthian ones are very simple. They use one pebble where advanced mosaicists might use fifty or more prepared *tesserae* (wedges or cubes of clay or marble, or even glass, with their smooth surface uppermost).

Many of the devices used in Hellenistic and Roman floor mosaics make their appearance in early Greece, such as the practice of outlining the position of important articles of furniture like beds or dining-couches (*triclinia*) in mosaic on the floor. With increasing ability in the handling of pebble mosaics, this technique was brought to a high level of competence, as in the superb coloured example from the capital of Macedonia, Pella (Plate 2), dating from about 300 BC and signed by the artist Gnosis. Using blue, brown and yellow pebbles along with the traditional black and white, this mosaic probably reflects contemporary developments in painting since it incorporates perfect perspective, depth, and the illusion of movement in the wind-swept cloaks. From such pebble mosaics, it was only a short step to the introduction of *tesserae* in the second half of the third century.

Pliny records the evolution of such flooring:

The Greeks were the first to introduce paved floors, which they decorated with painting until mosaic took its place. The most celebrated worker in mosaic is Sosos, who laid the floors of a

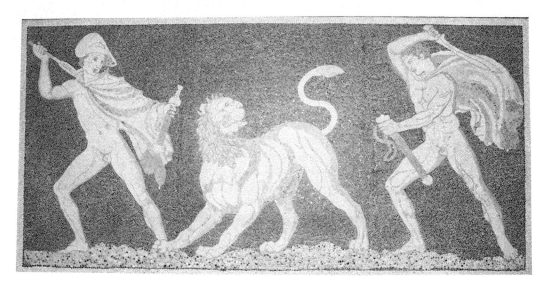

house at Pergamum, known as the *Unswept House*, because he represented in small pieces of many-coloured mosaic the scraps from the table and everything that is usually swept away, as if they had been left lying on the floor. Among these mosaics is a marvellous dove drinking and casting the shadow of its head on the water. Other doves are pluming their feathers in the sun on the tip of a goblet.

The fame of the dove mosaic is borne out by the number of copies which continued to be made well into Roman times. Techniques and applications are discussed below, but it is worth noting that by the first century BC three principal types of mosaic were in use: *opus segmentatum* (the coarsest variety), *opus tessellatum* of medium size and most commonly used, and *opus vermiculatum* using minute *tesserae* to convey the subtlest gradations of colour and tone as in painting. Although mosaicists often invented their own designs, there must have been considerable demand for reproductions of famous paintings through the medium of *opus vermiculatum*.

As in most hot climates, furniture was used sparsely, yet the quality of almost all surviving Greek furniture makes it clear that such restraint was the perfect foil for pieces of startling beauty. A number of furniture types were adopted from Egypt or the Near East, but the Greeks also evolved many of their own, and brought the art of furniture design to unprecedented levels of elegance and sophistication. Beds were now also used for reclining on while dining; most items in the Greek interior were seating furniture, often with extremely fine proportions and bearing inlays in many precious materials, or painted. Homer describes Penelope's chair in the *Odyssey* as 'inlaid with ivory and silver'. Upholstery did not exist, but great play was made with textile covers for the many cushions used on seating furniture. Since curtains often took the place of doors in the Greek and Roman world, these hangings assumed some importance in many interiors. (The potency for an Early Christian audience of the symbolic rending asunder of the great Temple curtain at the Crucifixion must therefore have been far greater than we can imagine today.)

Greek vases reveal the frequency with which fabrics of all kinds appeared on chairs, couches and walls; they were often suspended in arcades as they still are today. Women in Greek society passed much of their time in spinning and weaving – the story of Arachne and the goddess Athena in Ovid's *Metamorphoses* is a vivid illustration of this. Helen of Troy in the *Iliad* weaves 'many battles of the horse-taming Trojans and the brazen-coated Achaeans on a purple cloth of double fold'. The making of textiles was common to women at every social level and was regarded as a sign of household stability. Fragments of Greek cloth found in the Crimea show that designs were woven into the material or embroidered or painted on it. Not only decorative patterns appear but also historical or mythological events, anticipating Roman wall-hangings and medieval tapestries. We can only imagine the sumptuous effect of such fabrics, which Pollux describes in his dictionary, the *Onomasticon*, as 'delicate, well-woven, glistening, beautifully coloured, manifold, purple, dark green, scarlet, saffron, strewn with scarlet flowers, with a purple border, shot with gold, with figures of animals, with flowers of different colours, with gleaming stars . . .'

Initially, wool and linen were used and with the limitations imposed by animal and vegetable dyes the principal colours were very strong. Green, saffron, gold, violet and crimson were favourites. From an early stage, purple was associated with royalty, and Pliny calls it 'the colour of heaven'. Vitruvius, discussing colours, says that purple 'exceeds all those so far mentioned both in costliness and in the superiority of its delightful effect. It is derived from a marine shellfish.' Some fabrics were embroidered, using the complete repertoire of Classical motifs including scrolls, geometric designs and stylized animals; others were painted or decorated with a combination of techniques. A piece of linen in the Victoria and Albert Museum, London, possibly

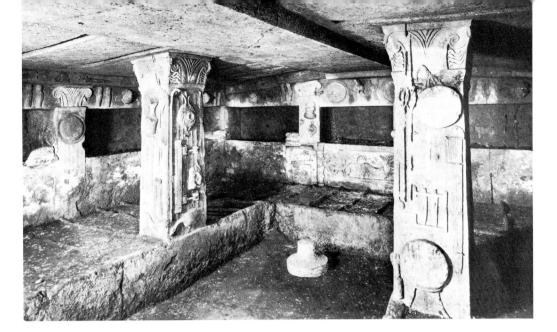

3 Tomb of the Capitals and Reliefs, *Cerveteri*

dating from as early as the eighth century BC and found at Koropi in Attica, is embroidered with a diaper pattern in silver-gilt with a walking lion in the centre of each unit. Couches are recorded with 'smooth Persian hangings' between the legs, indicating the importation of fabrics noted for specific characteristics. There is no doubt that such fabrics were used in decoration with superb skill, balancing elaboration with telling, simple areas as in the finest Athenian vases.

Although the Greeks differentiated between coverings for furniture (*stromata* or *hypostromata*) and wall-hangings (*parapetasmata*) as described in the inscription lists of the confiscated property of Alcibiades (450–404 BC), the range outlined by Pollux was probably used for both mural and other decorations. Their effect when seen against white or boldly coloured walls must have been impressive, if somewhat overpowering by modern standards. For a civilization which considered its architecture and statuary incomplete without extensive surface colour it was, however, quite appropriate. Such draperies were either hung flat against the wall or looped and gathered in bunches as in the Vatican sarcophagus showing Protesilaus and Laodamia. On occasion, multi-layered draperies of many different colours were used. Internal doors were rare in Greece, and curtains provided privacy (although the modern practice of firmly separating each room by doors, which evolved during the Middle Ages, would have amazed the ancients). Pollux describes 'curtains at the doors of bedchambers ... of various hues ... with beautiful designs of figures woven in them with great skill ...' In the court-yard houses of the Hellenistic world and Rome, they also provided much-needed draught-proofing. Even beds – the most important single article of furniture in Greek and Roman homes – were sometimes hung with 'embroidered bed-hangings on rings' according to Theophrastus.

Ideas were frequently borrowed from temporary structures. Thus the splendid canopies erected in gardens for *symposia* (learned banquets) later appear transformed and even more fantastic in Pompeian mural paintings, and their internal decoration seems to have mimicked in a lighthearted way the heavier developments of architectural interiors. One such structure, erected for the *symposium* of Ptolemy II in Alexandria, was described by Athenaeus over four centuries later (around AD 200): 'This pavilion contained 130 couches for guests and consisted of wooden columns ... set up at regular intervals ... upon these was set a square epistyle which held up the entire roof draped with a circular canopy, in scarlet edged with white ...' In the famous Nile mosaic from Palestrina, a similar structure is seen as an extension of a permanent building. It may be imagined that in such lavish canopies, both internally and out of doors, the supports were emblazoned with the same inlays which adorned other furniture, and were no doubt hung with many additional decorative features.

Ceilings in Greek houses appear to have taken their cue from developments in religious architecture, where coffering was extensively used. Since the arch was unknown to the early Greeks, all ceilings, such as those of major temples like the Athenian Parthenon, were basically flat or beamed in wood or marble. Pliny says that Pausios was the first to paint flat ceilings, and that before his time (fourth century BC) it was not customary to have painted decorative vaults, implying that, if architectural detail was not used, the ceilings were plain. Vitruvius, who devoted much attention to the various properties and regional origins of building materials, analysed the woods available to architects and noted that cedar was ideal for ceiling coffers because of its straight grain. Another attraction of cedarwood may have been its distinctive smell, particularly relevant in Classical interiors, where cloth hangings, textiles and clothes were often perfumed. In his recommendations for the perfect ('Greek') house type, Vitruvius suggests that the 'colonnades of peristyles [open columned courtyards] be decorated with polished stucco in relief or plain, and with *coffered ceilings of woodwork*'.

Since large trees were rare in Greece, the extensive use of wood in decoration carried connotations of wealth.

All the ideas evolved in Greece, especially under the impact of Hellenistic luxury, culminate in Rome, notably during the late Republic and Imperial times. Certain aspects of Roman life and art were inherited from the civilization of the Etruscans, who flourished in northern and central Italy between the eighth and fourth centuries BC. Although many Italian towns such as Orvieto, Volterra and Fiesole were originally Etruscan, the most important remains of their world are the magnificent tombs which they constructed in places like Cerveteri, Tarquinia and Chiusi. It is from these tombs that we can glean much information regarding the type of decoration which the Romans inherited from Etruscan patrician interiors, of which none survives. In tombs like the Tomb of the Lionesses at Tarquinia, of around 520–500 BC, are wall frescoes showing lively scenes of figures engaged in banqueting, dancing and wrestling, arranged in a continuous frieze and painted in limited tones of blue and brown. Also included are stylized plant and flower motifs, together with animals and birds. The tombs at Cerveteri near Rome show how Etruscan domestic architecture evolved from the seventh to the fifth centuries BC, during a period of local prosperity. Although strongly influenced by Oriental culture, particularly that of the Near East, the Etruscans were also susceptible to Greek art and it is probable that Greek artists and craftsmen were employed throughout Etruria. Thus there grew up a practice which accelerated during the supremacy of Rome: not only were many Greek works of art and ideas imported into Italy, but Greek craftsmen were eagerly sought out and employed by the Romans. In the Tomb of the Capitals and Reliefs at Cerveteri (Plate 3), we see fluted pilasters, Orientalizing capitals, stucco relief friezes showing weapons, helmets, vases, cups and animals. The ceilings are carved in imitation of beams with decorated areas between them. A fifth-century BC tomb at Chiusi retains its original stone doors, each cut from a single block. Like the Greeks, the Etruscans reclined on couches while dining, and their domestic surroundings may have been brightly coloured in a way combining both Eastern and Greek influences.

From around 616 BC Rome was ruled by Etruscan kings, but in 509 the Republic was established after the expulsion of the last Etruscan king. The simple, circular huts of the earliest settlements in Rome, on the Palatine and Campidoglio Hills, are recorded in the form of terracotta funerary urns, but these give no indication of the internal decoration which might be expected in a modest dwelling. After 275 BC, Rome was undisputed ruler of southern Italy, and with the defeat of Carthage in the Second Punic War (218–201) her empire advanced triumphantly east into Greece, Asia Minor and Syria. Rome's conquering of the Hellenistic kingdoms of the eastern Mediterranean was to have immense influence on the development of the arts, not least that of furnishing and decoration. Signi-

ficantly, among those destined to take the greatest advantage of the new trading possibilities were the inhabitants of Campania, the area of the Bay of Naples. Puteoli, the modern Pozzuoli, was the chief sea-going port of Rome, until Claudius (41–54) created an artificial harbour at the mouth of the Tiber, and Pompeii and Herculaneum lay close at hand on the opposite side of the bay.

It is from the Vesuvian cities of Pompeii and Herculaneum that much of our direct information comes regarding the Roman interior. A note of caution should be struck, however: Pompeian houses represent only one type of Roman domestic dwelling, the town house or *domus*, and show it at an advanced stage in its evolution. The other principal types are the palace, the villa – in the suburbs, in the country or by the sea – and the *insulae* or apartment blocks in cities. The *insulae* provided mass housing for the poorer classes and were often shoddily built and lacking in any form of comfort, sanitation or privacy, but there were also blocks of luxury apartments.

The Romans established finally the hierarchical divisions in domestic architecture which have prevailed to the present day. In town, a palace or house provided the base from which government, business or simply the pleasures of urban life were pursued; while a villa offered the delights of a rustic existence amid one's crops or vines, or with good fishing and swimming close at hand. Although the Imperial palaces of Rome were undoubtedly breathtaking in their splendour, the rich generally preferred to escape to their villas in the heat of summer, Augustus and Tiberius using the whole island of Capri as the setting for theirs. The refinements of these villas seem incredible even by modern standards, and Cicero attacks their shameless expense in his *Paradoxa*, as does Horace in several of his *Odes*.

As in the eighteenth century in France, when aristocratic taste demanded constant novelty, Roman taste advanced so quickly that it was easy for a villa to become *démodé* within a short space of time, despite the fortunes which were regularly spent on interior decoration. Pliny tells us that in 78 BC, the house of Lepidus in Rome was considered the finest of its age, but thirty-five years later it had not even kept the hundredth place in fashionable esteem. This would account for repeated remodellings of many interiors as taste changed, and one style replaced another, most notably in wall painting. Vitruvius, arch-defender of absolute standards, describes what we now regard as a progression in wall painting as 'The Decadence of Fresco Painting' in one of his chapter headings. The assumption of the title of Augustus by Caesar's heir Octavian, in 27 BC, marks the beginning for the rich of a period of luxurious living even more intensive than in the preceding century, when Hellenistic extravagance had become the norm in Roman architecture and decoration. Despite having 'found Rome all brick and left it all marble', Augustus' own taste was restrained, while that of his successors, the degenerate Tiberius, Caligula and Nero, was outrageously spendthrift. This ever-growing spiral of opulence culminated in Nero's Golden House, which is discussed below.

A visitor to Pompeii in the middle of the first century AD would have found a much greater number of conspicuously large, well-appointed houses belonging to the affluent than we are used to seeing in cities today. The fully developed 'Pompeian house' stands midway between the early Italic variety with a large hall and the complex ground plans of the houses and palaces of the rich in Imperial Rome. From the second century BC examples like the House of Sallust, with its inward-looking aspect centred on a large *atrium* courtyard topped by a sloping roof opening (*compluvium*) to lead rainwater down into the basin (*impluvium*) for household use, the Pompeian house developed to a larger scale, incorporating a peristyle or courtyard garden. Examples of the latter are the House of the Vettii or the House of the Menander. Basically, these houses consisted of an entrance porch (*vestibulum*), followed by a short corridor (*fauces*), and on either side of the *atrium*, small, square bedchambers (*cubicula*). In these, as we have seen, the outline of the couch would often appear marked on the floor and occasionally on the ceiling. Directly ahead lay the principal reception room of the house, the *tablinum*, separated from the *atrium* by a curtain or wooden screen and taking advantage of the garden (*hortus*) beyond with a window, a feature not found in many of the other rooms. To one side was the dining room (*triclinium*), so named from the placing at right angles of the three dining-couches or *klinai*. Only much later did upper storeys begin to appear on the street front, and these could incorporate windows omitted from the ground floor for safety and sound insulation. Many variants on this pattern occur, but it was within these rooms that most of the decoration which concerns us was found. Villas such as those on the slopes of Vesuvius (see Plate 13) or the *villae maritimae* on the coast where architectural caprice resulted in advancing and receding wings, galleries, porticoes and domes, had more open plans to ensure a good view. Vitruvius distinguishes firmly between private and public rooms:

The private rooms are those into which nobody has the right to enter without an invitation, such as bedrooms, dining rooms, bathrooms. The common rooms are those which any of the people have a right to enter even without an invitation: that is, entrance courts, peristyles ... hence, men of everyday fortune do not need entrance courts, *tablina*, or atriums built in the grand style, because such men are apt to discharge their social obligations by going round to others rather than having others come to them.

From the simplest to the most complicated construction and decoration, Vitruvius gives sound advice, which relates to much that is found in Pompeii and Herculaneum. 'Lay the floor,' he advises, 'either of large cubes or burnt brick in herring-bone pattern, and floors thus constructed will not be spoiled.' This refers to the *opus spicatum* type

of flooring called 'wheat-ear' by Pliny, because the pattern recalled the arrangement of grains in an ear of wheat. Pliny also describes 'Greek' flooring, which was commonly used in place of brick or mosaic, as in dining rooms, where its properties of absorption and warmth for servants' bare feet were valued:

The ground is well rammed and rubble or a layer of pounded potsherds laid on it. Then charcoal is trodden into a compact mass, and on top of this is spread a mixture of coarse sand, lime and ashes to a thickness of six inches. This is carefully finished to rule and level, and has the appearance of earth. But if it is smoothed with a grindstone it will pass for a black-stone floor.

Such a 'black-stone floor' would have been made with lava cement coloured with charcoal dust, into which were sometimes set marble fragments in decorative patterns, an inexpensive way of obtaining a moderately rich effect. Terracotta (*opus signinum*) – still widely used for floor tiles in Italy – was also popular and could be easily decorated with various patterns.

With the expansion of Roman artistic horizons through contact with Hellenism, a wide variety of materials came into use for flooring – materials which we now regard as the height of luxury, such as mosaic and marble of all kinds. Suetonius says that Caesar transported whole mosaic pavements with him during his campaigns, and records the general astonishment that Augustus' house on the Palatine was internally 'without any marble decoration or handsome pavements'. Although Pliny singled out Caesar's friend Mamurra as the first to apply marble in domestic interiors, it seems that the practice had already been current in the second century BC. From that period dates the House of the Faun at Pompeii, from which the famous Alexander Mosaic (Plate 4) comes. Throughout houses of this degree of pre-Roman Hellenistic elegance a variety of different pavements appear to have been laid; in the House of the Faun, for example, are also found fragments of coloured volcanic glass set into cement floors along with pieces of limestone, while lava cement is used in the *atrium*. One of the house's most attractive features is the unity achieved through the use of mosaics with widely differing designs of great beauty, contrasting with the restraint of the stucco wall decorations in relief.

Apart from representations of deities, animals (including delightful surprises like the fish mosaic from Pompeii showing edible sea creatures (Plate 5), now in Naples), birds, masks, portraits and other themes, many mosaics had complex astrological and other esoteric subject matter. There was generally a precise relationship between pavement and ceiling design, especially in Imperial interiors, and an iconographical programme referring to the patron must often have existed (see below). Sometimes, as in the case of the fish mosaic, pictorial mosaics of particular beauty made of *opus vermiculatum*, which were regarded as show pieces, might be set in the middle of *opus tessellatum*. Such pieces are called *emblema*.

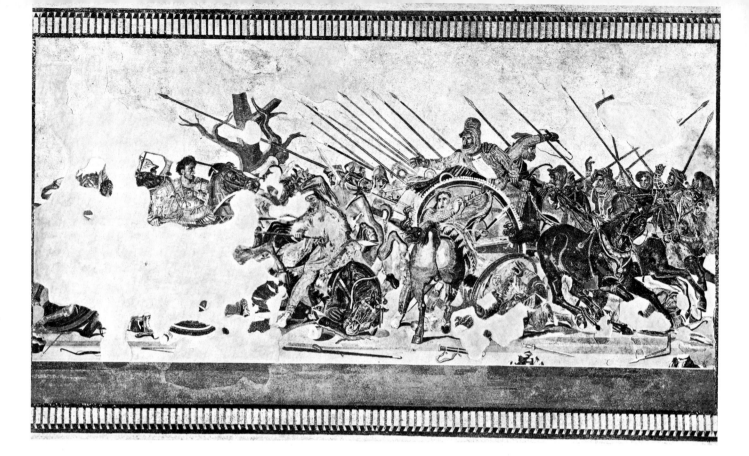

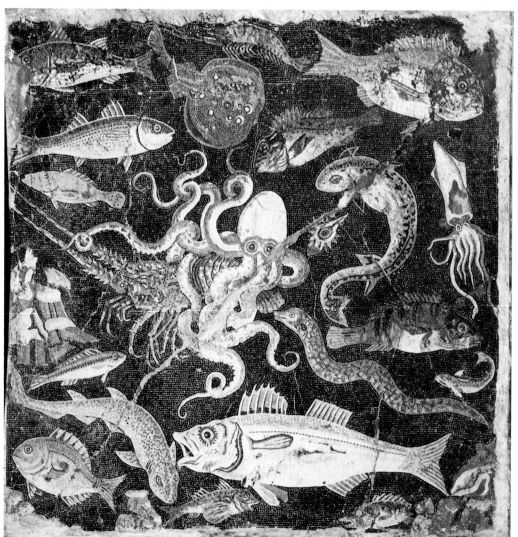

4 *(above)* The Battle of Issus. *Mosaic, second to first century* BC. *Naples, Museo Archeologico Nazionale   Probably deriving from a late-fourteenth-century* BC *painting, this is perhaps the most impressive pictorial mosaic to have survived from Roman times. It is a huge extension of the small type of highly sought-after pictorial mosaic called* emblemata, *often bought as a work of art in its own right and set into decorative schemes. Created out of thousands of minute tesserae by craftsmen of great skill, it celebrates Alexander's victory over Darius. The four colours – black, white, yellow and red – convey a sense of depth as well as drama*

5 *(left)* Fish mosaic from Pompeii. *Before 79* AD. *Naples, Museo Archeologico Nazionale*

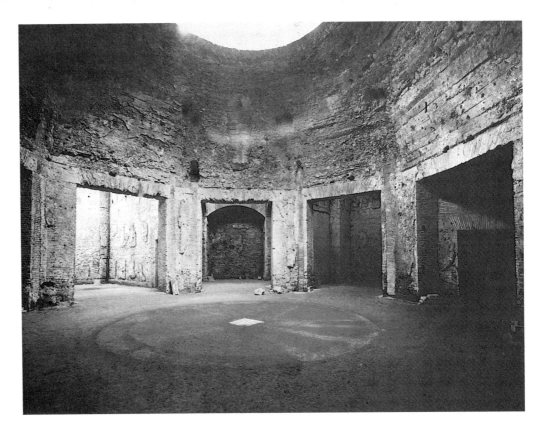

6 The Octagon, Golden House of Nero (*Domus Aurea*), Rome *This complex structure with its skilful lighting from above gives some idea of the subtle and complex internal architecture of the Golden House, which provided the setting for costly mosaics and painting, as well as for intricate mechanical devices. It was here that the Laocoon group was discovered in 1506*

The use of coloured marbles for columns and pavements was obviously confined to the rich, and was a distinctive feature of the great palaces and villas. During the reign of Augustus, the importation of foreign marbles increased considerably, and in Italy itself the quarries at Carrara (Luni) were opened. In Rome, both white and coloured marble wall and floor revetment in major public buildings was a commonplace by the turn of the first century AD. Porphyry, with its characteristic crystals of white or red feldspar in a dark red ground-mass, and granite were the most commonly used, while the most sought-after rarer marbles came from Egypt and the Aegean. Many pieces of marble were roughed out before transport, and had only to be completed and polished on arrival to make mouldings, sheets or columns of various sizes – from the gargantuan eighty-four-ton red and grey Egyptian granite ones of the Pantheon to smaller ones for domestic interiors. One ton of marble could provide around one hundred square yards of wall revetment or between thirty-five and forty-five square yards of paving.

In the Augustan period straightforward geometrical designs of contrasting colours had been favoured, which respected the proportions of the interior and enhanced the architecture. By the time of Nero's *Domus Transitoria* (which preceded his *Domus Aurea* – Golden House – and was completed in the early 60s) the art of paving with marble had reached a high level of skill: a wide variety of marbles was used, and the patterns were richly inventive. Shaped tiles of coloured marble, known as *opus sectile*, were also common. A hundred years later, marble paving

patterns often had little connection with the interior architecture and were used for their own effect. We have noted Pliny's disapproval of marble-lined walls, yet these were the norm by Nero's time not only in bathrooms but throughout domestic interiors. Pliny describes 'six celebrated monochrome pictures in red on white marble slabs let into the wall', and many works of art of considerable importance must have been exhibited in this way. Because of their permanent stucco setting, Caligula was frustrated in his desire to have 'two nude figures of Atalanta and Helen by Ekphantos of Corinth, both of great beauty, which he would undoubtedly have removed if the composition of the stucco had allowed of it.'

Apart from marble, the other resilient and durable type of mural decoration which gained enormously in popularity in the first century AD was mosaic. In a letter of 64 AD, Seneca warns that it is most unfashionable to be without wall mosaic! The Romans made a distinction between pavement mosaic and mosaic on walls and vaults. Floor mosaic was referred to as *lithostratum* or *tessellatum*, and was created by craftsmen known as *tessellarii*, while wall or vault mosaics may have had no specific name but were referred to as *opus musivum*. These were made by *musivarii*, and their evolution was intimately associated with the major architectural development of the period – concrete construction.

Great inventiveness went into finding new materials suitable for increasingly elaborate walls and vaults. Although glass *tesserae* appear at Delos long before Imperial times, Tiberius was among the first Romans to use them

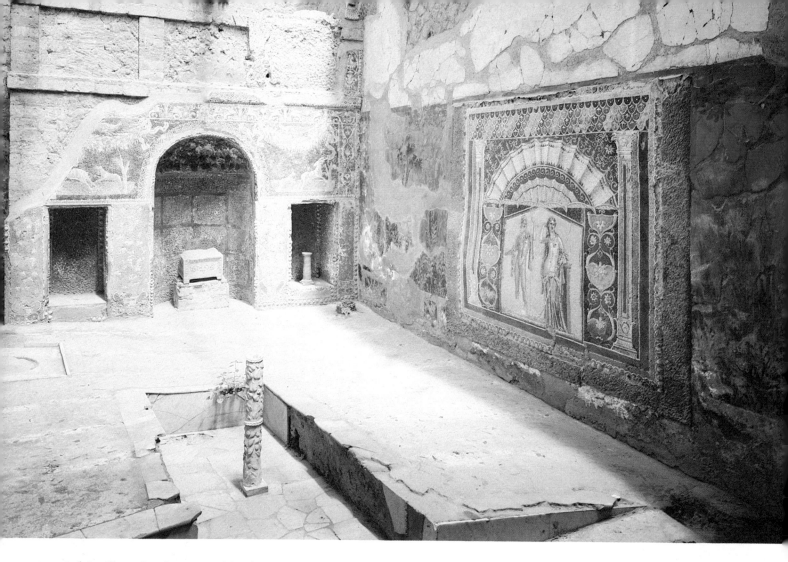

in his villa at Sperlonga, and by the second century Lucian describes baths as 'glass houses'. Glass mosaic, especially when combined with gold or colour, gave a glittering effect which further enhanced the new vault shapes made possible by concrete, blurring transitions from one zone to another. Thus it was naturally favoured for the most sophisticated interiors such as the Golden House, where gold glass mosaics made one of their earliest appearances, on vaults like that of the octagon (Plate 6). Their luxurious effect can be gauged from the domed vestibule of Diocletian's palace at Split (Spalato) and the Serapeum of Hadrian's villa at Tivoli.

Other materials used included twisted glass rods in yellow, white or blue, glass discs, broken glass vessels, mica and other minerals, pumice (as in the Golden House vault, with mosaic medallions set in a pumice ground) and shells, particularly pointed whelks and cockles. Egyptian blue, a pigment made by firing at 850°C a paste of silica, a copper compound (usually malachite), calcium carbonate and natron, was also very popular; Vitruvius calls this *caeruleum* and says it was invented at Alexandria. It was used extensively at Hadrian's Villa, where other imaginative inventions appear, such as the use of white marble chips set into plaster, brightly painted red, blue,

7 (*above*) Wall mosaics from the House of Neptune and Amphitrite, *Pompeii*

8 (*right*) Wall paintings from the Villa of the Mysteries, *Pompeii. c. 50 BC   It is not known whether these high-quality paintings in a villa outside Pompeii are by a Greek or a southern Italian painter; their mysterious theme appears to be an initiation rite. Mortals and immortals appear together in an elegant frieze, which is superbly related to the shape and proportions of the room. Such an interest in 'expanding' real space with illusionistic devices became increasingly characteristic of Roman interiors from the Augustan period onwards*

yellow or green. Wall mosaic was not only applied over large areas, but could also be used for individual sections of decoration. A group of eight mosaic pilasters were found at Hadrian's villa, and a number of columns were completely covered with mosaic. At Pompeii, many mosaics were carefully positioned so as to be visible from the front door of houses, such as the House of the Grand Duke, and at Herculaneum the House of Neptune and Amphitrite (Plate 7). This shows the prestige attached to owning fine mosaics and also the Romans' love of spatial and colouristic variety – since the eye would reach the

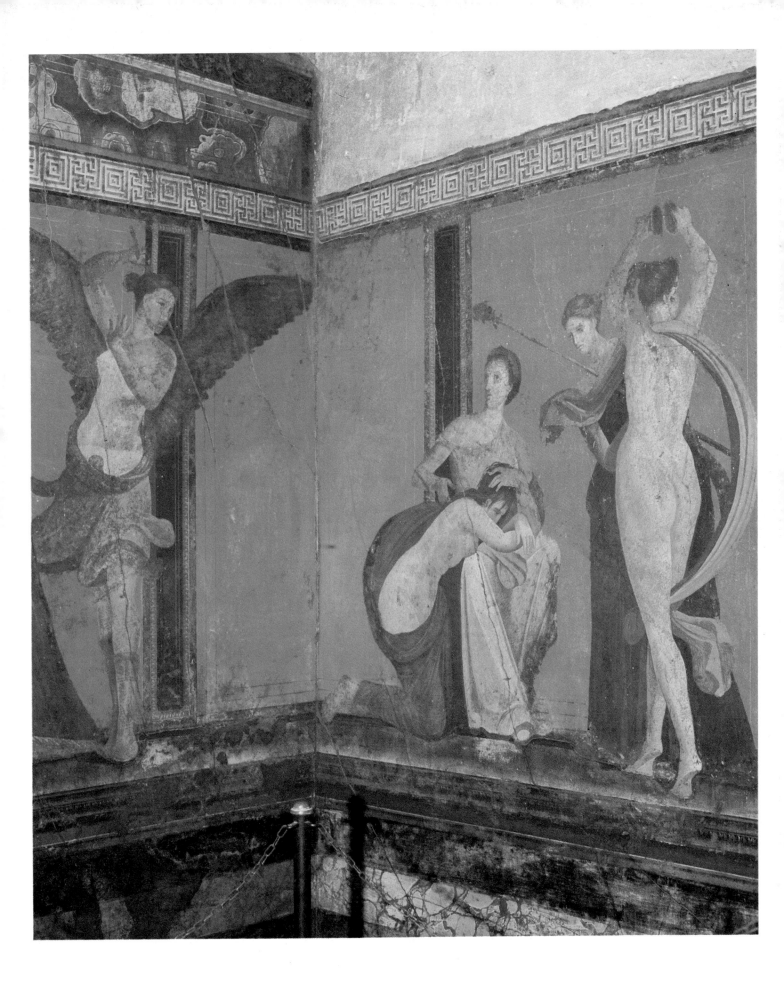

brilliantly lit mosaic through strongly contrasting areas of light and shade, reminiscent of the interiors of the huge Roman public baths.

The greatest degree of attention has always been focused on the wall paintings of the ancient Romans, and their various transformations provide some of the most beautiful and original interior decoration of any period. It is probable that fine Etruscan residences had inherited the Greek practice of painting a simple, colourful dado around the entire room, which they elaborated with continuous bands of decoration like the wave pattern found in a tomb at Ardea, of about 300 BC. We have seen that the Greek 'Masonry' style (Plate 9) was known throughout the Greek world from the fourth century BC onwards; practised in Sicily by the third, it was probably used in Rome and Pompeii by the early second century and is known as the First Pompeian Style (or Incrustation Style). Until the middle of the first century AD few Pompeian houses had windows larger than slits in the wall, and Seneca, who died in 65 AD, claims that the introduction of window-glass occurred only within his lifetime. The amount of wall space left for decoration was therefore considerable, especially in rooms with only one small doorway, and the small size of the windows must have contributed to the desire to extend space through the use of illusionistic paintings with simulated architecture.

Shortly after 80 BC, when Pompeii became a Roman colony, the Second Pompeian or 'Architectural' Style began to appear (Plate 9). The first Pompeian Style emphasized the flat, structural nature of the wall, but the subsequent three 'Pompeian Styles' increasingly broke down the division between reality and illusion, creating *trompe-l'œil* effects. At first, the Second Style placed the wall surface behind an illusionistic screen of painted columns on a plinth, supporting a cornice below ceiling level. Then, around the mid-first century BC, the upper part of the wall was 'opened' to the sky as if one were in a garden room, as in some rooms of the Villa of the Mysteries (Plate 8). The *cubiculum* from a villa at Boscoreale is a fully evolved example of this (Plate 11). The Boscoreale room shows how the Second Style's fictive architecture faithfully followed the room shape, and it was against this that the last phase of the style reacted. Now, the architecture became independent of its setting, and consisted of a build-up of separate units, often framing decorative figures, scenes or motifs. It was this fantastic element which was to dominate the subsequent development of Roman painting, but it should be recalled that many of the apparently capricious structures were probably based on real architectural prototypes. In the frescoes from the Villa of

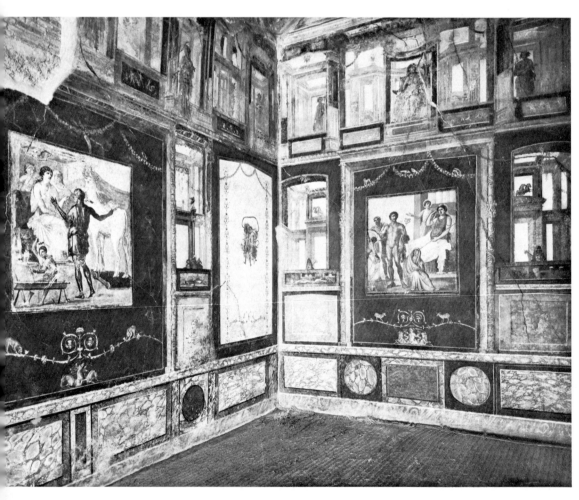

9 Ixion Room, House of the Vettii, *Pompeii. First century* AD *This room in the house of a rich merchant combines the Four Styles of Pompeian wall painting: above the dado of simulated marble panels are set pictures in simulated three-dimensional frames through which we glimpse light architectural structures beyond. Above, statues are set against further views, as it were, into real space outside. These wall and ceiling paintings were among the first examples of* trompe l'oeil

Publius Fannius Sistor at Boscoreale, for example, three large painted doorways form the centre of elaborate architecture, and in the recently excavated villa at Oplontis there is a tantalizing glimpse through an ornate screen of columns to a porticoed courtyard with a circular *tempietto* in its midst.

It is worth quoting one of Vitruvius' most critical passages at length since it gives us an exactly contemporary account of this development. He says that, after the 'Masonry' (or First Pompeian) Style, the ancients

... made such progress as to represent the forms of buildings and of columns, and projecting and overhanging pediments; in their open rooms such as exedrae, on account of the size, they depicted the façades of scenes in the tragic, comic or satyric style, and their walls, on account of their great length, they decorated with a variety of landscapes, copying the character of definite spots. In these paintings there are harbours, promontories, seashores, rivers, fountains ... in some places there are also pictures designed in the grand style with figures of the gods or detailed mythological episodes, or the battles at Troy or the wanderings of Ulysses with landscape backgrounds ... from real life.

But these subjects, which were copied from actual realities, are scorned in these days of bad taste. We now have fresco paintings of monstrosities, rather than truthful representations of definite things. For instance, reeds are put in the place of columns, fluted appendages with curly leaves and volutes instead of pediments, candelabra supporting representations of shrines, and on top of their pediments numerous tender stalks and volutes growing up from the roots and having human figures senselessly seated upon them; sometimes stalks having only half-length figures, some with human heads, others with the heads of animals.

Pliny credits Studius, 'a painter of the days of Augustus', with the introduction of 'a delightful style of decorating walls with representations of villas, harbours, landscape gardens, sacred groves, woods, hills, fishponds, straits, streams and shores, any scene in short that took the fancy'. Perhaps the finest examples of such scenes of the Second Style are the Garden Room from the Villa of Livia (Plate 12), where the garden almost invades the room, and the 'Odyssey Landscapes' illustrating Homer, from a villa on the Esquiline Hill in Rome and now in the Vatican Museums. The style which so displeased Vitruvius was therefore the last phase of the Second Style, and early Third. (Had he survived, the Fourth (Plate 9) would surely have enraged him.) Unlike its predecessors, the Third Style made no attempt to extend real space with an illusion of three-dimensional architecture. Instead, it concentrated on providing the most refined framework for pictures of every conceivable kind. This framework evolved from Second Style fantasy architecture, but was now reduced to the role of little more than a continuous trellis supporting decorative devices. These include elegant foliage arabesques, delicate candelabra, trailing tendrils, masks suspended on silken cords, and abstract motifs of all kinds – precisely the type of irrational design con-

demned by Vitruvius. There was also an increased attention to dominant areas of colour providing the perfect foil for the minutely detailed surrounding decorations. This colour was used with skill to emphasize the verticality of the patterns used, as in the *oecus* of the House of Menander at Pompeii. Here, there is a black dado, a green middle zone with black uprights and a white upper zone, all meticulously calculated in terms of colour balance, proportion and overall effect.

The earliest Third Style paintings in Rome are found in a villa in Trastevere, the Farnesina Villa, which may have belonged to M. Vipsanius Agrippa, Augustus' heir designate, who probably knew Pompeian painting at first hand. These document the transition from the Second to the Third Style, which occurred about 15 BC, and coincide with the formal court classicism of much of Augustus' taste. A late example of the Third Style is the *tablinum* frescoes in the House of M. Lucretius Fronto at Pompeii (Plate 10), out of which the Fourth Style grew. Since evolving taste often occasioned the replacement of the earlier styles as they went out of date, the Fourth (current at Pompeii's destruction in AD 79) is well repre-

10 House of M. Lucretius Fronto, *Pompeii. Before 79* AD

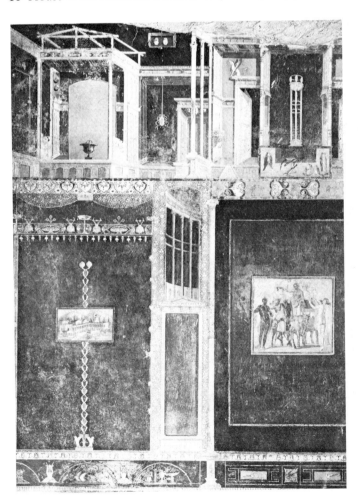

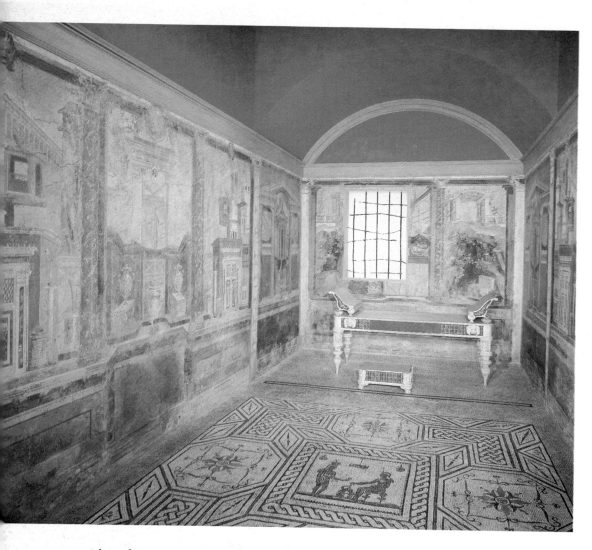

11 *(left)* Cubiculum from Boscoreale. *c. 50* BC. *New York, Metropolitan Museum of Art*

12 *(right)* Garden Room from the House of Livia. *First century* BC. *Rome, Museo Nazionale Romano The villa from which these delightful frescoes came was supposed to have belonged to Livia, wife of the Emperor Augustus. The freedom with which the artist has depicted the 'view' into the garden recalls Pliny's description of the work of the artist, probably Studius Ludius, who created '... landscape gardens, sacred groves, woods, hills, ... rivers and shores – any scene in short that took the fancy'*

sented in the Vesuvian cities. It was also the style most favoured by Nero. Pompeian examples include the House of the Red Walls, the House of the Centenary, and the House of Julius Polybius, which show the tendency to cover the entire wall with one colour as background to a network of linear and other motifs, or to offset rooms of one colour against those of another, as in the 'black' and 'white' rooms of some houses. The interpenetration of elements of one style with those of another sometimes makes precise categorization difficult.

Pliny affirms that 'No artists ... enjoy a real glory unless they have painted easel pictures.' Not one of these easel pictures survives, although they were probably painted on panel, or on canvas as in the case of the 120-foot painting of Nero noted by Pliny as 'an extravagance which must not be forgotten'. Many representational paintings on Roman or Pompeian walls are certainly records of celebrated pictures by Greek artists, and it is surprising to find that in all Campania only one fresco is signed with a Latin name. Apart from mythology and landscape, the Romans favoured Egyptianizing or Nilotic scenes, a preference which has been compared to the eighteenth century's passion for *chinoiserie*.

One of the most striking features of Roman mural paintings is their colouristic brilliance, which was probably achieved by repeated rubbing with cloth or with a special tool. An encaustic technique was confined to certain colours such as vermilion, and to use on walls exposed to the open air, or to work on marble, wood or ivory. Vitruvius describes the preparation of the wall, either to be left 'in the pride of its dazzling white' or painted:

with three coats of sand mortar and as many of powdered marble [the wall] will not possibly be liable to cracks or any other defect. And further, such walls, owing to the solid foundation given by thorough working with polishing instruments, and the smoothness of it due to the hard and dazzling white marble, will bring out in brilliant splendour the colours which are laid on at the same time with the polishing.

It is due to the skill of the artists in preparing the pigments used both for the foundation and for the final paint layer, and their use of a carefully proportioned amount of a fatty ingredient to neutralize the lime's causticity, that the Pompeian murals have survived so well. Occasionally, small decorative pictures were inset into panelled or

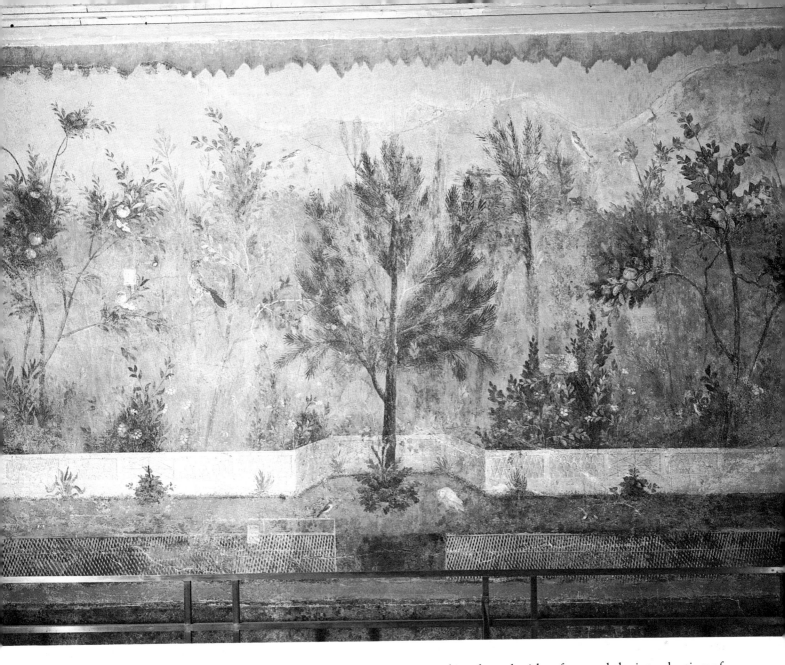

beamed ceilings, as in the House of Fabia at Pompeii. The Cella Dianea-Isiaca in the House of D. Ottavia Quartione at Pompeii still has its wooden beamed ceiling, reconstructed from surviving pieces.

Before we turn to the most spectacular of Roman interiors, that of Nero's Golden House, it may be useful to outline the treatment of door and window openings in domestic interiors. The smaller, unglazed openings usually had wooden sliding shutters, while larger ones often had gratings formed by iron grilles, or stone, terracotta or small marble blocks placed to leave a space. Sometimes star-shaped metal inserts with spikes were placed within the bars of the grilles. As we have seen, glass was a relatively late innovation, although the Romans in Britain soon realized it was essential to change their usual practice, and keep cold out while allowing more light in. Only when upper floors were built onto town houses could window openings be enlarged with safety, and the introduction of window-glass played an important part in the development of the *atrium* house (Plate 13); for exposed seaside villas, it was vital for the enjoyment of fine coastal views. Pliny says that the window-sills of urban *insulae* were often large enough to hold miniature gardens. Smaller windows were of one piece, but larger areas were filled by mounting glass rectangles in wood or bronze frames. Sometimes, the panes (*specularia*) were made of sheets of mica or gesso, which Pliny calls *lapis specularis*. Both large and small windows were often skilfully placed so as to shed light in one direction only, or highlight a particular area of the room, where a favourite painting or other work of art might be shown to advantage. The House of Obellius Firmus at Pompeii boasts an unusually large window with six openings and twelve shutters.

At Pompeii and Herculaneum, the position of doors can

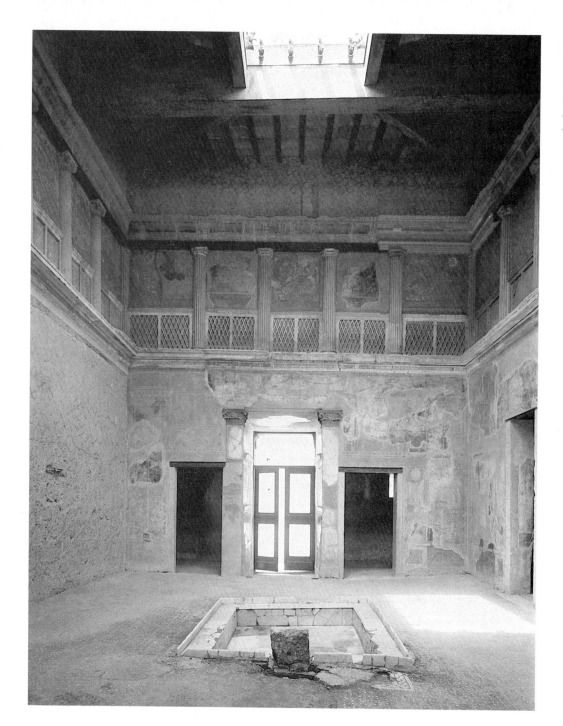

13 Atrium of Casa Sannatica, *Herculaneum* This splendid atrium *with its upper level of attached columns and false balustrade gives some idea of the grander Roman house*

be gauged from the plaster-filled negative spaces left when wood was carbonized (as in the House of the Carbonized Furniture). Many doors and their surrounds appear in wall paintings, and although Pliny says that 'in early times the thresholds and folding doors of temples were commonly made of bronze' such materials were probably reserved for the most lavish Imperial residences. There, double-grille doors in bronze, gilded or otherwise elaborated, would have added solemnity; some idea of their grandeur can be seen in the bronze doors of the Pantheon. Most smaller houses had double or folding doors with simple panelling, as in the House of the Tramezzo at Herculaneum, or with open trellises in their upper parts to admit light. Occasionally, doors were painted.

Of all the Imperial residences, the most notorious and stimulating to the imagination was the Golden House, incorporating all the latest trends in the arts, which Nero built for himself on the slopes of the Esquiline Hill in Rome between AD 64 and 68. The detestation in which his memory was held resulted in the subsequent destruction of much of this lavish pleasure-dome, set by his architects (Celer and Severus) amid rolling parkland in the centre of Rome – what Martial calls *rus in urbe*. The Golden House was the successor to the *Domus Transitoria*, destroyed in the Great Fire of AD 64, which gave Nero the opportunity to requisition the vast area necessary for his new project. Already in the *Domus Transitoria* he had revealed his taste for opulent interior decoration, using costly marble flooring with wide varieties of designs, and wall paintings encrusted with gems. Many features there prefigured the Golden House, and although little decoration survives in the remains beneath the Palace of Domitian, the fountain court with its air-cooling cascade anticipates the later building. The Golden House took its name from the façade, which Pliny says was gilded, and which set the tone of what lay within. Few palaces have rivalled the ostentatiously displayed luxury of the interiors, where apartments of all shapes and sizes followed each other in a blaze of colour using every device known to Roman ingenuity to astonish and delight the visitor. Nero's famous art collections completed the all-enveloping atmosphere of taste at its most rarefied.

Many of the features of the Golden House were made possible only by the great advances in the use of concrete construction during the preceding half-century. Roman concrete (*opus caementicum*) was not like modern concrete, but was an amalgam of lumps of aggregate (*caementa*) and mortar which could not be poured but had to be laid in horizontal courses. Its appearance was not important since it was almost always covered with a facing of marble, mosaic or plasterwork laid onto an underfacing of chequerboard stonework (*opus reticulatum*) or brick (*opus testaceum*). Once set, this cement formed a structure of immense strength and could support further concrete upperstructures of great weight and complexity, such as the Pantheon dome or the various buildings at Hadrian's Villa. Characteristically, Nero was the first to exploit the possibilities of this virtually sculptural architecture to mould interior space. Already under Augustus a taste had arisen for curvilinear and polygonal forms, and this reached its apogee in the Golden House, where the famous octagon opened a new chapter in architectural history (Plate 6). Now interiors could offer all types of domes, apses, semi-domes, interior colonnades, widely differing room shapes – all with rich decoration.

Nero was influenced in his thinking by the Hellenistic palaces of the Ptolemies in Egypt, and it is possible that ideas from the East had some bearing on his love of mechanical devices. Of these, the most famous was the fretted ivory ceiling described by Suetonius as opening to scatter flowers on those assembled below, while another ceiling contained pipes to spray perfumes. Petronius, in his *Satyricon*, mentions a similar device in the house of Trimalchio, and Heliogabalus is principally remembered for the ceiling of his *triclinia versatilia*, which poured flowers on his guests until they were stifled.

Throughout the Golden House there are indications that Nero was here to be envisaged as a celestial deity, most likely a sun god – much as Louis XIV at Versailles: the ceiling, for instance, 'revolved in time with the spheres'

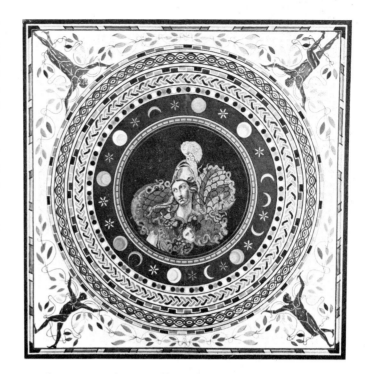

14 Floor mosaic from a villa in the Alban Hills. *Rome, Vatican Museum Astrological references in mosaic were common throughout Roman interior decoration, and the ceilings of rooms in which they were situated may well have had similar motifs, forming a coherent programme*

(Suetonius). It was probably operated by circling horses in the basement, whose concealed harness ropes were attached to the wooden framework of the dome. Seneca describes a dining room 'with a ceiling of movable panels [so] that it represents one appearance after another, the roof changing as often as the courses'. In many ceilings of this type (such as Varro's domical aviary at his villa at Cesinum) the separate parts probably moved independently of each other to further enhance the illusion. These ideas were later adopted by Islam (one Islamic dome is described as making the sound of thunder; another in Babylon was said to simulate the sound of rain!).

Such devices, however, constituted only a part of Nero's interiors; there was also the magnificent octagon with its revetment of precious mosaic, painted and moulded plaster – and possibly the 'great columns of costly marble', which Pliny noted in rich homes – together with extensive marble sheeting on floors and walls (Plates 15 and 17). Pliny singles out Fabullus as the artist most closely connected with the fresco decoration of the walls and vaults, saying that 'wearing his toga, he worked without a moment's respite on the Golden House, which became his self-allotted prison'. From the surviving painted interiors, together with Suetonius' descriptions of the extensive use of gilding and mother-of-pearl, the total effect can be fairly easily visualized.

One of the features which Nero most obviously derived from the palaces of Alexandria was the use of tent patterns

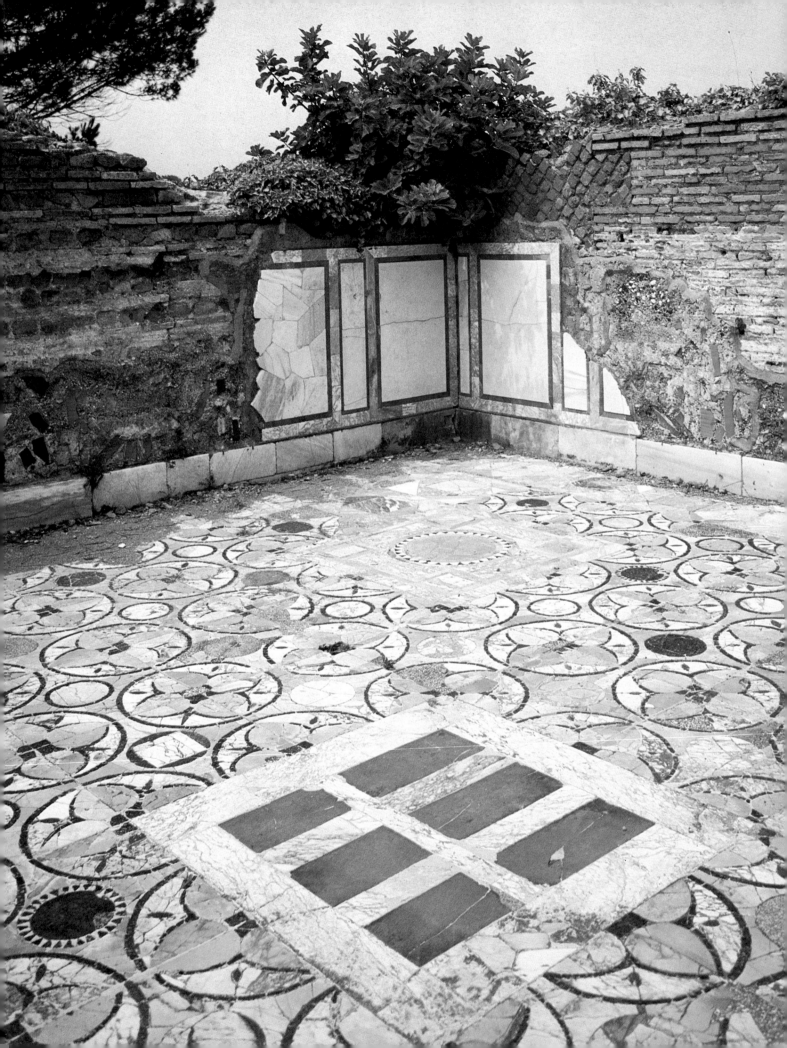

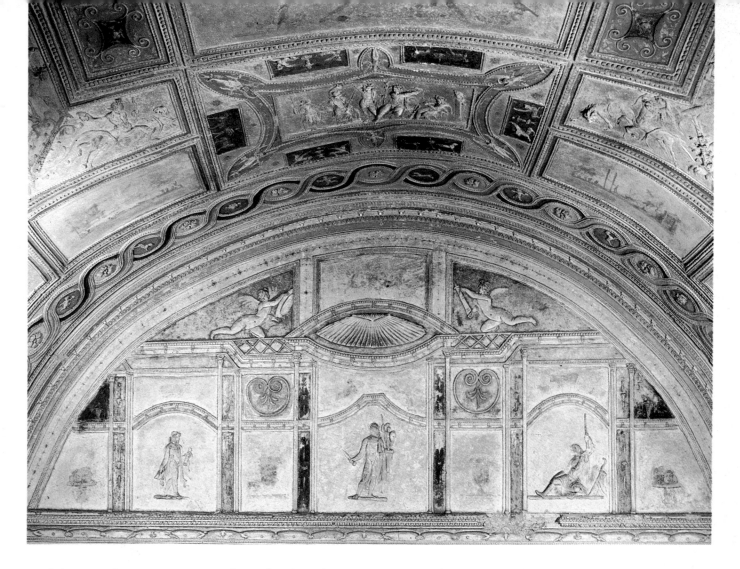

15 *(left)* View of an interior, House of Cupid and Psyche, *Ostia Both pavement and walls have marble revetment, the pavement being composed of pieces of coloured marble arranged to form an elaborate decorative pattern. The walls have large sheets of marble set against the brick structure*

16 *(above)* The Tomb of the Pancrazi, *Rome (detail). Second century* AD *One of the best preserved Roman tombs, its stuccoes show the wide range of decorative motifs used by decorators – shields,* putti, *relief figures, fictive architecture, interweaving bands enclosing rosettes and frescoed landscape panels. Blues, reds and violets predominate in the painted areas, and were originally much stronger in colour*

on the ceilings. These patterns originated from the woven rugs which were suspended on poles over the heads of dignitaries in the East, in Egypt and even in Rome itself. The second-century Greek historian, Dio Cassius, writes that the 'carpets which were spread out through the air in order to protect the spectators [in an amphitheatre] from the sun ... were of a purple colour, and in their centre in embroidery appeared Nero driving a chariot, while around him golden stars spread their light.' Later, Septimius Severus is recorded as 'having paintings of the stars made on the ceilings of the halls in the palace in which he used to give judgement', and many ceilings with cosmological speculations are recorded at Hadrian's Villa. In one of these, the Hours (*Horae*) appear with other mythological planet deities, such as Jupiter, Venus, Mars and Leda-Luna, the four planets which combine destiny and time. These, as Phyllis Lehmann writes, presumably represent 'the religious order of the world of time and space as governed by heavenly persons and expressed in their sacred hierarchy'. A ceiling painting from a villa at Castellamare di Stabia shows an orrery or clockwork model of the planetary system (and see also Plate 14).

One of the delights of the Golden House must have been its stuccoes modelled in relief, since this was an art which came to its finest flowering in the first and second centuries AD. Many examples have survived in tombs, underground chambers and grottoes. (Hence the use of the term *grotesque* to describe this kind of decorative motif.) Among the finest examples are those from the Farnesina villa (Museo Nazionale, Rome), where the remarkably crisp figures are surrounded by landscape and abstract foliage, and those from the Tomb of the Valerii on the Via Latina. There, the vault is filled with interlinked squares and circles with figures, grotesques and rosettes, and consists

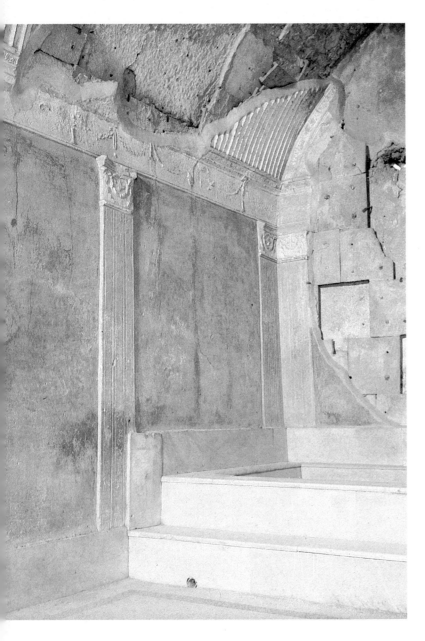

17 Interior view of the Stabian Baths, *Pompeii* *This is a particularly interesting example of how marble sheeting and stucco decoration were applied over the brick understructure of most Roman buildings, achieving great delicacy in the slim pilasters, flower garlands and fluted decoration of the barrel-vault*

they appear to have a life of their own, they never detract from the structural form of their setting. When seen in their pristine state together with all the other decorative devices of their period, the effect must have been quite spectacular.

Except for use on a small scale, the application of the Classical Orders in domestic interiors was confined to the grandest reception rooms of palaces, although examples such as the island villa and *triclinium* in Hadrian's Villa made considerable play on the spatial possibilities of rows of columns. This villa, built between 118 and 134, and in fact consisting of many individual structures covering the area of a small town, epitomizes many of the salient features of both Roman and Greek architecture and interior decoration. Although great interiors were created subsequently in Imperial Rome and throughout the Empire, they were to add little to the basic vocabulary as evolved by the middle of the first century AD. As we shall see, even the Early Christian and Byzantine world could only re-use the ideas perfected by the Romans in order to meet their own requirements.

of both moulded and incised plasterwork. A good idea of the vigour, colouristic boldness and immaculate decorative sense of such work at its best is obtained from the vault in the Mausoleum of the Pancrazi (Plate 16). This type of stucco relief combined with painted areas was to inspire later artists like Giovanni da Udine in the Renaissance and Robert Adam in the eighteenth century (see Chapters 3 and 6). Taking its cue from wall painting of the Second Style onwards, it united such a variety of devices that even single examples often baffle description, and only the original can convey the astonishing inventiveness of the craftsmen who made them. Never is there the slightest hint of pomposity in the use of the Orders, mythological figures, fantastic creatures, scrollwork, beaded mouldings, palmettes, shields, trellises. Strongly coloured areas are perfectly balanced with small subject paintings or landscapes which float in the middle of white panels, and while

2

Byzantium and the Middle Ages

Gold-embroidered tapestries
glowed from the walls

Beowulf

The very word 'Byzantine' conjures up visions of un-rivalled refinement, luxury and sophistication, and spectacular court ceremonial. If the Golden House of Nero stimulates our fantasies of sybaritic living, the domestic arrangements of the Byzantine emperors will amaze us further. The fact that nothing survives of their palaces only contributes to the rarefied aura surrounding their reputation. In Constantinople, the already lavish traditions of the Hellenistic and Roman world were mingled with those of the Orient to evolve an art even more opulent and costly. Byzantium forms a bridge between Imperial Rome and the Middle Ages, and the city which Constantine made his capital and to which he gave his name in the fourth century AD remained the centre of the Eastern or Greek Empire until it fell to the Turks in the fifteenth century. Rome's highly evolved sense of magnificence was combined with the Greek tendency to religious mysticism, and later with Islamic luxury, to give rise to a society where impressive ceremonial played an unprecedentedly important part. In Byzantine interior decoration, as throughout the arts of Byzantium, there was a desire to continue the achievements of the Classical world within the bounds of Orthodox Christianity. The function and decoration of almost all major buildings depended largely on ritual and ceremonial, and were given added impetus by the symbolic abstract art of Islam.

No domestic interior survives from Byzantium itself, and most of our information comes from two contemporary sources: the *Relatio de Legatione Constantinopolitana* of Liudprand, Bishop of Cremona (922–972), who was the Ambassador to Byzantium from the Emperor Otto I in 968, and two manuals by Constantine VII Porphyrogenitus (913–959) – *De Ceremoniis* and *De Administratione*. But it is possible to get some idea of the appearance of domestic interiors from rigidly formalized details in mosaics and from the surviving examples in

Byzantine style on the periphery of the Byzantine Empire – in Venice, Sicily (see Plate 34) and Spain. These allow us at least a glimpse of vanished glories.

Constantinople, largely laid out by Constantine, and rebuilt by Justinian in the sixth century, was altered and added to by successive dynasties of Macedonians, Comnenes and others. Almost all has now disappeared, with the exception of the church of the Holy Wisdom (the *Hagia Sophia*) and other religious monuments. Of the huge palaces of the emperors, and those of the aristocracy and merchants, scarcely a trace survives. Every great city of the Empire – Ephesus, Alexandria, Salonika, Trebizond – had palatial residences for its nobles and governors, who also built villas at coastal resorts – at Daphni, on the shore of the Black Sea, and on the Sea of Marmara. But because the Emperor rarely left his capital, except to wage war, the Court was the centre of all cultural activity, and major architectural developments took place in the capital. The Byzantine aristocracy disliked living in the provinces, which resulted in a further concentration of wealthy patronage in the city. Constantinople was also the trading centre for the entire eastern Mediterranean, and merchants thronged there from China, Russia, Palestine, Asia Minor, India, Italy, Spain and North Africa. The Court's cosmopolitan nature is typified by the Varangian Guard, successors to the Roman Praetorian Guard, which were composed of Scandinavian adventurers.

Constantinople was the largest city in the medieval world, with nearly one million inhabitants at its greatest period, twenty thousand of whom lived in the complex of the Great Palace. In this exotic society where to be orthodox in religion and to speak Greek were the only qualifications for citizenship, the immense wealth of the emperors, aristocracy and clergy was openly displayed with the utmost lavishness at every opportunity. Brick was the main building material of the city, due to the lack of good local stone, but versatile as brick was, the sensitive Byzantine aesthetic required that it be covered with plaster, stone-facing or marble. In this the Romans had led the way, and like them the Byzantines imported marble from every corner of the known world. The technique of marble revetment – slicing the marble as thinly as possible and placing the sheets side by side so that its veining patterns were mirrored – not only produced a pleasing effect, but was also more economical where a large area had to be covered. The mathematical precision and repetitive effect of such decoration reflect the Byzantine taste for 'nature, frozen and transmuted' and 'the rule of cool and temperate minds'. Proportion, rhythm and order, a sophisticated use of textures and light – all features which originated in Classical Greek and Roman art – now became suffused with an emotional wisdom, *sophia*, where art is a reflection of the mystery of the Deity, 'an echo that leads to ecstasy'. This fusion of art and religion accounts for the appearance of the Byzantine interior.

In domestic architecture, features inherited from Rome predominate. Flat surfaces were articulated by columns, pilasters, capitals and cornices, while simple barrel or groined vaults permitted artists and mosaicists greater freedom of invention. The houses of the aristocracy and wealthier classes presented a stern, windowless façade to the street, and the central *atrium* or courtyard was entered through doors of iron or brass – a precaution against the mob. That openness which had increasingly characterized the Roman house – and even important palaces like Nero's Golden House with its large windows opening onto colonnades – rapidly became a thing of the past, and houses became increasingly defensive. The main living rooms were on the first floor, reached by stairs of wood, or of stone in grander interiors. A central hall was the focus of the building, with roof gardens, terraces and balconies to catch the cooling breezes from the Bosphorus. The wet winter climate was kept at bay by warm rooms panelled with wood, hung with curtains and heated by a brick stove, and adequate if not perfect drains – guttering, drain-pipes and sewers – made the city far healthier than most in Europe.

The Great Palace stood on raised ground at the eastern end of the city between the Bosphorus and the Golden Horn. From its splendours, the upper classes took their

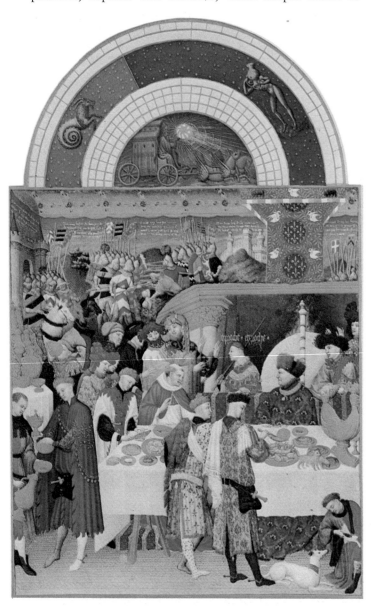

18 *(left)* Limbourg Brothers: 'January' from the Très Riches Heures of the Duc de Berry, *c. 1415. Chantilly, Musée Condé*

19 *(below)* Dirc Bouts: The Last Supper. *Central panel of triptych, c. 1463. Louvain, St Peter's*

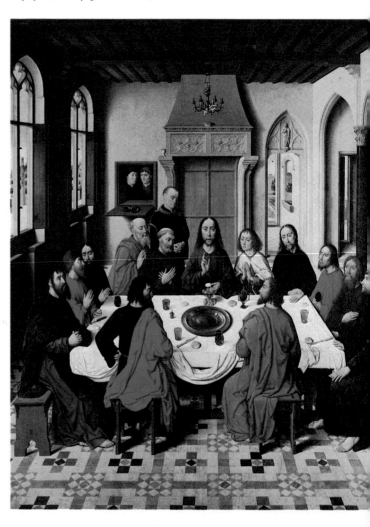

ideas on architecture and interior decoration. Like Hadrian's Villa and other great Imperial villas of Rome, the Palace consisted of many separate building complexes: state reception rooms for audiences, public feasts and the administration of justice; churches and chapels with offices for the clerical communities; barracks and guard-rooms; and the offices of the Imperial administration. Most important for the remarkably high level of artistic life in the Great Palace were the workshops, which were under the Emperor's direct patronage. These produced all the decorative materials used in the Palace – mosaics, carved marble and silks, together with the *objets de luxe* which formed so conspicuous a part of the major interiors, namely ivories, precious illuminated manuscripts, and gold and silver work. Completing the immense layout were treasuries, armouries, gardens, a polo ground and the private apartments of the Imperial family, which were connected to the sea below by staircases, colonnades, covered passages and terraces.

The main entrance to the Great Palace was through the Brazen House or *Chalkê* with its monumental bronze doors and a ceiling inlaid with bronze and mosaic. White marble veined with blue lined the walls, offset with green marble and red sandstone. Above the entrance stood two bronze horses, whose magical qualities, it was said,

prevented real horses from being noisy or quarrelsome at the Emperor's gate. In the centre of the floor lay the *Chalkê omphalos*, a circular porphyry plaque on which records of debts were ceremonially burnt by the Emperor on days of amnesty. The huge bronze doors were probably cast in pieces in damp sand, and fitted to a supporting wooden frame, although doors cast in one piece are known. Such doors were exported from Byzantium to the Balkans and Italy, and they were copied in France and Germany.

This dramatic entrance prepared the visitor for several major palaces beyond, which were constantly being re-built, enlarged and embellished. They resembled in their effect the Turkish seraglio or the Moscow kremlin. Among them were the *Boucoleon* (complete with its yacht marina), the *Scholae* and the *Daphne* with its royal box overlooking the Hippodrome. The great halls were basilican in plan and the heavily religious atmosphere was emphasized by the presence of holy relics; for example, Constantine's standard, the *Labarum*, was housed in the *Consistorium* or Council Hall, while in the *Pentapyriga* was found a great cupboard fashioned in gold with five towers or pinnacles. The *Chrysotriklinos*, which had doors of solid silver, sheltered the glories of the Imperial regalia, and in the centre of the room stood a solid gold table.

The most famous hall was in the Palace of the Great

20 Plate XLIII from Henry Shaw: Specimens of Tile Pavements Drawn from Existing Authorities, *London, 1858*

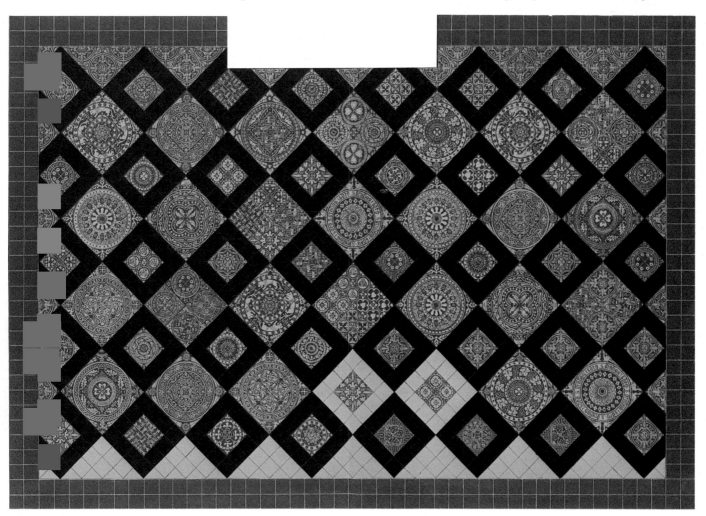

Breeze, the *Magnaura*, which contained the great throne made by Leo the Mathematician for the Emperor Theophilus in the ninth century. Here, surrounded by his most valuable possessions, the Emperor enacted the most spectacular of all Byzantine court rituals for his visitors. They would first see him lavishly attired and seated on the throne, but on raising their heads after prostration, would find that not only was the throne now miraculously suspended in mid-air but that the Emperor wore different clothes, while at either side golden mechanical lions roared and lashed their tails. In the centre of the hall stood a golden plane tree filled with mechanical birds which opened their wings and sang. Such elaborate devices recall those fashioned by the Romans to create moving ceilings, although Theophilus was inspired by detailed accounts of the Abbasid Caliph's court at Baghdad; the stupefied visitor was also regaled with music from two organs, one silver and one gold.

Whereas the Romans used couches for dining, in Byzantium they were used for ceremonial purposes only. In the principal Imperial dining room, the *Decanneacubita*, or Hall of the Nineteen Couches, the two side walls had nine apsidal niches, each containing a couch, and one niche in the end wall. The wooden ceiling had octagonal indentations carved with vine leaves and tendrils liberally sprinkled with gold. Its chandeliers were of gold and hung on silvered copper chains while carpets covered the floor and were strewn with rose petals on major public occasions. Other chains hung from the ceiling to raise the bowls of solid gold which contained the food from trolleys onto the tables, as they were too heavy to lift manually.

Many other rooms are described in some detail, including the *Zeuxippus*, containing part of the Imperial collection of Greek sculpture, and the *Kaenourgion*, with sixteen columns of green marble and onyx carved with vine leaves and spiral grooves (probably not dissimilar to those preserved in St Peter's in Rome). These supported a ceiling glittering with mosaics showing Basil I and his generals on a background of gold, dating from the late ninth century AD. More than in the late Roman world, mosaics were used to decorate important rooms, and the Byzantine craftsmen further developed Roman techniques. Glass *tesserae* with colour backing or gold or silver leaf were used as in Imperial Rome, but techniques became closely guarded secrets. One of the most memorable applications of mosaic must have been in the Imperial bedchamber. Of ceremonial rather than practical use, this was decorated with a mosaic ceiling showing the reigning Imperial family. At the centre of a floor fountain – as distinct from the type of internal cascade favoured in Imperial Rome and also elsewhere in Byzantium (see Plate 34) – was a peacock from which four channels ran to the corners of the room. Floor mosaics were generally made of coloured marbles, although sometimes semiprecious stones were used, such as lapis lazuli, various agates, chalcedony, porphyry or even rock crystal. The most beautiful feature of this interior may have been the walls, where, above a dado of marble revetment, sheets of glass were painted with flowers and fruit.

The Room of Porphyry played a vital role in the life of every Imperial family, since only children born in this room could ascend the throne. Porphyry revetment faced the walls and porphyry columns supported the ceiling; the silk hangings were of purple – the Roman Imperial colour transferred to Constantinople. Some of the smaller chambers had pavements of beaten silver and niello – a technique of staining silver with acid to produce a black lustrous effect. Breathtaking as pavements of mosaic, marble or silver were, there can be little doubt that other effects even more astonishing were certainly obtained. A description of a room in an imaginary palace on the Euphrates in a tenth-century poem by Dignes Akretes, no doubt reflecting a real interior, has the ring of a Hollywood extravaganza: onyx floors polished to look like ice, and white marble walls and windows set with alabaster or talc, cut so thinly that the resulting pure white light gave the illusion of being at the heart of a glacier.

Special exotic effects were highly prized by the Byzantines, and no finer example can be imagined than the *Triconch* in the Great Palace. This was a room on two levels with a trefoil whispering dome, which transmitted a double echo to the floors below. Oriental influence can be detected not only in the names given to some rooms – Pavilion of the Peal, the Chamber of Love, the Hall of Harmony – but also in the decorative *arabesques* and patterns suggesting Kufic inscriptions, the birds and flowers in mosaic and the delicate filigree carving in marble and wood. The *Mouchrontas*, or Domed Staircase, was a spiral stairway decorated with green, red and blue encaustic tiles of Persian workmanship, with geometric patterns of stars and polygonals in wood filling the dome.

As in Rome, it was the extensive use of textiles which made these marble- and mosaic-encrusted palaces and pavilions comfortable. Curtains – often on a vast scale – were suspended on rods between arches and could be wound or tied around the columns when open. Indoors, they were hung at dado level, a practice often depicted illusionistically in fresco. Carpets were popular imports from Persia and the Far East, and couches, stools and thrones were draped with a variety of textiles and piled high with cushions. Silk was produced in Constantinople under Imperial monopoly; the many pieces – especially those woven as gifts – which survive in western Europe give a good idea of its high quality, design and colouring. There is, however, a surprising contrast between the expert use of gold, silver, marble and precious stones in Byzantine interiors, and generally crudely made and poorly glazed ceramics.

The firm control maintained by the Byzantine Emperors over the production of luxury items for their palaces ensured a continuing high level of quality which was greatly admired throughout the West.

The art of Byzantium forms a bridge between Imperial Rome and the Middle Ages. It may seem daring to give a precise year and even a specific day for the beginning of the Middle Ages, but Christmas Day in the year 800 when Charlemagne, King of the Franks, was crowned Emperor of the West by Pope Leo III at Rome was the turning-point after the decline of the Roman Empire. It marks an end to the turmoil following the barbarian invasions, and the beginning of the continuous flow of the medieval world, its art and its clear-cut social and religious patterns.

The word medieval is often used loosely to cover the entire period from the ninth to the fifteenth century without differentiation, when society remained largely based on the feudal system. This is an over-simplification. The system which developed with the granting of lands in return for military service, and the dependence by the peasantry on landholders for protection, began to disintegrate in the eleventh century. By the mid-twelfth century the whole face of society had been transformed. Money provided a new basis for the economy, and a new learning, a new literature and art, and new social conventions emerged. So these 'Middle Ages' had no real middle, only a Romanesque beginning and a Gothic end. Even the word Gothic requires caution, since it was first used in the sixteenth and seventeenth centuries in a derogatory sense to imply pre-Renaissance and non-Italian styles.

Generalizations are easy to make in the discussion of 'the medieval interior', but they are difficult to substantiate with good or relevant examples. Single instances – descriptions, representations in art, or the odd extant interior – must often provide the basis for general observations. Consequently those interiors for which we have reliable, datable and detailed information must serve as somewhat exceptional examples. They come mostly from the very end of the Middle Ages and include the English royal hunting-lodge at Clarendon, Wiltshire, payments for the decoration of which are recorded in the Liberate Rolls of King Henry III and for which some archaeological evidence survives; and artistic sources such as the *Très Riches Heures* illuminations of Jean, Duc de Berry, painted by the Limbourg brothers around 1415, whose *January* (Plate 18) shows details of an interior of the period. Again in England, the inventory of Caister Castle, Norfolk, taken at Sir John Fastolf's death in 1459, is a useful guide to materials and fabrics used in a medieval house. In southern France, the Palace of the Popes at Avignon, and in Italy, the Palazzo Davanzati in Florence, provide a considerable amount of further information regarding medieval interiors in the Mediterranean area.

Three elements fundamental to the development of the medieval interior were Christianity, the feudal system and the peripatetic life-style of the ruling classes. After Constantine had made Christianity the state religion in the fourth century, the Church began its ascent up the ladder of secular power. Bishops and abbots became landholders on a vast scale, and were able to build extensively and to patronize architects, artists and craftsmen at a level unrivalled by secular princes. The Christian Gothic style was also favoured by medieval rulers, but their respect for representations of God and the saints precluded the excessive use of such images in secular settings. Nevertheless, the sophistication of the French courts of the fourteenth and fifteenth centuries epitomizes the achievements of the medieval age. The ceremony and veneration surrounding every aspect of the princes' life had a religious origin and was expressed throughout their surroundings; such ideas were vigorously preserved by the French kings until the Revolution.

The style of the medieval lords was inevitably imitated by their vassals, who lived in close contact with their masters. A warlike spirit dominated much secular, and too much ecclesiastical endeavour, with the result that the houses of the ruling classes were firmly set behind high walls. Cities, castles, keeps, towers and manors, all were fortified, some very heavily, so that attention to security often precluded elaborate interior arrangements.

The itinerant life-style of all classes often prevented any fittings of permanence in even the most civilized domestic interiors during much of the Middle Ages. Life – short, sharp and brutish as it may have been – was spent by a noble and his retainers largely on the move. Large, widely scattered estates or territories required constant supervision in the absence of an efficient or authoritative civil service, and very little furniture or decoration – especially if it was fragile or valuable – could be left behind. (The French word for furniture, *meuble*, means, literally, 'movable', and houses are often carefully distinguished as *immeubles*, 'immovable'.) The denuded appearance of so many medieval halls and chambers today is, in fact, how a noble would find and leave them on each visit. All life's comforts – and there were certainly many – were of necessity portable, and furnishings were neither fixed nor bulky, which is why there are comparatively few medieval interiors which we would regard as either 'furnished' or 'decorated'. Those that do survive help perpetuate the myth that medieval life was rigorous in the extreme, even at the upper end of the social scale.

Emperor Charlemagne (800–814), 'the new Constantine' who established an Empire in the West as a pendant to the Byzantine Eastern Empire, made Aachen his chief place of residence. There, he built a great palace, at 'Roma Secunda'. Its chapel, the Cappella Palatina, still stands, a domed octagonal basilica supported by marble columns taken from the Palace of the Exarchs in Ravenna. Charlemagne fondly imagined that his palace reflected the splendours of the Roman Empire he was recreating: its *Aula Regia* was a basilican hall with apses, two storeys of windows and a wooden roof. The main body of the palace was joined to the chapel by a long open *porticus* with a tower-like pavilion in the middle. We know little of the palace furnishings apart from a number of pieces in solid gold

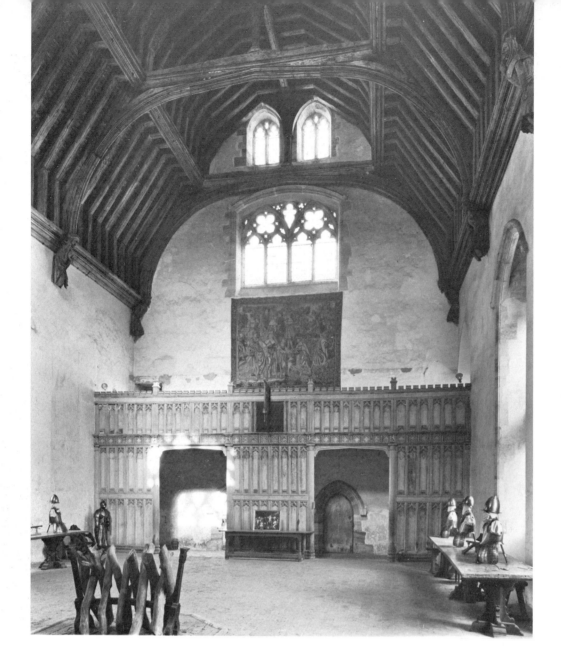

and silver, including a table engraved with a celestial map, which the Emperor is known to have owned. Our knowledge of Carolingian interiors is scanty to say the least, but Theodulph, Bishop of Orléans and Abbot of Fleury, had a villa at Germigny-des-Près with a gallery of paintings in fresco depicting such subjects as the seven liberal arts, the four seasons and a map of the world. Such gleanings are augmented by the decorative details found in manuscripts like the Utrecht Psalter, made in Rheims about 820, where curtains are shown hanging from rings on poles between arches in the Byzantine manner, looped or tied around columns, and elaborate lamps are suspended from ceilings by chains.

Carolingian metal workers, besides providing lavish sacramental objects in gold and silver, also cast bronze with a remarkable degree of competence. The Cappella Palatina has four pairs of bronze doors conceived in the most classical of styles, and the palace was probably similarly equipped with bronze doors, grilles and rails. Marble revetment is used in a way indicating knowledge of Eastern practices; direct mercantile and diplomatic contact with Byzantium is well documented also by artistic influences. Aachen was unfortified, but Charlemagne had fortress-palaces at Ingelheim and at the Weinhof, at Ulm, where terracotta tiles with animal and geometric patterns have been found.

Another important interior from this period survives at Naranco in Spain. This is an early throne hall, with elaborate architectural and sculptural decoration, built for King Ramiro I of the Asturias. It has a simple stone barrel-vault and twisted double columns dividing the walls into bays with floor-length windows between. Round-headed arches have classically inspired mouldings and roundels between them. At either end, doors open into loggias for addressing assemblies. Though comparatively small, it is a unique survival of a ninth-century secular

22 Great Hall, Palais des Contes, Poitiers *This was rebuilt for the Duc de Berry by his architect Guy de Dammartin after being burnt by the English in 1345. Its finest feature is the wall-length triple fireplace topped with a balustraded gallery and three arches with gable crowns and perforated Flamboyant tracery. The statues above show the duke, his second wife Jeanne de Boulogne, his nephew, King Charles VI and his queen, Isabeau of Bavaria*

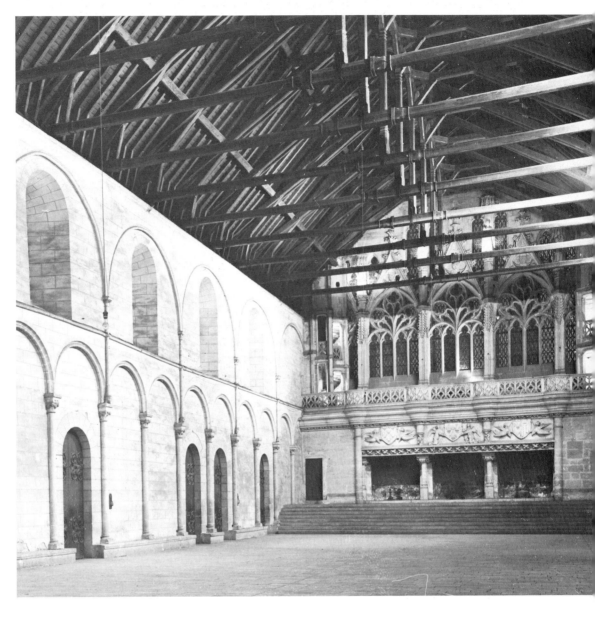

interior. Such halls were, up until the eleventh and twelfth centuries, the most important room in any princely residence. Even in the later Middle Ages, when the hall was no longer the main living room, its administrative and ceremonial functions helped it to keep its prominence (see Plate 21). There justice was administered, councils held, parliaments met, visitors and foreign ambassadors received; and there the household ate and often slept. The ritual and hospitality of the entertainment expressed the wealth and power of the princely owner. Privacy was scanty and only the most important persons would have a sleeping chamber. However, by the late fourteenth and fifteenth centuries privacy and comfort for the lord and his family began to replace the communal life. The hall was used for ceremony only by the lord, and the privy chamber became the focus of attention, and therefore the most lavishly decorated room.

Great halls could vary considerably, from the magnificence of Westminster Hall in London, which measures 239 by 67 feet, to the more modest 65 by 44 feet of Oakham Hall in Rutland. Like Oakham, Westminster was originally arcaded, but the elaborate hammer-beam roof constructed by Hugh Herland in 1399 meant that the whole hall could be roofed in one aisleless span. Such open timber roofs were common in all large halls throughout Europe when stone vaulting was not used, and the hall lasted longer as a functional interior on the Continent than in England. Although examples are to be found in England from the fourteenth century (like Penshurst Place, Kent, of 1335) they are still simple variants of the earlier theme. In France, the great hall of the Castle of Poitiers, built between 1384 and 1388, shows far greater elaboration in the triple fireplaces surmounted by a glazed screen of tracery with sculpture (Plate 22). The very end of the hall tradition is represented by the Vladislav Hall in Prague of 1486–1500, with its elaborate vault, originally

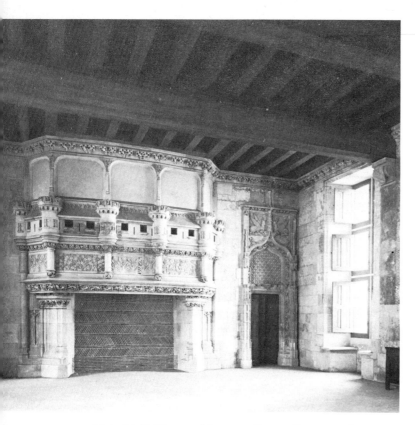

23 Main Hall, House of Jacques Coeur, *Bourges Jacques Coeur, merchant-financier on an international scale and one of the richest men of his day, began his palatial residence in 1443 at the pinnacle of his success. Its decoration was perhaps the most lavish of any such house of the period, with stained glass, wall and ceiling paintings, extensive sculpture and, no doubt, elaborate fittings of every kind. Although much restored, this hall gives an idea of the splendour in which the rich lived in the later Middle Ages, with every sort of convenience (including a steam-room), endless space, and decorations by leading artists. Another large building of similar date which has preserved much of its original decoration is now the Musée de Cluny, in Paris, built in 1485–98*

painted, and moulded fireplaces and doors. A spiral ramp leading up to the hall enabled knights to practise jousting indoors in bad weather.

Most medieval halls were much brighter than they appear today. Their walls were washed with white or colour, using powdered chalk and water. The habit of restorers of showing complete internal stone walls is wholly misleading since originally the walls were covered with plaster or tempera; the only visible signs of building construction would have been doorways, window surrounds, columns or piers. The washes were sometimes decorated with coloured lines, usually red, to form blocks representing masonry. Fortunately, our knowledge of this very basic wall treatment in England is fairly detailed. We know, for example, that Henry III ordered white-washing of 'the hall at Guildford within and without ... the Queen's Chapel and chamber and the Queen's great wardrobe'. Westminster Hall was freshly whitewashed for the coronation of Edward I in 1274. Besides whitewash, white plaster was used. This was of a coarse variety, made from lime, sand and hair, or, when a finer texture was required, of burnt gypsum. Fine plaster has been called plaster of Paris from an early date. In 1254, when Henry III visited Paris, the chronicler Mathew Paris reported: 'he took note of the elegance of the houses, which were made with gypsum, that is to say, plaster.' In 1251 Henry had ordered the Sheriff of Nottingham to finish the dais in the castle hall with French plaster – 'franco plastro'. (Gypsum was found in large quantities in Montmartre, but was also found in England, notably in the Isle of Purbeck in Dorset.) In 1312, plaster from Corfe was used at Windsor Castle, and in 1342, payments were made for 'digging white stone called chalk for making the walls of the chapel and chamber at Ludgershall of plaster of Paris'.

Remains of painted decoration on a plaster wall survive in the Old Deanery at Salisbury, Wiltshire, where traces of painted lime ashlar are combined with a short marginal frieze of stiff-leaf foliage decoration. Besides their plaster decoration, colour-washed, painted or even stencilled, the great halls were hung with devices relating to the owner – heraldic shields and banners, arms and armour, and mementoes of the chase. In Sir John Fastolf's hall at Caister were hung pikes and lances, fitting decoration for a knight who had fought at Agincourt, as well as eleven crossbows, six swords used for practice, twenty-one spears, a 'gay launce' and a great red-painted shield held before crossbowmen in battle. Although hunting trophies and military arms appear in Renaissance interior schemes, it was not until the eighteenth century that their full decorative potential was revived (see Chapter 6).

Fireplaces, where they existed, were usually placed in a long wall, although in earlier interiors smoke from a central fire was simply released through a louvre in the roof, as at Penshurst. The more enormous the fireplace, the less likely it was to be used for cooking, and separate kitchens were an early feature in castle life. The under-floor hypocaust heating systems which the Romans had introduced throughout the Empire were not adopted by subsequent civilizations, and the development of the ornamental chimney-piece forms a vital part of all interior decoration from the Middle Ages onwards. By the late Middle Ages, many fireplaces had developed into show-pieces of monumental architectural sculpture. The beautiful house of the banker Jacques Coeur in Bourges has a turreted and crenellated fireplace of immense proportions dated 1443 (Plate 23) with a frieze on which are carved huntsmen and knights riding donkeys to a mock tournament. Coeur was banker to many nobles as well as to the King, and this frieze possibly encapsulates his own wry attitude to some of his customers. Also incorporated are three sham windows where figures playing chess are seated.

It was difficult to heat very large rooms, even with three fireplaces as at Poitiers (Plate 22), and so the smaller privy chamber came into more regular use. Most fireplaces were provided with a hood – a vital necessity because of the deep projection of the hearth into the room. Although the hood had a large lintel, there was rarely a shelf above, and the hood was generally supported on projecting corbels to expose the fire as much as possible. The corbels were often carved, as in the twelfth-century Château of le Puy-en-Velay, or supported on free-standing columns like those in the Emperor Frederick II's castle at Gioia del Colle in Apulia. Several decorated fireplaces are recorded in England: in 1246, the mantel and hood in the King's upper chamber at Clarendon was painted with a Wheel of Fortune, while the mantel in the Queen's Chamber was carved with representations of the Twelve Months of the Year. In the famous Painted Chamber at Westminster, the fireplace surround contained a sculpted and painted Calendar.

Although the great hall, with its connotations of hearty, ribald communal life, on which the feudal lord gazed down from his dais, forms an important part of our image of medieval daily life, it is to the privy chamber that we must turn for a more realistic insight. In contrast to the vigour of the great hall, the solar, closet, wardrobe or privy chamber of a great house would have revealed a degree of luxury and sophistication very far removed from the barbarity of the lives of the majority. These rooms were in effect *grand luxe* bed-sitting rooms, a luxury in themselves when privacy was at a premium. They were often large enough to accommodate a bed, chests, settles and stools, together with treasured personal possessions.

A law of Henry VII's reveals that in England glass was regarded as part of the furnishings of a room, not part of the fabric of the house. Stored away in the absence of the owner, when wooden shutters kept out the elements, the large leaded panes were hung on stone or iron transoms by wire, or set on hinges leaded into the frame. Stained glass was not uncommon in secular buildings – the records of the Queen's Chamber at Clarendon refer to stained-glass figures of a Virgin and Child in a window overlooking the park 'well barred with iron'. Wooden shutters were often painted both inside and out, or pierced and fretted, and covered only the lower part of the window while the upper part was permanently glazed. This had the dual advantage of security and of allowing the passage of fresh air; hinged windows were rare. At Northampton, the King's castle had a window with one of Henry III's favourite themes – 'the figures of Lazarus and Dives painted in the same, opposite the King's dais, which may be opened and closed'. The *Annunciation* by the Master of Flémalle (Plate 24) shows several of these window features. There are glazed top-lights with stained-glass armorial bearings, while below, the hinged shutters open to reveal a wooden fretted screen. In St Joseph's workshop, the window shutters are hinged at the top rather than at the sides, and are kept open by wooden hooks suspended from the beamed wooden ceiling. These are, however, small windows when compared with the full-length oriels which developed to provide more light for the dais.

24 Robert Campin (Master of Flémalle): Mérode Altarpiece, c. 1425(?). New York, Metropolitan Museum of Art

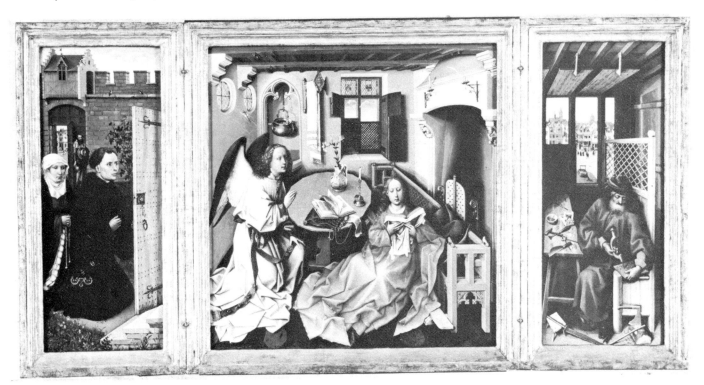

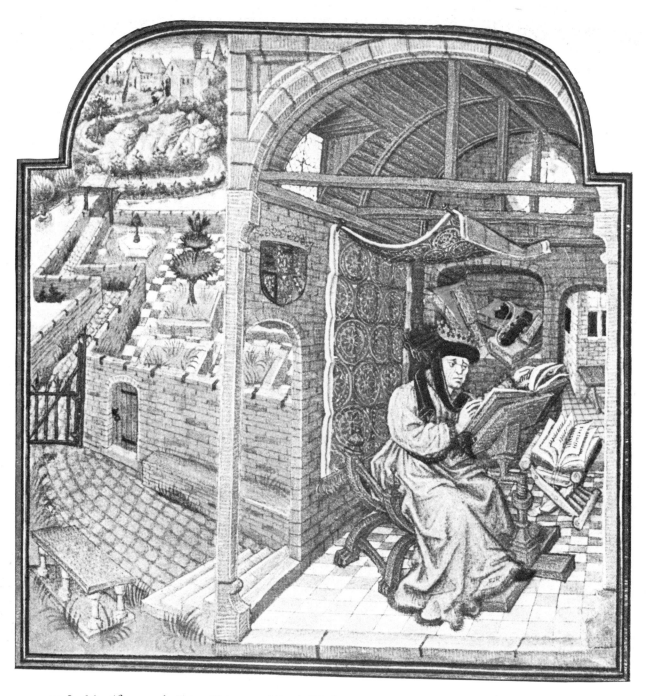

25 Le Mortifiement de Vaine Plaisance of René d'Anjou: King René in his study. *Mid-fifteenth century*

Polygonal and projecting, these windows often had window-seats, and the glass was frequently decorated with armorial and personal devices.

Courtly life in the Middle Ages was resplendent with ceremony, pageantry, and the symbolic trappings of chivalry – all of which were expressed in the apartments of the ruling classes. Painted decoration similar to that on window glass was found on the ceiling. On vaulted ceilings, the architectural elements of ribs, corbels, bosses and liernes would be used as frames and divisions for such decoration, as would the beams and lathes of a wooden ceiling. Personal motifs and devices used in such a way

were the forerunners of the *imprese* common throughout Renaissance interior decoration. In the cloth of state hanging behind the Duc de Berry (see Plate 18), apart from the coat-of-arms of gold fleurs-de-lys on an azure ground, are bears and white swans. These allude to the Duc's love for a certain lady Ursine – *ours* (bear) and *cygne* (swan). The ceiling here is a smooth barrel-vault of wood with banded decoration applied both lengthwise and crosswise, painted red and blue and with carved, gilded leaves. On the title-page of the *Mortifiement de vaine plaisance* of René d'Anjou, King of Sicily, dating from the mid-fifteenth century, we see a simpler version

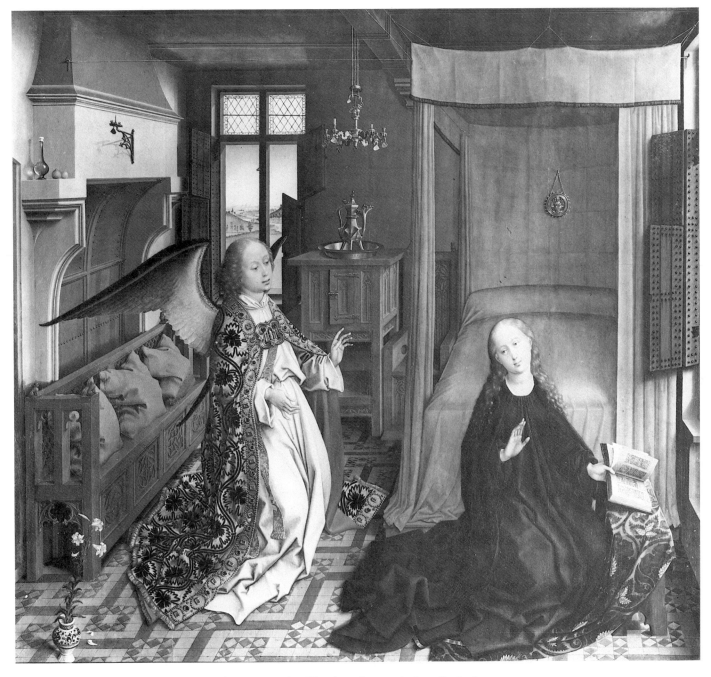

26 Roger van der Weyden: Annunciation. *Paris, Louvre*

of this ceiling type, set with rounded dormer windows (Plate 25). Tie-beams cross the ceiling, with vertical supporting joists joining them to the vault; a much-restored example exists in the Château de Chillon on the shore of Lake Geneva in Switzerland.

Flat ceilings were common in secular buildings within castle precincts or towns, where defence was not a primary consideration and thick walls or fireproof vaults were not required. Dieric Bouts' *Last Supper* at Louvain (Plate 19) shows a large, flat-ceilinged room, with the beams supported on moulded corbels. Several features already discussed also make their appearance – plastered walls,

a fine hooded fireplace with geometric sculpted decoration, and tall windows with shutters for the lower half only. It also shows an ornate tiled pavement, which, after wooden boards or stone flagging, was the most common type of flooring in the Middle Ages.

It is particularly unfortunate that none of the great domestic tiled pavements of the period survives intact, since these must have constituted one of the most splendid aspects of many interiors. The tiles were usually of decorated and glazed encaustic earthenware, square and varying in size from a few inches to a foot or more. A Continental development of the twelfth century, tiles

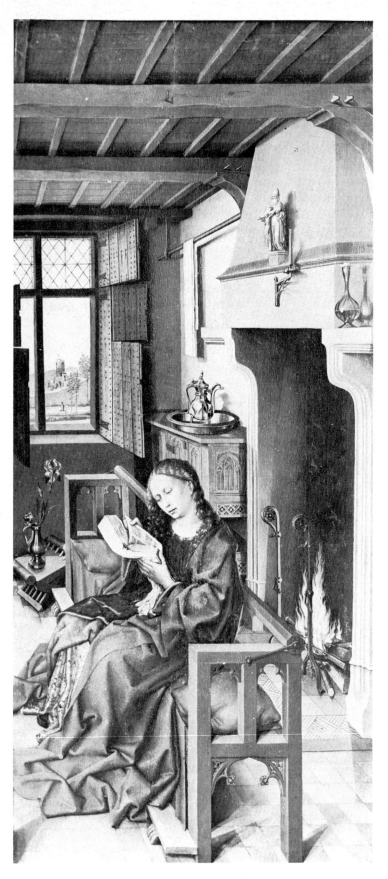

were introduced into England from the Low Countries about 1220, Clarendon Palace having some of the earliest examples. By the end of the thirteenth century, tiles were already less of a luxury and during the fourteenth century they were widely produced and readily available. Colour was largely dictated by the use of lead glazes, yellow, black, brown and various shades of green being the most common. Besides tiles of plain colour or of regular geometric pattern, placed in a chequerboard arrangement, animals, birds, human faces and heraldic devices were also used. At Clarendon Palace, sets of four or more were combined in a pattern separated by bands of plain tiles dividing the pavement into distinct areas. Sets of nine and sixteen tiles were also made with one overall continuous pattern when laid.

Though mosaic floors of the Roman or Byzantine type with tiny graded *tesserae* were not widely known in the Middle Ages, various types of stone flooring were adopted using engraved slabs or marbles cut into circles, with frames and decoration in semiprecious stones like porphyry, jasper and coloured marble. In the Master of Flémalle's *St Barbara* in Madrid, the fireplace has strips of tiles placed at angles to give the appearance of weaving (Plate 27). Woven materials were in fact used on floors, but carpets rarely were. René d'Anjou in his other poetical work, *Le Livre du cuer d'amour espris*, is, however, shown in a bedchamber which has two very beautiful Persian rugs on the floor, and King Henry VI of England had a leather carpet in his wardrobe. King Jean II of France is known to have had a bedside rug of green sendal which matched the hangings of his chamber. In the Duc de Berry's feast we see woven rush matting, plaited and then stitched to the required scale, which was probably the type of floor covering most used in great households; it was known as Egyptian matting.

Mural decoration naturally provided artists with their greatest opportunities for imaginative work (Plate 28). Painted murals were particularly common in houses in constant use, like the major palaces of a monarch or the sole residence of a lesser noble. It was the intermediate type of residence – great castles visited only occasionally – that went largely undecorated with permanent features. Since these tended to be fortified, they have survived in greater number and have led to the erroneous impression of stark empty rooms. Carolingian wall paintings are recorded, but it is only from the thirteenth century onwards that documents or actual paintings help us to comment more fully. Secular subjects were naturally more favoured in domestic decoration: Clarendon Palace, for example, had its Antioch Chamber, painted with scenes from the Siege of Antioch and the duel of Richard Coeur de Lion and Saladin – another favourite subject of

27 Robert Campin (Master of Flémalle): St Barbara, from the Werl Altarpiece. *Madrid, Prado*

28 Painted walls and ceiling in first-floor room. *Town Hall, Goslar, Germany*

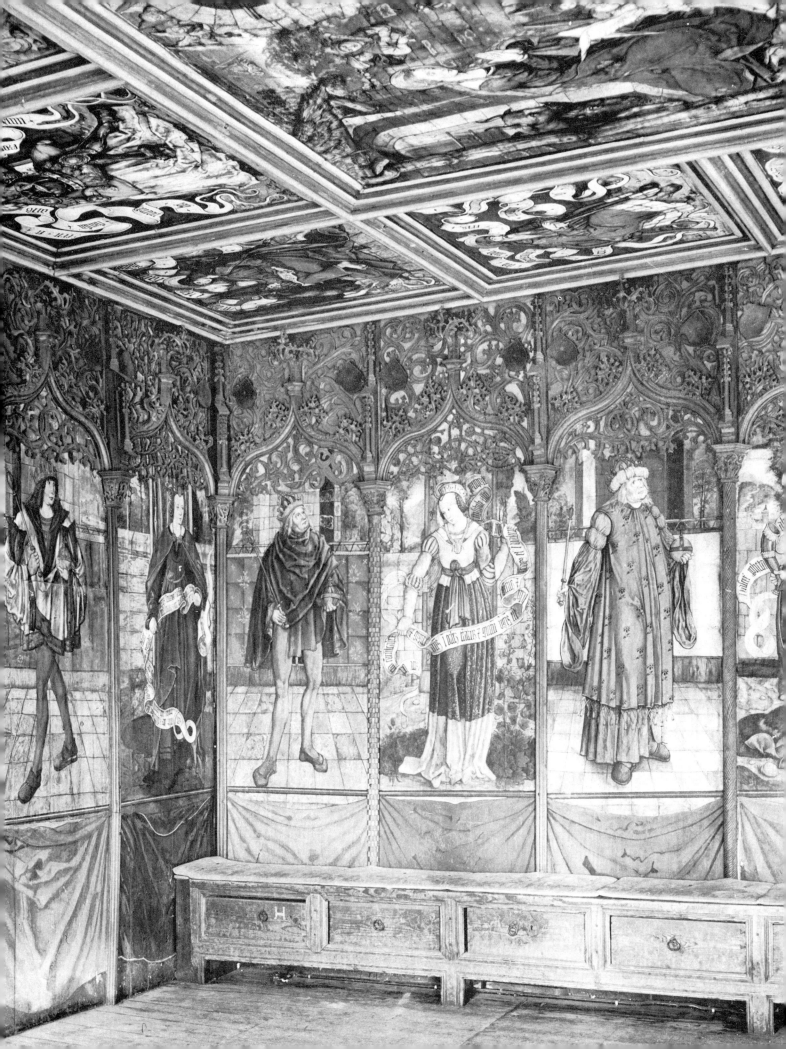

Henry III, who commissioned it. In Palazzo Davanzati in Florence, the story of Tristan and Isolde appeared in wall paintings, and similar chivalric scenes were no doubt popular. At Clarendon, religious subjects were to be found in the King's upper chamber, a sizeable room measuring some forty-two by twenty-five feet. A frieze of portrait heads in roundels ran round the room, and above were the Evangelists and St Margaret. A version of the Lazarus and Dives theme appeared in the hall at Guildford. The choice of themes was not arbitrary, and their symbolism was of great importance. Henry II ordered a room at Winchester Castle to be painted with various figures, but 'an empty space of wall should be left which will subsequently be filled with an eagle attacked by its four young, which, the King explained, was symbolic of the mutiny of his own sons'.

One of the most famous cycles of painting in a secular setting in England was in the Painted Chamber of the Palace of Westminster, destroyed by fire in 1835. Here, the combined audience room and bedchamber of the King's principal residence had a series of Old Testament scenes painted in three registers around the walls. Over the bed was the *Coronation of Edward the Confessor*, while guardians drawn from the *Song of Songs* were painted on either side:

Behold his bed, which is Solomon's, threescore valiant men are about it . . . every man hath his sword upon his thigh because of fear in the night.

A bestiary decorated the wainscoting, a Tree of Jesse the fireplace, and the highlight of the entire scheme was a *Mappa Mundi* painted by Mathew Paris, the monk chronicler from St Albans.

The inspiration for many of these decorations was drawn from illuminated manuscripts. In 1250, the Master of the Knights Templar of London was asked to lend a copy of the 'Psalter of Antioch' to the King's painter, Edward of Westminster, so that he could decorate a chamber for the Queen. Artists' names were rarely recorded, but apart from Edward of Westminster, we know of Peter the Painter who decorated the walls of the King's Hall at Marlborough with roses, and Odo the Goldsmith. Master of the shrine made for Edward the Confessor, Odo was ordered in 1237 'to displace without delay the painting which was commenced in the King's Great Chamber at Westminster, under the "great history" of the same chamber, with panels containing the species and figures of lions, birds and other beasts, and to paint it in a green colour in the fashion of a curtain so that the "great history" may be preserved unhurt.'

A most important example of a smaller fresco cycle has been preserved in the first-floor solar at Longthorpe Tower in Northamptonshire (Plate 29). Painted in the early fourteenth century for a member of the Thorpe family, probably by an artist from nearby Peterborough Abbey, the paintings show the *Ages of Man*, the *Hunt of*

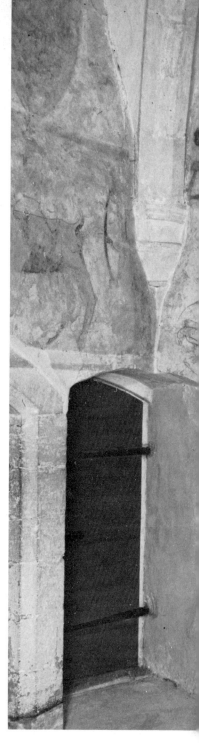

29 Longthorpe Tower, *Northants. Early fourteenth century*

the Bonnacon, a *Wheel of the Five Senses*, various saints and heraldic devices, and even some local Fenland birds. The idea of naming rooms after their decorative themes is Continental in origin, and was a common practice in French castles and palaces from the twelfth century onwards. The sources were varied – from the Bible, the spiritual romances, the *chansons de geste*, scenes from the lives of great men and contemporary events such as wars, hunting or hawking and courtly life. In 1235, Thibaut, Count of Champagne, had certain rooms in his castles at Provens and Troyes illustrated with scenes from his own

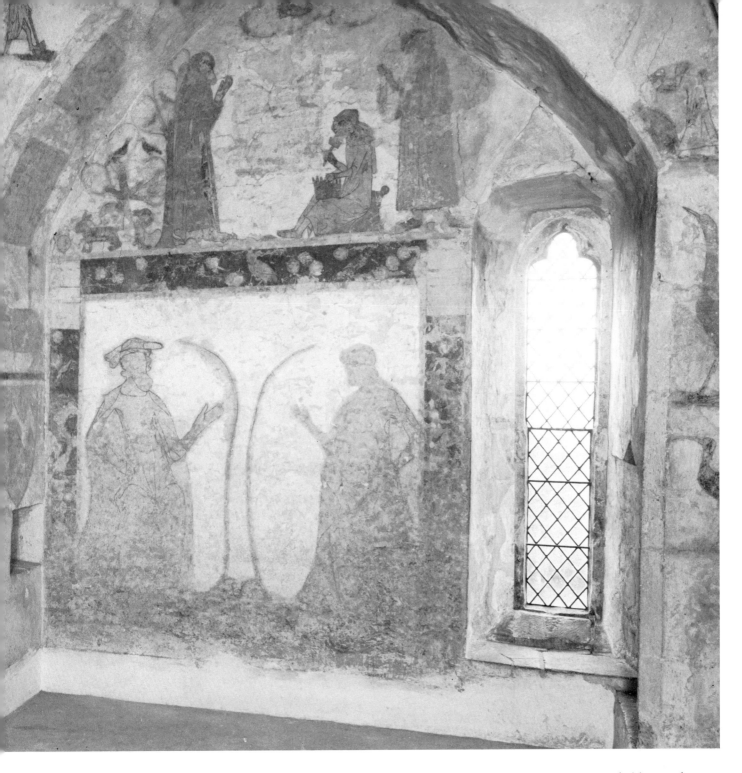

poems, and the Counts of Artois had a 'Salle de Chansons' at the Château de Hesdin painted with verses and illustrations from the *Jeu de Robin et Marion*. Books again provided inspiration for the decoration of the 'Salle des Caesars' in the Duke of Normandy's Château de Val de Recel in the fifteenth century: here the source was a book in the Duke's own library. King Charles V, like his brother the Duc de Berry a great patron of the arts, had a 'Chambre de Charlemagne', a 'Chambre de Matabrune' and a 'Salle de Thesée' in his Château de St-Pôl. The long gallery of this château was painted to represent a green forest of

apple, pear, cherry and plum trees with lilies and roses clustering at their base. Mahaut, Countess of Artois, created a memorial to her father by having the gallery of her castle at Conflans painted with scenes showing his feats of arms, rendered with meticulous historical accuracy. The *Songe de Vergier* records that '... the knights of our time have both infantry and cavalry battles painted in their halls ... taking much delight in battles which are purely imaginary'.

The instructions to Odo the Goldsmith quoted above referred to wooden wainscoting, a common solution to the decoration of the lower section of walls. When left unpainted, natural wood wainscoting, usually of oak or elm, was often divided into panels (Plate 26). These could frame carved folds of cloth scalloped at either end of vertically ribbed bands ('linenfold'), although this was a comparatively late medieval innovation. When painted, wainscoting was normally of softwood such as spruce or pine, which was sometimes specially imported. In 1252, Henry III ordered 'for our use, two hundred Norway boards of fir to wainscott therewith the chamber of our beloved son, Edward, in our castle at Winchester'. The wainscoting in the King's great chamber at Windsor was in radiating coloured bands. Not all of a room was necessarily wainscoted. At Cliff Castle in Northamptonshire, the King's great chamber was wainscoted only 'beyond our bed', and at Geddington, the dais end of the hall was treated in the same way. Usually, pine half-panelling, four to five feet high, was painted, green being the most fashionable, if also the most expensive, colour. The Queen's chamber at Woodstock was painted green with a red border, while in 1240 her chamber in the Tower of London was to be 'wainscoted without delay, thoroughly whitened internally and newly painted with roses'. The Antioch Chamber at Clarendon had a wainscot painted green and decorated with gold spangles – scintillis – and the King's upper chamber had a similar wainscot spotted with gold – auro deguttori. When the site was excavated in the 1930s, small lead stars and crescents with traces of gilding were found, with hooks and holes for nails to attach them to the woodwork. The combination of coloured tile pavements (fine examples from Clarendon are to be found in the British Museum; see also Plate 20), painted walls, stained-glass windows, carved and painted fireplaces, and painted wainscoting with shining metal-work must have created a dazzling impression.

Painted mural decoration was more common in Mediterranean interiors in the Middle Ages, and from the Renaissance onwards it was not unknown for virtually every wall surface even in the largest palaces to be completely covered with frescoes. In Italy, the political stability brought about by the rise of civic governments and the decline of Imperial power after the twelfth century, combined with swift economic expansion, gave rise to a new, affluent and comparatively stable aristocracy. This new class established residences within the safety of city walls, and these could be decorated and furnished with some hope of permanence.

Although restored at various times, Palazzo Davanzati in Florence provides a particularly well-preserved example of a late medieval palace on a large scale. It has a wide range of ceiling and mural decoration which gives a clear idea of the colouristic brilliance and love of pattern which must have been characteristic of many medieval interiors (Plate 33). Many of the rooms have geometric patterns on the walls painted in reds, greens and white, while others are decorated with fictive cloth hangings extending round

the walls to a height of about twelve feet. In some of these rooms, similar real hangings (of coloured wool for warmth in winter) would have been suspended on rings, as they appear in Giotto's fresco of the Confirmation of the Rule in S. Francesco at Assisi. In this fresco, the hangings have an all-over pattern similar to the wall decorations in Palazzo Davanzati, and are shown pulled back only at doors and windows.

In the space between the upper line of these decorations and the flat, beamed and painted wooden ceilings supported on carved corbels run continuous friezes, in which some of the most beautiful decorations in the palace appear. Gothic trefoil arches frame the arms of noble Florentine families, and, in a large second-floor bedroom, is an 'open' loggia in which figures walk or play chess against a background of bird-filled trees, illustrating scenes from the French romance of La Chastelaine de Vergi. This was probably painted to celebrate a marriage in 1395, and shows the Italian liking for Northern epic cycles, as does a fresco cycle illustrating Tristan and Isolde from the House of the Teri in Florence, fragments of which are now in the Museo di S. Marco. The practice of decorating the upper zone of a high wall with a continuous figurative frieze, while the lower part was hung with tapestries or pictures, survived throughout the Renaissance and Baroque in Italy, undergoing various transformations in the process.

Italian influence on the North at this time was remarkably slight, although Philippe le Bel of France sent his court artists to Rome to study and several Italians worked in Paris in the fourteenth century, including one Ziba da Firenze recorded there around 1410. The large wall surfaces, articulated by tiny windows placed at a height necessitated by the defence systems of most Italian town palaces, were ideal for large-scale fresco decoration. A fine example of an Italian medieval interior, almost classical in its simplicity, is seen in Pietro Lorenzetti's Birth of the Virgin in Siena. Dating from 1342, it shows St Anne lying on a bed in a room with a dark blue painted vault set with gold stars. Lozenge-shaped glazed windows pierce the lunettes in the wall, which is painted with a wash and a delicate frieze pattern. Around the walls are nailed long and very full linen draperies, with an embroidered border at the top. Such curtains were more suitable for warm climates than wooden wainscoting or heavy continuous tapestry. The floor is set with oblong border tiles and others inset with a glazed decorative pattern.

In the fourteenth century the schism within the Church and the increasing violence of the Roman mob forced the Papacy to move to Avignon in the south of France. Here, the Tour des Anges was magnificently frescoed around

30 Long Gallery of Little Moreton Hall, *Congleton, Cheshire. Fifteenth to sixteenth century*

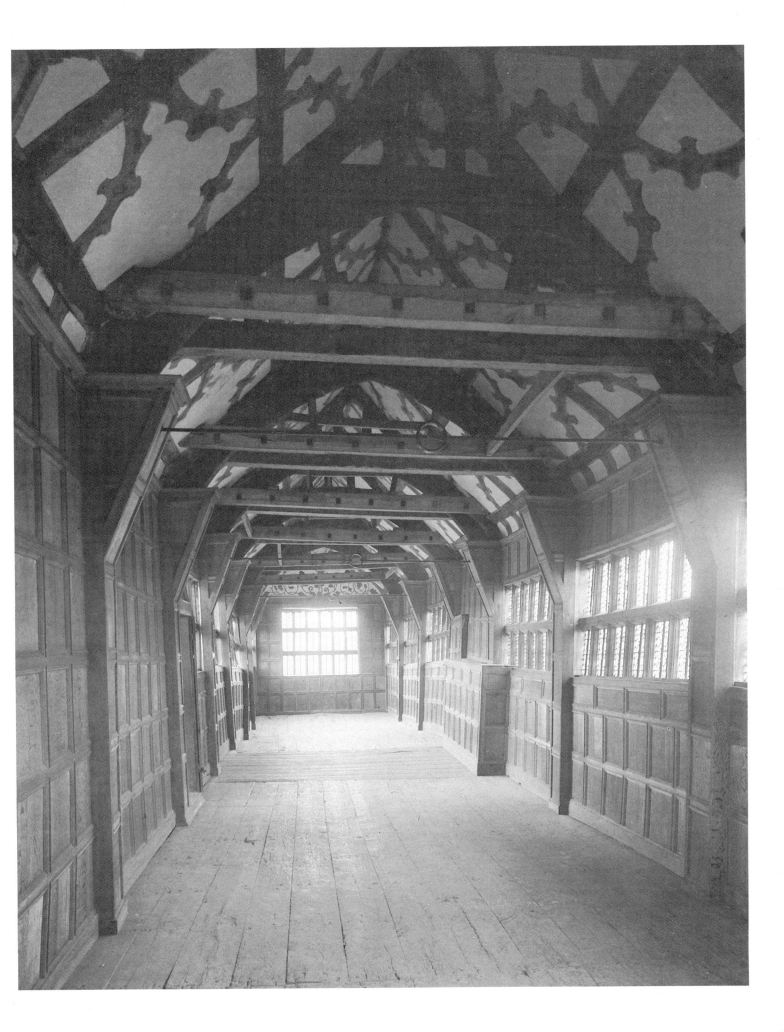

1340 for Pope Benedict XII (Plate 31). Giant vine scrolls cover the walls, rising out of a dado painted to simulate curtains, while a quatrefoil frieze high above contains somewhat flat scenic views. Although Italian artists probably executed these, French influence is apparent in the subject matter and in the emphasis on patterns inspired by the borders of illuminated manuscripts.

The nomadic life of the European aristocrat meant that the most important items of interior decoration had to be easy to transport and store. Rapid transformation could be achieved in even the barest rooms with woven tapestries of all sizes and stitched embroideries which could also be dyed or painted. Not only were these aesthetically pleasing, they also excluded draughts and retained heat. We have seen that embroidered hangings had evolved for similar purposes in the Classical world, and their use in the medieval interior began very early indeed. In Beowulf's Hall at Heorot,

> Gold-embroidered tapestries
> glowed from the walls, with wonderful sights
> for every creature that cared to look at them.

In the tenth century, Queen Adelaide, wife of Hugh Capet, gave an *orbis terrarum* embroidery to the Abbey of St-Denis, and in the eleventh century Peter Damien condemned the custom of hanging beds with embroidered curtains.

Woven hangings were first placed at the dais end of halls to give greater comfort and to emphasize the important part of the room, but when the noble moved to private chambers, the tapestries migrated with him, their quality improving in the more intimate setting. The fashion for full-length historiated and figurative tapestries – as opposed to plain cloth hangings – began at the courts of Burgundy and France, rapidly spreading to Germany and England. The custom of making lavish diplomatic gifts of sets of tapestries must have helped this process. Content, however, was always more important than visual appeal; for example, in 1393 Philip of Burgundy sent Henry of Lancaster a set showing Clovis, Pharaoh and Moses – Moses was long to remain an Old Testament favourite of monarchs.

A royal progress was accompanied by a huge baggage train containing several complete sets of tapestries. Mahaut, Countess of Artois, visited Artois twice a year, sometimes went to her estates in Burgundy, and stayed regularly at the royal castles in and around Paris, such as Fontainebleau, Vincennes and Pontoise. Her visits lasted a week or longer and in the apartments provided for her she would cover every wall surface with hangings. King Jean II of France had three sets for each of the year's great Christian festivals, Easter, All Saints and Christmas, and in the appropriate liturgical colours. The Christmas set comprised six wall tapestries, with the arms of France in the corners, a counterpane, a dorsal (for the back of a seat or bed), a tester and bed curtains, all of green sendal lined in blue linen and embroidered with silver stars. The ensemble was completed with chair cushions of blue velvet and green sendal, green serge window curtains and a matching carpet by the bed. A French royal bedroom of the late fourteenth century appears in the *Heures Boucicaut* with blue hangings embroidered with fleurs-de-lys (Plate 36).

Figurative tapestries, woven in the Low Countries, became fashionable only in the High Middle Ages. Wool was exported from England and the centres were at Tournai and Arras. The word 'Arras' came to be used to describe a certain type of material: the Black Prince had a room hung with 'Arras du pays de Saladyn'. Some tapestry weavers established themselves in London, and in 1317 Edward II bought from one Tomas de Hebenhith, mercer of London, a great hanging of wool '. . . wove with figures of the King and Earl' for use on solemn occasions. A border of green worsted was then sewn around it, to prevent its being damaged in hanging. Permanent pegs were used for this, usually at a height of eight to ten feet from ground level. Such tapestry sets were not exclusively for use on walls – in 1398, the Duke of Orléans purchased *une chambre portative*, 'a portable bedchamber', consisting of a canopy, a dorsal, curtains and a coverlet.

The secular themes illustrated on these fabrics were drawn from the same sources as wall paintings, but tended to emphasize the seasons. In autumn and winter, hunting and hawking scenes were popular, while pastoral and romantic ones were naturally associated with spring and summer. Sir John Fastolf's inventory lists numerous textiles, including a 'Cloth of the Nine Conquerors', one showing the Siege of Falaise at which he fought, and a 'clothe of arras with a geyannt in the myddell berying a legge of a bere in his honde'. The wars of the High Middle Ages, notably the Crusades and the Hundred Years' War, provided inspiration on a large scale, along with literary sources like the *Roman de la Rose* and the Arthurian and Trojan legends. In the Duc de Berry's chamber was a tapestry illustrating knights emerging from a city to give battle during the Trojan Wars, explained, as was so often done, in a text woven into the fabric above the scene. Not only is it possible to make out the hanging points immediately below the ceiling, but also where the tapestry has been tucked around the fireplace because it was too large for the wall – probably a common sight if hangings had to serve in several different places.

Also tucked under the tapestry is the cloth of state, which would be released in summer to cover the fireplace completely. Such cloths and canopies were made of damask from the Near East and were embroidered with the arms and devices of the owner, to which his vassals would continue to show respect even in his absence. René of Anjou, seated in his sparsely furnished study (Plate 25),

31 The Living Room, Tour des Anges. *Palais des Papes, Avignon. Fourteenth century*

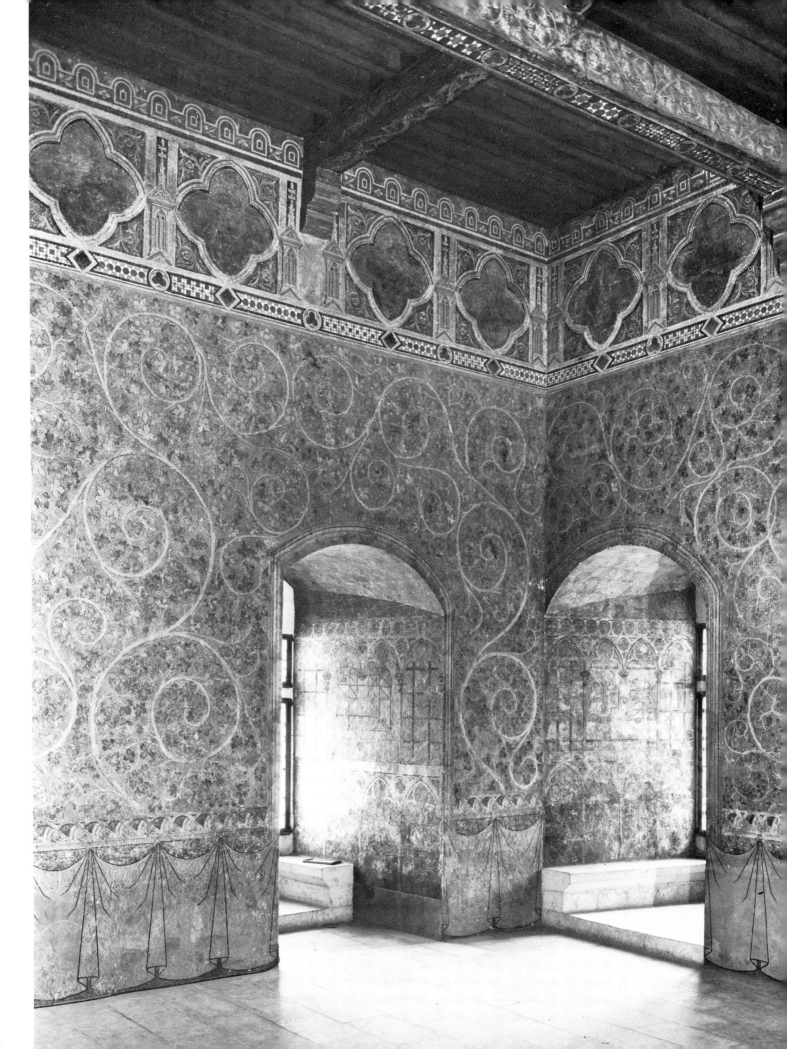

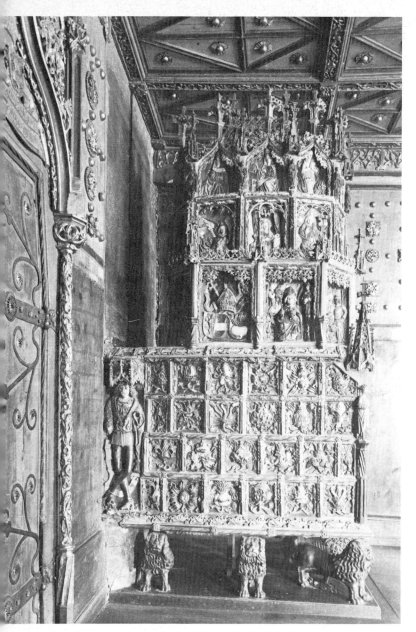

32 Detail of stove from the Golden Room. *Castle of Hohensalzburg, Austria. 1495–1519*

floor, creating an opulent effect. Tables too were covered with fabric; the Duc de Berry is shown seated (see Plate 18) at a table lavishly spread with gold and silver vessels on a white damask cloth. His table was undoubtedly, like so much medieval furniture, of a temporary nature: a simple board placed on trestles. Of the fitted pieces, wall cupboards were generally used for storing fragile items like glass or plate, and rarely for security. Closed with bolts or a simple latch, they were hinged with iron or leather; locks and keys were a luxury reserved for chests and important doors. Niches decorated with mouldings and carvings were found in privy chambers and held a water stoup, a basin and a ewer, with a towel-rail nearby. The only other built-in furniture which could be regarded as decorative as well as functional are the benches around the walls of halls and privy chambers. These were found everywhere in medieval Europe. The Castle of Gioia del Colle, built by Emperor Frederick II (1212–50) in Apulia, has a stone bench running along each wall, and Clarendon Palace had built-in benches topped with stone and faced with tiles.

One other important area where early medieval interiors survive is the Empire – Germany, Austria and the Habsburg possessions to the east. Nineteenth-century restorers, backed by the strength of patriotic nationalism, rebuilt, regilded or revarnished almost every vestige of German medieval interior decoration. As in France (for example at the Château of Pierrefonds), medieval ruins were ruthlessly converted into immaculate re-creations of Historicism's image of the Middle Ages, often with disastrous results. Two fine, if somewhat late interiors must suffice to show that French and Burgundian court taste of the fourteenth and fifteenth centuries had a profound influence on the German and Austrian interior. Local taste and style were modified to adapt the latest fashions from France, much as in later periods.

The Castle of Hohensalzburg, fortress of the Prince Archbishops of Salzburg, boasts the outstanding Golden Room decorated for Archbishop Leonhard von Keutschach (1495–1519). A flat beam and lathe ceiling has triangular coffering set with gilded hemispheres similar to the nearby Hall of Justice of the same date. The ceramic stove (Plate 32), seemingly resting on the backs of five wooden lions, is exuberantly decorated with saints, mythical beasts, fantastic fruit and flowers, fretwork balustrades and crockets and pinnacles – the whole confection glazed in many colours. A fine tracery of gilded Gothic mouldings in an ogee form with foliate terminals and bosses makes up the doorcases, and in the Hall of Justice the ceiling is supported by spiral columns of local blood-red marble, carved with the Keutschach arms – a turnip.

33 Sala dei Pappagalli, Palazzo Davanzati, *Florence. Early fourteenth century*

has his cloth of state hung from a rope between two beams to make a canopy. Walls of plain stone decorated only with his armorial bearings and his cloth, and an embrasure housing cushions and books, complete the simple furnishings befitting the author of a book called the *Mortification of Vain Pleasure*.

Cloth for wall-hangings was often painted, and Isabella of France, mother of King Edward III of England, had a dorsal and a banker showing a *Nativity*. In her hall was a cloth with the *Apocalypse*, but because this room lacked wainscoting, the space between hanging and floor was filled with worsted or coloured canvas. It was also common to use a long piece of cloth so that it would not only cover seating but also extend over a considerable part of the

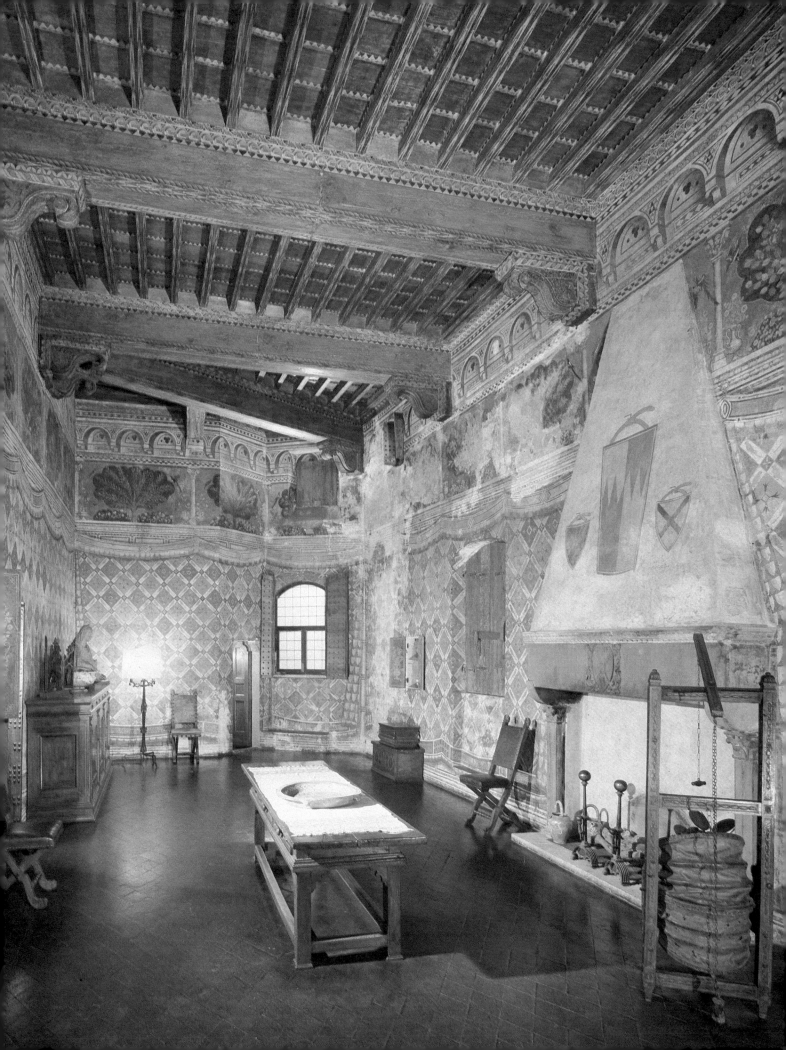

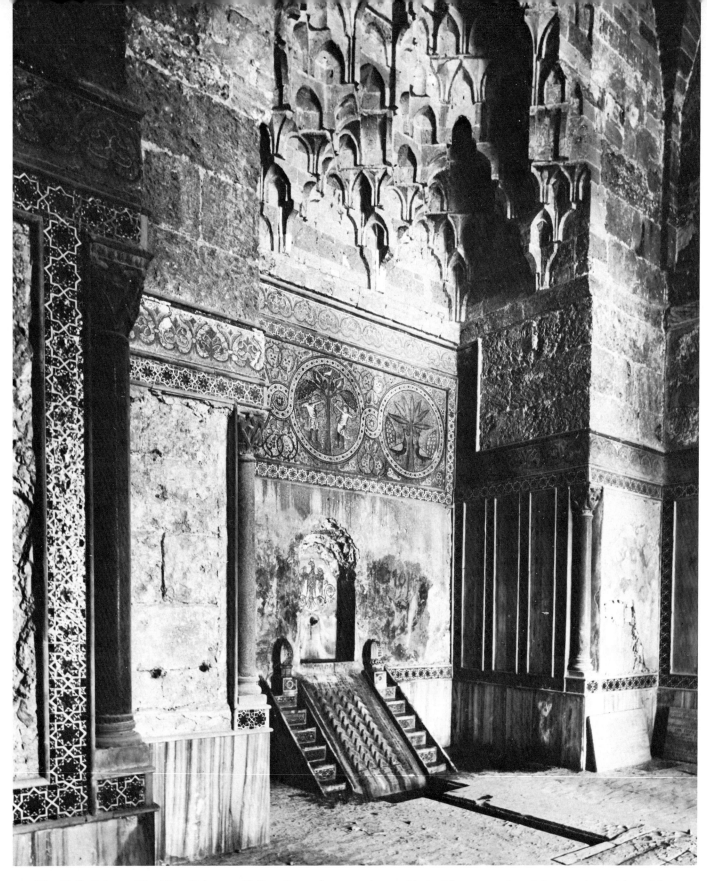

34 The Hall, Palace of La Zisa. *Palermo, Sicily   Begun by Guglielmo 1 in 1154–60 and completed by his son, La Zisa – the name comes from the Arab word aziz, meaning splendid – follows a typically compact and geometric plan. The hall* *is provided with rectangular niches on three sides with stalactite vaults, and a splendid mosaic frieze showing palms, peacocks and huntsmen, with the Imperial eagle in the niche above the water jet*

Similar extensive decoration survives in the Castle at Burg Eltz in the Moselle Valley, where plant forms of proto-Art Nouveau vitality creep over walls and beamed ceilings.

Karlstein in Bohemia was begun by the Emperor Charles IV (1348–78), and in its finest period must have compared favourably with any Valois castle for internal splendour. Little survives of its original decoration today, but the most outstanding feature must have been its walls covered with irregular fragments of marble and agate set in gilded plaster.

To balance the peripatetic marvels of the upper-class interior, it may be of interest to conclude with a mention of the type of room found in labourers' and peasants' homes, as recorded in the *Book of Hours of Catherine of Cleves* (Plate 35). The illustration is for the service of Nones in the Hours of the Virgin, and shows the Virgin and Joseph seated in a tiny room with a wooden-framed but unglazed window. A bare wooden ceiling complements the tiled but undecorated floor. Joseph sits in a chair made from a converted barrel, while around the fireplace and on a nearby shelf are household implements. The crumbling plaster of the fireplace strikes a credibly humble note, and gives what must be a realistic picture of the interior of a medieval carpenter's home – a stark contrast with the life-style of the Duc de Berry.

Between 1100 and 1300 Western Europe was brought into the closest contact with the art of the Greek East. In the fifteenth and sixteenth centuries, Ghiberti and Vasari blamed the 'Greek style' (*maniera greca*) for all the faults of painting in Italy before Giotto's genius ushered in a new era. We now appreciate the immensely valuable contribution not only to painting but also to design and decoration made by Byzantium, and see its art as part of a pattern rather than as mere decline. The flow of artistic ideas from the East received a sudden stimulus in 1204, when the diverted Fourth Crusade attacked and sacked Constantinople for the basest of motives, greed, and carried back its trophies to Italy. Well before that date, however, south Italian magnates and the Norman Kings of Sicily had commissioned Byzantine artists to decorate their palaces and churches. During the 1060s a flow of orders came from Italy for sets of cast bronze doors. In the 1070s, the first workshop of Byzantine mosaicists in Italy was set up at Montecassino, and throughout the twelfth century further teams were imported, notably by the Kings of Sicily and the Doges of Venice. These centres naturally became instrumental in spreading Byzantine styles and motifs into the West, most commonly through the portable arts of metalwork, painting and ivory carving. Thus, Byzantium became midwife at the birth of the true Gothic style of the thirteenth century, after its and many other influences had been assimilated.

The warring princes of southern Italy, wishing to break free from Byzantine rule in the eleventh century, engaged Northern adventurers or mercenaries, notably Tancred de

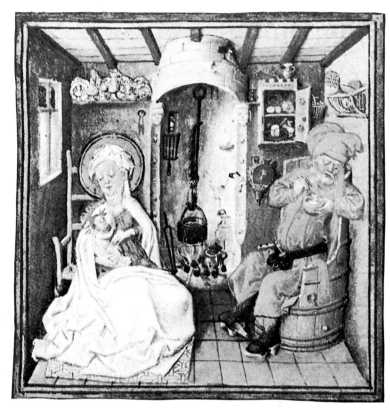

35 The Holy Family at Supper, from the Hours of Catherine of Cleves. *New York, Pierpont Morgan Library*

Hauteville, who led such spectacularly successful expeditions that his son Robert I founded a dynasty in Sicily. In 1130, Robert II was granted the title of King by the Pope. He and his grandson William II were inveterate builders and patrons of the arts, and to their reigns are attributed the most beautiful surviving 'Byzantinesque' interiors in the West: at the La Ziza and Cuba Palaces and at the Sala di Ruggero in the Royal Palace in Palermo (Plates 34 and 37). La Ziza is in very poor condition and the Sala di Ruggero heavily restored, but the combination of secular mosaics of flowers and animals, with marbles, tiles, plaster arabesques and the use of water typifies the courtly style of kings whose royal charters were in Greek, Latin or Arabic, and who spoke French.

Byzantine influence spread even further afield, into the Moslem world. In 711, Arabs and Berbers swept from Morocco into Visigothic Spain, moving North until halted in 732 by Charlemagne's grandfather, Charles Martel, when they had almost reached Tours on the Loire. After that, the Arab settlement of Spain became well established. A cruel, highly sophisticated, fanatically religious and artistically brilliant civilization, it was centred on the cities of Córdoba, Seville and Granada. It survived until 1492, when the Alhambra of Granada surrendered to King Ferdinand of Castile and Queen Isabella of Aragon.

The Alhambra, perched over the ravine dividing the city of Granada, shines out like a precious jewel on an immense scale. Constructed as a fortress and palace over

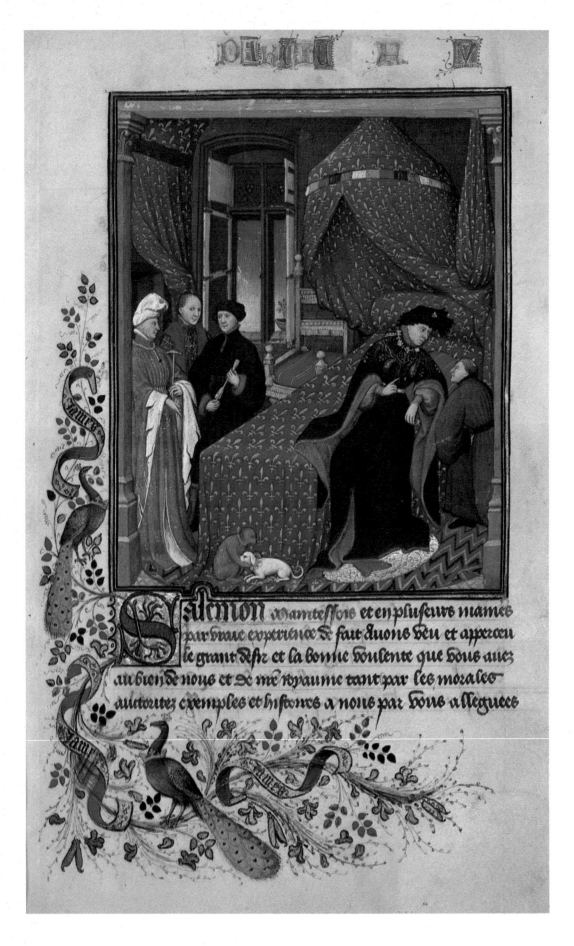

36 *(left)* Interior of Bedroom, from the Heures Boucicaut. *Late fourteenth century. Geneva, Bibliothèque Publique et Universitaire, MS fr. 165, f.4*

37 *(right)* Sala di Ruggero, Palace of the Normans *(formerly Royal Palace), Palermo, Sicily The combination of marble revetment with mosaics above on walls and vault gives a clear picture of a sumptuous Byzantine domestic interior. It was created by Arab and Byzantine craftsmen called in by the Normans during their enlargement of the existing ninth-century Arab structure. The mosaics date from around 1170, and include animals and trees, heavily restored*

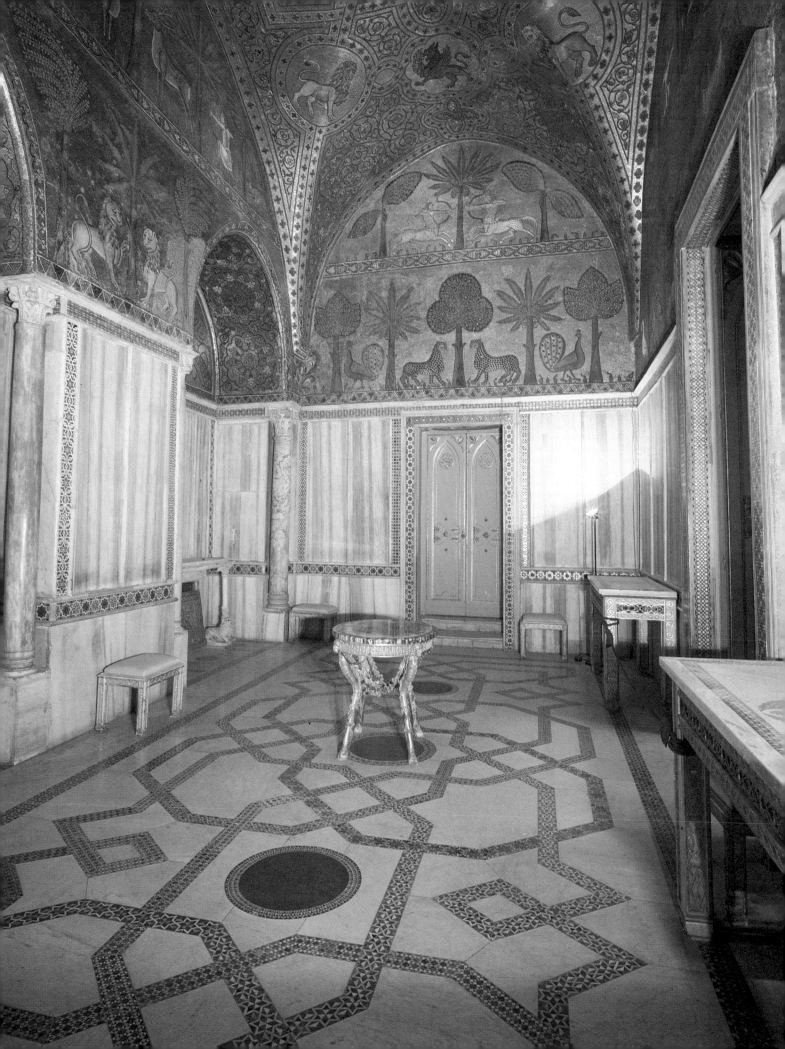

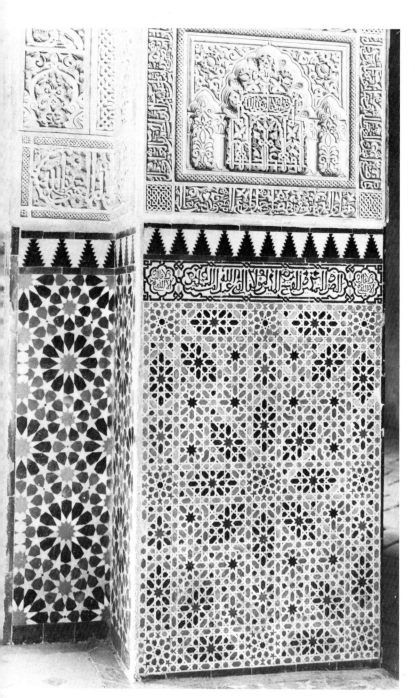

38 Tile decoration from the Alhambra, *Granada, 1354–91*
*The integration of exterior and interior which characterizes
the Alhambra is accentuated by the carved, moulded and
tiled decoration of its walls and complex vaults. Every
surface is covered with decoration, and ceilings are often
painted (as in the Hall of the Kings), or made of cedarwood
(as in the Hall of the Ambassadors) or have an elaborate
honeycomb or stalactite pattern as in the Hall of the
Abbencerrages. Tiles of every shape and colour are one
of the Alhambra's most striking features, and decorate
fountains, alcoves and even columns. They were mainly
manufactured in the ceramic workshops of Malaga*

several centuries, it was largely rebuilt between 1309 and
1354 by Abd-el-Walid and his successors. In this palace,
interior and exterior architecture intermingle as in few
other European buildings. The famous Court of the Lions
contains a fountain supported on lions' backs from which
water flows into four channels. Water – in basins, pools,
canals and running in streams through courtyards and
rooms – is combined with elaborate plasterwork and
glazed tiling on walls, domes and apses to create a pleasure
palace unrivalled in Europe. The transition from columned
halls to columned courtyards is barely discernible, and the
rich greenery of trees and flowers is reflected in the elaborate patterns of the wall tiles within (Plate 38). Its influence outside Spain was less widespread than Byzantine
styles of decoration, since Moorish Spain was cut off from
Europe not only by the Pyrenees but also by religious
differences. Contact between the mainstream of European
artistic development in the Middle Ages and Byzantium
did not always take place under conditions of war,
however. Between 961 and 976, the Caliph of Córdoba,
El Hakin, received from the Emperor Nicephorus Phocas
325 tons of mosaic *tesserae* – and the loan of one artist.

A last pathetic note on the decline of empires, and of
Byzantium in particular, is struck in the very heart of a new
order – Florence – where one of the Three Kings riding to
Bethlehem in Benozzo Gozzoli's fresco in the Medici-
Riccardi Chapel is Constantine XI Palaeologus, the last
Roman Emperor. He met his death defending the walls
of Constantinople against the victorious Turks in 1453.

3

Renaissance and Mannerism

… non aedifizio umano anzi divino

Giovanni Santi, speaking of the Palazzo Ducale
at Urbino in his *Cronaca*, LIX, 25

Historians of the Renaissance as a whole have not been inclined to admit that the domestic interior was one of the finest expressions of the culture of the period. If such an interior contained famous works of art, or carried an iconographical programme related to some noble prince's aspirations, then it deserved mention. However, because so many domestic interiors of the Renaissance *do* or did contain the finest art of their day (Mantegna's Camera degli Sposi, Veronese's Villa Barbaro decorations, the Salone of the Villa Medici (Plates 41, 42 and 44), and so on), the room as a whole often received little attention. In this respect, the selective aspect inherent in photography has played a detrimental role. Virtually no interior of the Renaissance retains its decoration and original furnishings intact, but now, for the first time, inventories enable us to visualize the contents of many of the more important rooms. Paintings too constitute one of the prime sources of information, especially those which set religious events in contemporary domestic surroundings.

Although the beginnings of the Renaissance are clearly defined in early fifteenth-century Italy, its spread throughout Europe and the precise dates of its various manifestations are not easy to date exactly. The Quattrocento in Italy presents a fairly coherent picture of discovery, evolution and resolution in the visual arts, dominated by great masters like Masaccio, Donatello and Brunelleschi. With the High Renaissance (*c.* 1500–20) came the consolidation of these trends in the classic works of Leonardo da Vinci, Michelangelo, Bramante and Raphael. In their wake follows the problematic period of Mannerism (*c.* 1520–1600), generally regarded as the final phase of the Renaissance. These dates refer specifically to Italy, but Italian ideas spread to other European countries with varying degrees of rapidity and intensity. While, for example, Italy was discarding Mannerism's conventions for the nascent Baroque style (see Chapter 4) France, Germany and England were still evolving their variants of the Renaissance artistic language. Since the principal advances and manifestations of the Renaissance occurred in Italy, it is with that country that this chapter is mainly concerned.

The Renaissance, with its increased emphasis on secular display, rapidly altered the medieval pattern of creating the principal works of art for ecclesiastical settings. While most Italian artists continued to work extensively for the Catholic Church, a greatly strengthened system of private patronage resulted in a vastly increased number of secular commissions for domestic interiors. The relative stability of the larger, more ambitious Italian families such as the Medici, the Farnese and the Gonzagas in comparison with their constantly feuding ancestors permitted the creation of new and imposing palaces, castles and villas on an unprecedented scale. Despite the centralized power of the Papacy, the continuous rivalry of the many city-states of Renaissance Italy had highly beneficial results for the arts. Under the Medici, Florence became Italy's leading centre of learning and artistic patronage. Lorenzo the Magnificent, himself a poet and scholar, patronized artists like the young Michelangelo and thinkers such as the Neo-Platonist Pico della Mirandola. His great library and his collections of ancient coins, cameos and medals were famous throughout Italy and contributed to the growing desire of the Florentines to live in 'classical' surroundings; the pedimented doorways, vaulted rooms and chimney-pieces decorated with details drawn from ancient sculpture (such as those in Palazzo Strozzi with cornucopias and other Roman motifs) all testify to this enthusiasm. The grafting of classical elements on to the Tuscan building tradition resulted in such work as that of Brunelleschi, who created interiors of unparalleled harmony and simplicity.

Distinct changes occurred in the type of houses required by the ruling and moneyed classes. During the later Middle Ages the city houses of the well-to-do crept upwards, within the necessary protection of the city walls, in the form of towers, sometimes expressing power and affluence through sheer height, as in many-towered San Gimignano in Tuscany. In Florence, the finest example of this type of

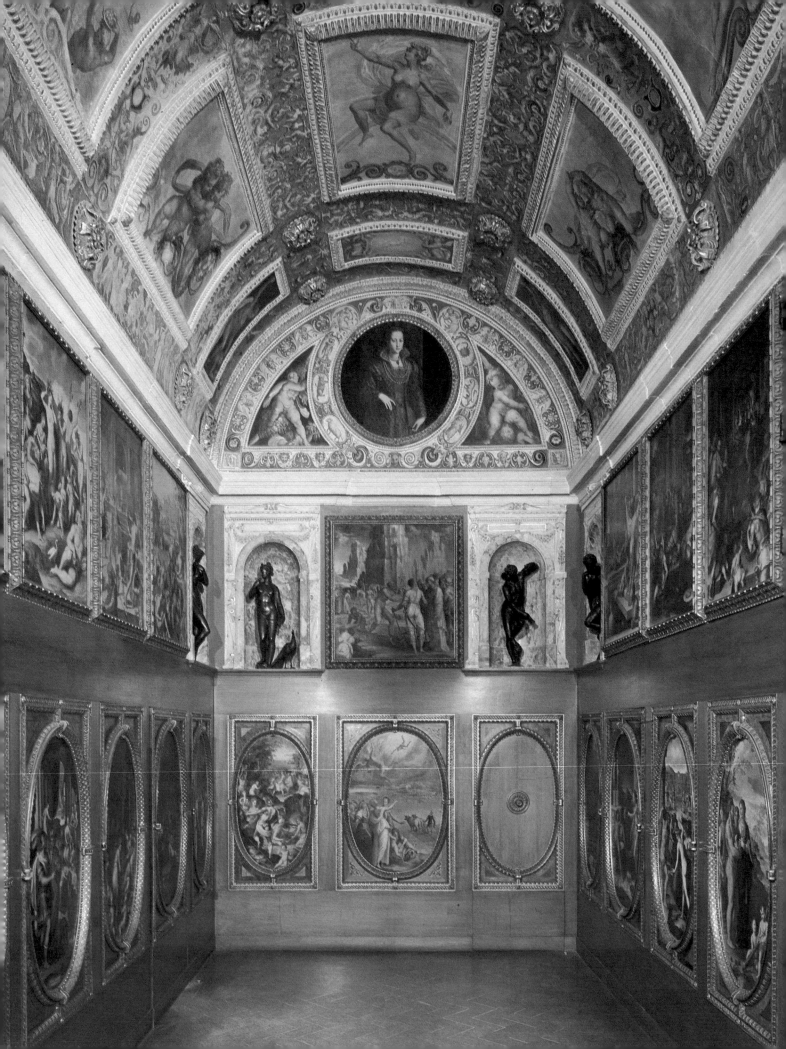

growth within restricted space is the Palazzo Davanzati. With the Renaissance, the concept of the city palace altered radically, and a new departure, the unfortified country villa, became possible through the greatly decreased threat of warfare.

From the fifteenth century onwards, many of the most beautiful and important schemes of interior decoration in Italy were realized in suburban or country villas, mainly centred around cities such as Rome and Florence and on the *terraferma* of the Veneto. In both villas and urban palaces, windows increased greatly in size, the small openings of the medieval *torre* giving way to large glazed spaces shedding copious light on the great collections of

sumptuous tapestries, paintings, sculpture, ceramics, metalwork and furniture which now became an integral part of civilized life. Many of the leading figures of the Renaissance were patrons and collectors of antique and contemporary art: Leon Battista Alberti in his book *Della famiglia* points out that the building and decoration of fine houses and the increasing accumulation of beautiful possessions and contemporary art are among the principal preoccupations of family life. The removal of most of these objects from their original setting has not only changed the appearance of many Renaissance rooms, but in certain cases altered the iconographic meaning intended by the humanistic 'programme' of the decoration.

During the Renaissance, man's new consciousness of his place in an increasingly less mysterious universe went hand in hand with the rediscovery of Classical civilization. The influence of the ancient world on architecture was immense, and during the Quattrocento the most imposing domestic interiors were predominantly architectonic in appearance. Alberti hailed the completion of Filippo Brunelleschi's famous dome of Florence Cathedral in 1435 as the first major achievement of the new art, rivalling and even surpassing Roman architecture. But the rediscovery of the antique progressed spasmodically. Fifteenth-century

39 *(left)* The Studiolo of Francesco I de' Medici, *1570–72. Palazzo Vecchio, Florence   The studiolo or study in the Renaissance provided an excuse for complex allegorical decorations, in this case devised by the room's designer, Giorgio Vasari, with the aid of Vincenzo Borghini. The Mannerist period's love of preciosity is seen in the richly detailed paintings and sculptures by a wide range of contemporary artists*

40 *(below)* Pavement of Room of Leone X. *Palazzo Vecchio, Florence*

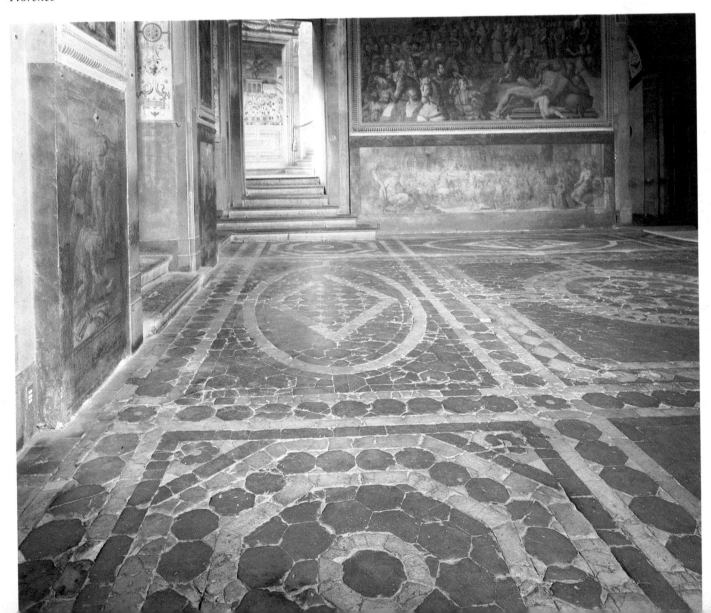

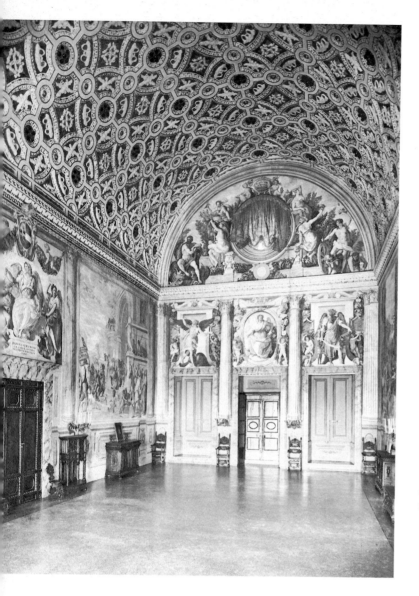

41 *(left)* Salone of Villa Medicea, Poggio a Caiano, near Florence, *by Giuliano da Sangallo   In 1480, Lorenzo the Magnificent commissioned Giuliano da Sangallo to convert the Villa Ambra at Poggio a Caiano. Sangallo's principal innovation was the introduction of this large central Salone rising through two storeys, in place of the more typical Tuscan villa's courtyard. The decoration, undertaken in two stages, includes frescoes by Andrea del Sarto, Franciabigio and Pontormo (the famous* Vertumnus and Pomona *lunette), begun in 1521; the second stage was carried out under Alessandro Allori in 1579. All of the frescoes allude to events in Medici history, such as Cicero's return from Exile, which refers to the return of Cosimo the Elder after his three-year absence from Florence. The elegant barrel-vault is typical of Cinquecento stucco coffering*

42 *(right)* Room of Bacchus, Villa Barbaro, Maser. *Frescoes by Paolo Veronese, c. 1561   Veronese's frescoes in the magnificent Villa at Maser, built by Andrea Palladio for the brothers Marcantonio and Daniele Barbaro, constitute one of the most harmonious schemes of fresco decoration of the Renaissance, and one of the most intact programmes of Italian Humanism. Amid a setting of fictive architecture and sculpture are found some of the most important early examples of Italian landscape painting, areas of finto marmo, illusionistic 'bronze' statues in niches, and open pergolas frescoed on the vault. The central vault fresco shows Bacchus revealing to mankind the mystery of wine. The large marble chimney-piece is a typically Venetian sixteenth-century version of earlier hooded prototypes, with classical consoles, Greek key frieze and a grotesque Mannerist mask. Throughout the villa, illusionistic fresco is used not only to extend real space on both walls and ceilings, but to suggest the presence in certain rooms of contemporary figures*

Italy's theories of beauty, in which Alberti's and Brunelleschi's contributions were of primary importance, were expressed through harmonic geometries based on the ideal proportions of the human body; from this period until the end of the sixteenth century (in the works of Palladio) proportional perfection characterized the finest interiors. This explains why such masterly interiors as those of the Ducal Palace in Urbino retain an astonishing dignity in spite of the removal of the original furnishings (Plate 46). The secret of this system of proportion lay in a 'multiplicity of spatial units . . . mathematically evolved from a module and grouped in a perfectly symmetrical whole [creating] that absolute harmony which was the culmination of the new concept of beauty' (Heydenreich).

Brunelleschi's pure, simple interiors (as in the Pazzi Chapel at S. Croce in Florence) had an immense effect on subsequent Renaissance interiors, contrasting white or pale blond plastered wall surfaces with smooth or sculpted grey stone mouldings and details. Unfortunately, there is little evidence to prove the existence of the many houses and palaces he is reputed to have designed. He never set out to imitate Roman architecture, since he combined in his buildings many elements of the regional architecture of Tuscany. Indeed, it was his application of antique motifs to the simplest architectural forms which laid the foundations of European architectural types for the future; to him we owe the acceptance (or re-acceptance) of the dome, the drum, the pendentive, coupled orders and many other features. The concepts of interior space evolved in fifteenth-century Italy are constants even today and still dictate our standards in evaluating the appearance of a room. While the medieval interior might spread out and take on any proportions required by function, in the Renaissance proportion dictated the basic forms which were applied to any given problem. Thus a huge interior like the Throne Room at the Ducal Palace of Urbino displays the same proportional system as the tiny *Studiolo* of Francesco I de'Medici (Plate 39), an interior whose

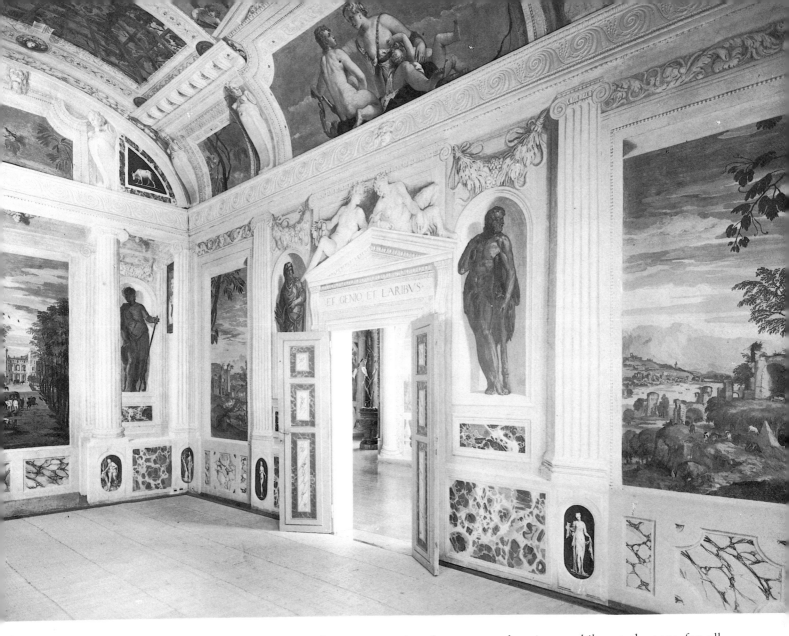

beautifully scaled proportions ensure its elegance. Alberti's and Brunelleschi's codification of perspective led to a new consciousness of both real and pictorial space. Not only is this reflected in the fifteenth century's new interest in room shapes and sizes, but also in their interrelationship. (As a virtual science, the latter was to reach perfection in the hands of Palladio.) It was at this time also that the desire to 'extend' real space by means of fictive distance in fresco, painting or even sculpture was born. This was to be of the greatest consequence for many of the major ecclesiastical and secular decorative schemes of the next four centuries.

Michelozzo (Michelozzo di Bartolomeo, 1396–1472) was an important architect of Florentine domestic buildings such as the Medici villas of Careggi, Trebbio, Caffagiuolo and Fiesole – mostly later remodelled. He also designed one of the most important buildings of the Renaissance, the Medici-Riccardi Palace in Florence, whose vast scale, and whose emphasis on the magnificent

suite of rooms on the *piano nobile*, set the tone for all subsequent great urban residences. It was, however, Leon Battista Alberti (1404–72) whose theoretical and practical work exercised the most immediate widespread influence. Born in Genoa of banished Florentine patrician parents, Alberti was primarily concerned with architecture, which he conceived of as the natural conjunction of the arts and sciences. His *Ten Books of Architecture* was first published in Latin in Florence in 1485; the first Italian translation appeared in Venice in 1546. Whereas Vitruvius' *Ten Books* had retained their value throughout the Middle Ages for their concern with cosmology and engineering, Alberti's writings were esteemed by his contemporaries for their practical application. Much of his advice on decoration, which, like Brunelleschi and Michelozzo, he saw as necessarily subservient to architecture, is austere: 'I, for my part, hate everything that savours of luxury (*lussuria*) or profusion . . .' Throughout his writing on art, Alberti places great emphasis on *decorum*, or the strict appro-

43 *(below)* Detail of Giovanni da Udine's grotesques in the Loggie of Raphael. *Rome, Vatican*

44 *(right)* Camera degli Sposi, 1465–74. *Palazzo Ducale, Mantua   The Camera Picta (Painted Room), or Camera degli Sposi as it was called, represents one of the triumphs of Renaissance courtly humanism and also of illusionistic fresco decoration. Starting with the ceiling, Andrea Mantegna (1431–1506) decorated the room as if curtains had been drawn back over the arches to reveal assembled Gonzaga courtiers set against distant landscapes. In the centre of the ceiling is painted an open oculus over whose balustrade figures peer down into the room. It is uncertain whether the frescoes depict specific scenes in the lives of the various Gonzagas. Of particular beauty is the chimney-piece, with its carved frieze* all'antica *and its supporting consoles*

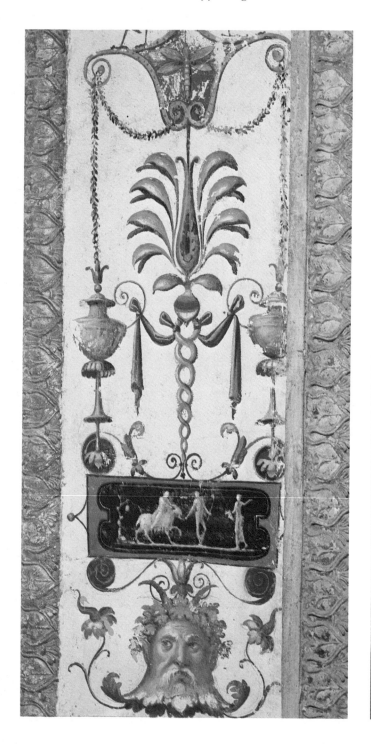

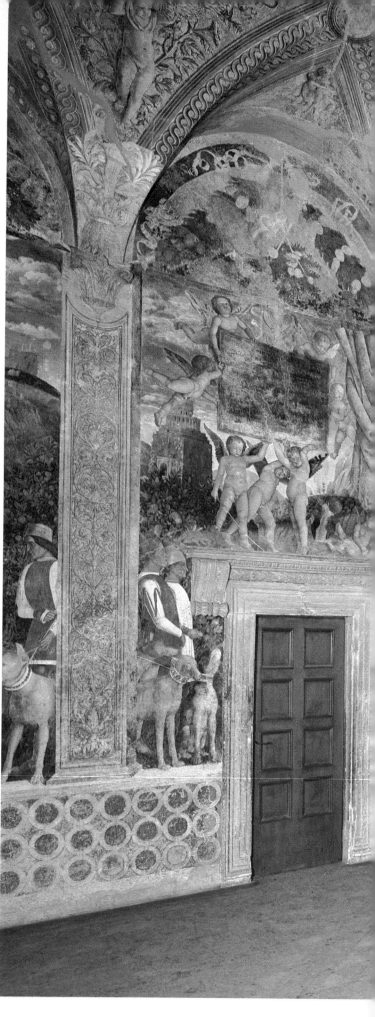

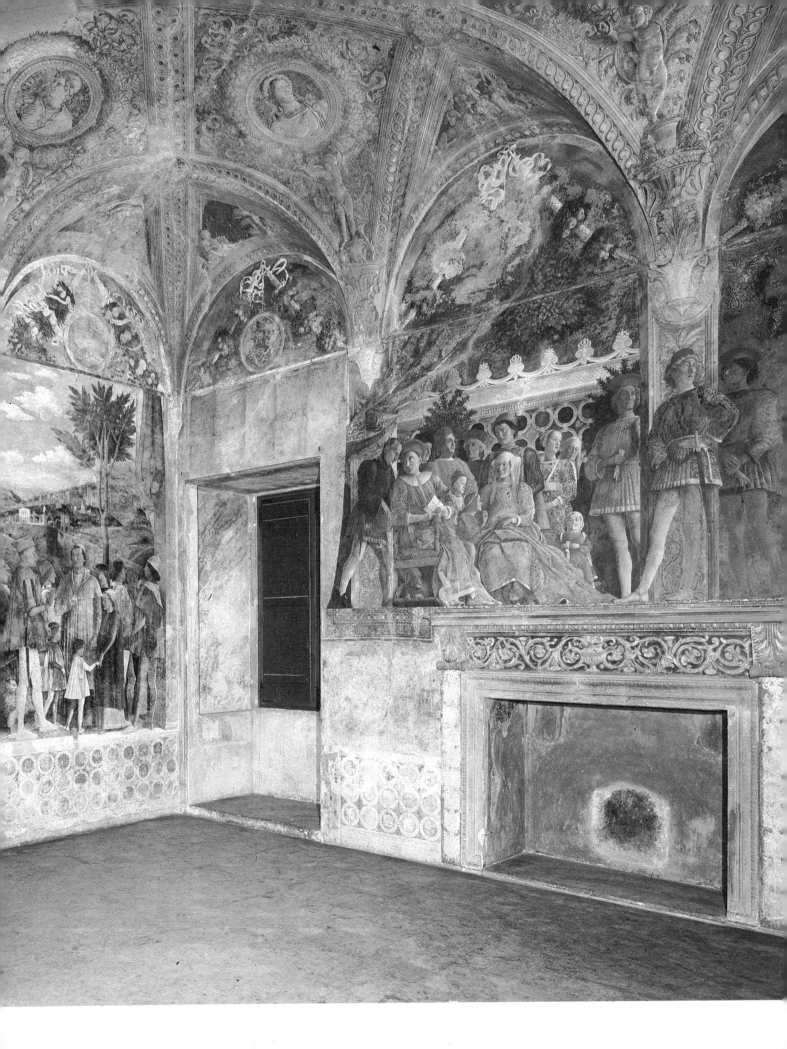

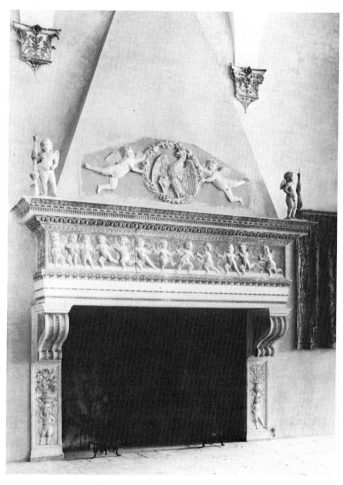

45 Fireplace, Sala degli Angeli. *Palazzo Ducale, Urbino*

pieces. Baldassare Castiglione in his *Book of the Courtier* writes, 'In the rugged place of Urbino he built a palace which is, in the opinion of many, the most beautiful which can be found in Italy; and he furnished it so well with every fitting thing that it appeared to be not a palace, but a city in palace form.' In 1450, when Federico began the palace, he had few models on which to base his ideas, and so the results are all the more surprising. The pictorial ideas of Piero della Francesca regarding classical architecture and space, as expressed in his *Flagellation of Christ* (Urbino, National Gallery of the Marches), almost certainly inspired Federico; Piero had had contact with Alberti in Rimini in the early 1450s. Like the forms of this picture, 'set jewel-like in the transparent air and silvery light' (Venturi), the decorative details of Federico's wonderful palace strike us with their crisply sculpted, incredibly rich profusion of classical motifs.

The palace is the perfect illustration of a great domestic interior created at the time of the full flowering of the early Renaissance. The architect was Luciano Laurana (1420/5–79), a Venetian-trained Dalmatian who had direct experience of Roman Imperial architecture at its most grandiose in the Emperor Diocletian's Palace at Split. Laurana's work was continued by Francesco di Giorgio.

The sumptuously decorated monumental staircase is the first example of its kind. The larger rooms such as the Sala della Jole, Salone del Trono, Sala degli Angeli and Sala delle Voglie display unprecedented virtuosity in the combination of perfectly harmonious proportion with a wealth of decorative detail baffling description. Most of the rooms have plain, whitewashed walls, offsetting the richly sculpted chimney-pieces (Plate 45), door-cases, window-frames and ceiling-mouldings which articulate them. Ceilings are of every description; in several, vaults spring from carved stone capitals, while in others the ceiling is flat above a deep cove framed by two richly moulded cornices. In the Duchess's bedchamber, a free-flowing pattern of ribbons surrounds a central stucco *impresa*, while in the library, stylized rays of flame emanate from the central circular device of the Montefeltro eagle framed by a pattern of angels' faces and wings. Doorways and chimney-pieces present the richest source of decoration. Above frames of egg-and-dart moulding are straight friezes of honeysuckle and other plant designs, incorporating griffins, *putti*, vases, cornucopias, ribbons, garlands, portrait-heads within wreaths and shells. Perhaps the most beautiful doorway of all is that of the Sala della Jole, which attains the highest sculptural level, transcending its mere function as a frame. To a lesser extent the same may be said of the chimney-pieces, which, as well as a medieval-derived kind with a hood (here often bearing a *stemma* or other sculpture), also include a novel straight carved entablature supported on twin pilasters, the whole in shallow relief against the wall; the entablature provides a very narrow upper ledge. It was only in eighteenth-century France and England that this type of chimney-piece was

priateness of every feature of any work of art. In this, he followed in Vitruvius' footsteps (see Chapter 1).

Alberti's interest in the scale and variety of ancient architecture, which struck a new chord in Italian architectural thinking, dates from his first period in Rome. Because he maintained close relations with many members of the Medici, Gonzaga, Este and Montefeltro families, his ideas of monumentality spread rapidly. Between 1450–80 in Florence he designed, or advised on, many domestic buildings, leaving his mark on the architecture of that city and its environs. He was a regular visitor at the court of Federico da Montefeltro in Urbino, and probably influenced Federico's desire to create a splendid new palace which would reflect not only his own wealth and culture but also the exciting new spirit of the humanistic age. Federico himself seemed to combine all the best qualities of the Renaissance prince. A brilliant soldier and able ruler, he was also a liberal patron of the arts, a scholar and a humanist. The portrait in his *Studiolo* characteristically shows him in realistic profile, fully armed and reading a book. Elsewhere in the palace his presence is consciously evoked by the use of his arms, devices and inscriptions in the decorative detail of doorways, windows and chimney-

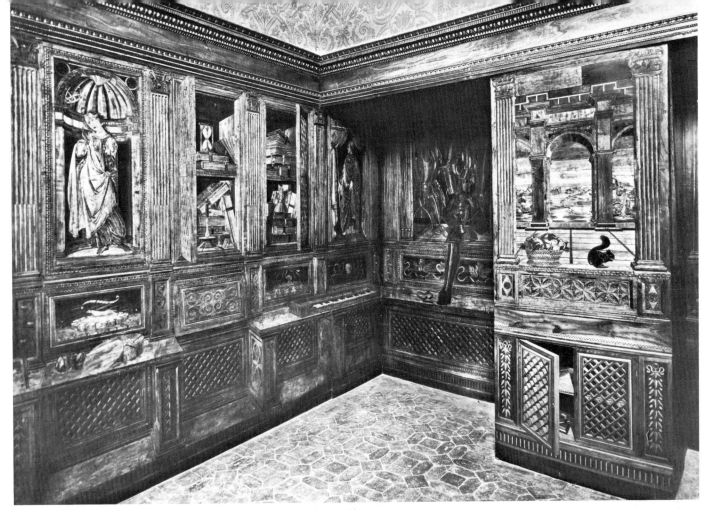

46 The Studiolo of Federico da Montefeltro, Duke of Urbino. *Palazzo Ducale, Urbino Despite its tiny proportions, this room was one of the most important interiors of the Renaissance, both from the point of view of its decoration (tarsie panels below, paintings on the wall above) and its iconography. The tarsie, in a wide variety of woods, show musical instruments, books, armour, caged birds, hour-glasses, candles and so on, arranged to suggest ledges, recesses and open or closed cupboards. All of these pertain to the humanistic studies dear to Federico. Above, centred around the famous portrait of the Duke with his son Guidobaldo by Pedro Berruguete(?), were affixed portraits of twenty-eight famous men ranging from Moses and Solomon to Plato, Aristotle, Dante and Petrarch. On the ceiling are the emblems of the Ermine and the Garter together with Federico's personal device. The privacy of the study is emphasized in the contrast of this room with the great Sala delle Veglie, where the court gathered for evening entertainment, music and conversation. While the tarsie and sumptuous ceiling remain, the rest was dismantled by Cardinal Antonio Barberini in 1631, and the paintings are scattered throughout various galleries*

adopted wholeheartedly, and it seems highly likely that the Urbino examples were known to designers like Adam. Much of this sculpture reflects an increasing study of Roman reliefs, especially on sarcophagi and triumphal arches. As no domestic interior by Alberti survives, his conception of decorative detail can only be surmised from such sculptural work as the Rucellai Chapel in S. Pancrazio, Florence.

As has been noted in Chapter I, it was not until the eighteenth century that direct imitation of Roman domestic interiors was either possible or considered generally desirable. No architect of the Quattrocento had any notion of the appearance of the average domestic interior of ancient Rome, apart from the descriptions of Vitruvius. Thus, although the exteriors of their palaces may have resembled those of antiquity (especially Bramante's House of Raphael, which was closely based on Roman *insulae* or apartment blocks above shops), the interiors did not. Robert Adam attacked British Palladian interiors on precisely these grounds – that, like Palladio (1508–80), the architects had taken their cue for their domestic arrangements from the public rather than the private architecture of Rome.

Through their reading of Vitruvius, however, architects and patrons developed an increased interest in specifying the function of rooms in a way unknown to the Middle Ages. Whereas 'the fixtures of the medieval household were equipment, chairs to sit on, beds to sleep in, icons to pray before, so much and no more' (*The Culture of Cities*), the dignity and order essential for the life of the

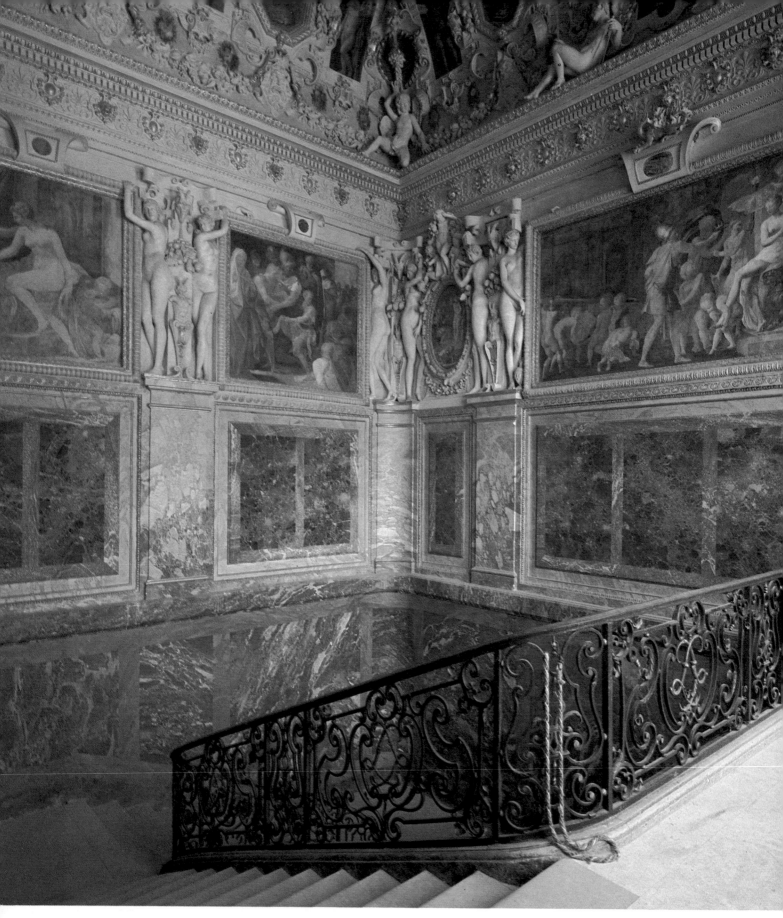

47 Staircase to Royal Apartments, Fontainebleau, *by Primaticcio*

Renaissance prince, were best expressed through the display of taste and wealth in public apartments. In the Apartment of Federico of Urbino, state and private rooms were combined – Antechamber, Audience Chamber, Bedchamber, *Studiolo* (Plate 46), Temple of the Muses and Chapel are all *en suite* and have specific functions. Most clearly defined during the Quattrocento are the vestibule (for the reception of visitors), the library (hardly surprising in the wake of the invention of printing and the dissemination of printed and bound books), the *studiolo* and the *galleria*. It was in the *galleria* that most of the antique sculpture, gems and other objects belonging to such connoisseurs as Federico da Montefeltro, the Medici – Giuliano, and Lorenzo the Magnificent – the Gonzagas, Lodovico il Moro and others were displayed. During the Baroque age, the *galleria* became one of the principal rooms in any great palace or villa, often receiving the most lavish treatment (Plate 76). Dining rooms were virtually unknown, and *tavole smontabili*, or folding tables, which could easily be dismantled or enlarged, were used, often in the delightfully appointed *loggie* which formed an important part of both urban and rural residences.

The medieval tendency to culminate vertically emphasized rooms with a pointed cross-vault was gradually replaced during the Quattrocento by vaults *all'antica*, springing from corbels forming lunettes, flat or coved wooden ceilings, and stuccoed and frescoed ceilings and vaults; most staircases had barrel-vaults. Ceilings made of wood were common to all levels of society; the poorest homes had strong wooden beams, often still with their natural irregularities, set into the masonry of supporting walls. Across these were laid smaller beams, which in turn supported the terracotta tiles of the upper floor – a system surviving almost unchanged from ancient times. Frequently the tiles are visible from beneath and their upper surfaces would attain a fine patina after continuous polishing. Terracotta ceilings appear to have been rare, despite the popularity in Florence of the Della Robbia family's work in coloured and glazed terracotta; an example survives in the Museo del Castello Sforzesco, Milan. Throughout most of the Quattrocento, the ceilings of the finest rooms were of wood, often elaborately carved, painted and gilded; during the sixteenth century, combinations of wood, stucco and even paintings and metal appear. Most of the wooden ceilings visible in Italian Renaissance palaces are of the so-called *soffitto morto*, or 'dead ceiling', type, so called because they do not form part of the building's structure, but are attached to the supporting beams by pegs and other means. The Latin origin of the Italian *soffitto* – *sub fictum* – seems to point to an ancient pedigree for this practice. False ceilings composed of light materials were almost certainly very common in the Middle Ages, and may have been used during winter months in unheatable interiors; they appear in Trecento paintings as the simplest of cross-struts with an in-filling possibly even of cloth or leather.

Painted ceilings were of course common during the Middle Ages both in Italy and in the North, and the art never died out. A particularly superb example painted on the eve of the Renaissance is that in Palazzo Chiaramonte in Palermo, executed by Simone di Corleone and Cecco di Naro (Plate 48), while in Florence in 1387 payments are recorded from Lapo da Castiglionchio to 'Francesco, painter, living in Piazza dei Priori, for painting the beams, cornices, brackets and supports for the bedroom ceiling and the room upstairs'. Although most of these late fourteenth-century ceilings were subdivided into sections containing representations of the human figure, animals, plants and abstract forms, they show little awareness of Roman precedents, and this was altered radically in the Quattrocento.

As on exteriors, cornices increased in depth, often to enormous proportions, and included classical motifs of all kinds, notably egg-and-dart. The ceiling of the Urbino *Studiolo* presents a particularly rich variant on Roman coffering, with circular bosses forming separate decorative articulation between the coffers. In the Palazzo Vecchio in Florence there is another important group of such ceilings, such as the Del Tasso brothers' octagonal coffers framing lilies in the Sala di Eleonora da Toledo (*c.* 1482) or the same craftsmen's much heavier Audience Chamber ceiling with its deeply carved frieze of animal heads and garlands of fruit (Plate 49). The Ducal Palace at Mantua also retains many outstanding Quattrocento ceilings of great richness. These wooden ceilings were paralleled in ecclesiastical architecture by similar experiments in stone or stucco, and towards the end of the Quattrocento, stucco became increasingly popular for the decoration of ceilings and vaults. Venice, however, retained a preference for wooden ceilings, often carved in shallow relief with a delicacy scarcely rivalled elsewhere in the Quattrocento, as in the various *Scuole*, or confraternities: particularly beautiful examples are the Sala di Adunanza in the Accademia, a collaborative work showing God the Father and four Prophets by Marco Cozzi, Alvise Vivarini and Domenico Campagnola. During the sixteenth century, Venice excelled in carved ceilings of immense richness and complexity.

As we have seen at the Palace of Urbino, the chimneypiece occupied a place of prominence unknown in the Middle Ages except in the great hall. The hooded type survived from earlier usage, sometimes self-supporting as in Paolo Uccello's painting *A Woman redeeming her Cloak at the price of a consecrated Host* (Plate 50), where the hood is painted with a coat of arms. The type of straight-topped, hoodless chimney-piece noted at Urbino may have originated with the Brunelleschi school; fine examples are found in the Faenza Museum and in the main *sala* of the Badia at Fiesole. One of the most monumental of these early fireplaces is that executed by Giuliano da San Gallo for the *sala* of the elaborate Palazzo Gondi in Florence, one of the prime sources of decoration surviving from the

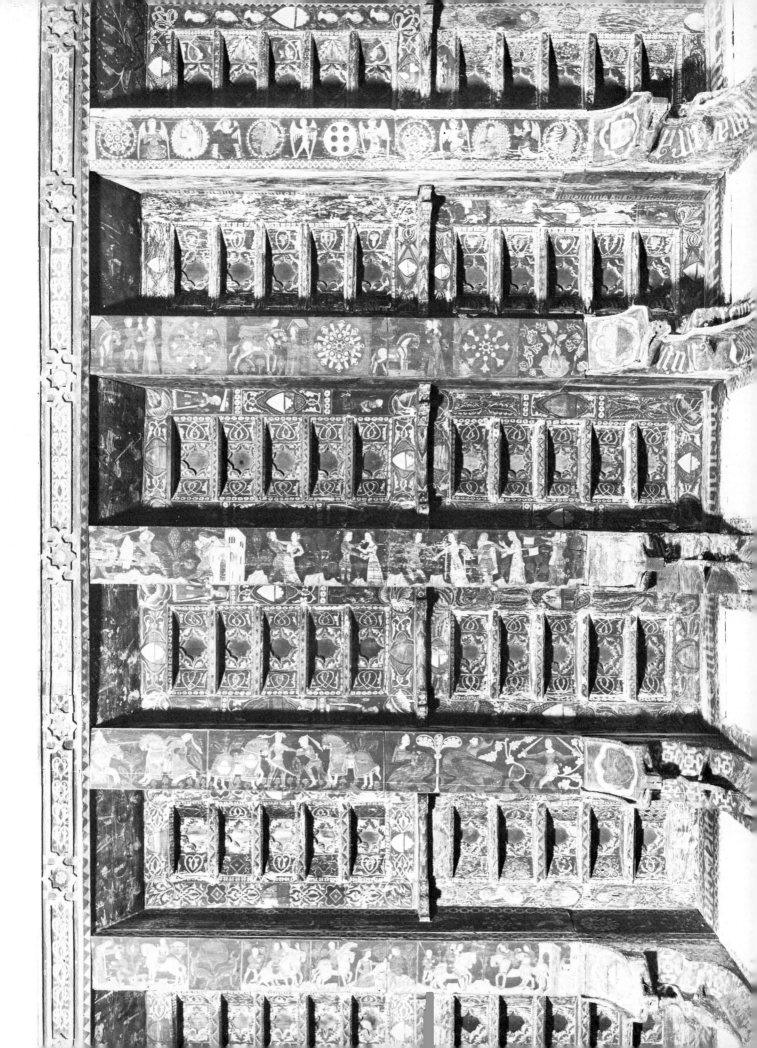

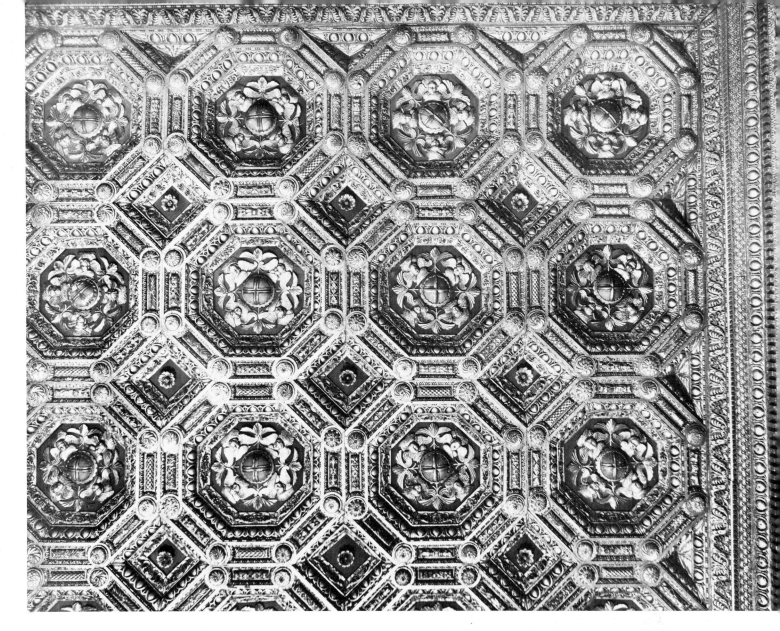

48 (left) Painted ceiling by
Simone di Corleone and
Cecco di Naro, 1377–80.
*Palazzo Chiaramonte,
Palermo*

49 (above) Coffered ceiling
by the Del Tasso Brothers.
*Audience Room, Palazzo
Vecchio, Florence*

50 (right) Paolo Uccello: A
Woman redeeming her Cloak
at the price of a consecrated
Host, 1456–9. *Urbino,
Galleria Nazionale delle
Marche*

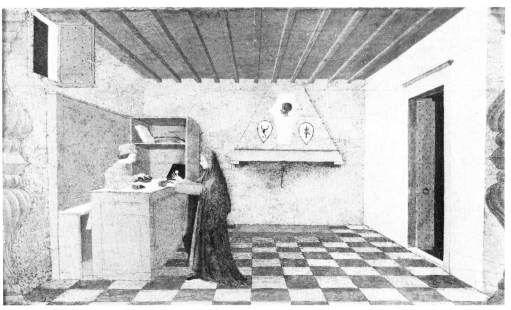

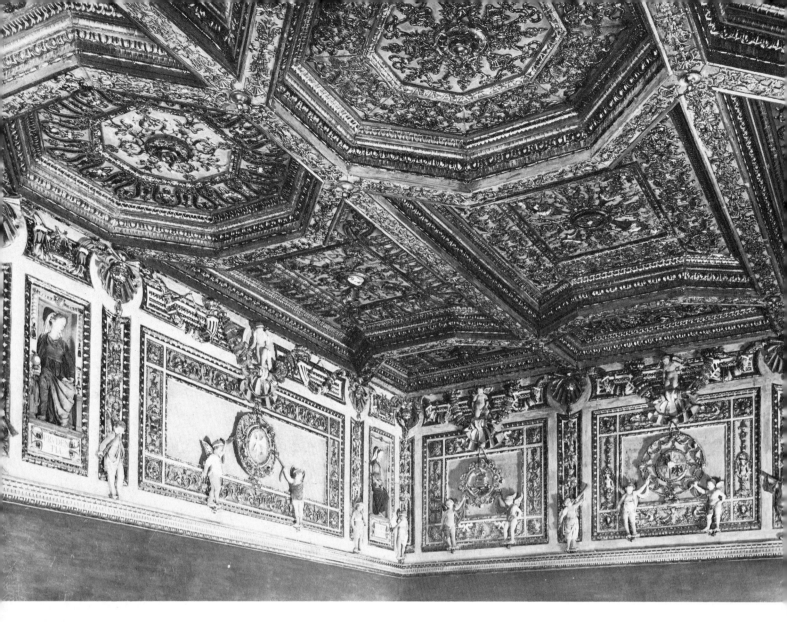

51 Frieze and ceiling from the Sala degli Stucchi. *Palazzo Schifanoia, Ferrara After the Sala dei Mesi, which has the largest series of secular frescoes of the Italian Renaissance, this room is one of the most beautiful. The elaborately carved and gilded ceiling of 1467 by Domenico Paris typifies a style found throughout Italy at this time, with minor variations on the basic theme of large carved beams forming octagonal, lozenge-shaped, square or circular compartments, also containing elaborate carved decoration. The frieze niches contain figures of the* Virtues

period. The Victoria and Albert Museum has a fine example attributed to Desiderio da Settignano with *putti*-consoles, portrait medallions and *putti* holding a wreath at the centre of the frieze. Despite the evident care and expense lavished on these chimney-pieces, their function in the Italian climate was much more limited than in the North, where the hooded variety survived far longer; certain exceptions (Plate 45) were well in advance of fashion.

The *mattoni*, or terracotta tiles, which we have noted as common to every stratum of society, could be laid in a variety of patterns (Plate 40). In Palazzo Gondi in Florence, they are hexagonal, and in paintings they sometimes appear in white and ochre-coloured designs. Alberti notes that *mattoni* called *mezzane* were laid in parallel lines,

while other types were placed in circles or fishbone patterns. Mosaics constructed of small pieces of marble in simple designs generally imitated the more lavish floors of great houses, and large marble tiles of contrasting colours appear in many Quattrocento paintings. Small coloured *mattoni* with lead glazes could also be adapted to realistic or abstract designs, and in the second half of the century lead-glazed maiolica tiles of dazzling colours were used domestically. Vasari writes in his life of Luca della Robbia, 'The magnificent Piero di Cosimo de'Medici, among the first to commission coloured ceramic work from Luca, ordered him to decorate the whole barrel-vault of a writing-room in the palace built ... by Cosimo his father, with various fanciful designs, and in the same manner, the

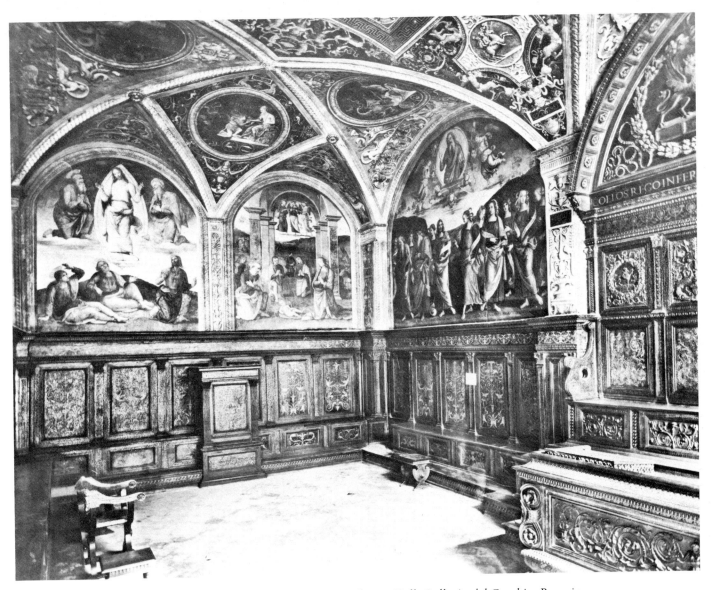

52 Frescoes by Perugino, *1498–1507. Audience Hall, Collegio del Cambio, Perugia*

floor ...' Vasari goes on to note that the effect was not of separate tiles but of a unified whole. In 1488 Giuliano da Maiano placed an order for twenty thousand glazed *mattonelle* for the decoration of one of the royal palaces of Naples, and it seems likely that the Tuscan fashion spread rapidly throughout Italy: suffice to note that it was the Della Robbia family who were commissioned to provide the maiolica pavements for one of the most important decorative undertakings of the early sixteenth century, the Vatican Loggie of Raphael. Among the most famous centres of maiolica production of this type was Montelupo, which was most active during the seventeenth century. Sometimes, where the decoration of walls and ceilings was particularly lavish or colourful, plain-coloured *mattoni* could be laid creating the shallowest of relief-patterns, as in the Sala dei Fasti Farnesiana in the Farnese Palace at Caprarola.

Wall-surfaces not covered with tapestries, paintings, cloth or leather hangings, were generally frescoed, or embellished with a combination of fresco and stucco relief – a fashion which became increasingly popular from the early sixteenth century. In rooms of any height where hangings were to be used, the uppermost part of the wall had a decorative frieze since large tapestries presented not only financial problems but also difficulties in hanging and handling. One of the earliest fully extant schemes with this type of elaborate frieze on the upper zone of the walls is in the Sala degli Stucchi of Palazzo Schifanoia at Ferrara (Plate 51), but its use is extremely common throughout the Renaissance, Mannerist and Baroque periods: Annibale Carracci, creator of one of the greatest interiors of the early Baroque – the Farnese Gallery in Rome (Plate 76) – began his career as a decorator with friezes of this type (see Chapter 4).

Towards the end of the Quattrocento, the simplified grotesques (see Chapter 1), which had appeared in a

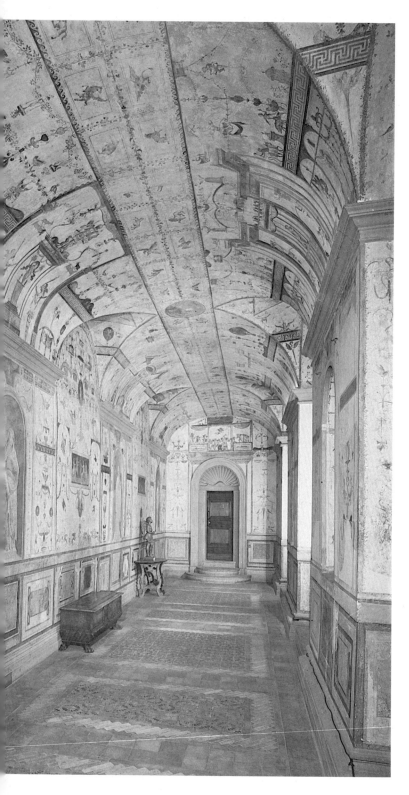

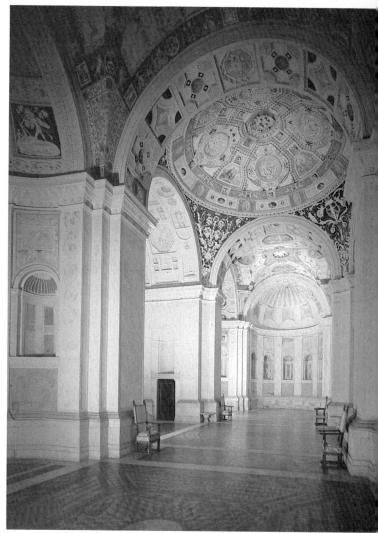

53 *(left)* The Loggie of Raphael. *Rome, Vatican (see also Plate 43)*

54 *(above)* The Loggia, 1517–23. *Villa Madama, Rome Raphael designed this villa for Cardinal Giuliano de' Medici, later Pope Clement VII. Although never completed, and damaged during the Sack of Rome in 1527, the Loggia is one of the most beautiful of the Renaissance's recreations of Classical ideas on decoration. Raphael partly based his design on Pliny's descriptions of his villas in the* Letters. *The vault grotesques by Giovanni da Udine and the wall stuccoes by Giulio Romano combine with Raphael's architecture to recreate the atmosphere of the bath-houses of ancient Rome, whose proportions the Loggia recalls. While dependent on Roman originals for inspiration, Giovanni da Udine's grotesques remain astonishingly inventive*

restrained form in the framework of many frescoes as well as on carved or painted pilasters (as at the Ducal Palace of Urbino) began to assume a new importance. One of the first notable uses of grotesques is in the Collegio del Cambio (Plate 52) at Perugia (1498–1507) and they also form an important part of Pinturicchio's Libreria Piccolomini decorations in Siena of 1502–9. Raphael, who had worked with Perugino in Perugia, was the artist mainly responsible for the true revival of interest in ancient grotesque decoration; two archetypal interiors where such grotesques constitute the main part of the decoration are the Loggie of the Vatican, and the Loggia of the Villa Madama (Plates 43, 53 and 54).

From this time onwards, grotesque decoration becomes

highly important, not only in European interiors of all kinds, but also in all the decorative arts. Grotesques, along with arabesques, evolved through various permutations during the Baroque and Rococo, and were revived in pure Classical form in the eighteenth century (see Chapter 6). It is worthwhile quoting Vasari's account of the events which precipitated the interest in fully developed grotesques (themselves a rare survival from antiquity outside the Vesuvian cities), from his *Life of Giovanni da Udine* (1487–1564):

… excavations being made at S. Pietro in Vincula, among the ruins and remains of the Palace of Titus [actually the Golden House of Nero, see Chapter I] in the hope of finding figures, certain rooms were discovered completely buried under the ground, which were full of little grotesques, small figures and scenes, with other ornaments of stucco in low relief. Whereupon Giovanni, going with Raphael … they were struck with amazement … at the freshness, beauty and excellence of these works, for it appeared to them an extraordinary thing that they had been preserved for so long a time; but it was no great marvel, for they had not been open or exposed to the air, which is wont in time, through the changes in the seasons, to consume all things. These grotesques – which were so called from their having been discovered in the underground grottoes – executed with so much design, with fantasies so varied and so bizarre, with their delicate ornaments of stucco divided by various fields of colour, and with their little scenes so pleasing and so beautiful, entered so deeply into the heart and mind of Giovanni, that, having devoted himself to the study of them, he was not content to merely draw or copy them once or twice; and he succeeded in executing them with facility and grace, lacking nothing save a knowledge of making the stucco on which the grotesques were wrought. Now many before him, as has been related, had exercised their wits on this, but had discovered nothing save the method of making the stucco, by means of fire, with gypsum, lime, colophony, wax and pounded brick, and of overlaying it with gold; and they had not found the true method of making stucco similar to that which had been discovered in those ancient chambers and grottoes. But at that time, works were being executed in lime and *pozzolana* … for the arches and the tribune at the back of St Peter's, all the ornaments of foliage, with the ovoli and other members, being cast in moulds of clay, and Giovanni, after considering that method of working with lime and *pozzolana*, began to try if he could succeed in making figures in low relief, and so, pursuing his experiments, he continued to make them as he desired in every part, save that the outer surface did not come out with the delicacy and finish that the ancient works possessed, nor yet so white, on which account he began to think that it might be necessary to mix with the white lime of travertine, in place of *pozzolana*, some substance white in colour … [finally] he mixed in powdered marble of the finest white with white lime of travertine, and, convinced that this was what the ancients had used, shewed it to Raphael, who was delighted.

Giovanni da Udine's investigative nature also led him to the study of other ancient decorative methods, and motifs such as the 'pleasing invention of the pergola canes counterfeited in various compartments, all covered with vines laden with grapes, and with clematis, jasmine, roses, and various kinds of birds and beasts'. Whole rooms came to be frescoed in this way, while echoes of the idea recur in the coved ceilings of the Rococo period (Plate 93). Vasari also notes Giovanni's 'imitations of variegated marbles of different kinds, similar to the incrustations that the ancient Romans used to make on their baths, temples and other buildings'; few subsequent Italian interiors lack examples of this *finto marmo*, the demand for which gave rise to artists specializing in this craft. Its use was not confined to dadoes and other mouldings, and it is found covering entire walls and even ceilings.

Vasari was right in regarding Giovanni da Udine as the originator of the fashion for grotesques, as although Raphael enjoyed a role equivalent to 'superintendent of Antiquities' in Rome, he appears to have had little interest in decorative detail. The real birthplace of the revived grotesque style is the tiny *stufetta*, or bathroom, of Cardinal Bibbiena in the Vatican (1516). This jewel-like room is as precocious as it is beautiful, and represents the first attempt to recreate a true antique interior, with 'Pompeian' red walls, strictly Classical niches and a frescoed vault reminiscent of the *volta dorata* in Nero's Golden House. Although strictly speaking the decoration is not grotesque, the mood adheres to antique prototypes; the same applies to the little *Loggetta* leading to it, a perfect recreation of a Roman Fourth Style interior. What distinguishes the Loggia and Villa Madama decorations, however, is their combination of relief stuccoes with fresco, using a decorative vocabulary of inestimable richness. Even if Raphael left the detail to Giovanni, it is important not to underestimate the quality of the architectural proportions which he provided as the setting.

The influence of this novel style was immediately felt in Rome, and is visible as early as 1517–18 in Baldassare Peruzzi's corridor in the Villa Farnesina and in the *volta dorata* of the Cancelleria Palace in Rome: none of these early imitations approaches the quality of Giovanni da Udine's work. Through Raphael's pupils, Perino del Vaga and Polidoro da Caravaggio, the grotesque style quickly became current, culminating in the vault of the Sala Paolina in the Castel Sant'Angelo. Del Vaga exported the style to Genoa, Polidoro to Naples; in Genoa, it was reinterpreted in an increasingly sumptuous manner (as in Lucio Romano's execution of Perino's designs at the Doria Palace), and the delicate compartmentation of Da Udine's originals evolves into heavier stucco frames leading through the splendid mid-century work of Galeazzo Alessi (such as Palazzo Marino) to the Baroque. As early as 1522, grotesques were made for the Sala di Leonbruno in the Ducal Palace at Mantua, where the Loggia di Eleonora also has them: at Pesaro fine examples exist in the Villa Imperiale and the Palazzo della Prefettura, while some of the most sumptuous were ordered by Francesco d'Este for the house he built at Ferrara for his daughter Marfisa. Many of these schemes included the type of upper wall

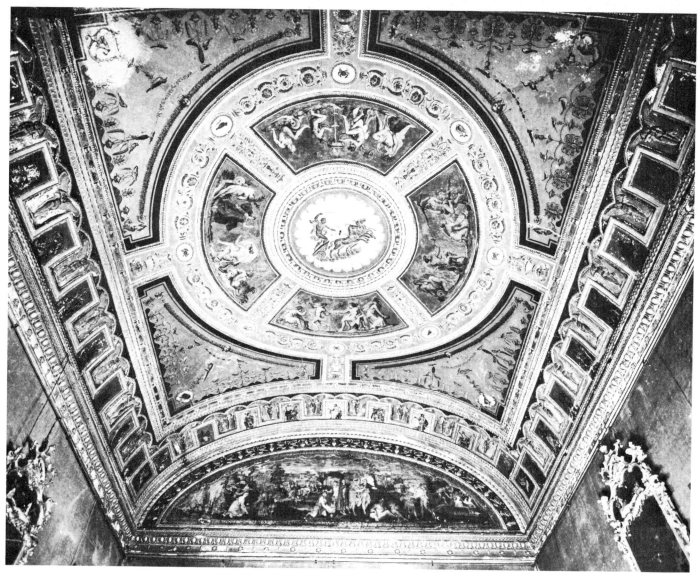

55 The Room of Apollo, *1539–40, in Palazzo Grimani,
Venice, by Francesco Salviati (1510–63) and Giovanni da
Udine (1494–1564)   With this room and the other surviving
interior by Da Udine in this Palace, the Room of Callisto,
the latest style of the Papal court made its Venetian début.
Executed for the noted collector of antiquities, Giovanni
Grimani (1501–93) (who probably designed other rooms,*
*including the massively architectural Antique Study which
contained more than 130 Greek and Roman sculptures),
these delicate ceilings show the increased weight visible in
Da Udine's later works. The Callisto ceiling incorporates
inset mirrors, and both prefigure the work of Robert Adam.
Da Udine's skill as a stuccatore was unrivalled in the
sixteenth century*

frieze discussed earlier. Surprisingly, the style was late in
reaching Venice, but was brought there by Giovanni da
Udine himself, who executed the breathtaking decorations
of the Palazzo Grimani from 1537 onwards (Plate 55).

Through the medium of engravings, often by foreign
artists like Jacques Androuet du Cerceau, Cornelis
Floris and Cornelis du Bos, grotesques spread rapidly
throughout Europe. During the second half of the sixteenth century work inspired by such engravings became
increasingly used in conjunction with the 'strapwork' (see
below) so characteristic of much Mannerist decoration,
and the purity of Da Udine's ideas was sadly debased.

The stuccoes of Giovanni da Udine in the Vatican, in
the Villa Madama and also in the Palazzo Massimo in
Rome form the first major group of such works in the
Renaissance; although as we have seen the style spread
rapidly, the quality of these early stuccoes was hardly if
ever rivalled. Of a different type are the grotesques in the
Sala Paolina of the Castel Sant'Angelo by Giovanni da
Udine, Raffaello da Montelupo, Perino del Vaga, Luzio
Luzi, Polidoro da Caravaggio, Giulio Romano and others.
This scheme shows much greater freedom in the applica-
tion of the basic Classical formulae, with much heavier
framing panels, large stucco reliefs recalling antique

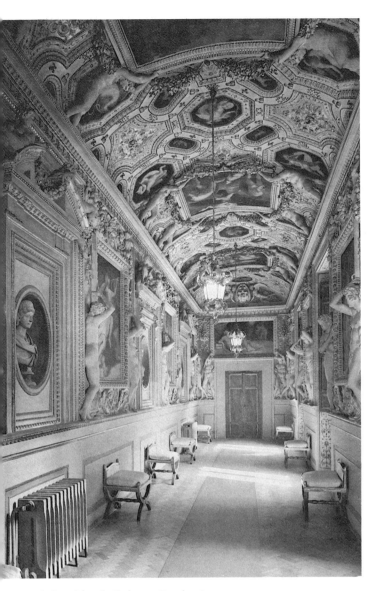

56 Corridor in Palazzo Spada, *Rome*

cameos, and an extensive use of gilding; the latter now became one of the hallmarks of much sixteenth-century stucco decoration, the moulded stucco figure assuming much greater importance – all leading to the Baroque splendours of Pietro da Cortona (Plate 73) and beyond. Another early example of the new, heavier manner is Perino del Vaga's magnificent stucco-coffered ceiling and frieze in the Sala Regia of the Vatican (and see Plate 56).

Papal patronage resulted in the creation of many of the most significant and beautiful programmes of sixteenth-century stucco decoration, such as Tempesta's Third Vatican Loggia, where such Mannerist elements as broken and curling pediments (more like scrolls than pediments) add a novel richness to the decorative repertory. Masks, festoons, garlands, caryatids and other figures of extreme elegance are combined with brilliant colour (as in the Sala Paolina) to dazzle the eye. Vignola's ceiling stuccoes

of the 1550s in the ground-floor rooms of the Villa di Papa Giulio in Rome show a surprising restraint, but the greatest Papal decorative complex of all is the interior of the Casino of Pius IV in the Vatican gardens. The decoration, begun in 1561, was supervised by Federico Barocci, and led Burckhardt in *Der Cicerone* to describe it as 'the most beautiful resting place for the afternoon hours which modern architecture has created'. Not only is this Casino the culmination of a series of superb Papal villas from the middle of the fifteenth century onwards, it is also one of the best preserved, with almost all of its interior decoration intact. Sacred and profane imagery mix in an astonishing array of decorative motifs, applied with the delicacy and fantasy of a Mannerist jeweller such as Cellini. Vasari lists the artists involved as Santi di Tito, Federico Zucchero (whose engraved cartouches exercised a widespread influence), and others, but the interior was the work of a remarkable army of painters, mosaicists, *stuccatori* and *scarpellini*. Throughout the decoration, flattering allusions to Pius IV are included, but nowhere does the iconography intrude on the beauty of the craftsmanship, which reaches its finest conclusion in the sumptuous Galleria. Here, yellows, blacks and ochres, colours typical of late Roman wall-paintings, enrich the effect, and a synthesis between antique originals and the innovation of Da Udine is achieved.

Outside Rome, one of the most important complexes of stucco work of the Raphael-Da Udine school is found at the Palazzo del Te in Mantua, decorated by Giulio Romano and assistants from the later 1520s not only with superb stuccoes but also with extensive frescoes (see below). An entire room – the Sala degli Stucchi – is devoted to a scheme of classical serenity with two magnificent stucco friezes of figures, an elegantly coffered barrel-vault and panelled lunettes.

Of all the decorative media utilized in Italy from the later Middle Ages onwards both in secular and ecclesiastical settings, fresco predominates. Vasari devotes considerable space to painting techniques, but it was fresco which he valued most highly: 'Of all the other methods which painters use, fresco painting (*il dipingere in muro*) is the most masterly and beautiful, because it consists of doing in a single day the work which can occupy many days' retouching in the other media...'. As Millard Meiss has noted,

The Italian word *fresco* means fresh, and a fresco is made by applying pigments mixed with water to freshly spread, damp plaster. Some pigments cannot be applied in water without soon undergoing chemical change – the widely used azurite blue for instance, turns green. These pigments must therefore be mixed with a binder and painted on dry plaster, a technique known by the Italian word for dry, *secco*. Thus, because of the special requirements of such pigments, for which no practical substitute was known, murals executed entirely in fresco are extremely rare. Fresco was, however, the technique most highly prized from 1300–1450, and it was still employed in a more or less modified form for several centuries afterwards. It has a peculiar and very important property; when the wet plaster made of slaked lime dries, the carbonation that occurs binds the pigments into a solid crystalline mass. These crystals are reflective and highly durable unless subjected to moisture combined with chemicals in the wall or in the modern polluted air.

It is worth noting also that by the mid-sixteenth century, when Vasari was writing, true fresco was very rarely used.

During the Middle Ages, plaster was applied in large horizontal bands, but later it was laid on in irregular patches often corresponding to the outline of the forms represented. The fresco had of course to be painted from the top, to avoid drips, and Vasari was right in regarding fresco as the supreme test of an artist's ability since he had to know how colours would change when dry. Fresco retained its popularity throughout Italy – except in Venice, where the damp atmosphere ruined it quickly – until the mid-nineteenth century, and has occasionally been revived for twentieth-century domestic interiors.

The patrimony of domestic fresco decoration in Italy is so vast that any discussion is bound to be cursory. In the Renaissance, mural frescoes generally fall into two main types, of which the most common during the fifteenth and sixteenth centuries is the continuous frieze running around the room with its base just above eye level or slightly below, at the level height of the larger pieces of furniture. One of the earliest and surprisingly little-known examples of this is the group of rooms in the Palazzo Trinci at Foligno (1407–21). Of these, the finest is the Camera delle Stelle, with the adjacent room decorated with a series of Famous Men represented three times life-size. This was to become a very popular theme during the Renaissance, as in

Castagno's magnificent series from the Villa Carducci at Soffiano, and in the frieze formerly decorating the *Studiolo* at Urbino (Plate 46). Humanistic historiography found its natural outlet in such cycles, often incorporating portraits of well-known contemporaries – a practice culminating in the Camera degli Sposi at Mantua (Plate 44). This uninterrupted frieze-type is a survival from medieval art, and other early examples include the splendid frescoes in the castle of Challant di Issogne in Piedmont, where delicate landscapes are seen through marble columns and exotic hangings.

Themes such as the hunt, the seasons and the ages of man are common, and in the only remaining Ferrarese fresco cycle of the Quattrocento, the Salone dei Mesi in Palazzo Schifanoia, another major inspiration of Renaissance decoration – astrology – is visible. Over each month presides one of the Olympian deities in this multi-tiered decoration vertically divided by chiaroscuro pilasters, and below this appear the signs of the zodiac. The frescoes by Cosmè Tura, Ercole dei Roberti, Francesco del Cossa and others thus form a huge mural devoted to astronomy and astrology.

A completely different offshoot of humanistic interest in the Classical world is seen in Pollaiuolo's delightful dancing nudes above an attempted reconstruction in fresco of the Roman hypocaust system, in the Villa La Gallina at Arcetri. It is interesting to note that Pollaiuolo's joyous figures were covered over at an early date, probably by scandalized members of the family who were followers of Savonarola. Tragically, what must have been one of the most perfect fresco schemes of the Quattrocento – Botticelli's figure scenes in Villa Lammi near Florence – has been partly dismantled, with two of the frescoes now

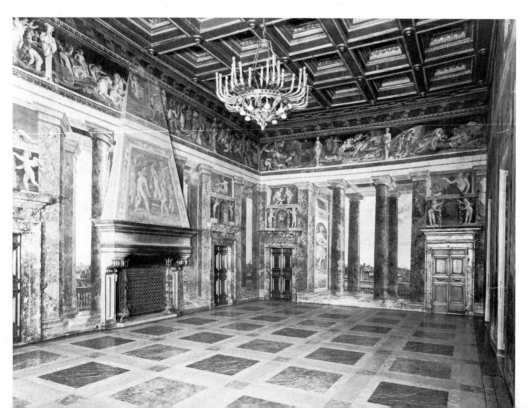

57 The Perspective Room, Villa Farnesina, *Rome, by Baldassare Peruzzi Peruzzi designed this villa on the banks of the Tiber for the wealthy and cultured banker Agostino Chigi. The frescoes are among the first to use architectural perspective to create an illusion of reality from a given position (here on arriving at the top of the staircase). Originally, the interrelationship of the villa and its setting would have given further meaning to the tantalizing glimpses of landscape beyond the fictive architecture*

moved to the Louvre, although the third remains *in situ*.

Although the frieze-type fresco persisted, with the end of the Quattrocento a new interest in illusionism was born. Mantegna's Camera degli Sposi, with its pageant of figures gazed down upon by *putti* who appear to lean over a circular balustrade in the frescoed ceiling, initiated the trend, which reached its most dazzling conclusion in the work of Tiepolo three centuries later (see Plate 105). In complete contrast to the rigidly contained forms of grotesque decoration, Giulio Romano introduced at Mantua the fashion for multi-figure scenes which appear to be set in a space extending the confines of the room. In Rome, Baldassare Peruzzi did the same with architectural illusion (Plate 57). Giulio's Sala di Psiche in the Palazzo del Te introduces an orgiastic rendering of the Cupid and Psyche myth, very different from the serene classicism of Raphael's fresco on the same theme done for Agostino Chigi in the Villa Farnesina, Rome. Before going to Mantua, Giulio had been Raphael's principal assistant, working on the frescoes in the Sala dell'Incendio in the Vatican, and, after Raphael's death, completing those in the Sala di Costantino. The Mantuan fresco is, however, still in a frieze form with lunettes above and a compartmentalized vault; it was in the nearby Sala dei Giganti that Giulio liberated the figures from any constraint of 'architectural' space. Begun in 1532, wall and ceiling decorations interpenetrate with no architectural members defining the individual zones. The giants crash around the spectator amid crumbling architecture and landscape, while the cloud-borne deities of Olympus gaze down in triumph, forming an 'apocalyptic cyclorama'; there is however, a precise iconographical relationship to the rest of the Palace's decoration.

A more timid precursor of this unique room was Dosso Dossi's Sala degli Eliadi at the Villa Imperiale of Pesaro (1530) where landscape predominates behind a framework of palms supported by allegorical caryatids: the idea of transforming a vault into an arbour of trees or plants goes back to Leonardo da Vinci's Sala delle Asse of 1498 in the Castello Sforzesco at Milan. Also at Pesaro, Girolamo Genga's Sala delle Calunnia develops the Peruzzian idea of painted architectural perspectives (see Plate 57) to include framed figure groups set behind open loggias approached by flights of steps – a feature subsequently to be widely exploited, even as late as Tiepolo's *Sacrifice of Iphigenia* fresco of 1757 in the Villa Valmarana at Vicenza. Indeed, it is in the villas of the Veneto that many of the most beautiful sixteenth-century frescoes are found, such as the Villa Pagello a Caldogno, where Palladio's architecture and Sansovino's sculpture find direct reflection in frescoes of contemporary figures moving among idealized buildings. One of the delights of many of these frescoed interiors of the Veneto is the contrast of their festive forms and colours with simple ceilings of massive undecorated wooden beams.

A final note should be made of the Mannerist style in mural frescoes at its most extreme, before the reaction of the Baroque in the seventeenth century. Vasari and his school advocated iconographical and visual complexity for their own sakes, and the result can be seen in such decorative undertakings as the Sala dei Cento Giorni in the Cancelleria Palace at Rome (Plate 58), or the less well-known Sala delle Udienze of the Palazzo Ricci Sacchetti in the same city. The work of Francesco Salviati, it reveals the entire Mannerist repertory of decorative devices; gone is the relaxed geniality of the Veneto frescoes, and in its

58 Sala dei Cento Giorni, Cancelleria Palace, *Rome*. *Decorations by Vasari and School*

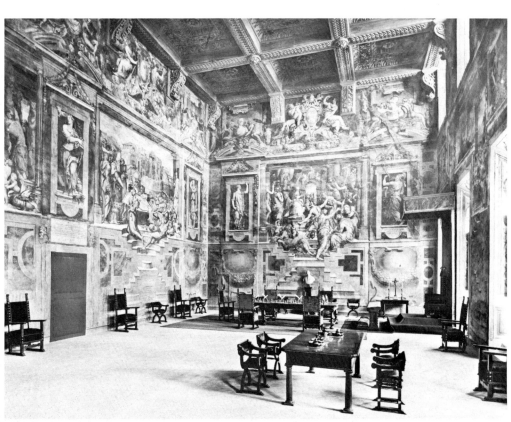

place a rigorous subdivision of the wall surface into myriad compartments offers little visual repose. Fictive frames capped by bizarre pediments, which contain narrative scenes and are replete with masks, swags and *putti*, jostle massive festoons of fruit, flowers, ewers and helmets, while Michelangelesque nudes recline uncomfortably on draperies over the windows. The entire *ensemble* is set against a background of columned architecture, caryatids and cornucopias, with the final touch of confusion in the form of real marble busts inset into carved, recessed overdoor shells. The *horror vacui* typical of all Mannerist art, combined with its delight in the bizarre (see Plate 59) and complex, is perfectly expressed in this somewhat suffocating build-up of decorative devices, also seen in the interiors of the great Villa Farnese at Caprarola.

The Italian interest in illusionism and *trompe l'oeil* (see Chapter 2) was not confined to the fresco tradition, and reached perfection in the Quattrocento in *tarsia*, or inlay in woods of differing colours, used not only in furniture but also in fixed decorative schemes of all kinds. Although fourteenth-century *tarsie* are known (such as the much restored examples in Orvieto Cathedral and in the Chapel of the Palazzo Pubblico at Siena), the Quattrocento saw in it a distinct art form. Vasari speaks of 'this work of putting together woods of differing colours, to make perspective ... and many other diverse fantasies' noting that the art was reborn in the time of Brunelleschi and Uccello. He goes on, however, to specify that Francesco di Giovanni, called il Francione (born 1428), was the real originator, and that it probably began to flourish around 1450. Ideally suited to large pieces of fitted furniture, it naturally developed in ecclesiastical settings like the New Sacristy of Florence Cathedral (possibly to Baldovinetti's designs) and the Sacristy of Modena Cathedral, where Piero della Francesca's designs were translated into *tarsie* by the famous Cristoforo da Lendinara. The greatest expression of the art both in design and execution is Lorenzo Lotto's magnificent screen in S. Maria Maggiore at Bergamo, and one of the foremost exponents of the art was Fra Giovanni da Verona.

As in the most famous surviving Renaissance interior decorated with *tarsie*, the *Studiolo* of Fedrico, Duke of Urbino (Plate 46), sometimes the entire lower walls were covered with such decoration. Usually, however, this expensive and delicate art was applied only to individual parts of the room, as on the doors of the Sala degli Angeli at Urbino; here, Apollo and Minerva stand in niches framed by grotesque decoration (all attributed to Botticelli), with *The Liberal Arts* by Francesco di Giorgio on the outside. Botticelli's name is also connected with the doors of the Sala degli Gigli in the Palazzo Vecchio, Florence, where the figures of Dante and Petrarch were executed to his design. Florence's main exponent of *tarsia* work seems to have been Giuliano da Maiano, working mainly in the Palazzo Vecchio, but also in the Duomo and at Pisa and Perugia. One of the greatest dynasties of

marangoni or *tarsia*-makers was the Canozi family from Lendinara, and although Lorenzo Canozi's masterpiece in the choir of the Santo at Pisa was destroyed by fire in 1749, a description survives by a visiting Sicilian monk which might apply to many such domestic decorative schemes. The monk, Matteo Colaccio, noted '... everyday objects ... among which are books in *tarsia* which seem real. Some freshly read and hard to shut ... candles ... rising smoke ... peaches rolling out of a basket ...' No theme proved too difficult to render, and examples range from land- and townscapes (as in Cristoforo da Lendinara's window-covers in the Lucca Pinacoteca, midway in style between Piero della Francesco and de Chirico) to the *trompe-l'oeil* table in the *Studiolo* from Federico da Montefeltro's palace at Gubbio (New York, Metropolitan Museum of Art). In the various residences of Lionello d'Este at Ferrara, the inlayer Arduino de Baisio possibly included even picture frames in *intarsia*. It was probably Piero della Francesca who transmitted the interest in perspective inlays to Northern Italy and beyond through, for example, his geometric projection drawings of vases. Piero de' Medici's *scrittoio* in Palazzo Medici in Florence had combined *tarsie* which illusionistically enlarged the room with brilliantly coloured Della Robbia maiolica on floor and ceiling; so famous was this interior that Diomede Carafa's Neopolitan palace – the first example there of the latest Tuscan style (1460s) – was decorated and furnished by Florentine artists, including Giuliano da Maiano, and equipped with a copy of the *scrittoio*. Vasari even asserts that there were copies of this room throughout Europe.

Throughout sixteenth-century Italy, but notably in Venice and Florence, oil paintings of varying dimensions occupied an important part in many decorative schemes both public and private; in Venice, Pietro Aretino had a Tintoretto ceiling painting of *Apollo and Marsyas* (1545, now in the Wadsworth Atheneum), and huge canvases inserted between carved and gilded beams on both walls and ceilings distinguish the Venetian Renaissance interior; a superb example of this sort is the Sala del Anticollegio (Plate 60) in the Palazzo Ducale which contains works by the leading Venetian artists of the day. In the Scuolo di San Rocco Tintoretto executed two immense cycles of painting: the scenes from the Life of Christ in the huge upper hall and the scenes from the Life of the Virgin in the lower hall. The interiors of Palazzo Vecchio in Florence as decorated for Duke Cosimo de' Medici by Vasari and his school are also notable for this combination of paintings with rich sculpted settings, culminating, albeit on a tiny scale, in the *Studiolo* of Francesco I (Plate 39). The majority of these schemes have been disbanded, and their contents dispersed throughout the museums of the world. One of the greatest losses is from the so-called *Camerino d'Alabastro* of Alfonso d'Este, part of a magnificent suite of rooms. In the bedroom alone were nine ceiling paintings and a frieze of sixteen landscapes, while the *Camerino* itself was initially

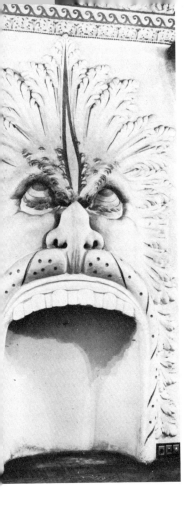

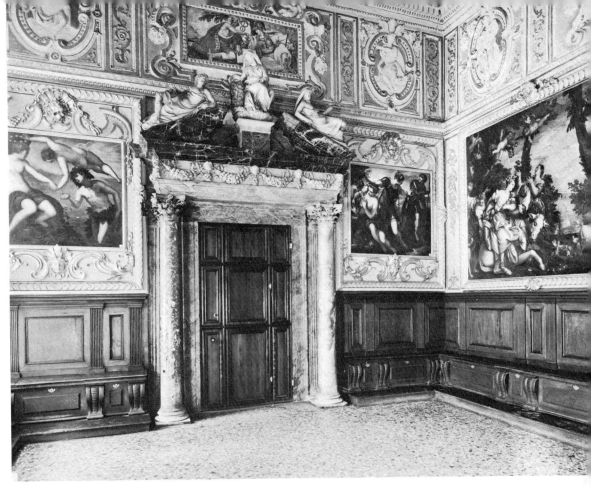

59 *(above)* Fireplace by Bartolomeo Ridolfi, Palazzo Thiene, *Vicenza*

60 *(above right)* Sala del Anticollegio, Palazzo Ducale, *Venice   Reconstructed to the designs of Palladio and Vittoria along with other rooms in the palace after a fire in 1574, this room combines elaborate stuccoes, marble carvings, oil and fresco paintings in a way typical of Venice's aristocratic taste in the mid-sixteenth century. Vault stuccoes by Marco del Moro frame a Veronese fresco, and a stucco frieze by Alessandro Vittoria encloses works by Montemezzano. The monumental chimney-piece is by Vincenzo Scamozzi, while Vittoria's* Venice, Concord *and* Glory *sculptures surmount the doorway; the paintings on the walls are by Veronese, Tintoretto and Bassano. Around the walls are wooden seats for dignitaries waiting for an audience with the Doge*

destined to contain works by Raphael, Bellini and Fra Bartolommeo. In the event, it housed masterpieces by Bellini and Titian, including the latter's *Worship of Venus* and *Bacchanal of the Andrians* (Prado, Madrid) and *Bacchus and Ariadne* (London, National Gallery). Few interiors could rival such a selection of the finest painters of the day, although in Florence Pier Francesco Borgherini commissioned a marriage chamber inset with paintings (both on the walls and the furniture) by Andrea del Sarto, Jacopo Pontormo and others. During the Siege of Flor-

ence, Borgherini's wife went so far as to say that she would defend the decoration with her life!

Although the feature most envied by foreign visitors to the great Italian courts was their opulence, many Italian rooms of the period would appear sparsely furnished to modern eyes. They relied heavily on the rich patterning of floors, walls and ceiling as a foil for the magnificent costumes of the day. Apart from tapestries (reserved for the very richest interiors), painted and gilded leather hangings, and hangings of wool or decorated cotton, there were few fixed pieces of furniture in most rooms. A contemporary description of the apartment in Palazzo Foscari specially furnished for King Henry III of France on his visit to Venice in 1574 shows that the rooms were by no means overfull, despite Venice's reputation as the centre of luxurious living. The bedchamber contained only three pieces of furniture: a gilded bed curtained in crimson silk with gold-hemmed sheets, a gilded armchair under a cloth of gold canopy and a black marble table covered with a green velvet cloth. Carpaccio's *Dream of St Ursula* (Plate 61) also reveals the comparative emptiness of even the most important interiors. Such furniture as was left more or less permanently in individual rooms – beds, *cassoni*, large cupboards, sideboards (introduced increasingly during the sixteenth century), the *cassapanca* or wooden settle containing a chest, and centre tables – was often of monumental proportions, and was decorated with motifs reflecting the interior decoration. The elaborate carving of wooden furniture, *intarsia* decoration on cupboard doors and such luxuries as the immense tabletops of brilliantly coloured *pietra dura* so popular in sixteenth- and seventeenth-century Florence all contributed to the dazzling impression; another important decorative element was the Turkish carpets, which entered Italy mainly through Venice, and were used everywhere – except on floors.

By 1500, the Italian houses and palaces were the envy of Europe. In the words of one contemporary they were 'so richly and beautifully decorated that they astonish the visitor, and whoever seeks to describe them will be accused of lying'. The period of consolidation of Renaissance ideas in Italy, however, corresponded, according to the historian Francesco Guiccardini, with the years of her 'calamity'. After a period of unparalleled prosperity, much of Italy fell to the French and subsequently to other invading foreign armies – and these invasions swiftly carried Renaissance ideas to the North. In France, Italian artists like the sculptor Francesco Laurana had already begun to lay the foundations of French interest in Italian ideas and King Charles VIII returned to France with twenty-two craftsmen to 'practise their craft in the Italian manner'. The French, however, had been used to the exuberance of the Flamboyant Gothic style in interior decoration, and did not adapt readily to the severe demands of the great Tuscan innovators of the Quattrocento. Consequently,

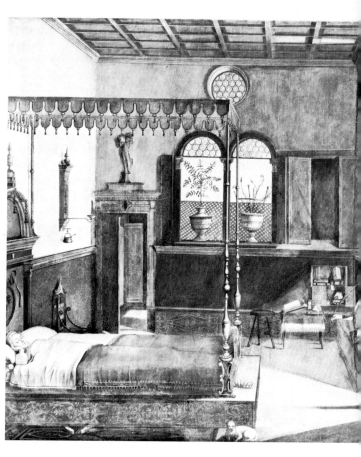

61 *(above)* Carpaccio: The Dream of St Ursula. *1490–95. Venice, Accademia*

62 *(left)* Gallery of François I, Fontainebleau, *1533–40. Decorated by Rosso Fiorentino and Primaticcio, later repainted*

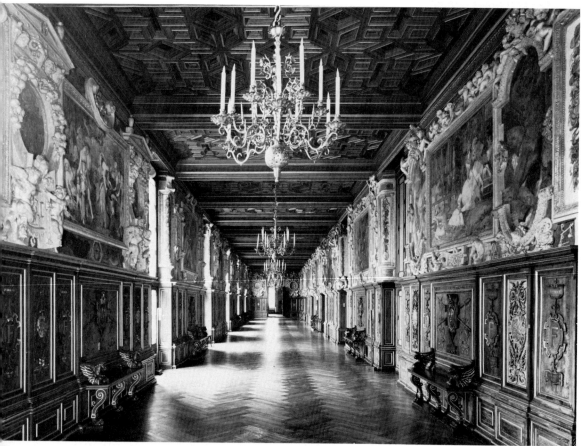

Renaissance style in France (and throughout Northern Europe) is much less clearly defined than in Italy and embraces the period from Charles VIII's reign (1483–98) to that of Henry III. In many cases, Renaissance motifs were simply grafted on to Late Gothic forms, often with incongruous results.

It was the reign of François I (1515–47) which saw the first real development of a French Renaissance style, at a time when Mannerism was gaining ground in Italy. François emulated at his castle of Amboise that feature of Italian life which had contributed so much to the development of the arts – the princely court; although unsuccessful in luring Michelangelo, he obtained the services of Leonardo and other Italian artists and craftsmen. At the Château de Fontainebleau François created major French Renaissance interiors with the aid of the painters Giovanni Battista Rosso, called Rosso Fiorentino, and Francesco Primaticcio. These two Italians had had considerable success in their native country, and with the aid of French and Flemish artists they altered the course of French interior decoration during the 1530s. Although by no means all of their transformations of the medieval château survive, the Galerie François I, the Chambre de la Duchesse d'Etampes and the Staircase of Primaticcio (Plate 47) display all the characteristics of an elegant, sophisticated style; many drawings and engravings connected with these interiors not only further our knowledge of the new style, but also exerted an immense influence on contemporary designers. Although Rosso was mainly a painter, Primaticcio had been Giulio Romano's assistant on the decorations of the Castello and Palazzo del Te for the Gonzagas at Mantua. Vasari says that 'the first labours in fresco of any account [at Fontainebleau] had their origin, it is said, from Primaticcio.' It appears indeed that the manner which replaced the grotesque style in Roman favour after 1530 at the Vatican's Sala Regia and the gallery of Palazzo Spada originated at Fontainebleau.

Throughout the decorations, the two artists introduced the entire repertoire of motifs found previously in Italy, but not in Northern design: moulded stucco nymphs of slender proportions with clinging drapery *à la* Parmigianino, chimerae, masks, garlands, playful *putti*, and stylized scrollwork in both the stuccoes and woodwork – executed by François I's finest woodcarver Scibec de Carpi, but replaced by copies during other alterations in the nineteenth century. Of all the multitude of motifs introduced by Rosso and Primaticcio at Fontainebleau, it was perhaps the strapwork which exercised the greatest influence on all forms of Mannerist decoration, not only in France but also in Italy, Flanders, England and Germany. Its origin may have been in rolled, folded and cut leather, which left sharp-edged, sometimes asymmetrical flaps and openings. The long Galerie François I at Fontainebleau is essentially un-Italian in form (Plate 62). It is the earliest survival of a feature which later became

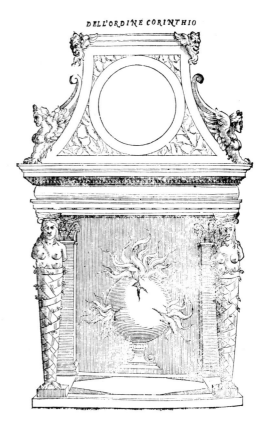

63 Plate 183 from the Sixth Book of Architecture, *by Sebastiano Serlio   Serlio's L'Architettura, which appeared in six parts between 1537 and 1551, deals with almost every aspect of practical architectural design, including examples of the architecture of Bramante, Raphael and Peruzzi, building plans, and details such as doorways, chimney-pieces and windows. Since he offered no precise indication of the proportional system of ancient architecture, many French, Flemish, English and German architects used his designs blindly, often further debasing their sources*

standard in French châteaux and *hôtels*, and which became popular in the great English houses of the Elizabethan and Jacobean period. Its strapwork decoration, subdivided into individual zones, is also a feature at variance with Italian practice, but one which was rapidly adopted throughout Europe. Rosso's inventive designs were rapidly propagated through the engravings of Fantuzzi, Domenico del Barbiere and René Boyvin.

The next phase of French Renaissance decoration was also heavily influenced by Italian artists and ideas. By the early 1540s Primaticcio had returned from Rome, the Bolognese pupil of Peruzzi, Sebastiano Serlio, had settled in France, and the French architect Philibert de l'Orme was back in Paris after an Italian journey. The Renaissance style began to spread, and was no longer confined mainly to Royal commissions in the Ile de France. The study of Vitruvius and the influence of Serlio's *Seven Books of Architecture*, which began to appear in 1537 with dedications to François I, were of prime importance in the growth of French classicism. The *Seven Books* were essentially

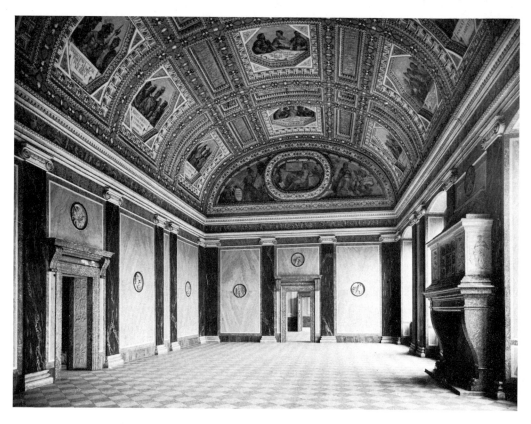

64 Italienischer Saal,
Stadtresidenz, *Landshut*,
1542

practical, unlike the writings of Vitruvius and Alberti, and
offered the basis of the Renaissance vocabulary even to
designers without the remotest idea of classical form.
However, many of Serlio's woodcuts (Plate 63) show
debased forms of the pure High Renaissance architecture
of Italy.

It was with de l'Orme and Pierre Lescot that an independent French Renaissance style emerged, as seen in
Lescot's revolutionary new wing of the Louvre which he
built for François I from 1527 containing one of the
major innovations in French interior decoration, the great
ground-floor gallery supported by Goujon's four large
sculpted caryatids. Lescot's incorporation of sculpture
into his interiors continued to play an important role in
France for the next three centuries, notably in many
rooms at Versailles (Plate 84). His collaboration with
Scibec de Carpi resulted in another of the finest works of
this period, the ceiling of the bedroom of Henri II, which
substitutes the richly carved Venetian beam for the
painted ones usual up to that point in France, even at
Fontainebleau.

Nothing survives of the domestic decoration of Serlio
and Philibert de l'Orme, although de l'Orme's superb
chapel at Anet shows how he conceived interior space as a
whole, articulated by classical decorations of extreme
refinement. Outside the Ile de France, Renaissance detail
was for a long time freely interpreted, and applied with
the richness of the Flamboyant style in such centres as
Toulouse and Rodez. The French, however, unlike the
Spanish, wholeheartedly adopted and absorbed Renais-

sance classicism, evolving a personal, national style. In
Spain, after the introduction of Italian Renaissance ideas
in Charles V's Alhambra Palace at Granada from 1526,
and Philip II's severely grandiose monastery-castle at the
Escorial, where Italians frescoed and decorated many
rooms, the Plateresque style (so called because of its
similarity to silversmiths' work – *plateria* = silverwork)
with its irrational decorative language deriving from the
late Gothic tradition once more overwhelmed architecture
and interior design.

Fundamental to the spread of Renaissance ideas were
the books on architecture and pattern-books which began
to appear in increasing number during the sixteenth
century. Antwerp produced and exported engravings by
artists of all nationalities, published mostly by Hierony-
mus Cock (1510–70). Strapwork and grotesques (called
compartimenti, as they were often engraved within long
oblong frameworks) dominated and exercised a widespread influence. The most notable books on architecture
were Hans Blum's *Five Orders* (1550), Du Cerceau's *Livre
d'architecture* (1559), Vignola's *Rule of the Five Orders*
(1562), Bullant's *Règle générale des cinque manières*
(1564), de l'Orme's *Architecture* (1568), Palladio's *Architecture* (1570) and Wendel Dietterlin's book on the Orders
(1593) and his *Architecture* (1594–8). Even England man-
aged to produce a guide, John Shute's *Chief Groundes of
Architecture* (1563). In Germany, Holland, Flanders and
England, the application of the Orders to interior decoration was generally confined during the sixteenth century to
carved wooden or moulded plaster decoration, although

the Italianate court at Munich commissioned or inspired some of the most monumental classical interiors outside Italy (Plate 64). Generally speaking, it was the influence of pattern books like Vredeman de Vries's collection of fantastic engraved ornament which made the greatest impact on the unclassical minds of non-Italian craftsmen for whom the Renaissance was still a mystery. From these, they could select at will and apply classical, or at least classically inspired motifs, to almost any decorative situation, often with bizarre results (see Plates 65 and 67).

This is particularly evident in England, where the Renaissance – inasmuch as it exists in interior decoration in the sixteenth century – was an amalgam of strapwork, the classical style of French châteaux such as Blois and Chambord, and stray Italian ideas imported direct by artists like Antonio Toto del Nunziata, Benedetto da Rovezzano and Giovanni da Maiano, all of whom came to England with Pietro Torrigiano at Cardinal Wolsey's invitation. Although Wolsey included 'Renaissance' detail at Hampton Court, the Hall there (1531–6) is still a Gothic interior, with a hammer-beam roof; however, some of its carved detail by Richard Rydge shows awareness of Italian ideas and standards. In 1538, Henry VIII began his palace at Nonesuch, possibly in direct rivalry with François I's Chambord; nothing survives of it, but John Evelyn's

description indicates that Italians provided 'antick' ornament for the King there. The immense strides in Italian interior decoration, which took it totally away from medieval practices by 1500, find no parallel in England. There, isolated details like the superb Doric chimneypiece at Lacock Abbey, Wiltshire, of 1540–9, record the hesitant and spasmodic acceptance of Renaissance ideas.

Throughout the sixteenth century, the English interior remained largely as it had appeared at the very end of the Middle Ages, with panelling in carved oak or other woods, simple plastered or beamed ceilings, and wooden or occasionally marble or stone floors. What has been called the 'negativeness of the Tudor style' resulted in most interiors being conceived as accumulations of decorative fragments (see Plate 66) – a concept totally antithetical to the new unity formulated by Italian and even French architects and designers. Even novel elements like the plaster ceilings of the watching chamber at Hampton Court (1536) or St James's Palace of the same period show the innate English tendency to adapt prototypes (such as classical coffering) to very different effect, resulting there in the type of pendant decoration framing compartmentalized areas which became so typical of the Elizabethan interior (Plate 69). It was only in the second half of the century that the Mediterranean concepts of

65 Hermann Tom Ring: Annunciation, *1594 (detail).*
Munster, Westfälisches Landesmuseum für Kunst und Kulturgeschichte

66 Staircase, Knole, *Kent, 1456*

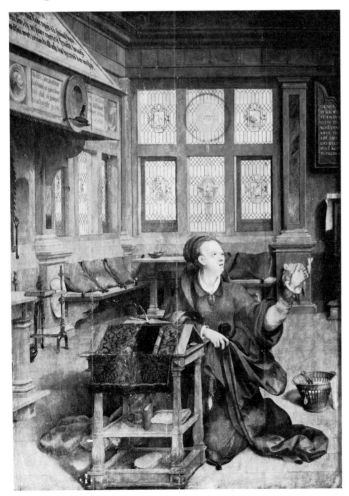

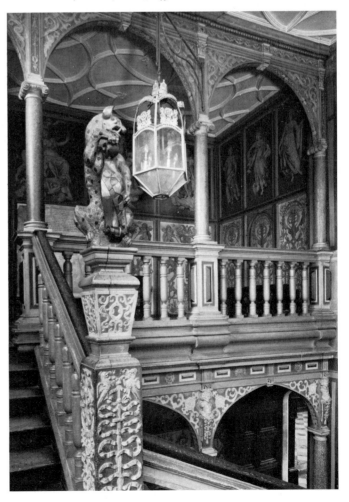

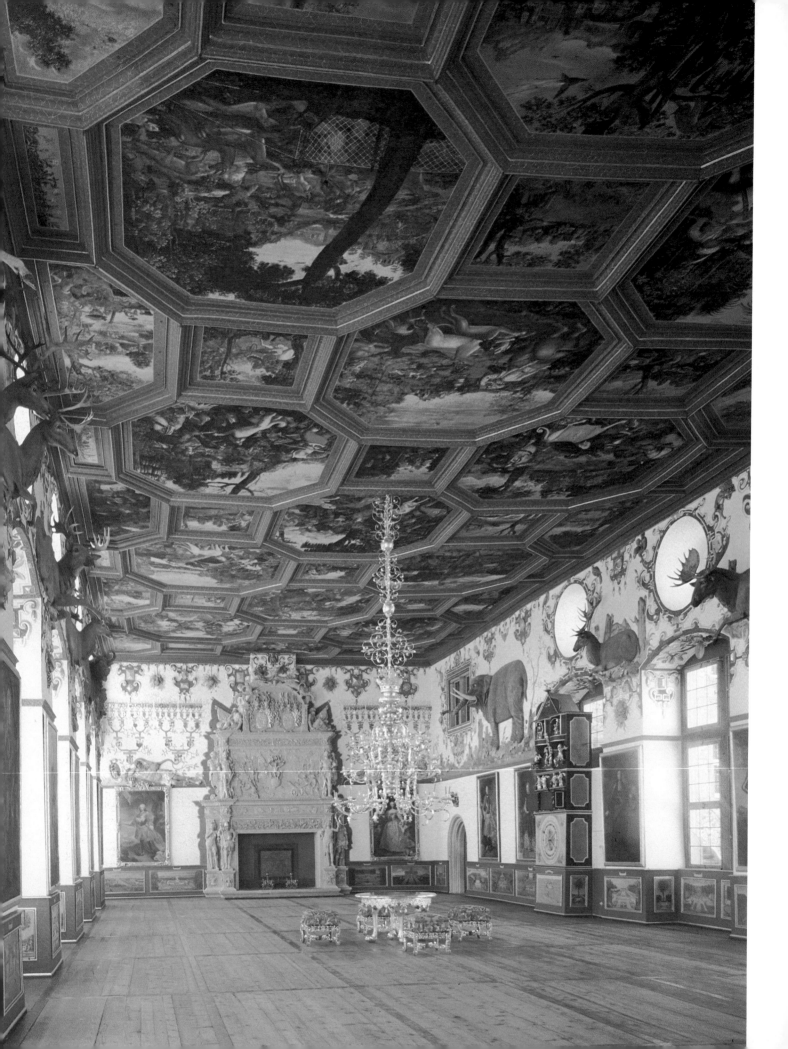

67 *(left)* Jagd oder Reisensaal ((*Hunting or travelling room*), *Weikersheim, West Germany*

68 *(right)* The Gallery, Lanhydrock House, *Cornwall. c. 1640 One of the most splendid English Renaissance galleries (it is 116 feet long), it forms part of the house built for himself by a Truro tin and wool merchant after 1620. Despite its date, its decoration is typical of the late Renaissance, with scenes of the Creation and other Old Testament themes, and elaborate plasterwork ceiling with pendants, probably done by plasterers who worked at Barnstaple and Rashleigh Barton in North Devon*

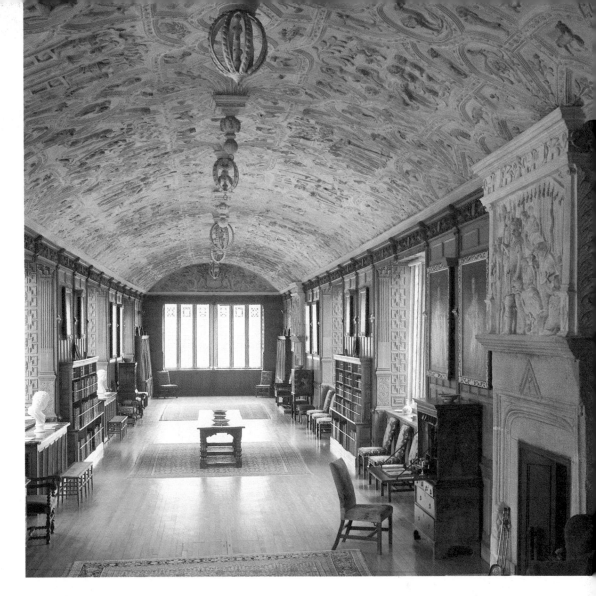

69 *(below)* The Long Gallery, Haddon Hall, *Derbyshire*

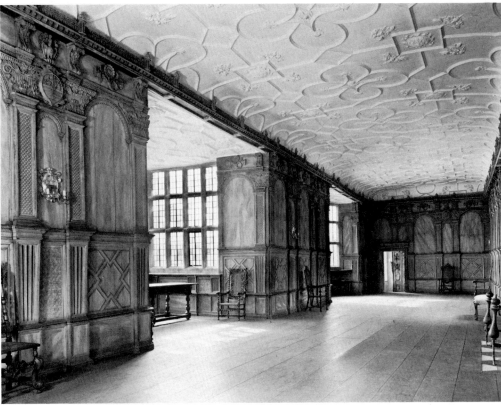

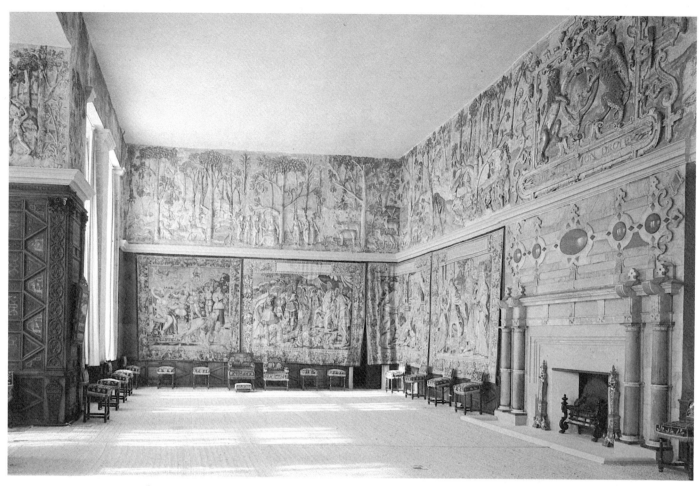

70 The High Great Chamber, Hardwick Hall, *Derbyshire, 1591–7*

grandeur and space begin to be felt, as at Longleat House, Somerset, by John Thynn (died 1580), 'an ingenious man and a traveller', and other great Elizabethan houses like Wollaton, Audley End, Kirby Hall and Hardwick. Longleat in Wiltshire and Hardwick (Plate 70) ('more glass than wall') represent the summit of English domestic building in this period, but despite the abundance of Classical detail, remain isolated from the mainstream of Renaissance ideas. The major concessions to Renaissance advances are in architecture and planning, with increased emphasis on privacy – with parlours, chambers and solars – in contrast to the typical Renaissance rooms of parade,

which find their echo in the gallery. From late Tudor times until the later seventeenth century the gallery, designed for conversation and even exercise, forms an important part of the English interior (Plate 68). A gallery such as that at Aston Hall, Birmingham, which dates from the early seventeenth century, shows the typical proliferation of Mannerist detail in the wooden panelling and carved chimney-piece, culminating in the flat plaster ceiling with its all-over patterning in shallow relief; it was against this background of homespun English Renaissance detail that the new classicism of Inigo Jones was born (see Chapter 4).

4

The Age of the Baroque

Everymans proper *Mansion* House and *Home*, being the
Theatre of his hospitality, the Seate of Selfe-fruition, the
Comfortablest of his owne *Life*; the *noblest* of his sonnes
Inheritance, a kind of private *Princedome* ...

Sir Henry Wotton, *The Elements of Architecture*, 1624

The seventeenth century – the age of the Baroque – gave birth to modern concepts of interior decoration and furnishing. Despite the overwhelming grandeur of many Baroque interiors, our ideal of a room as a unified combination of compatible elements dates from the Baroque, notably in France. During the Middle Ages, when those who could afford fine objects often led peripatetic lives, comfort was rarely the prime consideration in decorating a room, as a glance at the angular interiors of the time reveals. In the Italian Renaissance, architects became much more concerned with the design and selection of objects destined for particular rooms, but on the whole furniture answered the demands of architectural style rather than the needs of the human figure in repose. The rigidly upright wooden settles and chairs found in Renaissance homes make it difficult to imagine that prolonged relaxation was ever considered. The Baroque changed all of this.

Above all, the Baroque interior was considered as a magnificent framework for social events. This applied to both secular and ecclesiastical interiors, since the two often came to resemble one another, especially in Italy. Furnishings assumed an increasingly important role, underlining both social status and social stability. It was during the Baroque period that artists often portrayed their sitters not against simplified, generalized backgrounds, but in specific rooms surrounded by specific pieces of furniture, sometimes still identifiable. For the first time on any scale, suites of furniture were made to form part of specific schemes including fitted mirrors and paintings in wooden or stucco frames, frescoed or painted ceilings and walls, carved and painted or gilded panelling, consoles *en suite* with mirrors, candle stands, chairs, side tables, supports for sculpture, and so on. Something approaching a European language of interior decoration began to emerge, with strong similarities observable from Rome to Paris, London and even Russia and Scandinavia.

Allowing for obvious local differences, a comparison of the Colonna Gallery with rooms at Versailles and Chatsworth (Plates 71, 79 and 84) reveals that the basic vocabulary of design and decoration spread much more rapidly in the seventeenth century than in preceding periods.

Among the reasons for the spread of ideas was the dramatic shift from Italian to French dominance in matters of taste in the second half of the century, the rise of the United Provinces to bourgeois prosperity, and the return to England at the Restoration of nobles from both the French and the Dutch courts. The Baroque was the age of great monarchies, in France, Spain and England, while Germany and Italy remained divided under secular or ecclesiastical rulers. If Italian artists invented and perfected the Baroque style, it was the French under Louis XIV who gave it the royal stamp of approval and made it the official court art for the rest of Europe.

The Italian Baroque was first and foremost a Roman and a Papal style, which then filtered to the other cities of the peninsula, there to assume different forms at the courts of families like the Medici and Farnese. The palaces and villas of the period retained and accentuated the element of 'parade' already so important in the Renaissance, with saloons, galleries, cabinets and loggias where elegant gatherings were offset by splendid backgrounds. Today, when we see them in the glare of day, many of these frescoed, gilded interiors appear cold or false: they must be imagined in candlelight, filled with bejewelled animated crowds, dressed in colourful clothes. Italy's palaces were never conceived as intimate settings for private life, but as theatres for social activity on the grandest scale – balls, private and official receptions, banquets and so on. This accounts for the fact that, while the apartments of the ground floor and the *piano nobile* (where the principal bedchamber was also found) were lavishly decorated and furnished, the rooms above might be shabby or even completely unused.

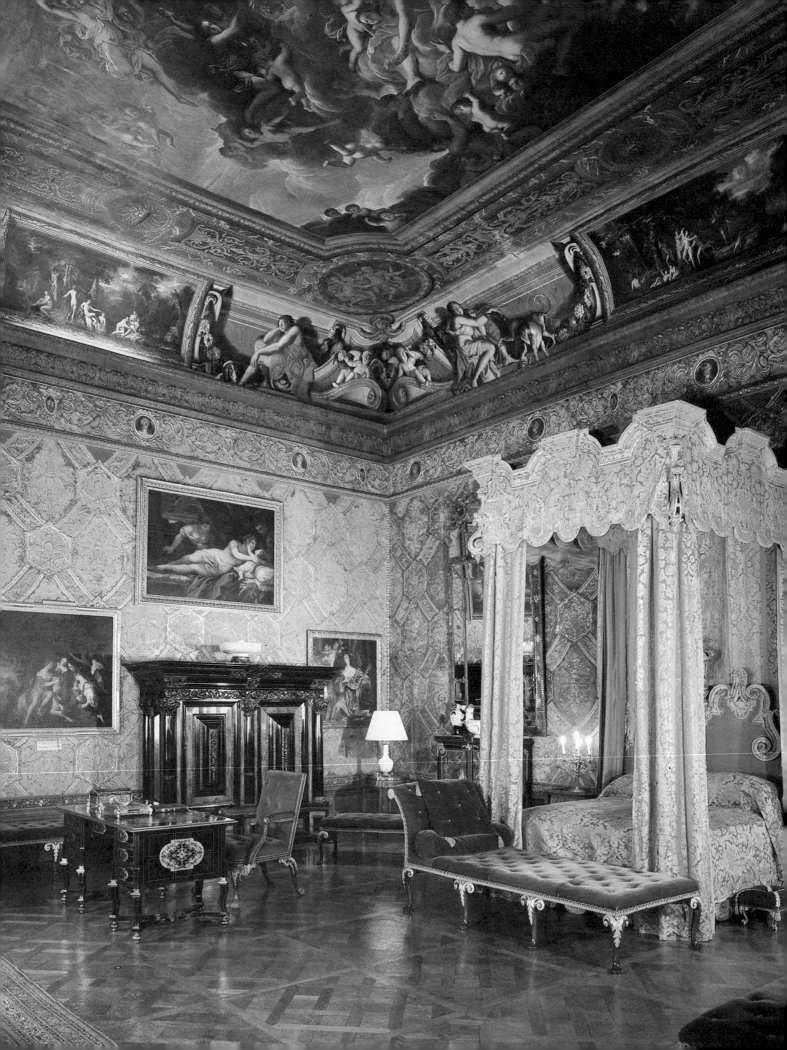

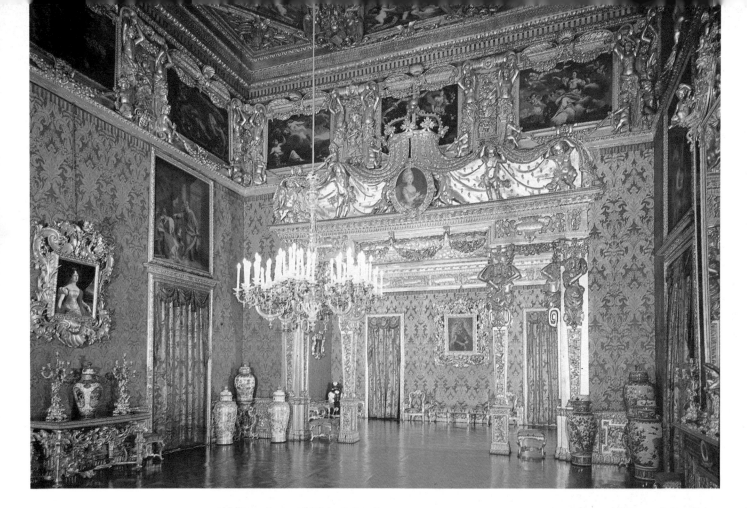

71 *(left)* The State Bedroom, Chatsworth, *Derbyshire. Late seventeenth century*

72 *(above)* Camera dell'Alcove, Palazzo Reale, *Turin*

73 *(right)* Vault of the Sala di Giove, Palazzo Pitti, *Florence. Paintings by Pietro da Cortona and Ciro Ferri*

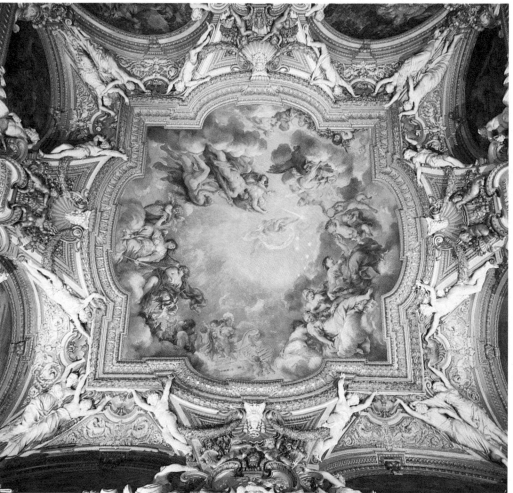

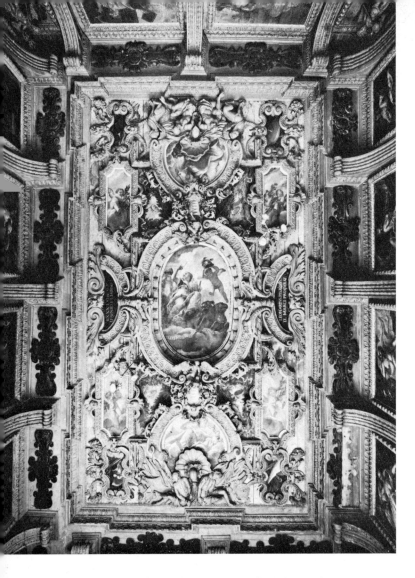

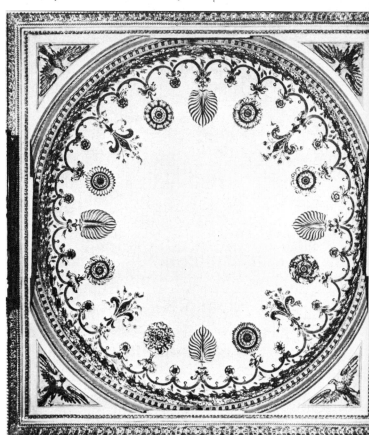

74 *(left)* Ceiling from Palazzo Pesaro, *Venice, with paintings by Niccolo Bambini, 1682*

75 *(below)* Ceiling of small room in the Palazzo Falconieri, *Rome, by Francesco Borromini, c. 1640*

Since the fifteenth century it had been the custom to build town palaces on the largest scale possible – the Florentine Strozzi and Medici-Riccardi Palaces and the Roman Cancelleria and Farnese Palaces are good examples. The Baroque continued and even amplified this tradition. The arts in Italy flourished on an unprecedented scale despite general and economic decline and the increasing intervention of foreign powers. Many new palaces sprang up, and every family of consequence obtained or built a country villa. Decoration and furnishing became a mania and the demand for fixed and movable decoration and furniture of all kinds increased; where collections do not survive, inventories of the period reveal the range and richness of household contents among the wealthy.

Rome was the centre of an urbanistic revival which had no equal in Baroque Europe. Under the Popes Paul V Borghese, Urban VIII Barberini and Innocent X Pamphili all of the visual arts enjoyed immense prestige. Papal monopoly of the leading artists and craftsmen ensured that the palaces of the Papal families led the way in architecture and interior decoration. The major artists of the period were called in to decorate domestic interiors on an unprecedented scale, and thus we find architects like Bernini, Borromini, Cortona and Juvarra not merely providing the architectural framework, but also supervising or executing the decoration; this was particularly significant in an age when artists such as the sculptor Bernini or the painter Cortona worked with equal facility as architects. This sense of an accomplished artist's versatility had a long tradition in Italy, but reached its apogee in the Baroque, and is reflected in the all-enveloping richness of many interiors of the period where the arts attain a previously unimagined unity.

Unlike the Baroque interior in other European countries, that of Italy has strong antecedents in the Mannerist period. The main features of the Italian Baroque interior are already found in the sixteenth century: fresco used extensively for walls and ceilings, elaborately moulded stucco ornament, carved woodwork either painted or gilded (as in the great Venetian palaces, see Plate 74) to frame inserted painted canvases (Plate 75). The creator of one of the first major Baroque interiors (the Farnese Gallery, Plate 76), Annibale Carracci, began his career as a decorator at the Fava and Magnani-Salem Palaces in Bologna with simple friezes of frescoes painted directly below the ceilings. This tradition was as we have seen (Chapter 3)

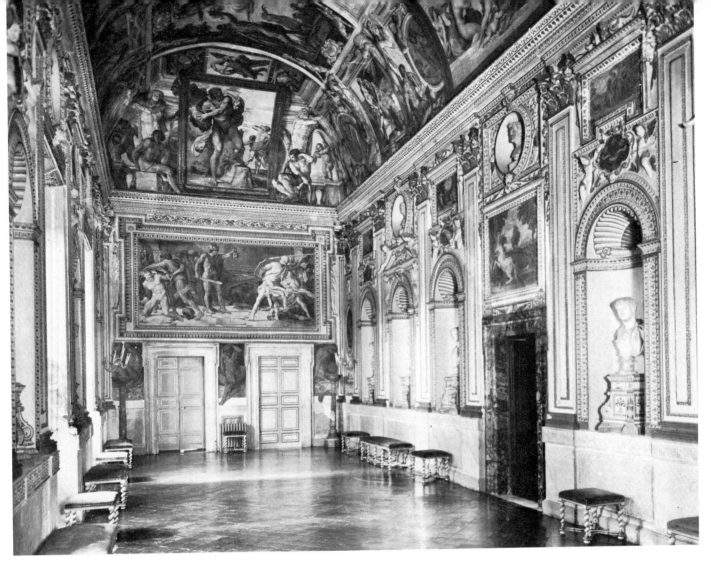

76 The Galleria Farnese, Palazzo Farnese, *Rome, 1597–1604*

a well-established one in the Middle Ages and the Renaissance, but was largely abandoned in the Baroque in favour of more illusionistic devices. Significantly, however, it was Bologna which first perfected earlier ideas on the use of painted illusionistic architecture (*quadratura*) and this became by far the most popular means of decorating large or small wall and ceiling surfaces in seventeenth- and eighteenth-century Italy. It was the Bolognese Pope Gregory XIII (1572–85) who introduced *quadratura* painting to Rome when he brought Tommaso Laureti and Ottaviano Mascherino from his native city to decorate the Vatican.

The creation of the Farnese Gallery between 1597 and 1604 signals the birth of the full Baroque style, in painting as much as in interior decoration. Annibale's frescoed vault with its brilliantly colourful combinations of illusionistic 'easel paintings' in fictive gold frames with 'bronze' roundels and 'stone' figures and other carving heralds the festive abundance of countless such ceilings: its vigorous and bright profusion is in perfect harmony with the white and gold stuccoed walls with their elegant articu-

lation of shell-headed niches, inset circular openings for busts and shallow pilasters, and small frescoes disposed as if they were hanging pictures. Unlike Mannerist decorative schemes of this kind such as the *sala* of the Roman Palazzo Ricci-Sacchetti (see Chapter 3), the aim of Baroque decoration was usually to achieve clarity, so that in spite of a profusion of motifs and colours, an interior would 'read' at a glance: in this context, the Farnese Gallery is a perfect example.

The development of the Baroque illusionistic fresco is a complete study in itself. The most important advances were made in Rome between 1600 and 1639, the year of the completion of Pietro da Cortona's Barberini ceiling. After the mixed illusionism of the Farnese ceiling, Giovanni Barbieri, called il Guercino, broke new ground in 1621–3 with the vault fresco of the Casino Ludovisi in Rome, where Aurora's chariot is represented as if actually crossing real space above our heads, clouds and figures penetrating the illusionistically painted 'ruins' of the upper part of the room. In 1624–5 Giovanni Lanfranco, significantly an admirer of Correggio's illusionistic ecclesi-

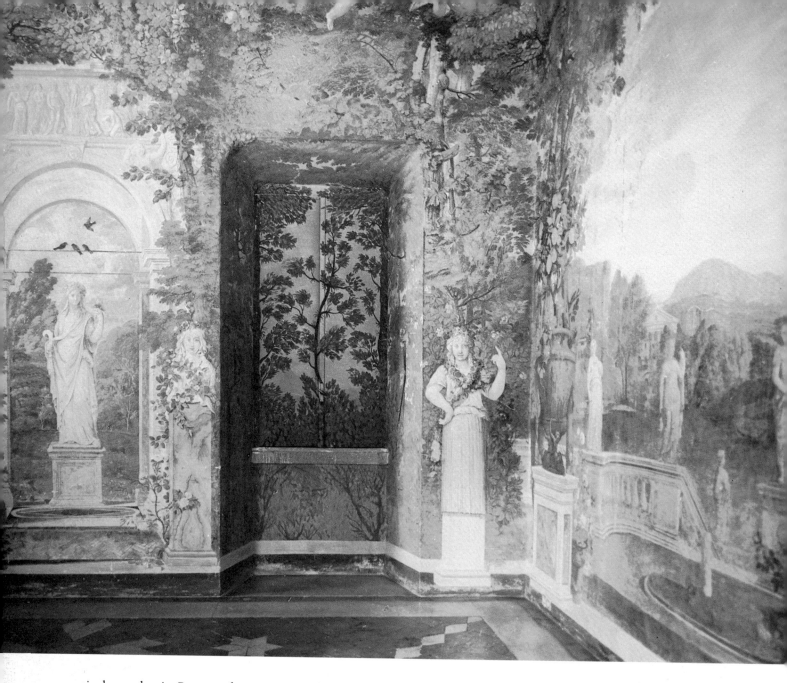

astical cupolas in Parma of a century earlier, painted a 'stone' framework of sculpted Atlantes supporting heavy architecture through which we are shown glimpses of real space, in the Villa Borghese, Rome. From all these precedents, Pietra da Cortona evolved a personal style, which was to have more far-reaching consequences than that of most of his contemporaries in the field of decorative painting.

Pietro Berrettini (1596–1669), called da Cortona after his Tuscan birthplace, came to Rome in 1612 or 1613. As a very young man he began to paint domestic fresco decorations, in the Villa Muti at Frascati and in the Palazzo Mattei in Rome, of 1662–3. In these his robust style is already evident. It was, however, during the 1630s that he perfected the equivalent in painting to the full Baroque sculpture of his contemporary Bernini. The gigantic ceiling

77 (above) The Stanza della Primavera from Villa Falconieri 'La Rufina', *Frascati, 1670s*   *The walls of this delightful room were frescoed with garden scenes by Giovan Francesco Grimaldi (1606–80).* The Triumph of Flora *on the ceiling is the work of Ciro Ferri (1634–89). There is no division between walls and ceiling and architecture: tree-lined avenues, statues, fountains and distant views are all seen under the same 'open' sky frescoed above. The room opens onto Borromini's splendid balcony outside, and was conceived with a central fountain which would have further emphasized the link between interior and exterior. This room and Clérisseau's 'Ruin Room' (Plate 132) are the natural conclusion of the* trompe-l'oeil *tradition initiated by Peruzzi's Villa Farnesina frescoes (Plate 57)*

78 (right) Bedroom from Palazzo Sagredo, *Venice, c. 1718. New York, Metropolitan Museum of Art*

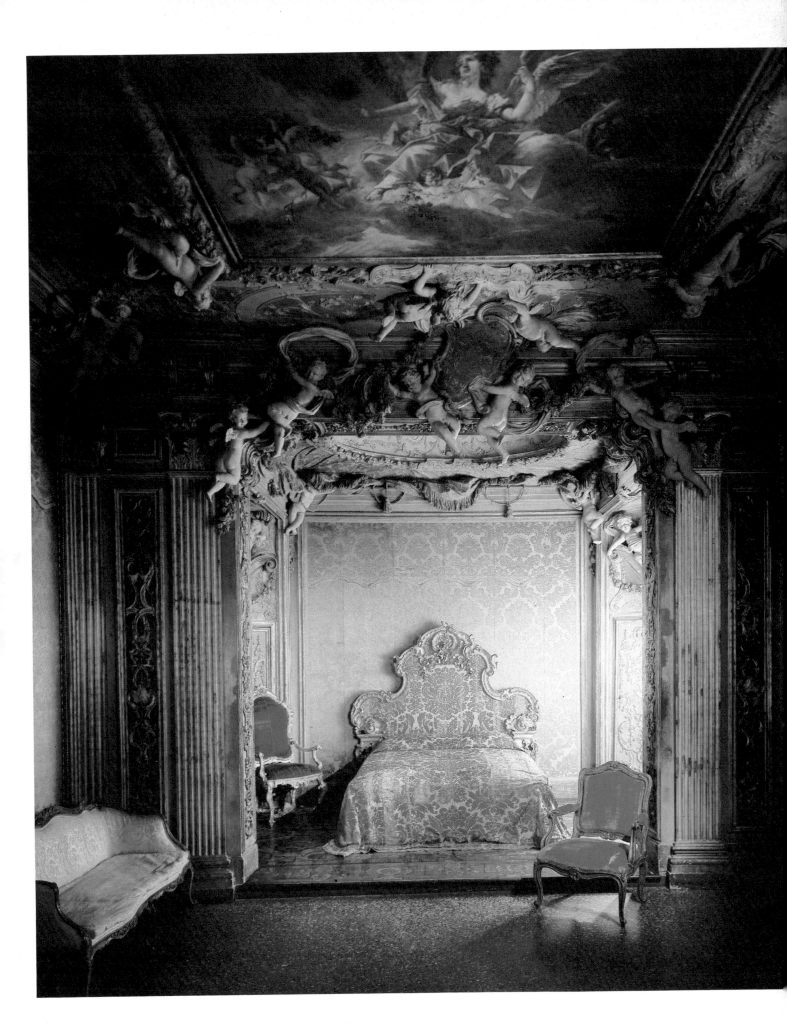

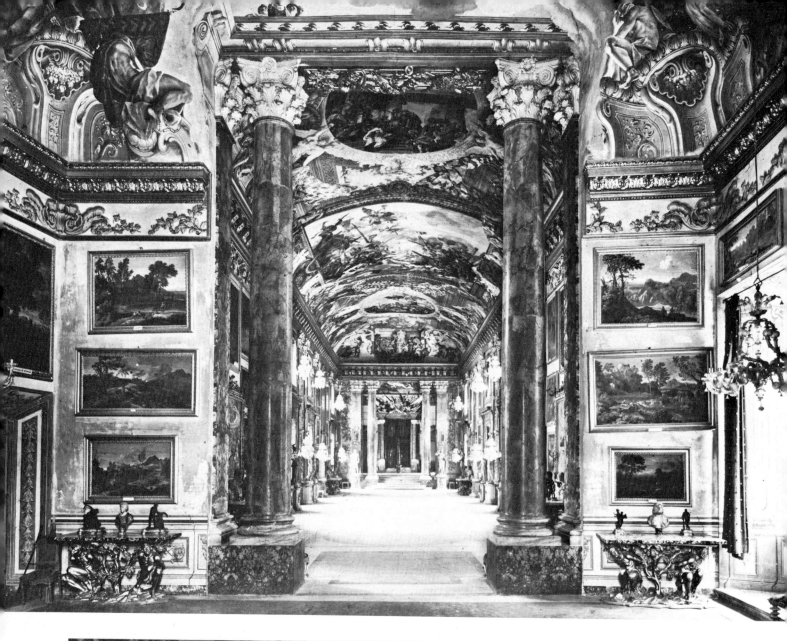

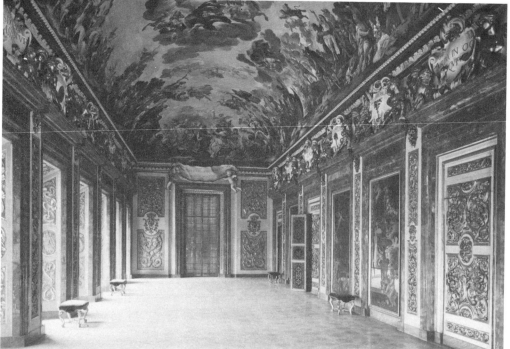

79 (above) Salone in
Palazzo Colonna, Rome

80 (left) Ceiling frescoes
by Luca Giordano, Palazzo
Medici-Riccardi, Florence,
1682–3

of the Gran Salone of the Palazzo Barberini is one of the largest frescoed spaces in Europe, and dominates a room in which the hand of Borromini is visible in the fantastic pedimented door-cases with their Michelangelo-derived detail. Its theme, *The Triumph of Divine Providence*, typifies the allegory preferred by the Baroque, and the profusion of forms leads directly to Cortona's most sumptuous and influential decorative scheme, the Planetary Rooms of the Palazzo Pitti in Florence.

While working on the ceiling Cortona also went to Venice and then to Florence where he painted his first interior decoration for the Grand Duke Ferdinando II de' Medici, the walls of the Sala della Stufa. He spent the years 1640 to 1647 in Florence, painting the series of rooms dedicated to the planets Venus, Apollo, Mars, Jupiter and Saturn. These interiors, now the Palatine Gallery, were the Grand Duke's reception rooms in the Palazzo Pitti and preserve largely intact one of the most ambitious decorative schemes of the Italian Baroque. Although the tapestries, pictures and objects have been removed or rearranged, the breathtaking combination of stucco and fresco which constitutes the ceilings with velvet-covered walls and marble doorways still gives a clear idea of late Medici splendour (Plate 73). Rudolf Wittkower has left the best description of the Pitti ceilings, which were completed by Cortona's pupil Ciro Ferri:

The wealth of these decorations baffles accurate description. One meets the entire repertory; figures and caryatids, white stuccoes on gilt ground or gilded ones on white ground; wreaths, trophies, cornucopias, shells and hangings; duplication, triplication, and superimpositions of architectural and decorative elements; cartouches with sprawling borders incongruously linked with lions' heads, and with palmettes, cornucopias and inverted shells – a seemingly illogical joining, interlocking, association of motif with motif. Unrivalled is the agglomeration of plastic forms and their ebullient energy.

After the Barberini ceiling, several large frescoes were painted in Roman palaces, including the Gallery in the Quirinal Palace by a number of artists under Cortona's guidance, the Palazzo Pamphili in Piazza Navona by Camassei and Gimignani (1648 and 1649) and Cortona's own magnificent gallery there of 1650–4, the fresco cycle at the Palazzo Pamphili at Valmantone near Rome, the Palazzo Altieri and, most grandiose of all, the Gallery of Palazzo Colonna (Plate 79).

The densely packed, deep-toned type of fresco which had dominated Italian decoration throughout the century began to be replaced after the 1660s with looser compositions and fresher colour, as in Mattia Preti's Stanza dell'Aria in Palazzo Valmontese of 1661 and even the latest Cortona rooms at the Pitti. Now figures begin to create their own space, a tendency culminating in the weightless, spaceless Rococo frescoes of Tiepolo. Particularly important in the diffusion of the transitional style between late Baroque and the early Rococo was the

Neapolitan Luca Giordano, who worked in Naples, Rome, Florence, Venice and Madrid; his most notable domestic decorations are the great ceiling frescoes in the Palazzo Medici-Riccardi (Plate 80), Florence, and in the Royal Palace in Madrid. It required only the Venetian Sebastiano Ricci to transform Giordano's airy compositions and brilliant colour into the first Rococo, as in his decorations in the Pitti and Marucelli Palaces in Florence of around the turn of the century. In Genoa Gregorio de Ferrari created similar decorations at the same time, notably in the Palazzo Rosso, where his whirling figures are offset by the superb gilded stuccoes to the design of Arrigo Haffner. The number of artists at work on domestic fresco decoration in the second half of the seventeenth century throughout Italy from Genoa to Sicily is prodigious and their production was astonishingly prolific. Armies of pupils and assistants helped spread the ideas of the major masters. The Jesuit priest Andrea Pozzo, author of many grandiose *quadratura* frescoes both secular and ecclesiastical, wrote a highly influential treatise on the art, *Perspectiva pictorum et architectorum* (Rome, 1693). This gave technical advice on problems such as relating the perspective viewpoint to a fresco's setting, and also outlined ways of facilitating the creation of huge frescoes – a subject that was to prove of the greatest importance for German and Austrian decorators, who were then coming into their own as frescoists, outdoing even the Italians in scale. Throughout the seventeenth century, grotesque decoration remained in fashion, especially in Florence where Bernardino Poccetti's inventive frescoes set the standard.

Although now stripped of its tapestry decorations, the Gran Salone of the Palazzo Barberini in Rome was typical of the precise iconographical relationship often created between tapestries, frescoes and even sculpture in Italian Baroque interiors. Urban VIII's nephew, the highly refined collector and connoisseur Cardinal Francesco Barberini, founded the Barberini tapestry factory; its first gesture was to send the *History of Constantine* series, designed by Rubens and Cortona, to King Louis XIII of France after its weaving in 1632–41 (Philadelphia Museum of Art). After the tapestry works founded by Cosimo I de' Medici in Florence in the preceding century, the Barberini factory was the most important in Italy, although it never produced enough to rival those in France or Flanders. The series for the Gran Salone shows the *Life of Christ*, woven in 1643–6 to the designs of Giovanni Francesco Romanelli and Pietro da Cortona, and is now in St John's Cathedral, New York. Its theme complemented that of Cortona's great vault fresco showing *The Triumph of Divine Providence*. Obviously only the richest families could afford such decorative schemes, and the tapestries used in many Italian seventeenth-century interiors were often earlier Italian or imported examples.

Particularly associated with the name of the greatest Italian Baroque sculptor, Gianlorenzo Bernini, is the use of coloured marbles on walls in conjunction with metal,

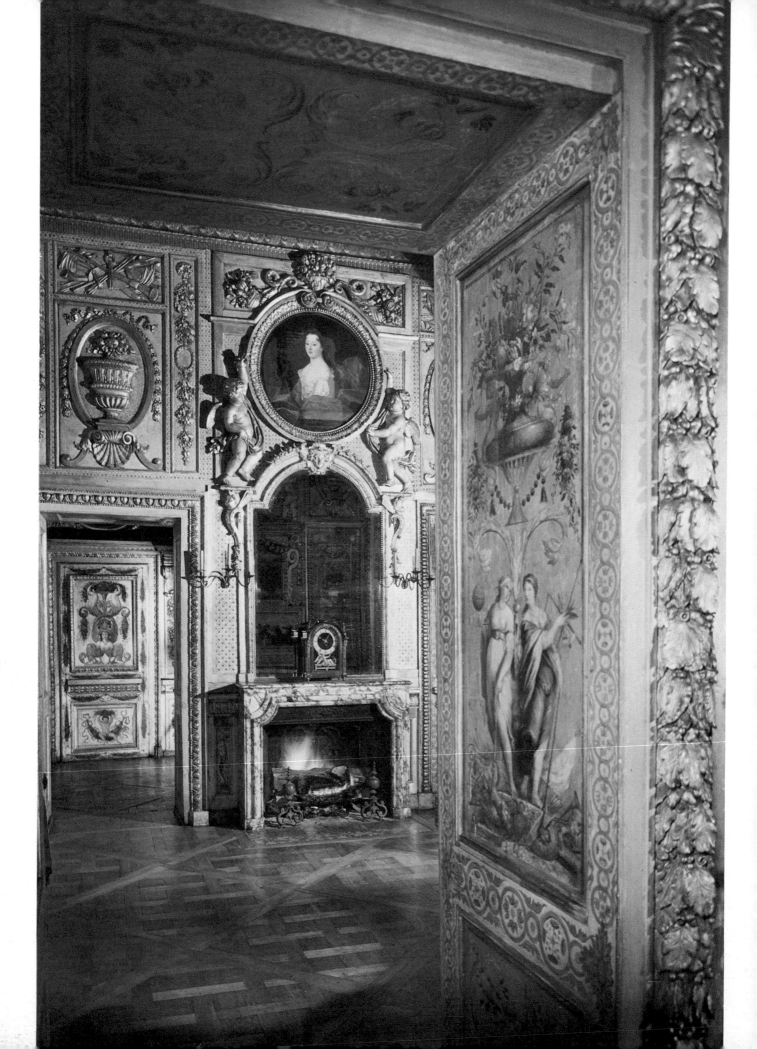

stucco and other decoration, including fresco. Bernini applied such mixed media decorations almost exclusively to ecclesiastical interiors, such as the famous Cornaro Chapel in S. Maria della Vittoria, Rome, containing his *Vision of St Theresa* (1645–52), and his church of S. Andrea al Quirinale of 1658–70. Because of the cost of coloured marbles, their use was confined to the very rich, and apart from flooring, large-scale application of marble to domestic interiors is extremely rare in Italy. When it does occur, its effect is sumptuous, as in the gallery of Palazzo Colonna, Rome (Plate 79). In most cases, wood painted to resemble marble was used (*finto marmo*), a technique brought to the highest degree of perfection in the seventeenth and eighteenth centuries; whole walls could be decorated in this way without vast expense, and the fashion spread throughout Europe. Even in England,

it had its vogue; Celia Fiennes records that at Newby Hall in Yorkshire 'the best roome was painted just like marble' and seventeenth-century marbling survives at Dyrham Park in Gloucestershire, Ham House, Richmond, and Belton in Lincolnshire. It was however at Versailles, as we shall see, that marble decoration on any scale first came into its own outside Italy for domestic interiors in the seventeenth century.

That most lavish feature of the earlier Renaissance interior in Italy, the chimney-piece, came to assume less importance in the Baroque, partly because the old hooded type intruded too much into decorative schemes. In 1665 the Frenchman Jean Le Pautre published his set of engravings of 'cheminées à l'Italienne', and it is interesting that by this term he meant chimney-pieces much closer to the modern type, often consisting of little more than a carved

81 *(left)* Boudoir, Hôtel Lauzun, *Paris*   82 *(below)* Dining Room, Rubens House, *Antwerp*

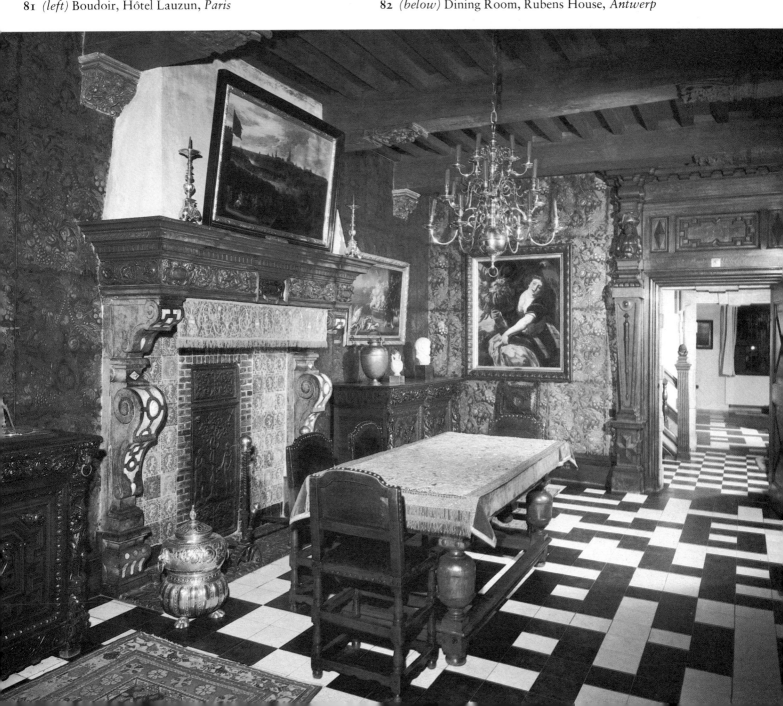

surround, or, in the case of 'à la romaine', with flanking figures. Even very elaborate rooms, such as the Gran Salone of Palazzo Barberini, had fairly simple chimney-pieces, or at least ones which did not intrude into the room, and many interiors were entirely without them. Decorative stoves were a rarity in Italy before the eighteenth century, although north of the Alps they were fairly common by this time.

The one other area in which Italian craftsmen continued to excel during the seventeenth century was that of plasterwork. Building on the traditions and expertise of the Mannerist period, the stucco workers continued the earlier tradition of elaborately wrought plaster, either white or gilded, as a framework for paintings or fresco panels. Increased freedom characterizes the motifs; illustrative of this are the stuccoes in the Salone dei Corazzieri in the Quirinal Palace, Rome, dating from 1605–21, and those in the Salone of the Riccardi Palace in Florence. But while figurative decoration won the day – culminating in Cortona's Pitti ceilings (see Plate 73) – the antique still provided inspiration for many schemes, like the series of vaults in Palazzo Mattei, Rome, which shows fantastic variations on classical models. Some of the finest plasterwork of the period is found in northern Italy, in Genoa's Palazzo Rosso with Arrigo Haffner's Sala d'Estate and Sala d'Inverno, and in Venice in the spectacular Palazzo Albrizzi. Dating from the later part of the century, Palazzo Albrizzi's stuccoes are attributed to Abbondio Stazio from the Ticino. The ballroom or Sala dei Putti is perhaps the culmination of Italian Baroque plasterwork, not so much for its scale (which is not large) as for its *brio*; the entire ceiling consists of a gigantic white drapery 'held' in place against the ceiling with two gilded motifs supported by swarms of flying *putti* who appear and disappear under the folds where they meet the cornice. How such decoration was to lead directly into the Rococo is illustrated by another Venetian room, now in the Metropolitan Museum of Art, from Palazzo Sagredo. Dating from around 1718, this combines a painted ceiling with stucco, marble and wood to form the perfect transition between the richness of the Baroque and the new lightness of Rococo decoration (see Plate 78). Another stucco worker whose decorations come close to Rococo forms is the Sicilian Giovanni Serpotta (1656–1732) who came from a family of carvers and stucco workers. Many examples of his work are to be found in Palermo.

Italian decorators of every kind travelled to other parts of Europe during the seventeenth century, where their unique skills were in great demand, particularly at the courts of Germany, Austria and Russia, where elaborate carving, metalwork and stucco decorations were increasingly in fashion. The important innovations of Borromini, Bernini and Cortona in architecture and decoration found their most immediate following in Southern Germany, while France, Holland and England all borrowed cautiously from them. Italy's dominance in fresco decoration (and indeed in any large-scale mural or ceiling decorations at this time) made it the object of emulation throughout Europe, although few decorative schemes in the Italian manner can be said to live up to the original models.

The story of French interior decoration in the seventeenth century is particularly rich: *le Siècle d'Or* established the French as leaders of European taste for three centuries at precisely the moment of Italy's decline. During the ministries of Richelieu and Mazarin (*c.* 1630–60) French supremacy was confirmed, and under Louis XIV (reigned 1643–1715) all European monarchs turned to the arts in France for guidance. It was at this time that the middle classes gained their immense wealth and power in France. The most important commissions in architecture and the other arts came at this period from the bourgeoisie, with scarcely any aristocratic patronage. It was the intelligence and taste of the bourgeoisie which encouraged the rise of the great period of French classicism, with the tragedies of Corneille, the painting of Poussin, and the architecture of Mansart.

In Italy professional architects had long been established as the designers of their own interiors, whereas the French and English sixteenth-century interior had often been the creation of craftsmen or artisans working from Italian engravings. Although this persisted, notably in the provinces, the major French interiors of the seventeenth century are all the work of well-established architects and designers, such as François Mansart, Louis Le Vau and Charles Le Brun. Since the most important commissions under Louis XIV were almost exclusively for the Crown and wealthy bourgeois, the best artists and craftsmen tended to gravitate to Versailles and to Paris, where the King monopolized as many of them as he could.

A major factor in the centralization of the decorative arts in seventeenth-century France was the formation of the Manufacture Royale des meubles de la Couronne in 1633. Commonly known as the Manufacture des Gobelins from the hôtel of the brothers of that name where the manufactory was situated, outside Paris, it was established by Louis XIV's Minister Colbert to provide furnishings for the royal residences, but it was also seen as the means of instigating a national style (see below). This and the other activities of Colbert, who wanted to make Versailles the centre not only of European power but also of the arts, have tended to diminish the achievements of the earlier part of the century in interior decoration.

Henry IV had already installed craftsmen in special workshops in the Louvre in 1608, although many of these were Flemish or Italian. After his assassination in 1610, the Florentine Marie de Médicis acted as regent during the minority of Louis XIII, and established a high level of taste in her Palais du Luxembourg with its famous gallery containing Rubens' huge series of paintings showing the history of the Queen. Her example encouraged a rash of private building, with many private houses springing up around the Luxembourg, on the Ile Saint-Louis, and in the Marais. Indicative of the new trend to luxurious interiors were the decorations carried out by the Marquise de Rambouillet in her father's Parisian hôtel from 1619. These rooms were said to be 'proportioned and ordered with such art that they impress the onlooker and seem much larger than they actually are'. Her celebrated 'Chambre Bleue' – the bedchamber in which she held her *salon* – created such a stir with its blue walls, hangings and furnishings, that the Queen sent her architects to study it.

Cardinal Richelieu tried to establish a national style for Louis XIII, setting an example of great luxury in his own château at Richelieu. Subsequently the Italian Cardinal de Mazarin imported many Italian artists, including Romanelli, Borzoni and Grimaldi, to decorate his own and the royal residences; the result was a version of the latest Roman Baroque with elaborate stuccoes, wall and ceiling painting, gilding, and fine furniture (Plate 81). The effect of all of this on the French, who until this time had continued to decorate their homes in the style of the Second School of Fontainebleau, was considerable, but the desire for a national, French style with its own characteristics was growing.

The architect who first fully realized these ideals and set high standards for his successors was François Mansart. Born in Paris in 1598, Mansart almost certainly never visited Italy and evolved his 'sophisticated and luxurious classicism' in France. His first known private house commission was in 1635 for the Hôtel de la Vrillière, which boasted a Galerie painted by François Perrier incorporating large paintings by Poussin, Guercino, Guido Reni and others on its walls. It was here also that Mansart introduced the feature which became one of the constants of his interiors, a staircase whose flights followed the outer walls of a square space, with an ample central well. Mansart's interiors are never 'decorated'; they are of as pure an architecture as his exteriors, relying on the juxtaposition of plain, even severe wall surfaces with areas of rich sculptural decoration. This is combined with the ingenious planning which subsequently became the hallmark of French, and especially Parisian, domestic architecture.

Mansart is said to have had the difficult character of many geniuses, and his career was uneven, to say the least. Of his many interiors, including the Château de Blois for Gaston d'Orléans (with its breathtaking staircase using unusual spatial and lighting devices), the Château de Balleroy and the Hôtel du Jars, only those of the Château de Maisons (now Maisons Laffitte) survive to convey the full scope of his talent. The adjoining vestibule (Plate 83) and staircase form one of the most beautiful interiors of the century. Whereas his contemporaries used gilding and colour, Mansart relied on the contrast of solids and voids, plain and decorated in the great classical tradition of Bramante, with the additional attraction of a highly personal manner. Typical of Mansart's classicism is his

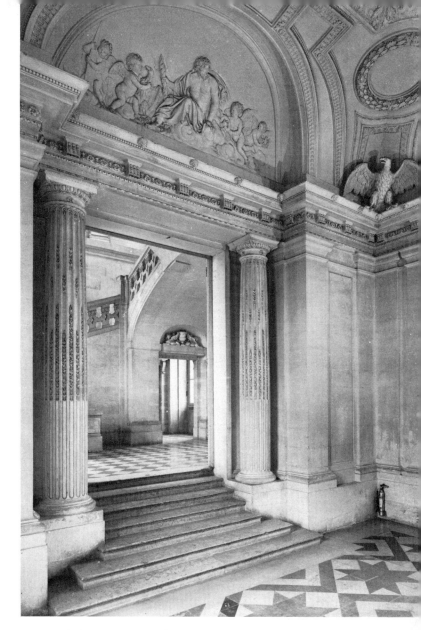

83 Vestibule, Maisons Laffitte, *by François Mansart, 1642–51*
This country house near Paris was built for René de Longueuil, who allowed Mansart great freedom in the design

placing of carved *putti* representing the arts and sciences (executed like the other sculpture at Maisons by Guérin, Buyster and Van Obstal to the designs of Jacques Sarrazin) above projecting undecorated stone panels on the staircase; also of great individuality is the balustrade with its complex interlocking pattern and acanthus decoration. A similarly magnificent staircase in the Hôtel d'Aumont is recorded in engravings, but it was Maisons which was said to have inspired Voltaire's lines:

> Simple en était la noble architecture;
> Chaque ornement en sa place arrêté
> Y semblait mis par la nécessité:
> L'art s'y cachait sous l'air de la nature
> L'oeil satisfait embrassait sa structure,
> Jamais surpris et toujours enchanté.

In spite of Mansart's unquestionably superior talent, Louis Le Vau (1612–70) was destined to become the architect most closely linked with the official style of the Sun King. Le Vau was, unlike Mansart, the perfect civil servant and, more important, a brilliant organizer of the talents of others. He demonstrated his ability as early as 1642 when he headed his team of decorators, which included the painters Bourdon, Le Brun, Le Sueur and Dorigny, and the sculptors Sarrazin, Guérin, Le Hongre and Van Obstal, at the Hôtel Hesselin. It was at the Hôtel Lambert in Paris and at the Château de Vaux-le-Vicomte in the Île de France that Le Vau first revealed the decorative manner later to reach perfection at Versailles. Much of their original decoration survives.

The Hôtel Lambert is notable not only for its richly varied room shapes, including ovals and octagons, but also for the combination of spatial ingenuity with considerable grandeur, especially in the Cabinet de l'Amour with its dado and frieze filled with landscapes and mythologies (now mainly in the Louvre) by an international array of painters. The Galerie is the culmination of the Hôtel in every sense, with its original splendid view of the Seine and its gold and bronze-coloured stucco reliefs by Van Obstal, large upright Rousseau landscapes and Le Brun's painted ceiling with illusionistic tapestries showing *The Labours of Hercules*, to whom the room is dedicated. Compared with an Italian interior of the same period, its rigid vertical emphasis, carefully contained decorations, and the richly severe classical entrance wall composed of two pairs of Corinthian columns and pilasters surmounted by an unbroken straight entablature, all appear restrained. The only Italianate element is the long form of the gallery itself, typical of Parisian houses of the early seventeenth century.

Le Vau's involvement with the proto-Versailles (Sainte-Beuve called it '*ce Versailles anticipé*') of Vaux-le-Vicomte prepared him directly for royal employment. Nicolas Fouquet was Louis XIV's *Surintendant des Finances* and established private workshops at Maincy to furnish this gigantic château. It was Le Brun's real début as a grand manner decorator, and he formed part of a distinguished team. On 7 August 1661, Fouquet staged the famous party for the King, the Queen, Mlle Louise de la Vallière and the entire court where a Molière comedy-ballet with Le Brun's décor was given with music by Lully and spectacular fireworks. Within weeks, Fouquet was thrown into prison for malversation and the King appropriated a ready-made team of unparalleled artistic talent for his works at Versailles. On the model of Pietro da Cortona's Pitti interiors, Le Brun made masterpieces out of Le Vau's somewhat uninspired rooms. The Italian influence is especially evident in the King's bedchamber with its elaborate combination of stuccoed and painted (not frescoed) ceiling in white and gold, velvet-hung walls, and its originally sumptuous furnishings.

It is at this point that Charles Le Brun emerges into the artistic limelight, to become one of the first all-round *decorators*, involved with every aspect of interior design at the highest level. Born in 1619 of a Parisian family of painters and sculptors, he first worked as a painter in a rather sombre manner. In 1642 he went as a *pensionnaire* to Rome, studying the antique and the great masters. In 1648 he was closely involved with Colbert in the foundation of the Académie Royale de Peinture et Sculpture which was designed to bring these, and subsequently, with the other academies, all the arts under State control. His success as a painter of domestic decorations and the fall of Fouquet led to his being put in charge of the Gobelins in 1663, controlling all the decoration and furnishing for the royal residences – a position of power unprecedented in interior decoration history. The striking uniformity of Versailles's interiors resulted from his régime. In his work at the Tuileries (destroyed) and the Galerie d'Apollon of the Louvre with its white and gilded stuccoes, paintings and arabesque panels, he created the *style Louis XIV*.

Between 1671 and 1681 Le Brun decorated the Grands Appartements of Versailles, producing interiors which stunned every visitor to the château, and inspired every European court to emulation. It is a tribute to Le Brun that within the unified style of these interiors he succeeded in creating rooms of great diversity, from the famous Escalier des Ambassadeurs (destroyed) to the Galerie des Glaces, and the Salons de la Guerre and de la Paix (Plate 84) which completed the ensemble in 1686. These rooms are based, like those of Pietro da Cortona at the Pitti Palace, on the planetary system, with a highly organized propaganda campaign carried out through art. The rooms culminated in the Salle d'Apollon, appropriately for the monarch who identified himself with Apollo, the sun-god. Visitors started their symbolic journey towards the sun by ascending the Escalier des Ambassadeurs. A suitably stunning introduction to the glories to follow, this staircase was constructed along one long side of a huge oblong space. Its steps, balustrade and lower walls were covered with a revetment of brilliantly coloured marbles, with a fountain at the first landing where the staircase divided into two. Around the upper walls immediately beneath the lavish above-lit vault was a series of illusionistic murals showing many figures gazing down on the ascending visitors. The staircase's immense scale was rivalled only by the Galerie des Glaces itself, erected by Jules-Hardouin Mansart in the space of Le Vau's great terrace facing the gardens. One other notable interior largely faced with marble was the Appartement des Bains, where in dalliance with Mme de Montespan the King passed long periods to escape the heat of summer in its water-cooled air. Mme de Montespan's interest in interior decoration was such that her château at Clagny became known as '*la maison des délices*' not only on account of the royal favourite's own presence there.

The Salon de Vénus and the Salon de Diane were also panelled with marble in rigid rectilinear patterns com-

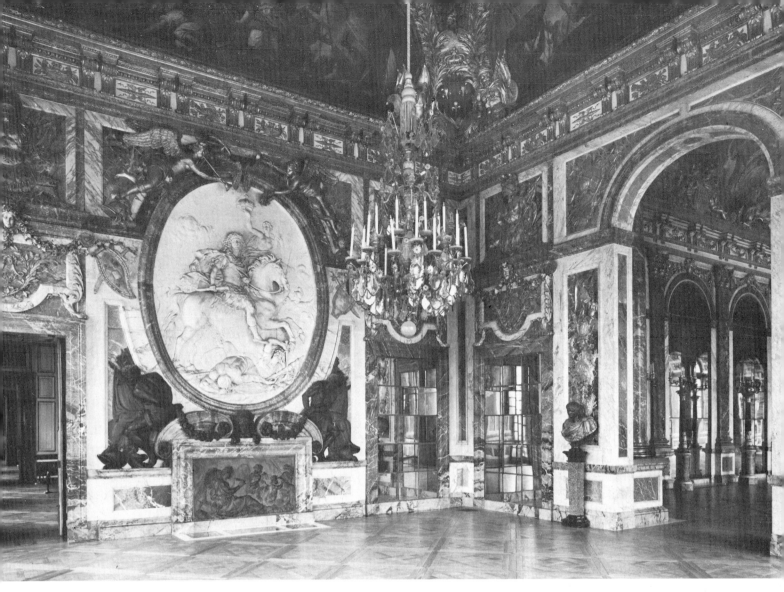

84 Salon de la Guerre, Versailles, *by Le Brun and J. Hardouin-Mansart, 1678–86*

plemented by marble floors, while other rooms were hung with patterned bottle-green or crimson velvet as a background for some of the King's astonishing collection of old master paintings, hung in gilded frames. Following sixteenth-century Italian precedents, such as that of the Tribune in the Uffizi, Florence, pictures were often arranged in patterns on walls, rather than for their intrinsic content, creating pleasing symmetrical arrangements of form and colour against a uniform background. This method retained general acceptance until the later nineteenth century, mixing artists and schools indiscriminately in the widest variety of frames, ranging from carved and gilded or silvered for Italian and French pictures to heavy black or mixed, stained wood ones for Dutch and Flemish works. Unlike his successors in the eighteenth century, Louis XIV loathed Dutch and Flemish realism, saying of such pictures: 'Get these horrors (*magots*) out of my sight!', with the result that the majority of paintings displayed at Versailles were of the 'grand manner', Roman, Bolognese, Venetian or French.

Apart from marble, velvet and tapestry (discussed below), an important feature of Versailles interiors which stamped them as extravagantly regal was the mirrors. The earliest surviving mirror room is a circular one at Maisons dating from around 1660, although Catherine de' Medici (1519–89) had a Cabinet de Miroirs with 109 Venetian mirrors set into the panelling. Venice had dominated the European market for plate glass, but in 1665 the Manufacture des Glaces de Venise was founded in Paris, soon to become the Manufacture Royale des Glaces de Miroirs and to provide the vast quantities of mirrors for Versailles. In 1684, Louis XIV planned the Petite Galerie at Versailles, where his impressive collection of gemstone vessels (in the best Medici tradition) was to be displayed to great advantage on brackets set against mirrored walls. Like most large paintings, single mirrors in frames were hung canted forward on cords which provided ample scope for decoration with silken ribbons, tassels, and so on. Sometimes, mirrors were painted with fruit and flowers, as in the Medici-Riccardi and the Colonna Galleries (Plate 79).

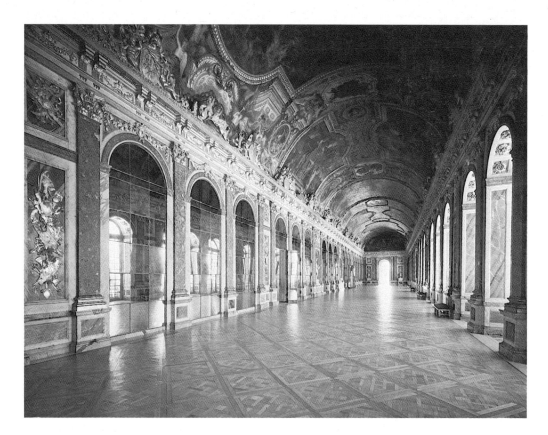

In the early Louis XIV interiors at Versailles, the furniture played a most important role in the final effect. The *Mercure Galant* noted that most of the furniture of the Grande Galerie, the Salon de la Guerre and the Salon de Mercure (the King's bedroom) was almost entirely of silver. The latter room contained a complete set of silver furniture, including the balustrade surrounding the bed alcove, eight two-feet candlesticks, four silver basins, two pedestals for perfume burners, a pair of firedogs, and a chandelier! Mlle de Scudéry's description of the King's Appartement des Collections leaves us in no doubt of the remarkable degree of luxury:

... it is lighted by rock-crystal chandeliers, and ... there are vases to match ... of excessive height and wondrous beauty, inlaid with gold and diamonds; together with busts and figures in the Antique; a gold vessel ornate with diamonds and rubies, all manner of porcelain articles from Japan as well as from China; vases made of agate, with all the varieties to be found ... vases made of emerald, turquoise, jade, fire-opal, jasper from Germany and the Orient, star-stone, oriental cornelian and chrysolite; several figures in the Grotesque style set with pearls, emeralds, rubies and agates ... excellent pictures, looking-glasses ... all the treasures of the earth can hardly vie with the wealth and beauty of the rare or precious articles to be found in this room.

Tragically, almost all of the silver pieces were melted down after the first sumptuary edict of 1689 to pay the crippling costs of wars; despite their splendour, Versailles's interiors today are but a pale reflection of their former glory.

The iconography and the unparalleled magnificence of the Château directly reflected the rigid protocol imposed by the King on his Court in the first great period of his reign at Versailles. Such a life, lived entirely in public, led Louis to seek escape in various buildings outside Versailles itself, such as the Grand Trianon and the Trianon de Porcelaine of 1670–2, which was decorated externally with faience and internally with painted plaster in imitation of Dutch blue-and-white ceramics. In designing the interiors of the Trianon, Mansart (see Chapter 5) decided upon rectangular panelling, painted white and occasionally picked out in gold and framing mirrors – already looking forward to the anti-Baroque spirit of the Rococo.

The importance of tapestry in French interior decoration of the seventeenth and eighteenth centuries cannot be overemphasized. In 1607, Henry IV had founded the first important Parisian tapestry manufactory, granting special privileges to two Flemings, Marc de Comans and François de la Planche (van der Planken). Its most important production was the series showing the *Story of Artemisia*; later the painter Simon Vouet (himself one of the major decorative artists of the period along with François Perrier) provided inspiration for tapestries with his paintings of *Rinaldo and Armida, The Loves of the Gods* and *The Old Testament*. The first set woven by the Gobelins manufactory was *The Acts of the Apostles* after cartoons by Raphael, setting the tone for the three major royal commissions, the *History of Alexander*, the superlative *Life of Louis XIV* and the *Royal Residences*, all woven between 1664 and 1681. The importance which Louis XIV attached to interior decoration is best revealed in two of the tapestries from the *Life: The Audience of the Papal Legate*, which is set in the royal bedchamber amid a profusion of pictures, precious furniture, metalwork and tapestries, and *The Visit of the King to the Gobelins in 1667*, where the manufactory's astonishing range and quality are fully displayed. In 1664, Louis XIV had opened another Manufacture Royale de Tapisseries at Beauvais which, like the workshops at Aubusson and Felletin, grew in importance in the seventeenth century.

Most tapestries were woven in wool, in special cases enriched with gold or silver threads together with silk for highlights. Almost all the tapestries for the Crown depicted themes found throughout the royal decorative schemes – history, allegory and religious subjects, all of which were directly related to King and State. In less wealthy circles, tapestries often had repeat patterns and were known as *Tapisseries de Bergame* or *verdures d'Auvergne*.

Other wall-coverings ranged from plain tawny serge to damask and velvet which were made and hung in vertical strips and hence could be used regardless of a room's size. Genoese velvet retained its exclusivity throughout the century, being of a particularly luxurious pile which rendered rich colours even richer in appearance. Embossed leather – usually calfskin – was widely used, decorated with tinfoil either silvered or gilded and often elaborately painted with bright colours in a wide variety of motifs. Such leather coverings – paralleled in exoticism by the new fascination with the East – were first used in Moorish and Islamic interiors and their adoption in Europe may have come through Spain, since the city of Córdoba was one of the main centres of production. Despite the advent of all these lavish hangings during the Baroque, plain wooden panelling retained its popularity on account of its warmth, comfortable appearance and relative inexpensiveness. Oak and pine were the preferred woods, although deal, painted to resemble more costly woods, was also used. As the century advanced, wooden wall panelling tended to be painted in pale colours, white, pale green or blue, sometimes combined with dadoes or other areas picked out in marbling.

The splendour of Versailles and other great houses depended largely on spectacular lighting from tall and numerous windows; the Galerie des Glaces is unimaginable without them (Plate 85). By the end of the sixteenth century it was *de rigueur* to have all windows glazed, although the breakage rate in the manufacture of glass kept the cost high and small panes were the norm except for the wealthy. Sometimes even window-glass was painted on the inside with scenes, figures or portraits, and in Holland, Flanders and England inset stained glass panels showing coats-of-arms remained popular. By 1700, the sash window (the name derives from the French word for the wooden frame *chassis*) was in common use throughout Europe, with the exception of Italy. For ground-floor windows or those of important first-floor rooms, which often opened onto balconies, the French preferred the so-called french window (see page 117), whose floor-length design remained an integral part of external and internal architecture.

The multiple interior shutters appearing in so many Dutch paintings of the seventeenth century were considered *démodé* elsewhere, and in Mediterranean countries external slatted shutters were the rule. Velvet for large curtains remained expensive and very heavy, and after the mid-century silk curtains became more common, with a cheaper woven fabric being widely used even in lavish interiors for warmer hangings. Festoons of silk or other delicate materials which could be raised and lowered by cords were already in use in the Baroque period and became even more popular in the eighteenth century. Undeniably the most elegant window covering, they have the added advantage of being the least obtrusive when drawn up. Painted blinds of silk or linen were decorated with all types of figurative elements, seen to effect against daylight. Venetian blinds of wooden slats, called *jalousies à la persienne*, appear by the early eighteenth century.

Italy's dominance in the field of engravings of architecture and ornament had already been challenged in the sixteenth century by such publications as Jacques Androuet du Cerceau's *Les plus excellent bastiments de France*, which appeared in two volumes in 1576 and 1579. Its uniqueness lay in the inclusion of ornament suitable for interior decoration. Concurrently with increased French consciousness of the decorative arts, a spate of engravings of every possible detail of the domestic interior – doors, chimney-pieces, panelling, ceilings, mouldings, and so on – began to emerge from Paris from the 1630s onwards. The ceiling designs of Jean Cotelle and the chimney-piece engravings of Jean Barbet had an instant success as far afield as England and Scandinavia. Jean Le Pautre's (1618–82) engravings of the designs of Le Brun had immense influence, and transmitted Le Brun's fame beyond France. Jean Berain (1638–1711), architect and designer, became the most influential engraver of the later part of the century, developing his personal variant of the grotesque style as evolved from antique precedents by Raphael and, in France, by Primaticcio at Fontainebleau. These arabesques, which lead directly to the Rococo (see page 112), are light-hearted and filled with a wide variety of motifs, ranging from monkeys, exotic figures, vine-tendrils and draperies to pedestals and festoons. They quickly entered the repertoire for the decoration of walls, ceilings and furniture, and much of the furniture by or associated with the celebrated cabinet maker André-Charles Boulle is derived from them.

The difference in materials used by French and Italian designers accounts to some extent for the very different effects obtained in the two countries. Even the most grandiose French interiors sometimes employed wood extensively, as in the splendid Galerie of the Hôtel Lambert by Le Vau (1650–60). It was principally under Italian influence that expensive marbles were preferred for the interiors of Versailles, not only for floors but also for the revetment of walls. Although many pavements in ground-floor rooms might often be of marble, those on the upper storeys were generally wooden, of varying degrees of opulence and complexity. As early as the 1620s, Marie de Médicis (who after all had inherited a long family tradition of lavish taste) had the floor of her closet made of parquetry inlaid with silver. Later, Pierre Golle, *ébéniste du roi*, created a series of outstanding wooden floors for the Dauphin: in one instance, André-Charles Boulle was called in to make a floor as valuable as his tortoiseshell and silver-inlaid furniture, also for the Dauphin. Such cases were, however, exceptional.

Most important interiors had simple wooden flooring, although during the seventeenth century parquet came increasingly into vogue, the word deriving from the raised, separated or otherwise distinguished area of a room set aside for the King. In France, parquet is generally arranged in lozenge shapes and is usually of oak. Elaborate inlays of the kind first adopted in Italian *intarsie* found little favour in France, while in Germany, Russia and other Northern countries they were taken to their richest conclusions; one of the most perfect surviving examples is the Rococo *Intarsienkabinett* of 1756 from Schloss Fantaisie, now in the Bayerisches Nationalmuseum in Munich. On top of these inlays straw matting was laid, surprisingly even in royal interiors, where richness was provided by Turkish carpets; not until the eighteenth century does all-over carpeting appear in the form of separate pieces sewn together. The rarity of Persian carpets, which were normally diplomatic gifts from the Shah, preserved their exclusivity; indicative of their splendour is a contemporary description of a pavilion with Persian carpets with 'gold and silver backgrounds' and others 'of crimson velvet decorated with abundant gold and silver'. Such carpets were only laid on the floor for special occasions. In many cases, they were displayed over tables, where their beauty could be appreciated without risk to their fabric. The Chapel at Versailles had a crimson velvet carpet, and Cardinal Mazarin (noted for his love of luxury) possessed a crimson leather carpet tooled in gold like a book binding!

The French seventeenth century is particularly associated with the development of the decorative chimney-piece, and engravings were fundamental in the spread of ideas in this sphere. For obvious reasons the fireplace had far greater importance in Northern interiors, becoming the focus of almost all indoor life during the winter months. Except in out-of-the-way places the hooded chimney-piece vanished during the seventeenth century, and generally speaking the preferred type became the flat-fronted projection running from floor to ceiling at the same depth, sometimes surmounted by an overmantel mirror and a pediment or a carved or moulded cornice following that of the room itself. Although chimney-pieces with overmantel mirrors appear as early as 1601 at Fontainebleau, it was not until the end of the century that they became widespread.

The importance of the chimney-piece as a vehicle for elaborate decoration and even fantasy was recognized in the sixteenth century, notably in Italy (see Chapter 3), and both Serlio and Philibert de l'Orme included them in their treatises. The influence of such engraved works is felt throughout Europe in the predominantly architectural approach to chimney-piece design which continued to dominate well into the seventeenth century; the magnificent multicoloured examples of the 1650s in the Castle at Rosenberg in Denmark are indicative not only of the new internationalism of certain aspects of decoration but also of the continued influence outside the main centres of much earlier manuals throughout the Baroque. Jean Le Pautre's engravings of chimney-pieces published in 1665 (see page 95) indicate the new taste for lighter types; the earliest example of the new mirror decorations may have been in the Chambre du Roi of 1684 at Versailles. Daniel Marot's set of engravings, *Nouvelles cheminées à panneaux de glace à la manière de France*, are among the first direct results of such innovations and had immense influence in Holland and England.

During the 1690s Jules Hardouin-Mansart created several interiors at Versailles, Trianon and Marly whose design rejects all the grandeur of the preceding decades in favour of a new style soon to be transformed into the early Rococo; the Classical Orders vanish, or are reduced to mere strips, heavy panelling gives way to the lightest of mouldings, overmantel mirrors proliferate, cornices are elegant rather than imposing and the general atmosphere is one of intimacy after the grandeur of the Baroque. Instead of strong colour and contrasts, panelling and ceilings are painted overall in one pale colour, usually white or grey. Mansart's plans for private houses in this period show rooms with rounded ends, breaking with the rigidity of Versailles's rectangular forms. Well before Louis XIV's death in 1715 the reaction to the magnificence of the *Grand Siècle* had begun, and France was preparing for a revolution in the decorative arts – the Rococo.

Louis XIV's European supremacy also affected Holland in a decisive way, although the Republic of the United Netherlands evolved a culture independent of the rest of Europe. In 1609 the United Provinces had concluded a twelve-year truce with Spain, thereby freeing themselves of Spanish domination. Under Prince Maurice of Orange (1567–1625) they rose to being the major seapower in the world with vast colonial possessions – which had a considerable effect on certain aspects of their art. During the seventeenth century, the Dutch evolved what might be termed 'bourgeois classicism' in their interior decoration, at one end of the scale massive and somewhat pompous (Plate 82), but at the other small-scaled, intimate and unassuming; it is perhaps in these last qualities that their greatest contribution to the period lies.

The ample interiors of Vermeer's pictures exemplify those of the Dutch seventeenth century. Dominated by strong verticals and horizontals – emphasized by immaculately neat floor patterns of black and white marble tiles – the main feature of these interiors is their light, streaming in from large windows. Often the chimney-piece is surprisingly classical, and remains the only architectural feature of the room, apart from occasional pedimented door-cases. One of the most striking features of almost all Dutch interiors is the number of oil paintings, hung everywhere – above doors, chimney-pieces and windows, and on any available wall space. In 1640, Peter Mundy wrote of the Dutch:

as for the art of Painting and the affection of the people to Pictures, I thincke none other goe beeyond them, there having bin in this Country Many excellent Men in thatt Facullty, some at present, as Rimbrantt, etts, All in general striving to adorne their houses, especially the outer or street roome, with costly peeces, Butchers and bakers not much inferiour in their shoppes, which are Fairely sett Forth, yea many tymes blacksmithes, Cobblers, etts., will have some picture or other by their Forge and in their stalle. Such is the generall Notion, enclination and delight that these Countrie Native(s) have to Paintings.

In 1641, John Evelyn noted in Rotterdam that the number of pictures was matched only by their cheapness.

The artist who most influenced decorative detail in early seventeenth-century Holland was Hans Vredeman de Vries (1527–1606) from Leeuwarden. His book *Variae Architecture Formae* of 1601 contains prints of his fantastic compositions showing colonnades, perspectives and fountains of astonishing vulgarity in comparison with French or Italian work of the time. De Vries in his turn had been influenced by Cornelis Floris de Vriendt (1514 ? –75) and Wendel Dietterlin (1550–99). It was against this background of wilful Mannerism and rather clumsy Baroque that Daniel Marot (1661–1752) established himself in Holland as the leading modern designer, especially of interiors.

Marot grew up in Paris and came to Holland along with many other French Protestant refugees after the Revocation of the Edict of Nantes. Their influence on the arts was to be considerable. As architect-designer to William of Orange, for whom he designed the interiors of the royal palace of Het Loo, Marot had a position not dissimilar to Le Brun's in France and like him he readily turned his hand to every aspect of interior and furniture design. In his Trêveszaal in the Binnenhof at The Hague (Plate 86) the French-influenced decorative ensemble has, typically, a more Dutch solidity and decorative detail. Such interiors show the triumph of the late Louis XIV style in Holland over equally monumental but rather different Dutch Baroque interiors such as Jacob van Campen's vast central hall in the Amsterdam Royal Palace, begun in 1648, and the ponderous Oranjezaal decorated by Jacob Jordaens in the Huis ten Bosch of the same period.

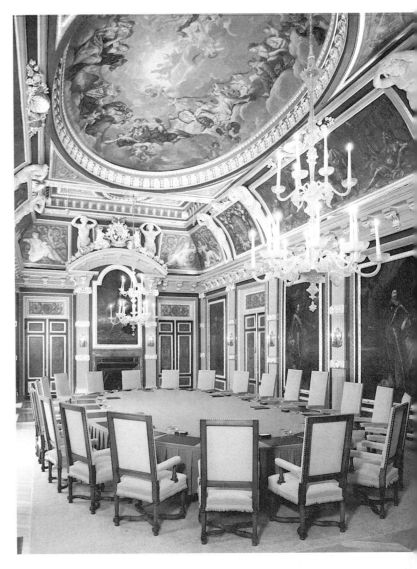

86 Trêveszaal, 1696–8, by Daniel Marot. Binnenhof, The Hague

Marot, like his near contemporary Jean I Berain (see page 101), exerted his greatest influence as an *ornemaniste*, and his designs range across the whole sphere of decorative detail. In furniture design his most notable productions were the spectacular four-poster state beds (beds were the most important single item of furniture in any seventeenth-century household) which, like his other furniture and detail, substituted sculptural Baroque forms for the existing rectangular ones of the period in Holland. His designs included tasselled drapes and valances of great richness, and plumed canopies. Another area in which his designs broke new ground was chimney-pieces with supports for porcelain and faïence vases, and these appear in rooms for Queen Mary at Hampton Court: it was she who introduced the fashion for the collecting and display of Oriental porcelain and European tin-enamel ware (delft) into England, a fashion which played so important a part in the appearance of both Dutch and English rooms at this time. Marot's designs for panels also deserve mention with their combination of strapwork, acanthus scrolls, grotesques, floral garlands and popular allegories.

The seventeenth century saw greater political change in Britain than in any other European country with the unification of England and Scotland under James I, the execution of his son Charles I in 1649, the ensuing Commonwealth, and the Restoration of Charles II in 1660. This had little direct effect on interior decoration, which progressed from the extreme late Mannerism of the Jacobean style through Inigo Jones's elegant Palladianism and its offshoots to the Baroque of the Restoration. Unlike the Baroque elsewhere in Europe, in Britain the style did not evolve naturally into the Rococo, but represented an interlude between two major Palladian revivals.

The interiors of the great Jacobean houses were often the creation of Flemish and other foreign craftsmen, who provided chimney-pieces, doorways and other detail derived from such engraved books as Dietterlin's extravagant *Architectura* published in Nuremberg in 1594–8. H. Vredeman de Vries's book of the same title appeared in Antwerp in 1563 and its ubiquitous strapwork ornament was influential in Britain. Among the foreign craftsmen recorded in this period are the families of Colt, Cure, Stevens, Johnson and Holleman. The decoration of Audley End, Essex (after 1603–1616), with its somewhat coarse Anglo-Flemish ornament, the vestigial hammer-beams and large screen with male and female terms in the hall, and Italianate grotesques, is typical of 'Jacobean' as distinct from Elizabethan style.

It is against this background of carved wooden, plaster or stone decorations employing the whole range of Mannerist detail and set in room shapes which owe nothing to the proportional lessons of Palladio and other Italians that Inigo Jones's achievement must be seen. Jones was the son of a Smithfield clothworker and may have paid his first visit to Italy in 1596 at the age of 23, where he presumably learned his considerable skill as a draughtsman – far in advance of any of his designer contemporaries in England. In Italy with Lord Arundel in 1613–14 he made a study of antique detail which placed him in a unique position as an architect, the first in England to have mastered the Classical language from the original buildings. His court career began with the design of masques, and from 1615 until the outbreak of the Civil War in 1642 he was Surveyor of the King's Works, with responsibility for the royal residences. His first interior may be the Haynes Grange Room now in the Victoria and Albert Museum, supposedly from Houghton Conquest House in Bedfordshire. Dating from around 1615, it is the first English room to be panelled entirely in pinewood and has impressive Corinthian pilasters from floor to ceiling, framing inset raised 'aedicules' recalling Palladio as interpreted by Serlio. 'Masculinity should be at the basis of all ornament', wrote Jones, and it is impossible to think of another English architect of that date who could have designed such a simple and monumentally classical room. In spite of its severity, it has a richness later adopted by Jones and his pupil John Webb in their domestic interiors: 'For as outwardly every wyse man carrieth a graviti in Publicke Places ... yet inwardly has his imaginacy set on fire, and sumtimes licenciously flying out ...' Jones's words perfectly describe the contrast between his simple monumental exterior architecture and rich interiors like that of Wilton (Plate 87).

Jones's most monumental surviving domestic interior, the Banqueting House at Whitehall (1619–22), is, like the entrance hall in his Queen's House at Greenwich, somewhat bleak, despite its richly Baroque ceiling paintings by Rubens, *The Apotheosis of James I* and *The Allegory of the Birth of Charles I*. It was originally built with a huge coffered niche at one end, and must have created a great stir at the time on account of its pure Classicism. It was, however, in smaller interiors that the new style must have made its finest impression, combining elegance with comfort. In this context, it is interesting that the most elaborate were made for Charles I's Queen, Henrietta Maria, who no doubt brought with her from France the latest ideas and even influential books such as Jean Barbet's *Livre d'architecture*, first published in Paris in 1633. For her, Jones altered Somerset House, creating with the painter Matthew Goodrich the sumptuous Cabinet Room, reconstructed from the accounts by Sir John Summerson:

It was completely panelled, each panel having 'grotesques' on a white ground, while the stiles and muntins were enriched with gilded and shadowed guilloche with small flowers at the crossings. The ceiling was white with a central circular panel marked with a leaf-enriched moulding, shadowed and gilded. The entablature, too, had shadowed and gilded mouldings. A stone window had gold arabesques on its white surfaces and an edge of gold next to the glass; hinges, lock and staples were gilded. The chimney-piece had an Ionic order below painted like white marble, gilded, and above, a Corinthian order in blue and gold. The doorcase was painted like white marble, with enrichments picked out in white and gold.

Such advanced regal taste had little if any following in England, but a faint echo of its splendour is captured in other interiors for the Queen at the Queen's House, Greenwich, such as the Cabinet Room and Queen's Cabinet. The only interiors to survive which probably reflect Court taste in the 1630s are those at Ham House, Surrey (Plate 88).

The culmination of the Jonesian Palladian style with its French-derived decorative detail is the elegant and assured series of interiors at Wilton House (Plate 87) dating from the early 1650s. Surprisingly, only a few years previously the gentleman amateur Sir Roger Pratt had observed on his return from Italy that 'Architecture here has not received those advantages which it has in other parts, it continuing almost still as rude here as it was at the very first.' It is interesting to note that in the same year

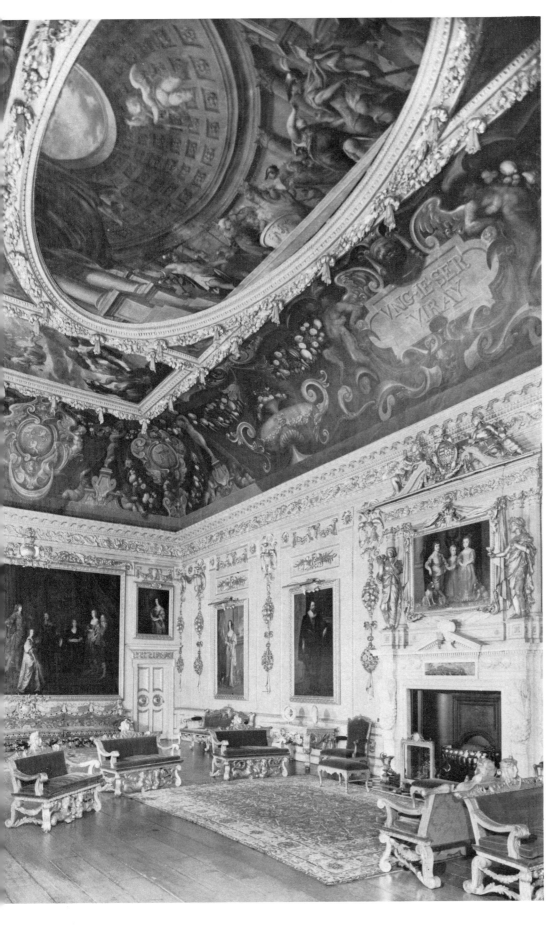

87 The Double Cube Room,
Wilton House, *Salisbury.*
c. 1653 No single country-
house interior can be firmly
attributed to Inigo Jones,
but the rooms at Wilton,
which were probably
decorated by John Webb
'with the advice of' Jones,
represent the fullest
realization of many of his
ideas. The Double Cube
Room, 60 feet long, 30 feet
wide and 30 feet high,
adjoins the Cube Room
which is based on the same
proportional system. The
wall panelling is of pine,
decorated with carved swags
of fruit, flowers and foliage
suspended from cartouches.
Its chimney-piece and
magnificent east double
doors are derived from
Franco-Flemish sources, and
from Jean Barbet's Livre
d'architecture. The ceiling
cove was painted by the
elder Edward Pierce, while
the ceiling paintings are
probably by Emanuel de
Critz, the decorative painter
who with his two brothers
Thomas and John worked
for Charles I. A magnificent
set of Van Dyck portraits –
the room's raison d'être –
culminates in the vast canvas
showing the Herbert family,
on the west wall

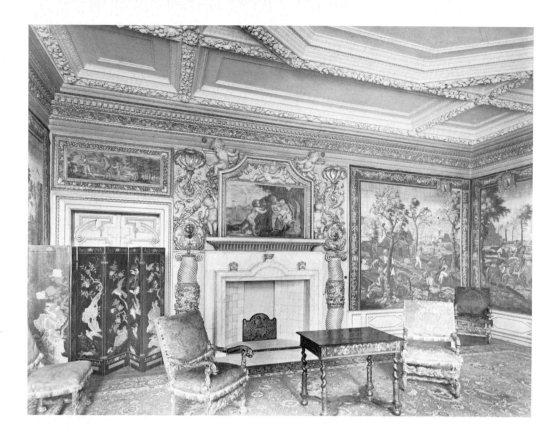

Pratt designed the superb Coleshill in Berkshire, one of the most magnificent of all country houses, decorated throughout in a personal interpretation of the Jones manner and tragically destroyed in a fire in 1953. Such building was undoubtedly confined to a handful of enlightened patrons, and during the Commonwealth there was little new building: one of the reasons was certainly lack of money, Sir Roger Verney noting that 'Of all my acquaintance there is scarce an honest man that is not in a borrowing condition'.

The career of John Webb, Jones's best pupil, spans the period from the heyday of royal patronage in the 1630s through the Commonwealth to the Restoration. His style was closely dependent on the older man's ideas and experience, but nonetheless Webb succeeded in evolving a personal manner, as is seen in his Saloon at Chevening, Kent, of 1655. This room bridges the gap between Jones's more academic Palladianism and the early English Baroque; heavier than Jones might have liked, it has wood-panelled blank arcading articulated with Corinthian pilasters and a pedimented door-case. Like Jones, Webb did not approve of the Commonwealth, but nonetheless he worked for its leading figures and established a healthy practice in the 1650s. His fine draughtsmanship carries on the Jones tradition of Italian and French source materials muted for English taste.

At the Restoration, building and decorating were taken up again with gusto, and the name to the fore in the formation of the English Baroque is that of Christopher Wren (1632–1723). Wren's Paris visit of 1665 opened his eyes to the high quality of French craftsmanship, and after seeing 'the incomparable Villas of *Vaux* and *Maisons*' and many others he returned to London with 'a great deal of Taille douce [copper-plate engraving] that I might give our Country-men Examples of Ornaments and Grotesks, in which the *Italians* themselves confess the French to excel'. He noted an army of no fewer than a thousand men engaged at the Louvre in 'Carving, Inlaying of Marbles, Plaistering, Painting, Gilding etc.' which must have inspired him to train his craftsmen in such skills for the decoration of the royal palaces, St Paul's and the City of London churches.

England was ready for a new style expressive of the restored grandeur of the Stuarts, but the most notable achievements of the English Baroque were created for private patrons. While English Baroque architecture has a strongly distinctive flavour in the hands of Vanbrugh, Hawksmoor, Talman and Archer, most interiors of the period are by comparison disappointing. In general, the grander the attempt, the less satisfactory the result, especially where large decorative paintings are concerned. The Baroque always remained outside the mainstream of English taste, unlike Jones's subtly anglicized Palladianism, and there is often a strong whiff of provincialism about even the most elaborate decorative schemes.

From the 'joiner's baroque' of an interior like Ashburham House, Westminster, of around 1660, with its delightful staircase surmounted by a large oval opening with gallery above, the desire for grand effects increased noticeably in the 1670s and 1680s. Plasterwork, the glory of the Elizabethan and Jacobean interior, reached new heights of elaboration; this was due to the introduction of harder, quick-drying *stucco duro* mounted on wire, wood or even leather, and replacing the Tudor mixture of lime and plaster of Paris which was cast in a mould and applied with nails before hardening. Some of the most skilled plasterers in English interior decoration were active at this time, the most notable being Goudge, Grove, Martin, Bradbury and Pettifer. In dynasties of plasterers such as the Abbotts of Barnstaple in Devon – whose notebook designs survive – technique was handed down from father to son. Plasterers of the quality of Edward Goudge could design their own ceilings, as in the case of his drawing for Hamstead Marshall, Berkshire.

The beamed and moulded ceilings of the Jones type, described by Pratt as 'divided artificially into noble squares, ovals or circles ... either filled with painting, or absolutely without' continued in the Restoration, but became vehicles for virtuoso plasterwork. Some of the finest English plasterwork dates from this period, among the outstanding examples being the huge Long Gallery of 1676 by Bradbury at Sudbury Hall, Derbyshire, and the Belisarius Room at Raynham Hall in Norfolk.

After plasterwork, the most characteristic medium used in English interior decoration at this time was wood carving, which reached unequalled heights of perfection in the work of Grinling Gibbons. The main areas where such carving was used were staircase balustrades, chimney-pieces, overdoors and other decoration applied to panelling. Partly under the influence of developments in the Low Countries, the solid, closed carving seen for example in the Double Cube at Wilton was replaced by lighter, open and more naturalistic sculpture; the Dutch Artus Quellin I's etched designs were highly important in this context.

Grinling Gibbons's name is inevitably connected with every piece of outstanding wood carving of the English Baroque, although few surviving pieces can be certainly attributed to him. Gibbons was born in Rotterdam of English parents, came to England as a youth and was discovered by John Evelyn in 1670. His earliest country house commission may have been the staircase at Cassiobury House, Watford (now in the Metropolitan Museum), of 1674, which shows the type of open-work, naturalistic carving which replaced strapwork for balustrade decoration in the 1630s; a particularly elaborate example is at Ham House, where military trophies fill the panels. Horace Walpole admired 'the loose and airy lightness of flowers ... the various productions of the elements with free disorder natural to each species' achieved by Gibbons's carving. Apart from his work at Windsor Castle, other securely documented carvings exist at Sudbury (Plate 89), Burghley, Badminton and Ramsbury; the work of his pupils and followers remains to be fully investigated – Edward Pierce, James Selden, Samuel Watson, Thomas Young and Jonathan Maine.

Oak wall panelling remained a firm favourite at all levels of affluent society, with bolection mouldings used

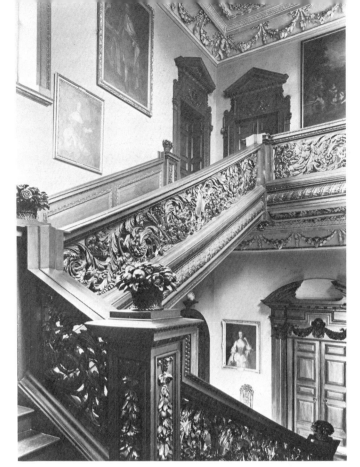

89 Staircase by Grinling Gibbons, Sudbury Hall, *Derbyshire. Seventeenth century*

for portraits inset into the panel. Where the chimney-piece had often been spectacular under Jones, the Restoration favoured plain marble moulding surrounding the fireplace opening, abandoning the overmantel decorations and continuing the panelling across the top. Leather hangings were popular, especially for dining rooms, since they did not retain odours as tapestry tended to do; they could either be of oriental pattern as at Honington, Warwickshire, or of geometric design like those of the 1670s in the Marble Dining Room at Ham House. The oriental fashion had spread from France and Holland, and oriental wallpaper probably of the 1690s survives at Longnor in Shropshire; lacquer panels decorate the Chinese Closet at Drayton, Northamptonshire.

During the last two decades of the century, plasterwork began increasingly to be replaced by wall and ceiling paintings; in 1710, a traveller noted that 'in England tapestry is no longer in fashion ... all is painted at great cost'. Although decorative painting had been popular before the Restoration, it was not employed on any great scale, except in a few houses such as Wilton. Apart from this, Castle Ashby's delightful Painted Bower, possibly by Matthew Goodrich and dating from after 1621, and some tempera ceilings at Ham House are the only work of any quality to have survived from the first half of the century. The new interiors at Windsor created the vogue for a Baroque fusion of the arts, with Hugh

May's architecture, Antonio Verrio's paintings and Gibbons's carvings, and the greatest of such schemes to survive are at Chatsworth and Burghley House. Although no major decorative painter of international stature such as Pietro da Cortona or Charles Le Brun was lured to England, the leading names were nonetheless French or Italian. Le Brun's pupil Louis Laguerre enjoyed great favour (see Plate 71) but his work is ponderous and often uninspired, while lesser-known artists like Chéron could realize such successful schemes as the Great Hall ceiling at Boughton House, Northamptonshire.

Among the other painters active in England were Lanscroon, Rousseau, Jean Baptist Monnoyer and Marco Ricci. Ricci and Giovanni Antonio Pellegrini were brought from Venice by the Duke of Manchester. It was said that Wren wanted Pellegrini to decorate the dome of St Paul's (it was finally given to the lumpish Thornhill, who was responsible for many second-rate decorative schemes) and Pellegrini was certainly the most talented foreigner in England. His work at Kimbolton Castle, Huntingdonshire, of 1711–12 is unrivalled in England for its brilliant colour and fresco-like delicacy; like all such schemes these decorations are painted on canvas mounted on the wall, fresco not being suited to the English climate. Pellegrini also decorated Narford Hall for Sir Andrew Fountaine

and Castle Howard in Yorkshire for Lord Carlisle, where his wonderful mural paintings in the High Saloon were on a qualitative level with any in Europe until their destruction by fire in 1940. Less wealthy clients had to make do with a painted overmantel or overdoor, 'chiefly', in Pratt's words, 'some pleasant landscape of ruins and trees' thereby adding 'much grace to the place where they are'.

A dominant note in many English interiors of the seventeenth century today is their sobriety, especially when they are oak-panelled, but it must be recalled that the effect of rich furniture would have considerably modified this. Silver-encased and decorated furniture incorporating many different woods and even tortoiseshell became popular, and mirrors added lustre to many interiors; in 1664 Samuel Pepys recorded his pleasure at having purchased 'a very fair glasse for five guineas'. The East India Company's imports included porcelain and brilliant fabrics, which played an important role in creating variety. With the Palladian revival after 1715 under Colen Campbell and Lord Burlington (see Chapter 5) much of the imaginative exoticism which must have coloured English Baroque interiors vanished, to be replaced with the classicism so characteristic of the eighteenth century in England.

90 The Alter Seidenhof, *1620. Zurich, Swiss National Museum*

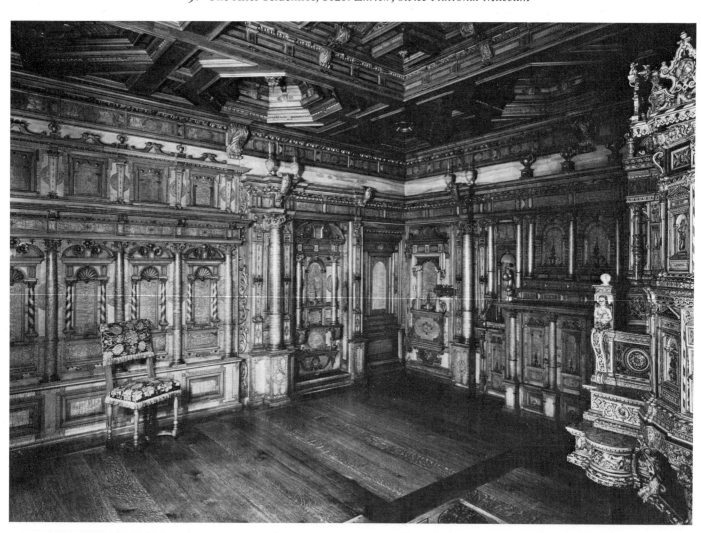

In the eastern American colonies, at the earliest period of expansion in the seventeenth century, the buildings at first emulated the Dutch Baroque, with some German and Scandinavian derivations. By far the strongest influence, however, was the English vernacular architecture of East Anglia, which was essentially late-medieval in character. The interiors of such houses were very plain; they were plastered and white-washed, with vertical boards on the doors and exposed beams (panelling came into use only in about 1700). They usually consisted of a hall and a 'parlor' or a hall with parlor and passage. The Adam Thoroughgood House near Norfolk, Virginia (1636) had its staircase in the main hall. Other examples of the type can be found throughout New England and Virginia.

In the Spanish colonies of the south-west – Texas, Arizona, New Mexico and California – the style was a blend of the Spanish Baroque with native Indian traditions. Virtually no domestic examples are extant from this period.

A final note must be added about the seventeenth century in Germany and Austria. In the early part of the century, Italian High Renaissance ideas were adapted in Germany (Plate 90), as at the court of the Elector Maximilian I in Munich, who made the Residenz the finest palace of its period in Germany. Rooms like the Hall of the Council of around 1612–16 with its stuccoed and painted frieze, marble door-cases and compartmented ceiling with allegorical paintings by Peter Candid show strong Italian influence; by 1667, the date of the Electress Adelheid's 'Heart Cabinet' in the Residenz, French and Venetian ideas are reflected in the elaborately carved, gilded and painted ceiling and frieze. Many of the palace interiors were decorated by Antonio Francesco Pistorini on the designs of Agostino Barelli. Italian craftsmen flocked to courts north of the Alps, and they, and the influence of Italian art *in situ* as seen by architects like Johann Bernhard Fischer von Erlach (1656–1723), determined the course of interior decoration until the Rococo.

Von Erlach left his native Graz in 1674 for a stay of about twelve years in Rome and Naples. Apart from the architecture of Bernini and Borromini, he was most impressed by the huge ceiling paintings of Andrea Pozzo, Giordano and G. B. Gaulli, and imported this fashion into his interiors in Austria and Moravia, as in the impressive great oval hall of the castle at Vranov (Frain) of 1690–4.

Here, the curving walls, giant order of pilasters and vast ceiling frescoes by J. M. Rottmayr dissolving space between huge oval windows all look forward to the essential features of the German Rococo. In 1685 he settled in Vienna and drew on Italian and French models for both his extensive church designs and his palace building, culminating in the Imperial Library, begun in 1722. Its scale, like that of many German and Austrian interiors of its kind, outstrips all its prototypes, combining carved and gilded woodwork, plasterwork and fresco, and leads directly to the next phase of Viennese interior grandeur with Johan Lucas von Hildebrandt (1668–1745). Hildebrandt's Daun-Kinsky Palace of 1713–16 and his Upper Belvedere of the early 1720s stand at the beginning of Austrian Rococo decoration.

In Prussia, the 1685 Edict of Potsdam admitted twenty thousand French Huguenot émigrés, among them many craftsmen who worked under Frederick III on the decoration of the royal palaces of Oranienburg and Charlottenburg. One great architect dominates the Baroque in Berlin – Andreas Schlüter (c. 1664–1714), who arrived from Warsaw in 1694. Schlüter favoured extensive sculpture in his interiors and was more involved with the minutiae of interior decoration than many of his contemporaries. His work at the Berlin Schloss (1698–1707) included Michelangelesque figures, notably in the Baronial and Elizabeth Halls, and gigantic architectural features accompanied by extensive figure sculpture on the massive staircase. In 1714 he moved to St Petersburg. In Russia, as in Scandinavia, late Baroque ideas on architecture and decoration were introduced and disseminated by foreign craftsmen and decorators. In Russia these men had been imported by Peter the Great as part of his endeavours to modernize the country, and they were also patronized by his daughter and successor Elisabeth. The primary architects of this phase were Jean-Baptiste Alexandre Le Blond (1679–1719), whose chief inspiration was Versailles; Domenico Tressini (1670–1734), who worked in the Dutch Baroque style and built the Tsar's Summer Palace near St Petersburg; and above all Bartolomeo Rastrelli (1700–71), who remodelled the four royal palaces in St Petersburg for the Empress. He was particularly skilled at inventing opulent decorative schemes such as the room at Tsarskoe Selo which was entirely floored in amber. Rastrelli's career spans both the Baroque and the style which was soon to sweep through Europe, the Rococo.

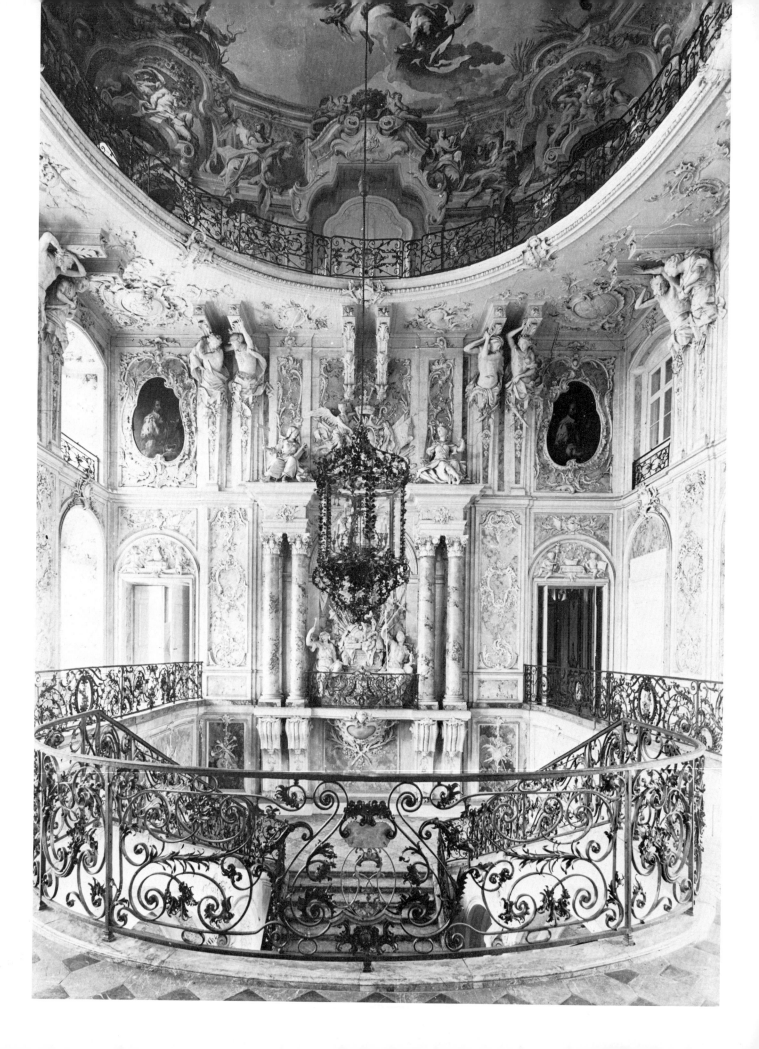

5

Europe and the Rococo
1700-1750

Tout est confort, politesse et convenance

Mme de Chatelet, *Discours sur le bonheur*

No style is more clearly linked to its historical period than the Rococo, and it was in the art of decorating interiors that the Rococo found its most complete expression. Ironically, since the Rococo was a style almost devoid of Classical derivation, its interiors were the first since antiquity to achieve a total synthesis between fixed and movable decoration and furniture. Superb as French Rococo furniture by the great master craftsmen Cressent, Gaudreaux, Dubois and Delanois is in isolation, it assumes its full decorative significance only in the interiors for which it was so often specifically designed. The same applies to much Rococo painting, sculpture, porcelain and textiles.

The Rococo is the last wholly original expression of the aristocratic ideal in European art. Its sources are many and complex, and the Italians and the French both claim to have invented it. Although it is arguable that Rococo painting was born in Italy with the work of painters like Sebastiano Ricci, the style's first appearance in interior decoration was certainly in France. We have seen how fashionable Europe turned increasingly from the influence of Baroque Rome to look for guidance in matters of taste

91 Staircase at Augustusburg Castle, *Brühl, near Cologne, 1743–8 Although the layout of this remarkable staircase was designed by Balthasar Neumann, its appearance is largely due to the court architect of the electors of Cologne, Michael Leveilly, and the designer Johann Adolf Biarelle. It is one of the most perfect examples of collaboration between craftsmen; the stucco supporting figures and other decorations are by Giuseppe Artario, Carlo Pietro Morsegno and Joseph Anton Brilli, and the wrought ironwork is by Johann Georg Sandtener. Carlo Carlone painted the vault fresco. Marble of intense blue, yellow and various shades of red decorates the ground-floor walls, while green and yellow dominate the upper parts. Augustusburg was built by Clemens August, who became Archbishop and Elector of Cologne in 1723*

to the Sun King's splendid new château at Versailles. Pocket-scale Versailles appeared throughout Europe, but what fascinated other princes more than the actual architecture of the château were the layout, appearance and symbolism of its interiors. The glittering Hall of Mirrors, unprecedentedly large and sumptuous (Plate 85), was the room they would most have liked to transplant to their palaces in Italy, Germany, Austria, Holland or England, although it was not until the nineteenth century that it was imitated on any scale. But the reality which lay behind Versailles's pomp was that Louis XIV had to escape periodically from the rigidity of the court life which he had created and carefully maintained. His refuge was at the Trianons and the Château of Marly.

In 1687, Jules Hardouin-Mansart (1646–1708), great-nephew of François Mansart (see pages 97–8 and Plate 83), replaced Le Vau's Trianon de Porcelaine with what is now the Grand Trianon. This single-storey building, whose two parts are linked by an open colonnade, had none of the heavy Baroque decoration of nearby Versailles. Instead, its simple rectangular wooden panelling was painted white, a perfect foil for the elaborate inlaid furniture of André-Charles Boulle and in keeping with the novel proximity of the rooms to gardens outside; at Versailles, all of the major interiors were on the first floor, the *piano nobile*, offering little real communication with the park beyond.

Mansart began his career as a Baroque architect of châteaux (such as Clagny) and hôtels (town houses), but was as flexible as he was inventive. Saint-Simon loathed Mansart, and claimed that much of his work was done by young architects who received no credit. Among these, Pierre Cailleteaux, called Lassurance (1655–1724), and Pierre Le Pautre (1660–1744) were probably responsible for much of the later decoration 'by' Mansart which directly prefigures the Rococo. Under Mansart's guidance, rooms at Versailles, Marly and Trianon were created or

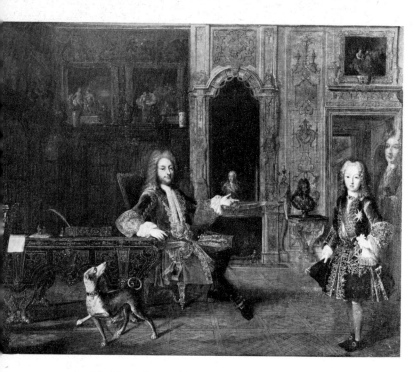

92 The Dauphin in his cabinet at Meudon. *Versailles, Musée du Château*

redecorated during the 1690s, and prepared the way for the new style. Gone are the columns and pilasters of the Baroque, gone too the heavy panelling and ponderous overmantels. In their place we find light panels, delicate cornices and, one of the most important innovations of the dawning Rococo age, large mirrors over the chimney-pieces. Pierre Le Pautre's book of engravings *Cheminées à la royalle* of around 1698 illustrates clearly projecting chimney-pieces surmounted by two types of mirrors. Already some of the features adopted later by the Rococo are present, such as brackets for vases forming part of the frame, sea-shells and arabesques.

It is to arabesques that we must turn to understand one of the principal sources of that free asymmetrical carved or painted decoration which is the essence of Rococo wall-panelling, plasterwork and even furniture. As its name suggests, the arabesque is of Arab origin, but many of its forms are derived from the grotesque decorations of Raphael and Giovanni da Udine (see pages 70–1 and Plates 43 and 53), which were eagerly adopted in France during the reign of Louis XIII and used in such interiors as the Cabinet de Colbert de Villacerf (Carnavalet Museum, Paris) and the decoration of the Arsenal of about 1640. Jean Berain (1640–1711) transformed the grotesque by thinning its elements, making it lighter and airier, and by connecting it with interlace derived from the arabesque, which had long been employed in France as an ornament in such arts as book-binding, inlay-work, embroidery and garden parterres. This interlace developed into an ornament in its own right – ribbonwork, or bandwork – which in Germany became the *leitmotiv* of Régence decoration.

Berain's engravings, along with those of Claude Audran (1657–1734), were instrumental in diffusing the new style of grotesque ornament. From these grotesques came much of that 'variety' regarded as an essential of fine interiors of the period: naturalistic plants and flowers, outspread bats' wings, figured medallions (often placed in the centre of wall or door panels), shells, flower and tendril festoons, and even waves. The two designers were also responsible for introducing Chinese motifs (*chinoiseries*) and humorous depictions of monkeys (*singeries*) into the decorations of rooms – the most famous examples of which were the Petite Singerie (1735) and the Grande Singerie at Chantilly by Audran's one-time collaborator Christophe Huet. The *chinoiserie* fashion spread rapidly in the early eighteenth century under Rococo influence. Dragons, exotic birds and picturesquely attired Chinese figures appear on walls, textiles, furniture and porcelain. Sometimes whole rooms were decorated in the Chinese style, as at Capodimonte, Aranjuez (Plate 95) or Claydon in Buckinghamshire (Plate 110). The designs of Huet and Jean Pillement were imitated all over Europe, and such was the influence of engravings after the latter's work that Rococo *chinoiserie* decoration was often termed *le style Pillement*.

Berain also produced many engravings for chimney-pieces. His designs, like those of Marot (see page 102), show the chimney-piece on a reduced scale, which contributes to the feeling of comfort we associate with Rococo rooms. In place of the fixed, often ponderous and elaborate carved or painted overmantel of the Baroque, the Rococo substitutes the *garniture de cheminée*, consisting of a large central clock flanked by symmetrically aligned porcelain vases, which has remained a constant feature of interior decoration up to the present day.

The portrait of the Dauphin in his Cabinet at Meudon (Plate 92) shows an interior which is transitional between the French late Baroque and the early Rococo. As in the Dining Room at Vaux-le-Vicomte of around forty years earlier, the arabesques are rigidly contained within their straight-edged frames, while in another interior of the same year, the Appartement de Nuit of the Duc de Bourgogne at Versailles, greater steps forward were taken. The room has two of the salient features of Rococo interior decoration – depressed arches (like those in Plate 93) and a frieze with consoles. Even the aged Louis XIV was prepared to allow the most important room at Versailles – his Bedchamber, setting of his symbolic *lever* and *coucher* – to be redecorated in what the early eighteenth century was already calling the *goût moderne* – the modern taste. Architecturally, the Bedchamber is still in the *grand goût* with Corinthian pilasters throughout but, significantly, handled with a new delicacy and painted in the latest colour scheme – white and gold. Two large overmantel mirrors face each other across the room, creating that illusion of endless space so beloved of the Rococo.

Although many of the important advances in the Rococo style occurred in ecclesiastical interiors like Notre

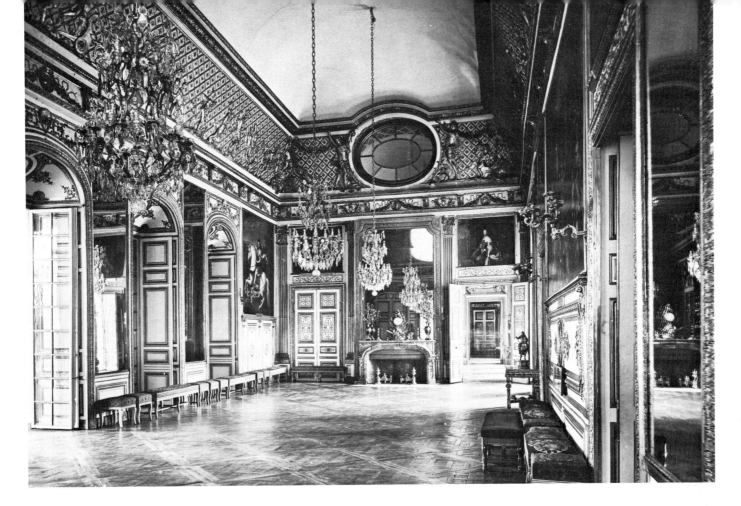

93 Antichambre de l'Oeil de Boeuf, *Versailles, 1701*
Completed fourteen years before the death of Louis XIV,
this room is perhaps the first in France to indicate the
direction which interior decoration was to take for the next
half-century. Depressed arches, large mirrors, and detail such
as the trellis decoration on the ceiling cove picked out in
gold, are all indicative of many Rococo trends. The room's
name comes from the two oval openings which break
through the ceiling cornice at either end

Dame and St-Sulpice, it was in domestic design in France
that it gained ground most rapidly. In 1699 Louis XIV
had instructed Mansart on the decoration of the small
Château de la Ménagerie for the thirteen-year-old Duchesse de Bourgogne. Mythological subjects, which were too
serious, should be replaced by 'a youthful note' which
'ought to appear in whatever is done' and 'there must be
an air of childhood everywhere'. The drawings for these
lost decorations are the work of Claude Audran. His
designs show a ceiling covered with arabesque patterns of
unprecedented delicacy. Interspersed among flower garlands, festoons and tendrils of acanthus leaves are young
girls, animals, birds, ribbons and arrows, all painted with
a disarming freshness, far removed from the heavily
meaningful allegories of the Baroque. The King was delighted with the results, and praised them as 'charming'
and 'magnificent', an indication that his taste had changed

since the creation of the Grands Appartements at Versailles. From its first appearance, the Rococo appears to
have captivated the fashionable mind, and was soon to
sweep through Europe.

Pierre Le Pautre created one of the first rooms which
clearly shows how the style was evolving – the Antichambre
de l'Oeil de Boeuf at Versailles (Plate 93). Its door and
window embrasures have depressed arches, above which
hang delicate flower garlands and shells. Above these a
frieze of alternating consoles and flower garlands is surmounted by the room's most distinctive feature. This is a
coved ceiling incorporating the *oeil-de-boeuf* (bull's eye
window) and a trellis against which *putti* cavort in gilded
relief. Large mirrors play an important part in the scheme,
their glittering expanse acting as a foil to the elegance of
white and gold carving. After the foundation of the
Manufacture Royale des Glaces de Miroirs in the 1660s
(see page 99) it had become easier to supply the royal
residences with mirrors of this size, and almost every
interior of any importance during the Rococo had to have
at least one.

The years leading up to Louis XIV's death in 1715 were
clouded for him by the deaths in rapid succession of several important members of his family – including that of
the young Duchesse de Bourgogne. Versailles became
oppressive, and younger members of the court drifted
away to the more intimate circles of the Duchesse de

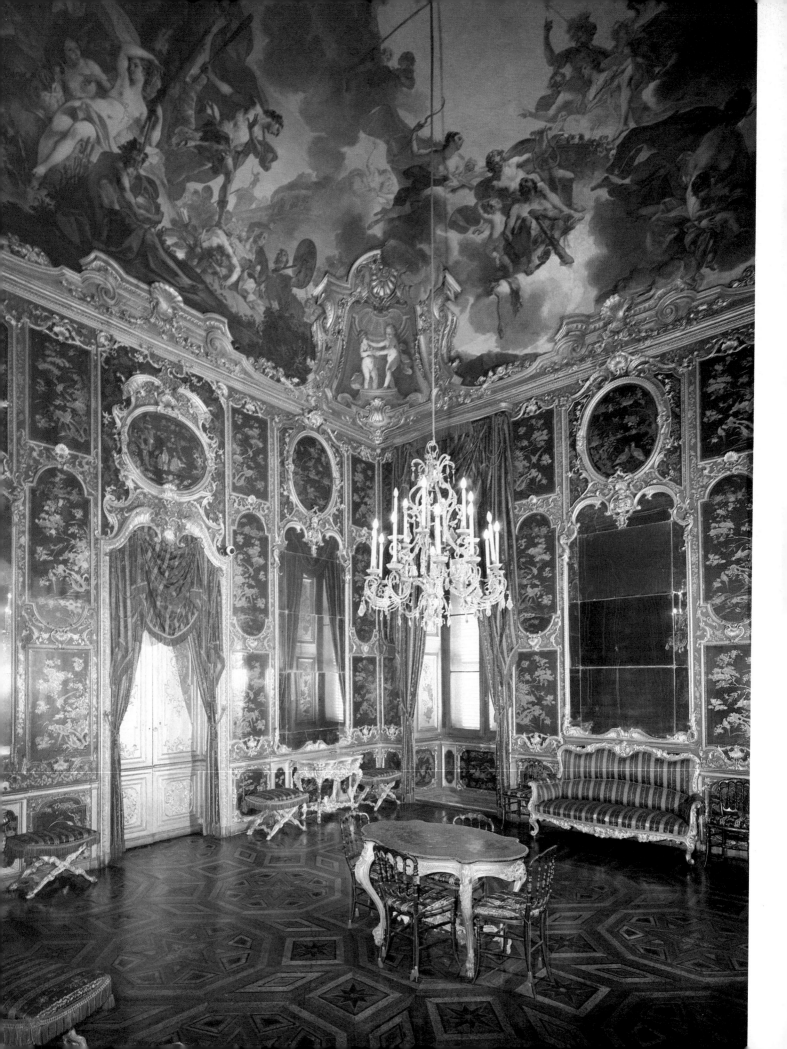

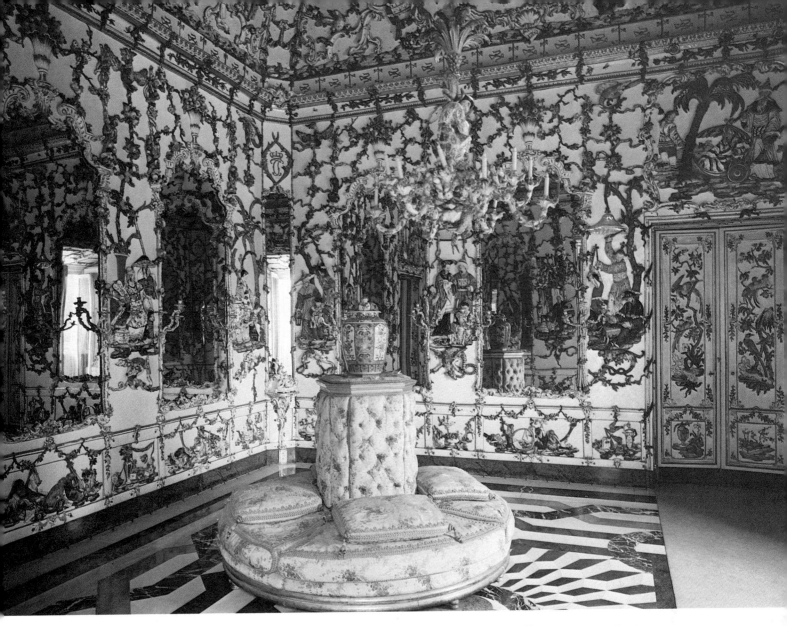

94 *(left)* Chinese Room, Palazzo Reale, *Turin*   The ceiling *fresco, c. 1735, is by Claudio Francesco Beaumont*

95 *(above)* Sala di Porcellana, Aranjuez, *Spain*

Maine and the Duc d'Orléans in Paris. It was in this atmosphere that the ideals of the *Grand Siècle* finally gave way to the new longing for greater informality, comfort and elegance. Grandeur was an aspiration of the past, and the desire to impress was replaced by the desire to please. Mme de Chatelet's *Discours sur le bonheur* (Discourse on Happiness), written in the 1740s although not published until 1779, encapsulates much of the Rococo's *raison d'être*: '... we have nothing to do in this world other than to procure for ourselves agreeable sensations and feelings.' Thus it was that most of the popular decorative motifs of the period are connected with pleasurable diversions such as the hunt, love-making, music and the countryside; fantastic themes such as *chinoiseries* and *turqueries* were also part of the search for diversion in novelty. This was in perfect keeping with the subject matter of much Rococo painting, from Watteau's pastoral *fêtes galantes* to the game-pieces of Desportes and Oudry and the still lifes of Chardin.

In 1710, the architect Le Blond outlined the rooms to be found in the principal part of a typical Parisian town house of quality – its *appartement de parade*, a term adopted for a suite of rooms designed entirely for entertaining and reception. There should be a vestibule, an anteroom, a salon, a bedroom (or *chambre de parade*) and a study; cabinets and dressing rooms might be added as discretion allowed. The old-fashioned two-storey *salle à l'italienne* of the seventeenth century was now often replaced by a one-storey salon, and an *appartement de commodité*, consisting of smaller, more easily heated rooms, designed for comfort not display, became the most important part of the main or even upper floors. Intimacy thus became one of the characteristics of the French Rococo interior, perfectly in accord with the small-scale nature of much of

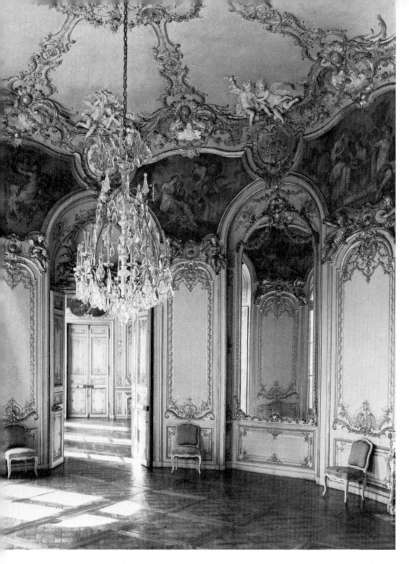

its decorative repertoire. Even a moderately grand room such as the Salon de la Princesse at the Hôtel de Soubise (Plate 96) is much smaller than its Baroque counterpart.

The first phase of the Rococo in France developed during the Régence period, when Louis XIV's nephew, the Duc d'Orléans, acted as regent for the young Louis XV from 1715 to 1723. The Regent made Paris his seat of government, and resided in the Palais Royal. Despite the Court's return to Versailles in 1722, Paris remained the artistic centre of Europe for the rest of the century – a position it was to hold intermittently until the present century. Unlike Louis XV, the Regent was a fine connoisseur with an interest in architecture and decoration, and the Palais Royal was the setting for some of the major artistic advances of the period: Antoine Watteau, the important decorator Gilles-Marie Oppenordt and the Toulon-based wood-carver Jean Bernard Toro (1672–1731) all found early favour there. Together with François-Antoine Vassé (1681–1736), Toro and Oppenordt exercised a profound influence on the growth of the Régence and early Rococo styles.

Oppenordt (1672–1742) lived in Rome from 1692 to 1669, where Borromini had been the main influence on his ideas. Coming from a background of craftsmen and decorators Oppenordt was able to translate his ideas readily into brilliant interior decoration, helped by his immense facility for drawing. His use of huge cartouches, trophies and flying *putti*, combined with fluted pilasters and vast overmantel mirrors, shows a love of sculpted ornament deriving from his Italian training. In 1716 Toro produced a series of engravings, including cartouche designs, which, with the grotesque designs of Audran and Gillot, certainly influenced Oppenordt. Oppenordt is also noted for his designs for elaborate wrought-ironwork, much used in the Rococo for staircases and balconies, external and internal. Totally anti-academic, the Rococo was a style of supreme fantasy and invention.

This is perhaps a suitable point to examine the constituent parts of a French Régence, or early Rococo, interior, such as those reproduced in Plates 93 and 97. The decoration centred around the chimney-piece, with its opening in the S-curve shape favoured for all aspects of Rococo design, and its tall overmantel mirror, which was echoed by one or more pier-glasses (*trumeaux*) above console-tables. Chimney-pieces were made either of white or coloured marbles, often with rich mounts in ormolu (gilded bronze) comparable with those on contemporary furniture. Vassé's designs for the Hôtel de Toulouse (see Plate 97) incorporate ornate ormolu candelabra as part of the chimney-pieces, a practice which was not uncommon. Sometimes entire walls were lined with mirrors (as in Marie-Antoinette's vanished bathroom), and they were also used on ceilings, to fill fireplaces in summer and, most glamorous of all, on sliding window shutters where, cunningly concealed in the panelling by day, they completely disguised the windows at night.

96 Salon de la Princesse, Hôtel de Soubise, *Paris, 1736–9, by Germain Boffrand Boffrand (1667–1754) added an oval ground-floor salon to the Hôtel de Soubise for Prince Hercule-Mériadec de Soubise on the occasion of his marriage to Marie-Sophie de Courcillon. The Princess's salon is above her husband's, and in keeping with the character of the room has spandrel paintings showing the* Story of Psyche and Eros *by Charles-Joseph Natoire. Door, mirror and window arches are linked to each other and to the ceiling by a system of cartouches and by the highly original wheel-like openwork plaster motif above. The colour scheme is one of the most sophisticated of the period, with white walls, a pale blue ceiling and detail picked out in gilding. Boffrand's fine rhythmic sense is seen in the juxtaposition of large arch-topped spaces, either windows, mirrors or doors, with smaller round-headed panels. The Salon du Prince beneath has the same articulation, but in place of the paintings has stucco relief spandrels by L. S. Adam and J. B. Lemoyne: white and flax-blue are used throughout, with gilding confined to the elaborate recessed mirror frames. Elsewhere in the Hôtel, Boffrand decorated the Cabinet Vert with carvings of Aesop's fables (now in the Hôtel de Rohan).*

Boffrand also designed the salons of the Hôtel du Petit Luxembourg for the German-born Duchesse d'Orléans around 1710. His influence on German Rococo architecture was to be considerable

The marble of the chimney-piece might be echoed in the slab on the console-tables. The variety of available types was considerable, ranging from the most sought-after *marbre d'Antin* with red, yellow, violet and grey streaks, through Italian red *griotte* and various violet stones to the black and white *grand antique*. Marble was also used for flooring, often in black and white, arranged in squares or lozenge patterns, but earthen and wooden floors were commoner, the latter varying enormously in quality from superbly inlaid parquets to simple wooden blocks.

All openings such as doorways and windows were now round or oval-headed, or with depressed arches, and mirrors followed suit. Windows were increasingly brought down to floor level, often opening onto a terrace or balcony – hence the adoption of the term 'french window' in England, where sashes were the norm. The principal features of the room, with the exception of doors, now generally reached to the cornice, and the walls had the appearance of rigidly defined areas with a strong vertical emphasis. Generally speaking, the French preserved the right-angled room and flat ceiling throughout the Rococo, and the contrast of elaborate walls with ceilings usually left plain, apart from a large central plaster rosette, was perfectly calculated to show off both surfaces to advantage.

Occasionally, the wall-panelling was left in natural wood, especially in the country, but more usually it was painted. The preferred colour scheme was ivory-white and gold. In 1730, the brothers Guillaume and Etienne-Simon Martin invented a varnish imitating Chinese lacquer, which was used on furniture and walls. Called *vernis Martin*, after its inventors, it is most usually associated with a rich green colour. The varnish itself was known as *cipolin* and gave a porcelain-like glaze to the treated surface. Its use was generally confined to fairly small rooms, such as Louis XV's Petits Cabinets at Versailles, where the King could escape from court formality, and there is a well-preserved room in the apartments of the Dauphin and Dauphine at Versailles which has carved flowers on the *boiseries* lacquered in bright, naturalistic colours. *Vernis Martin* was superior to any imitation lacquers previously produced, in France, although the fashion had existed since the later seventeenth century.

French Rococo rooms followed a rigid symmetry of layout (echoed in the *chaises meublantes* and *chaises courantes* – seating which was placed rigidly around the perimeter of the room, and seating which could be moved at will in the centre). Despite the increasing asymmetry of the wall-carvings, these were at first kept strictly within thin, straight mouldings which separated each panel from the next; the result was a strong vertical emphasis which required balancing features on each side of the room. If no real door existed where balance was needed, a false one would be made. The deep coving of the Antichambre de l'Oeil de Boeuf (Plate 93) gave way to the merest curve between wall and ceiling (Plate 100) where creeping plaster decoration now occasionally spread over the framework.

Paintings were allotted a carefully pre-ordained place, generally confined to overdoors, and it was to fulfil this role that many people in the period conceived the purpose of pictures. Symmetrical during the Régence, they increasingly assumed more wilful outlines, frequently composed of a series of S-curves. Among better known painters

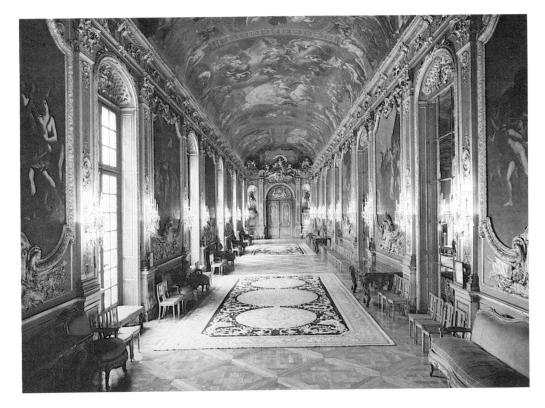

97 Galerie Dorée of the Hôtel de Toulouse, *c. 1720. Paris   The architect Robert de Cotte rebuilt the Hôtel de Toulouse in 1713–19, remodelling the earlier galerie to its present appearance. François Perrier's grisaille ceiling painting of around 1640 was coloured, and the original wall canvases by Pietro da Cortona, Guido Reni and others were set into François-Antoine Vassé's sumptuous carved panelling. A major interior of the Régence style, it has all the individual elements of Rococo decoration but these are still rigidly contained within their architectural framework. Copies have replaced the original wall paintings, which are now in the Louvre*

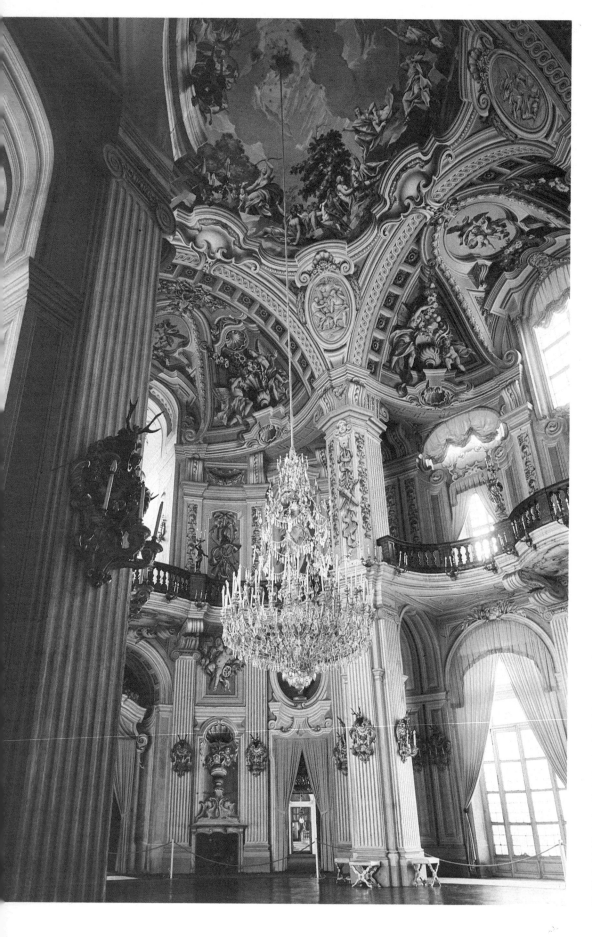

98 Central saloon of the Palazzina di Caccia at Stupinigi, *1729–33, by Filippo Juvarra Filippo Juvarra (1678–1736) was the greatest architect and decorator of the late Baroque and early Rococo in Italy. This remarkable salone in the royal hunting lodge of Stupinigi is composed of a great central domed space flanked by four enormous apses encircled by a continuous gallery at first-floor level. A gifted stage designer, Juvarra had the same love of fantastic architectural perspectives and elaborate decoration as his influential contemporaries, the Bibiena family, whose magnificent engravings spread Italian illusionist ideas throughout Europe – particularly in Germany and Austria. The saloon's layout resembles theatrical and festive decorations of the period, with its magnificent vault fresco showing the* Depature of Diana for the Hunt *by Giuseppe and Domenico Valeriani. Italian Rococo interiors retained much of the Baroque's spatial dynamics, and even a delicately exotic interior such as Juvarra's 'Chinese Room' in Turin's Royal Palace (Plate 94) is dominated by its ceiling fresco; no contemporary French decorator would do this, preferring plain white ceilings with moulded plaster decoration around the edge and at the centre. In southern Italy and Sicily, the Rococo reached even greater heights of fantasy; the breathtaking rooms of the Palazzo Genci in Palermo have ceilings with an outer and an inner plaster shell so that the frescoes are seen through a stucco framework, and floors are tiled with dramatic patterns and colours*

99 Room from the Tattenbach Palace, *c. 1775*, by François Cuvilliés the Younger. Munich, Bayerisches National-museum This fine example of a 'pergola' room has painted silk panels by Joseph Zachenberger set into carved frames by Possenbacher

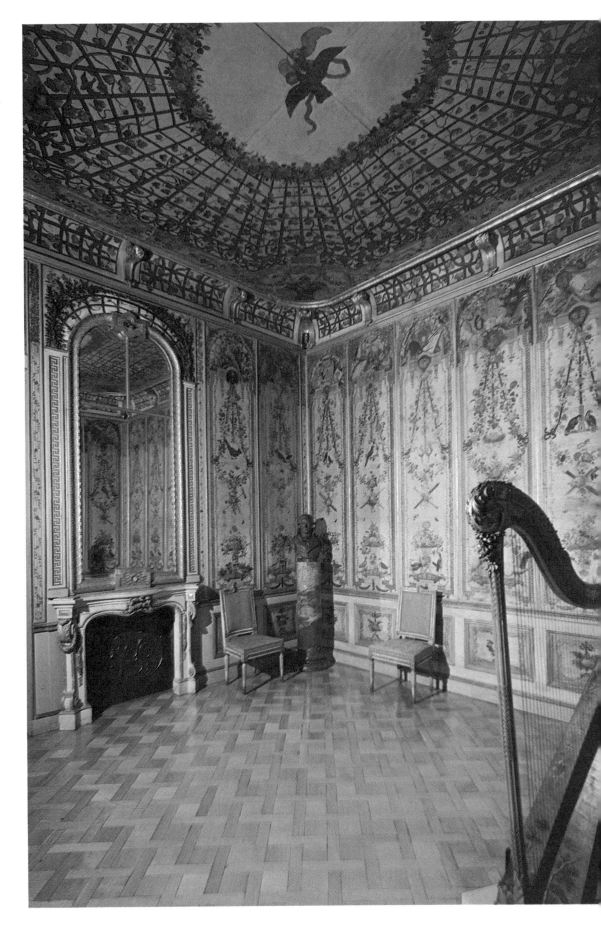

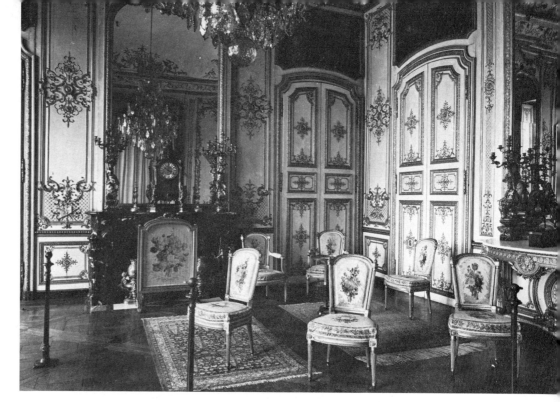

100 Salon de Musique, Petit Château, Chantilly, 1722, by Jean Aubert Aubert's exquisite decorations at Chantilly are the best-preserved ensemble outside Paris, and give an excellent idea of the variety possible in the use of net-like gold patterning, sumptuous rosettes in the wall panels, and fantastic grotesques. Particularly interesting is the use of concave corners on the already depressed arches of the doors. To ensure the symmetry of room layout, an essential requirement at the time, many Rococo designers provided false doors where there were none

who produced such decorative work were François Boucher, Carle van Loo, Charles-Joseph Natoire (see Plate 96), Pierre-Charles Trémolières, and Jean-Honoré Fragonard. Themes like the *Four Seasons* and the *Loves of the Gods* were popular. Since strong wall colouring was almost unknown in the French Rococo, the sparkling colours and pearly flesh tones of these paintings were perfectly offset by their elegant white and gold backgrounds.

Jean Aubert (d. 1741), who designed the Salon de Musique at Chantilly (Plate 100), began as one of Mansart's draughtsmen, but became court architect of the Duc de Bourbon-Condé and was one of the finest decorators of the Rococo. After his work at Chantilly, his major masterpiece is the suite of reception rooms at the Hôtel de Lassay, built between 1722 and 1728 for the Marquis de Lassay. (The Marquis was one of the few who made a fortune out of one of the greatest disasters of the period – the speculating schemes of the Scotsman John Law.) Although since altered, Aubert's original décor reveals a freedom and richness which usher in the true Rococo style: riotous gilded forms begin to break out of their surrounding restrictions, spreading over cornices (with larger corner cartouches) and *boiseries*. The *genre pittoresque* had emerged, and the underlying antithesis between French architecture and interior decoration reached its fullest conclusion; it is the coincidence of this fully Rococo style with the reign of Louis XV that gave rise to the term *style Louis Quinze*.

The next phase of the Rococo is marked by its spread throughout Europe, although resistance to imported French modes and the entrenchment of the Palladian school of architecture both conspired to limit its adoption in Britain. During the Régence, foreign rulers began to consult French architects for advice not only on building, but also on decorating their palaces. In Spain, now a Bourbon kingdom, as early as 1712 the Princesse des Ursins wrote to Paris seeking advice for her Cabinet des Furies in the Royal Palace at Madrid. In 1716–17 designs were provided for the Electoral Palace and the Buen Retiro at Bonn by the studio of Robert de Cotte (1656–1735), the dominant architect of the Régence, and in 1720 two major schemes of decoration were carried out by French decorators – at La Grange-du-Milion, to designs by Oppenordt, and at Peterhof, where Peter the Great's Cabinet was decorated with delicate cartouches and trophies, designed and carved by Nicolas Pineau (1684–1754). Increasingly, from the 1720s onwards, native talent began to emerge outside France, remaining, however, strongly under French influence as we shall see.

By 1730, the two salient features of fully developed Rococo decoration had emerged – asymmetry and the *rocaille*. *Rocaille*, sometimes used as a synonym for the Rococo, actually refers to a specific type of decoration, derived from shell-work in grottoes. Watteau has left us a superb drawing of a seashell (Paris, Institut Néerlandais) whose curving S-form and wave-like spiky outline encapsulate so much of *rocaille* ornament. The difference between the irregular cleft shell-type studies by Rococo *ornemanistes* (who designed panelling, plasterwork and so on) and the symmetrical shells used in earlier interiors is fundamental to the origins of the full Rococo. Along with Pineau, the other designer who dominated the period from the later 1720s until his death was Juste Aurèle Meissonier (1695–1750). Although born in Turin, Meissonier was a native of Provence, and his training as a goldsmith left him with a more three-dimensional approach than Pineau's. In 1726, he became the King's ornament designer as Jean Berain had been before him, and this position ensured his widespread influence and the rapid spread of the *rocaille*.

In 1734, Meissonier published his designs in the immensely successful *Livre d'ornements*, which includes not only decoration, but also architecture, fountains and other inventions. Fantastic structures consisting entirely of curves and abstract *rocaille* forms are enlivened by gushing waterfalls and fountains, curling plants, animals and fish. All of these elements, including water, immediately entered the decorators' vocabulary, and became known as the *genre pittoresque*: the painter Charles Antoine Coypel first used this term in 1726, describing the style as 'a piquant and singular choice of the effects of nature'. Oppenordt and Toro had made very tentative attempts at asymmetry, but it was Meissonier who perfected this important aspect of the Rococo, which was then known as '*contraste*'.

Meissonier's importance, like that of Jacques de Lajoue (1686–1761), lies not in his executed work but in his engravings, while Pineau remains the greatest designer of ornament. Pineau executed many important interiors in Paris, but few have survived intact, or *in situ*: those from the Hôtel de Villars are now at Waddesdon Manor, Buckinghamshire. Others exist at the Hôtel de Roquelaure, and the Hôtel de Maisons. Most of Pineau's drawings are in the Musée des Arts Décoratifs in Paris, and with the Parisian print-dealer Mariette's engravings, they record his incredibly fertile inventions. Almost everything is fashioned into plants of all kinds: the mouldings on wall panels become reeds, around which tendrils wrap themselves, and palm trees and other natural forms sprout around mirrors. 'Pineau's wall-systems,' one critic has written '– like the decoration in the Fourth Pompeian Style – sometimes only keep themselves upright like pieces of ephemeral garden architecture.' Pineau's profession was termed *sculpteur*, and demanded not only the ability to realize designs conceived on paper, but to improvise while maintaining the highest technical skill.

Pineau's fully developed style is seen in the Hôtel de Maisons, which dates from around 1750 and sums up the finest aspects of French domestic Rococo decoration. Its principal characteristics, which typify the French approach, are its rectangular form and flat walls – two features often shunned by the more Baroque approach of Italian and German architects and designers. Only one major interior in Paris of the period made use of the Baroque principles of dynamic movement inherent in the architecture of Bernini and Borromini – the Salon de la Princesse in the Hôtel de Soubise (Plate 96). Also Baroque is the importance given to painting, and the heaviness of the carved and moulded ornament throughout. Its designer, Germain Boffrand (1667–1754), worked first under Mansart and like Robert de Cotte devoted much of his energy to palace design for foreign princes. In 1711 he became First Architect to the Duke of Lorraine, while also working for the exiled Elector Max Emanuel of Bavaria (see page 124), and advising the Archbishop of Mainz and the Prince-Bishop of Würzburg. Typically of the period in France this architecture tells us little about his attitude to interior decoration, although he favoured varied room shapes and mathematically complex spaces, as at his hunting pavilion of Bouchefort of 1705 for the Elector of Bavaria, and the Château de Malgrange outside Nancy of 1712–15. Boffrand's designs for decoration were published in his *Livre d'architecture* of 1745.

The Rococo was created exclusively for the aristocracy and *nouveaux riches* in Paris, and it was only in the 1730s that the court at Versailles began to use the style. There, a talented young architect and a carver of Flemish origin – Jacques-Ange Gabriel (1698–1782) and Jacques Verberckt (1704–71) – collaborated on their first joint decoration in the Queen's Bedchamber in 1735. (Although he began as a brilliant Rococo designer under the King's patronage, Gabriel subsequently became one of the earliest French Neo-classicists, and as such is discussed in Chapter 6.) As in so many interiors for the Crown, the work had to be fitted into an existing shape, but their combined genius can be seen in the ravishing suite of rooms called the Petits Appartements du Roi and the first-floor suite, including Louis XV's Bedchamber and the Cabinet de la Pendule. In this room, as in the Cabinet du Conseil, the decoration is perhaps heavier than contemporary work in Paris. The same is true of Gabriel and Verberckt's work at the Palace of Fontainebleau, although the Cabinet du Conseil there with its brilliantly coloured painted panels by Van Loo, Peyrotte and Pierre is among the grandest of the time (1751–4). Mention must also be made of the exquisite decorations at Rambouillet (1730–35), probably by Verberckt. In many ways they are the most complete realization of gossamer-fine carved ornament which seems to spread naturally over every surface, and it is easy to understand why this delightful form of decoration should have riled pro-classical rational designers and intellectuals, for whom its apparent lack of purpose condemned it outright. The reaction against the Rococo began earlier than is often supposed, in the 1740s, and is discussed in Chapter 6.

Although major interiors from the Rococo period exist in Italy (Plate 98) and Spain, after France it was Germany which most readily adopted the style, and evolved it in a series of independent ways. It also spread to Austria, Hungary, Poland, Bohemia and Russia. The willing acceptance of the Baroque by the Central European countries made the spread of the Rococo easier there, and many features of Baroque architecture lingered on through the entire eighteenth century. In France as we have seen, the Rococo was almost exclusively a style of the court, aristocracy and *nouveaux riches*, but in Central Europe it was also eagerly adopted by the Church, and masterpieces in the Rococo style continued to be built long after Neo-classicism had swept the board elsewhere. Great as the

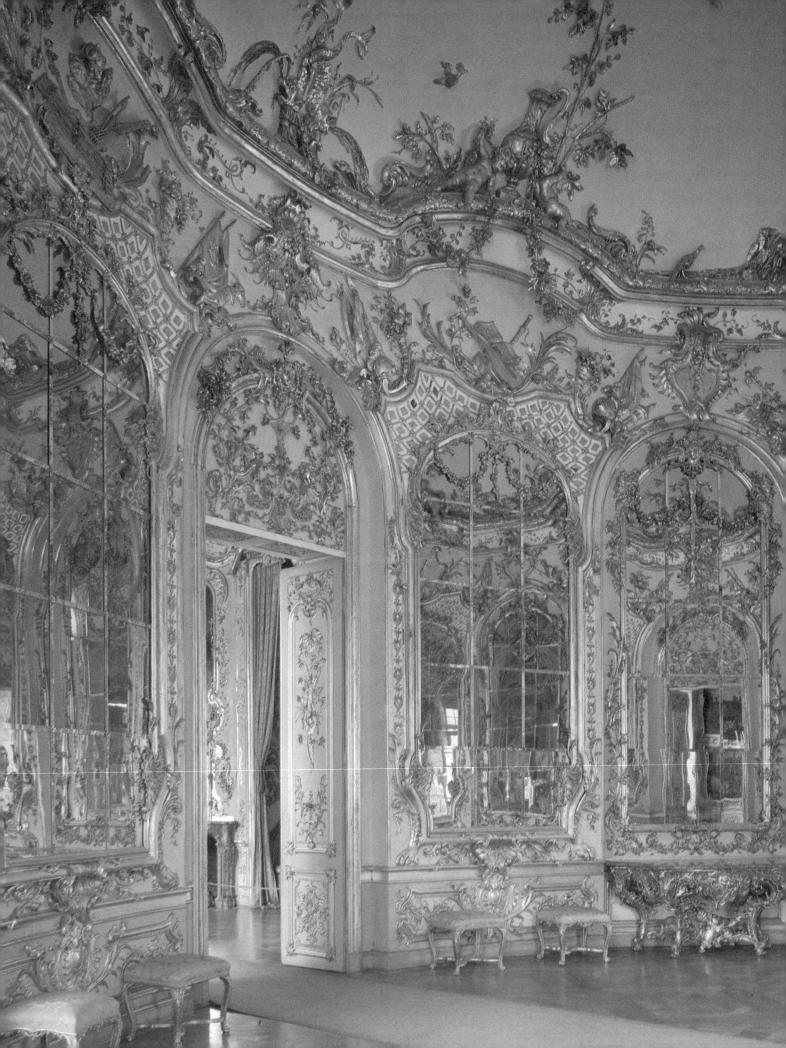

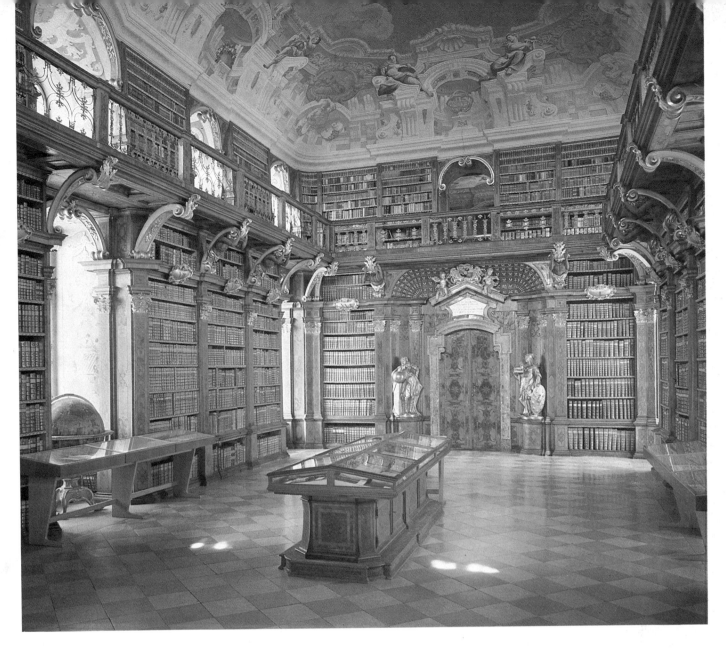

101 (left) Spiegelsaal in the Amalienburg, 1734–9.
Nymphenburg, Munich   *The Amalienburg was built as a
hunting lodge for the Electress Amalia by François Cuvilliés
the Elder with the circular Spiegelsaal (Hall of Mirrors) at its
centre. Johann Baptist Zimmermann executed the stuccoes
and Joachim Dietrich the woodcarvings; perhaps no other
interior rivals the wealth and exquisite delicacy of the detail
here. Silvered flowers, fruit, flags, vases, cartouches, musical
instruments, putti, fish, shells, palm branches, military
emblems, trellises and pheasants (a reference to those shot
from the balcony on the roof above) – all are picked out
against the white ceiling and pale blue walls, while fountain
jets and even carved three-dimensional fishing nets add to
the profusion of Rococo motifs. The silver-gilt console
tables may be by the Netherlandish sculptor-decorator J.
Gerstens. Adjoining the Spiegelsaal are the lemon-yellow
and silver Bedroom and Hunting Room*

102 (above) Library, Monastery of Melk, *Austria (building
designed in 1702)*

Rococo can be in domestic decoration in Central Europe,
it is in the churches that its finest ebullience is expressed –
perhaps the last real manifestation of religious intensity
on such a scale in European art. For the French, comfort,
politeness and convenience were the guiding force in
Rococo decoration, and it therefore never attained the
rich expressiveness that characterized the style in Germany.

French furniture in this period plays a very important
rôle in interior decoration, and its development owes
much to the Parisian dealers or *marchands-merciers*. They
supplied furniture to royal clients such as Louis XV,
Madame de Pompadour and the Prince de Condé, and to
many private patrons. Their influence on taste was considerable because they employed independent designers
and craftsmen, although they did not have their own
workshops. Among leading furniture-makers employed
by them were Martin Carlin and Bernard II van Risen-
burgh, known until recently only as B.V.R.B.; the latter is

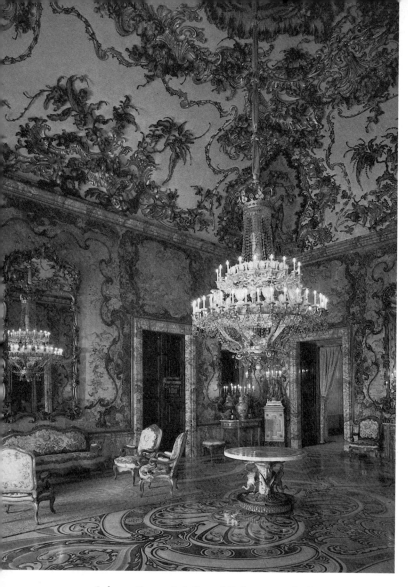

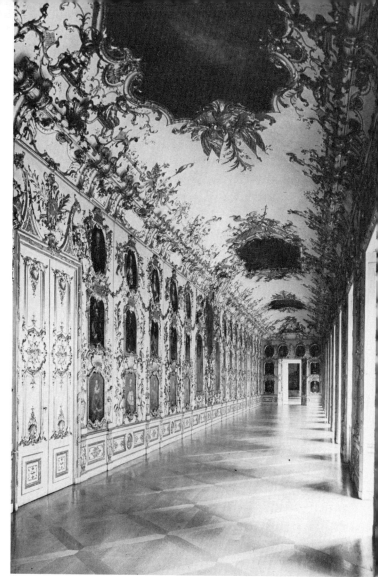

103 Salone Gasparini, Royal Palace, *Madrid*

104 The Ancestors' Gallery in the Residenz, *Munich*. 1726–31
*Originally a garden hall, this room was converted in the later
1720s to house portraits by a wide range of painters of
Wittelsbach ancestors and relatives. The 121 portraits are
framed in superb gilded carvings of vases, flowers, allegorical
figures, trophies and legendary beasts by Wenzeslaus
Miroffsky. Johann Baptist Zimmermann's gilded stuccoes
surround Balthasar Augustin Albrecht's ceiling painting.
This and the other rooms forming the Elector Carl Albrecht's
Reiche Zimmer ('rich rooms') are among the masterpieces of
the German Rococo; lit by 2000 candles they were opened
on 4 November 1737*

now regarded as one of eighteenth-century France's
greatest *ébénistes*.

One of the principal reasons for the richness and diversity of the Rococo in Germany is that the country still consisted of independent states, and rivalry between the various princes resulted in architectural magnificence, which in France was confined to Paris and its environs. During the later stages of the War of the Spanish Succession, from 1704 to 1714, two princes of the Wittelsbach family who had taken Louis XV's side in the dispute were exiled to France, and were therefore present at the birth of the new style. They were the Elector Max Emanuel (1662–1726) of Bavaria and his brother Joseph Clemens (1671–1723), the Elector-Archbishop of Cologne. De Cotte, Boffrand and Oppenordt were all instrumental in shaping these princes' future interest in Rococo architecture and interiors, but the real creators of the earliest manifestations of the style in Germany were Paris-trained Germans. Many of the best French furniture-makers of the century, such as Jean-François Oeben, Jean-Henri Riese-

ner, and David Roentgen were German by birth. The garden-designer turned architect, Joseph Effner (1687–1745), was also trained in Paris. Under his supervision the earliest surviving Régence interiors in Germany were decorated, namely those in the Pagodenburg garden pavilion in the grounds of Schloss Nymphenburg outside Munich (1716–19). Taking its name from the exotic taste for *chinoiserie*, which found particular favour in Germany, the Pagodenburg has interiors which would not be out of place in a Paris *hôtel*, with the added *frisson* of that delicacy that was to be so characteristic of the Bavarian Rococo. Another distinguishing feature also occurs there, the use of stucco and tiles for panelling, instead of the typical French *boiseries*, and the major triumphs of both domestic and ecclesiastical German Rococo decoration owe a great deal to the breathtaking achievements of the stucco and plaster-workers (see Plates 91, 101 and 105).

As in Italy, Baroque architectural influence remained strong in German Rococo interiors. Unlike the French, who adhered to basically rectangular room shapes on whose flat surfaces Rococo decoration was applied, the Germans allowed the potentially wayward forms of plasterwork to integrate as fully as possible with rooms of every conceivable shape. On entering a French Rococo room, one is immediately aware of its precise shape and size, an approach often consciously avoided in Germany. Decoration obscures rather than clarifies underlying structure, resulting in a blurring of the different zones of wall and ceiling. Ceiling frescoes, either in large single fields, or in a series of often irregular shapes scattered across the ceiling, can be either a colouristic complement to the rest of the interior or provide the sole note of colour in an otherwise totally white scheme. Under Italian influence, Germany made extensive use of marble, or plaster or wood treated to imitate marble, in domestic interiors, which, particularly in conjunction with the pale colours – white, pink, grey, green, yellow and so on – chosen for plasterwork and woodwork, lacks warmth and often creates a somewhat cold impression. Mirrors are extensively used, although rarely is the rigid symmetry of the French system sought. Instead, designers preferred to create dazzling effects with unusual placing of mirror glass (Plate 101) or massing of mirrors in a fragile setting which enhanced their reflections.

It is one of the delightful quirks of fate that the most accomplished designer of the bizarrerie-loving Rococo was a dwarf. François du Cuvilliés (1695–1768) was a page to Max Emanuel from 1711 and went with him to France when his patron was exiled there. Cuvilliés' genius lay in adapting and transforming his French sources into a wholly new version of the Rococo, and one where all its aspirations reach perfection. In forty-three years of Electoral service, he created several of the Rococo's greatest masterpieces of interior decoration. In 1720–4 he was again in Paris, studying with François Blondel the Younger, and on his return to Germany soon perfected the personal manner which makes its first triumphant appearance in the hunting lodge of Falkenlust at Schloss Brühl, near Cologne (1729–40). There, all the features later evolved in his pavilion of Amalienburg (Plate 101) are prefigured. Brilliant room planning and decoration of varying degrees of elaboration, ranging from the blue and white tile-clad staircase to the tiny mirror-cabinet, achieve a unity unrivalled in contemporary France.

In Munich, the Reiche Zimmer of the Residenz (Plate 104) established his reputation with their profusion of naturalistic motifs created in plaster by the famous Johann Baptist Zimmermann (brother of the architect Dominikus) and in woodcarving by Joachim Dietrich, Pichler and Miroffsky. What has rightly been characterized as the 'abundance and gaiety' of Bavarian Rococo culminates in the Amalienburg, both externally and internally. As much as any Neo-classical architect, Cuvilliés here perfectly expressed the nature of his interiors on the exterior. He made some 400 to 500 engravings, which were all published in Munich in volumes such as his *Livre de cartouches* (1738), *Livre de plafonds* and *Morceaux de caprice*; the decorative motifs included in them show a fecundity of imagination with no equal in the field. Ranging from ceilings, wall-panels and picture frames to cane-handles, locks and stoves – all revealing the interchangeable forms of the Rococo – they remained one of the prime sources for German Rococo designers of all kinds. Cuvilliés became Chief Architect to the Court in 1763, and his finest late designs were mainly for architecture, with the remarkable Residenz Theatre in Munich as his last major interior. Many of his Bavarian contemporaries such as Dominikus Zimmermann and Johann Michael Fischer were almost exclusively concerned with ecclesiastical architecture, and produced some of their best decoration in the libraries and other rooms of monasteries like St Gallen.

The Rococo found unparalleled favour throughout the German lands, where in many cases the immense palaces begun around the turn of the eighteenth century in a late Baroque style were eventually decorated internally by Rococo craftsmen, as at the Zwinger Palace at Dresden for Augustus the Strong, King of Poland and Elector of Saxony, at Pommersfelden for the Elector of Mainz (Plate 106), and in Würzburg (Plate 105). The decoration of Schloss Brühl with its breathtaking late Baroque staircase bristling with virtuoso Rococo plasterwork and sculpture (Plate 91) typifies the balance struck between dramatic architecture and decoration, a balance which distinguishes the German Rococo at its most sumptuous. In Vienna after the defeat of the Turks in 1683 the Emperor and the aristocracy devoted themselves to creating palaces suitable for the capital of the Holy Roman Empire and the Habsburg domains. There, as in Prague, the example of Versailles with its lavish use of marble, bronzes, mirrors and paintings inspired a grander version of the German Rococo, and Italian decorators of every kind were brought in to assist with the work. Mention too should be made of the fantastic Rococo style favoured by Frederick the Great for his various palaces around Berlin, such as Charlottenburg, Sans Souci and the Stadtschloss at Potsdam, where an army of stuccoists created fantasies (including delightful *chinoiseries*) outshining even Cuvilliés in invention if not always in the quality of their design. This was also the period of the great German porcelain factories. Meissen and Nymphenburg produced work of outstanding finesse and quality which had great fashionable appeal.

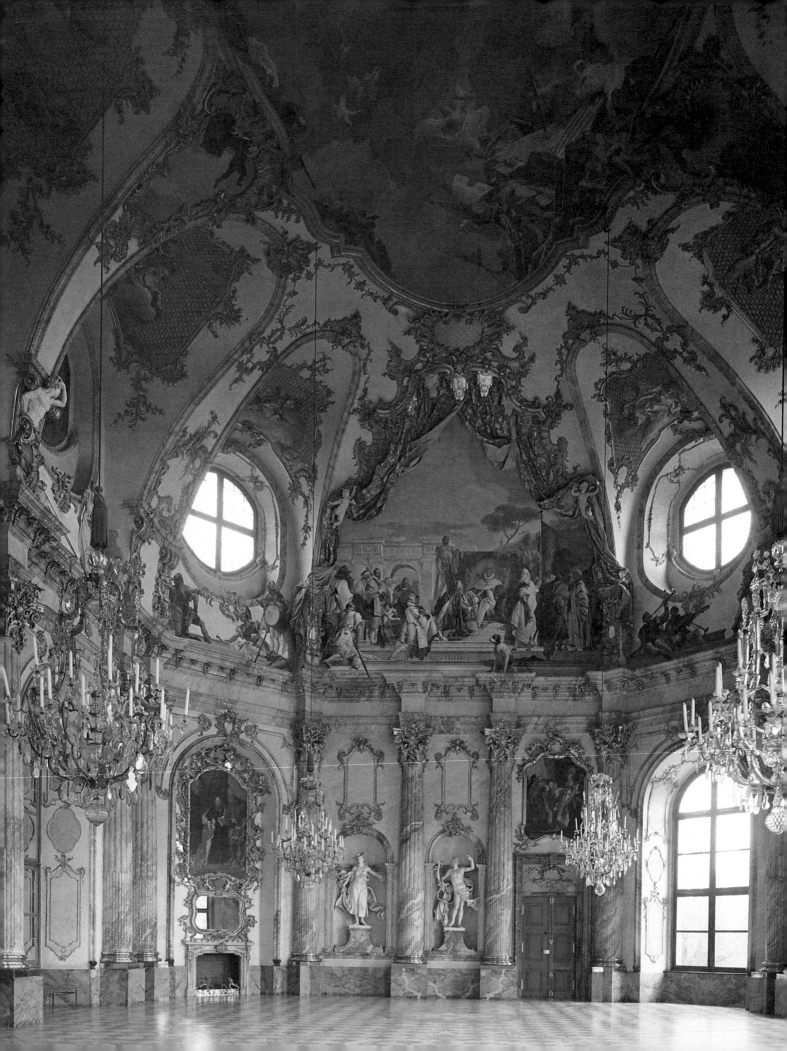

105 *(left)* Kaisersaal in the Residenz, *Würzburg, decorated 1749–53* The Kaisersaal or Imperial Hall was a feature of the architecture of the Electors and Princes of the Church in the Catholic regions of Germany. This is the finest Rococo example, and is a collaboration between three great artists – the architect Balthasar Neumann, the Italian painter Giovanni Battista Tiepolo and the stucco-worker Antonio Bossi. It is the culminating point of a sequence of rooms which include the magnificent staircase (also frescoed by Tiepolo) and the elaborately stuccoed Weisser Saal. The theme of Tiepolo's frescoes is the union of the Emperor Barbarossa with Beatrix of Burgundy, 'revealed' by Bossi's uplifted stucco curtains at the ends of the room and in the huge central ceiling panel. Inset into the vault are innumerable small mirrors intended to reflect and multiply the lights and movement beneath

106 *(right)* The Mirror Room, Schloss Pommersfelden, *West Germany*

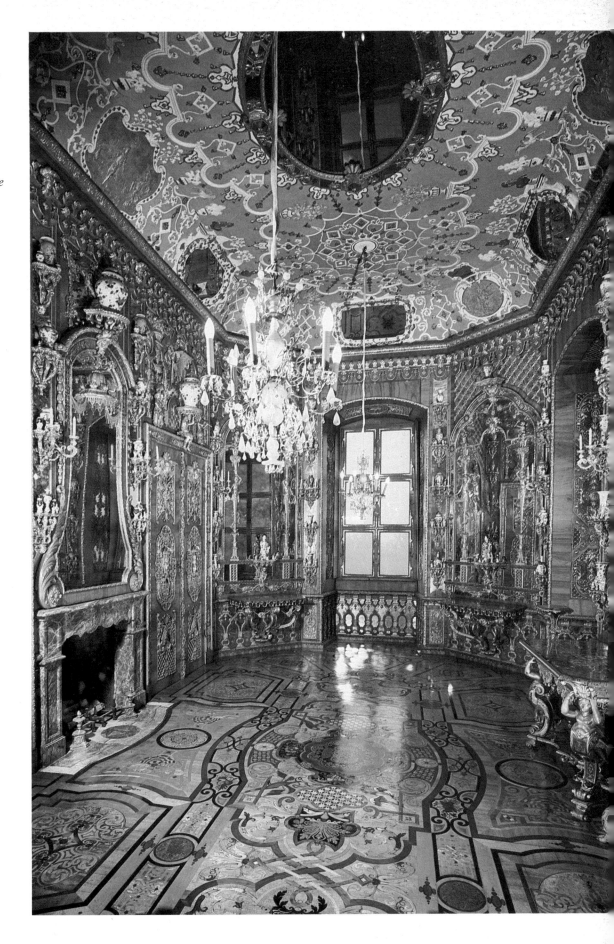

Britain was the only European country where the Rococo not only had little influence outside the minor arts, but was also consciously rejected by architects. The period 1715–60 saw a complete rejection of the late Baroque style of Wren, Vanbrugh and Hawksmoor in favour of a revival of the architectural principles of Andrea Palladio, whose ideas had already found fertile soil in Britain in the work of Inigo Jones a century earlier (see Chapter 4). Because of its dislike of the foreign art associated with the Stuart dynasty, the second generation of Whig aristocracy sought a 'correct' and 'polite' style which carried no whiff of the Baroque; Jones's version of Palladianism seemed the perfect answer. As with the Rococo, whose chronological rise and fall exactly parallels English Palladianism, books of engravings played a fundamental role in the style's growth and spread. In 1715, the first volume of the Scottish architect Colen Campbell's *Vitruvius Britannicus* appeared, and Nicholas Dubois's translation of Palladio's *Four Books* with plates by Giacomo Leoni was published. Richard Boyle (1694–1753), Earl of Burlington, returned from Italy in the same year, and it was his knowledge of Palladian architecture together with his splendid collection of the architect's own drawings which made him a key figure in eighteenth-century English architecture. Campbell was his protégé, as was William Kent, gifted interior and furniture designer and second-rate painter. The precise contribution of each of these three men to the growth of the Palladian interior is difficult to pinpoint, but it was almost certainly Kent's concept of the interior as a whole which was the most influential. In his famous *Epistle to Lord Burlington* of 1731, Alexander Pope sums up the new taste for classical restraint which rapidly began to replace the extravagances of the Baroque: 'You show us, Rome was glorious, not profuse, / And pompous buildings were once things of use.'

As Jones had discovered, Palladio's interiors were essentially like his exterior architecture in their reliance for effect on the immaculate proportioning and placing of every detail, and the subsequent decoration of many of Palladio's interiors had little or nothing to do with their creator's intentions. The English climate prevented the use of fresco as in the Veneto, and the English Palladian interior is based partly on the language of Palladio and Jones, partly on the decorative usages of the Baroque. The combination resulted in some of Europe's most impressive interiors, such as the entrance hall at Holkham Hall in Norfolk, which combines a Roman basilica and features derived from Palladio and Vitruvius with a flight of steps of Baroque *brio*. Basing their ideas on Palladian and Jonesian prototypes, Burlington, Kent, Campbell, John Wood of Bath and others created uniquely English versions of their prototypes – Mereworth Castle, Kent (1723), and Chiswick (Plate 107), both based on Palladio's Villa Rotonda near Vincenza, as well as Holkham Hall and Houghton, both in Norfolk, to name only the major examples.

Campbell's remodelling of Lord Burlington's town house in Piccadilly set the fashion for palatial town residences in the new style, and at 44 Berkeley Square in London, Kent (1685–1748) made one of the most sumptuous interiors of the period for Lady Isabella Finch, a relative of Burlington's. Kent drew heavily on Jones, notably for chimney-pieces, and in 1727 published his *Designs of Inigo Jones*. For Lady Finch, Kent created a drawing room summing up many of the aims of the first mature phase of English Palladian decoration. Silk- or velvet-hung walls are usually articulated by heavily architectural door-cases and windows, all surmounted by massive ceiling cornices and coved ceilings with classical coffering as in Berkeley Square and at Holkham. Woodwork is usually painted a pale colour with detail picked out in gold, creating a sumptuous yet restrained effect against dark wall-hangings punctuated with pictures. In some interiors, like the Green State Bedroom at Houghton, wall-tapestries offset dark wooden doors and floor against brilliant white and gold plasterwork and a large painted ceiling roundel: here, the State Bed with its gigantic double shell set into a broken pediment at the head typifies Kent's monumental approach to the furniture with which he filled many interiors of the period. Architectural features such as the much-used tripartite Venetian or Serlian window opening often dominate the Palladian interior, as at Chiswick Villa. While the French Rococo reflects the sophistication of Parisian urban life in its delicate, non-architectural approach to decoration, English Palladianism is perfectly representative of a landed aristocracy whose great palaces lay at the heart of their country estates.

More than the Baroque, Palladianism lent itself to the simplification necessary for smaller interiors, and many publications of the period provided an armoury of plans, elevations and decorative detail for the architect and craftsmen, who were often working far away from the main centres. Apart from Kent's book, Burlington's *Fabbriche antiche* with engravings of Palladio's drawings provided a clear picture of the original sources, and Kent himself entered the Palladian pantheon in John Vardy's *Designs of Inigo Jones and William Kent* of 1744. The perfect ease with which the style was adapted to less grand needs is shown in Kent's Painted Parlour at Rousham House in Oxfordshire of around 1738, where very simple wooden panelling and doors with straight entablatures find an ornate focus in the marble chimney-piece and carved, gilded overmantel; on the ceiling, Kent painted one of his better 'grotesques', and much of the furniture is his. This type of interior found great favour throughout Britain on account of its simple and harmonious marriage of the native tradition of wood-panelled walls with a straightforward Classical vocabulary. It also provided the ideal setting for the landscapes and portraits which are so characteristic of English eighteenth-century painting.

It is worth noting that apart from the elaborately carved and gilded furniture of Kent, the majority of great interiors

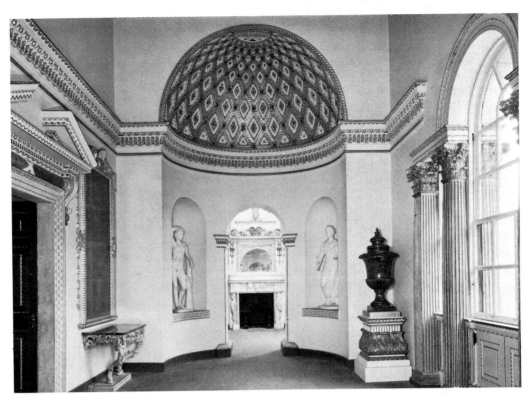

107 *(right)* The Gallery, Chiswick House, *London,* by William Kent, *c. 1725*

108 *(below)* The Dining Room, Nostell Priory, *West Yorkshire. Mid-eighteenth century*

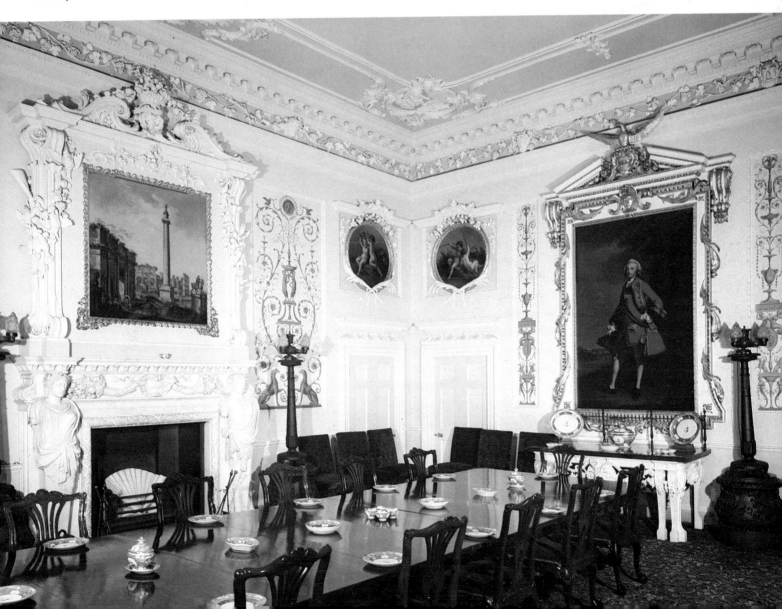

109 *(right, above)* The North Hall of Claydon House, *Buckinghamshire* *The quality of the carvings at Claydon, the work of Luke Lightfoot, about whom very little is known, is striking. Lightfoot may have derived his designs from Mathias Lock, the originator of the plates for Chippendale's 1754 Director. Applied to a Palladian double cube by Sir Thomas Robinson (who found Lightfoot's decorations 'the ridicule of all who have seen or heard of it') they recall German rather than French extravagances. In the Chinese Room (Plate 110), Lightfoot drew on George Edwards and Mathias Darly's book of* Chinese Designs, *in its turn based on the* chinoiseries *introduced by Sir William Chambers after his visit to China of 1748–9. Like the 'Gothick' style,* chinoiseries *were one aspect of the Rococo that found acceptance in Britain*

110 *(right, below)* Detail from the Chinese Room, Claydon House, *Buckinghamshire. Mid-eighteenth century*

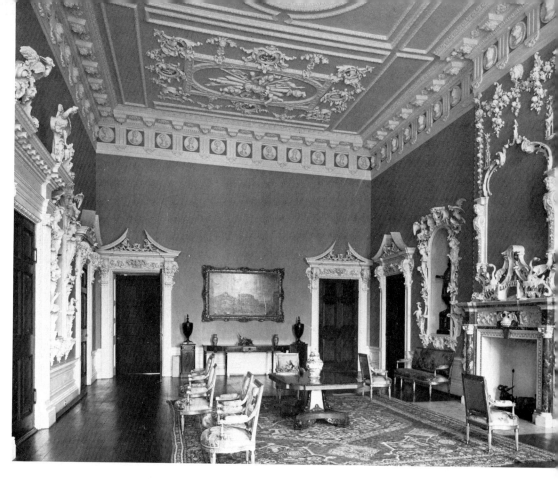

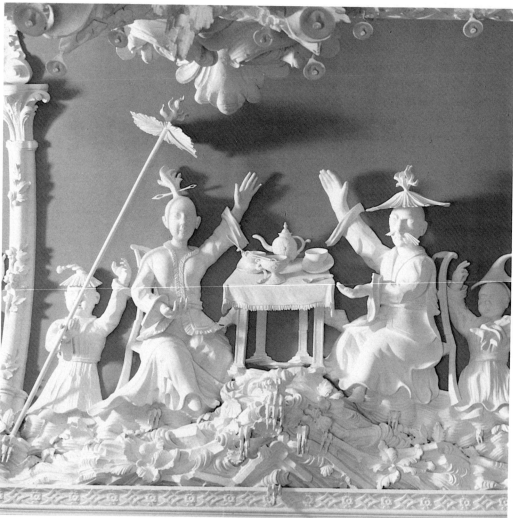

were still filled with Baroque furniture, and the taste for Italian masters, which became a mania in the age of the grand tour, turned major rooms such as the gallery at Corsham Court in Wiltshire into interiors whose principal function was to display the owner's collection. The rectilinear nature of Palladian interiors provided the best possible setting for such collections, where a unique balance is struck between fixed decoration – generally confined to functional areas such as doors, windows and fireplaces – and splendidly framed paintings hung from chair-rail to cornice generally according to size and shape. In the finest interiors is already apparent the contrast in room shapes and finish later so prized by Robert Adam (see Chapter 6), as at Holkham, where damask-hung rooms with paintings alternate with painted plaster walls articulated with niches for sculpture.

The tenets of Palladianism were maintained by a second generation of architects including Sir Robert Taylor, John Carr of York and James Paine, few of whose interiors, however, achieved the magnificence of those of earlier patrons like Coke of Norfolk, Sir Robert Walpole and Burlington himself. Although Rococo decoration in England was mainly applied to furniture, it also made sporadic appearances in interior decoration, usually as an extrinsic

rather than an intrinsic part of the scheme (Plate 108). Its principal attraction was that it could be added at will to almost any existing setting, and indeed this often happened with bizarre results. No important foreign architects of the Rococo worked in England, and contacts with the style came mainly through furniture designs and other engraved work. Commissions to foreign artists were rare (apart from painters such as Pellegrini and Sebastiano Ricci), and the Duke of Kingston commissioned from the great Juste-Aurèle Meissonier only designs for silver. Even by 1739, when William Jones published *The Gentlemens or Builders Companion*, the Rococo style had not been fully assimilated; it seems significant that the gifted carver of one of the most convincing Rococo decorative schemes in England, at Claydon House, Buckinghamshire (Plate 109), Luke Lightfoot, still remains otherwise something of a mystery.

Two offshoots of the Rococo produced a certain number of delightful interiors in Britain – *chinoiserie* (Plate 110) and the Gothick. The former was usually confined to details, or occasionally to whole rooms using Chinese wallpaper, while the Gothick style found a wider public after the printing of Batty Langley's *Gothic Architecture Improved* in 1742. This included engraved designs for 'Gothic'

III Room from 'Marmion', King's County, Virginia. *1750–75. New York, Metropolitan Museum of Art*

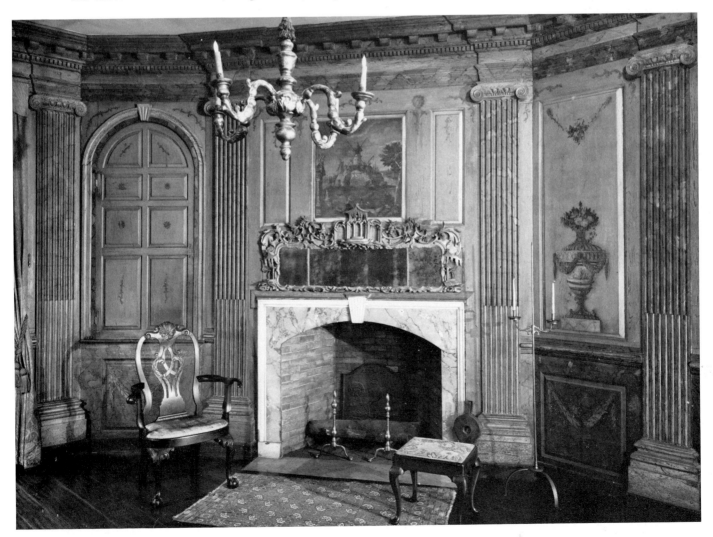

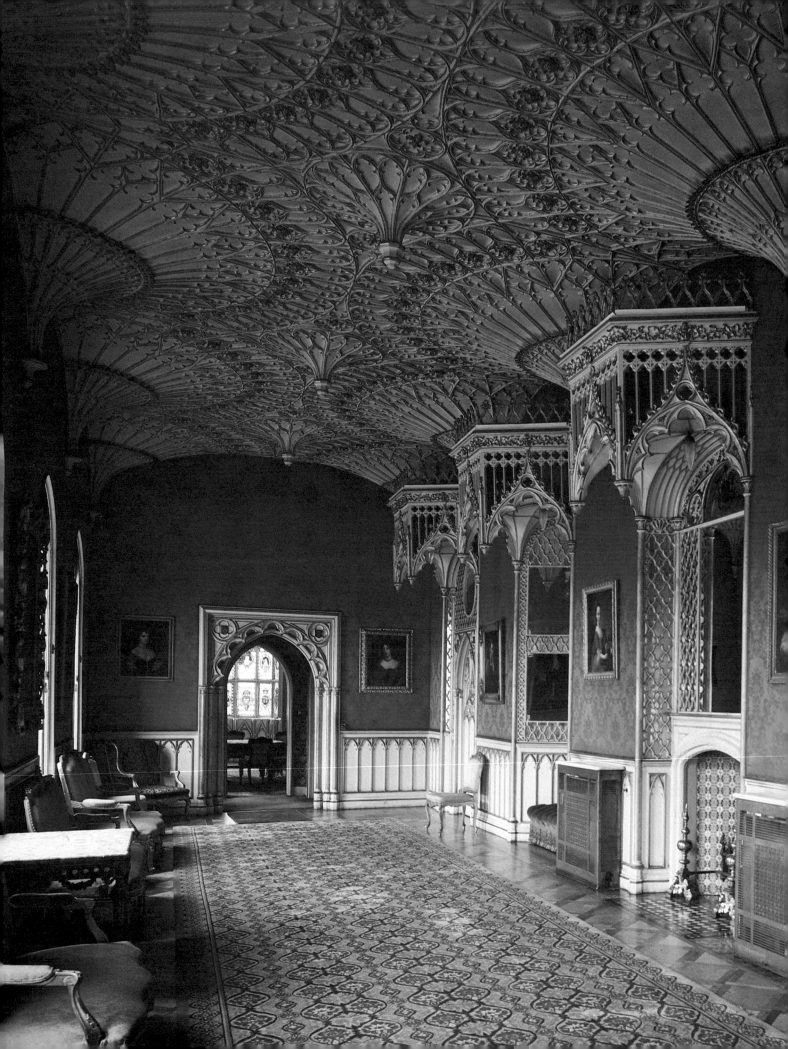

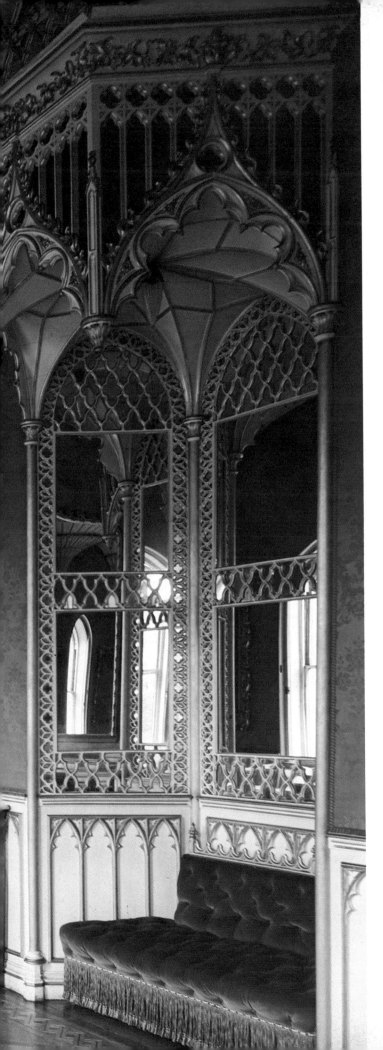

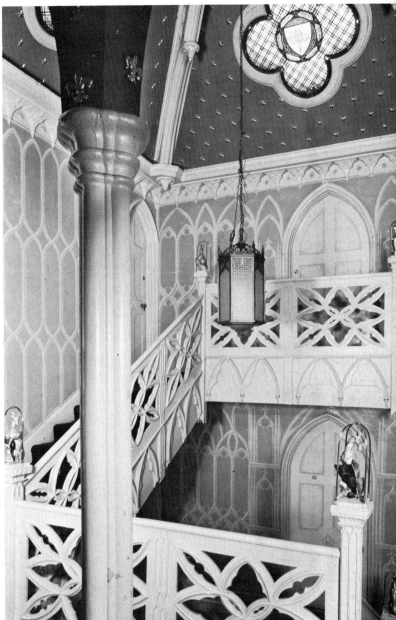

112 *(left)* The Long Gallery of Strawberry Hill, Twickenham, 1763 *The Long Gallery was designed by Thomas Pitt in what Walpole termed 'charming venerable Gothic'. The large door is copied from the north door at St Albans and the vaulting from the aisles of the Henry VII Chapel at Westminster. Its use of mirrors is typically Rococo, as is the Staircase Hall (Plate 113) with its spindly Gothick painted paper and thin detailing*

113 *(above)* Staircase at Strawberry Hill, Twickenham, *begun 1749*

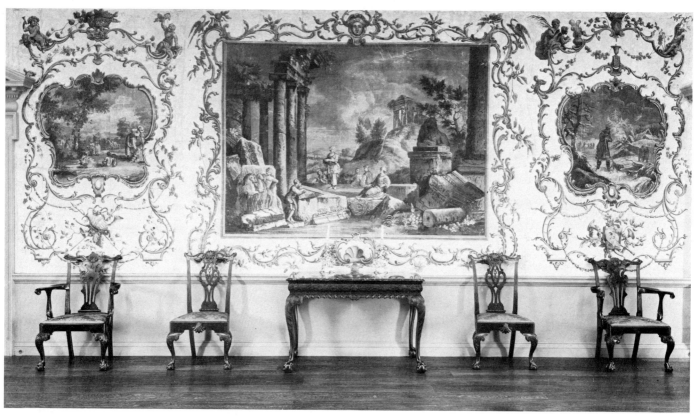

114 Entry Hall, Van Rensselaer Manor House, Albany, New York. *1765–9. New York, Metropolitan Museum of Art*

chimney-pieces, which bear little resemblance to anything in the medieval domestic interior. The style was encouraged by an amateur architect, Sanderson Miller, but reached its first real culmination in architecture and decoration with Horace Walpole's Strawberry Hill villa at Twickenham near London (Plates 112 and 113). In the gallery a wide variety of real medieval sources was plundered for details (such as the vaulting copied from the Henry VII Chapel in Westminster Abbey) and the effect – though often papery and unconvincing – looks forward to the beginnings of the Gothic Revival in the early nineteenth century. Adam, Wyatt and many other architects ensured the style's continued fashion through the second half of the eighteenth century.

In America during the early part of the century there was a change in approach to the treatment of interiors. Sash windows now became a distinctive feature, and panelling was handled in a more architectural manner. In Stratford Hall, Virginia (begun 1725), the wooden panelling was more elaborate than any in the seventeenth century. Such panelling was usually of painted pine; plain walnut and mahogany were used for doors and stairs. Drayton Hall, near Charleston (built 1738–42), was the earliest American house to reflect the Palladian ideas now widely published; the chimney-piece in the hall is based on a design by Inigo Jones. The first colonial example of *chinoiserie* is in the dining room of Gunston Hall, Virginia (built 1755–9), in which the woodwork was carved by the Englishman William Buckland (b. 1734). The drawing room is classical with an Adam-style marble mantel. Like Britain, America readily adopted Palladianism, usually rejecting the excesses of the Rococo in favour of the style which best represented 'that balanced combination of the useful and the beautiful, of prosperity and good breeding' (Summerson). Thomas Jefferson (1743–1826) developed many of his ideas from the English architect James Gibbs, but came to prefer the simplest classical forms both for his exteriors and interiors. His own villa of Monticello best shows his style, which gained widespread exposure as a result of his involvement in politics and philosophy in Virginia.

Jefferson's brand of Palladianism moved closer to the Neo-classicism of the Adam school in England with Samuel McIntyre (1757–1811), and the transitional styles of Charles Bulfinch (1763–1844) and the English-born Benjamin Latrobe (1764–1820) lead directly to the beginnings of Romantic architecture in America.

6

Neo-classicism

... on se flatterait en vain de trouver des formes préférables à
celles que les anciens nous ont transmises.

Percier and Fontaine, *Recueil de décorations intérieures*, 1812

The term 'Neo-classicism' strikes a note almost as chill as the most severe manifestations of the style itself. First used in the 1880s, it still brings to many minds a vision of uncompromisingly rectilinear interiors where physical comfort is sacrificed to the rigid verticality of all components, animate or inanimate. In fact, the term covers a wide variety of *different* styles and includes some of the most elegant interiors in Europe; the Empire style in France having perhaps the strongest claim to be regarded as the most *chic* in domestic decoration. All of the different stages of Neo-classicism shared one aim – to imitate, or at least evoke, the styles of art found in the ancient world. The result was an international style which found favour in France, England, Italy, Spain, Germany, Russia, Denmark and, for the first time in the history of interior decoration, in America.

In Chapter 1 of this book, it was noted that virtually nothing survives of ancient Greek interiors, a fact bitterly regretted by the greatest designers of the Empire in France, Percier and Fontaine, in the introduction to their self-advertising *Recueil* of 1812. Thus, although Greek architecture and its detail was known to Europe from the mid-eighteenth century onwards through publications like Robert Wood's *Ruins of Palmyra* (1753) and *Ruins of Balbec* (1757) and Stuart and Revett's *Antiquities of Athens* (from 1762), interior designers had to base their ideas of Classical houses on a somewhat haphazard selection of sources. The excavations at Pompeii and Herculaneum after 1750 provided new inspiration and the public architecture of ancient Rome could be seen both in the original remains and through the eyes of Alberti, Palladio and others. As we have seen, Palladio's superb reworking of Roman baths and temples to create domestic architecture for his own period had little or nothing to do with the houses and palaces of the ancient world; it was his legacy, however, which dominated interior design in Britain immediately prior to the Neo-classical period, and also, surprisingly, French academic thought during the Rococo period.

Although the language of Neo-classicism was international by 1800, the way in which it developed, and indeed the reasons for its development, varied from country to country. Italy had a profusion of Roman architecture in its midst, and remained a source of inspiration for Neo-classical artists of all nations: its own development of the style was erratic and spasmodic. France, with its eternal allegiance to Classicism, was ready – even at the height of the Rococo period – to throw itself wholeheartedly into the new style, and was among the first to produce the anti-Baroque and anti-Rococo theory which prepared the way for its adoption. Britain's Palladianism made heavy architectural interiors, bristling with columns and pediments, the norm, and although the early interiors of Robert Adam were later described as 'snippets of embroidery' his public were at least already classically minded. Other countries such as Russia and Scandinavia readily adopted the new vogue and thoroughly mastered it. Germany and Austria continued to create masterpieces of interior decoration in the Rococo style long after the rest of Europe had largely abandoned it, but when they did adopt Neo-classicism, their fervour almost outshone their rivals: J. J. Winckelmann, the first great enthusiast for a new revival of the antique was, after all, German. In America, newly independent, the revival of ancient architecture came at a singularly opportune moment since it most fully represented the recently won freedom.

This is not the place to list all of the main events of Neo-classicism as a movement in general, but it is worth noting a few of them. As early as 1693, Fénelon had expressed the idea that Classicism was a language which each of the arts could speak with equal ease: 'one must write as Raphael, the Carracci and Poussin painted'. Despite the Baroque and Rococo, this was an ideal cherished by many artists and thinkers, and the frequent re-discovery of Classical remains stimulated it. Great collections of antique sculpture and other objects had graced the palaces of the Medici, Farnese, Borghese, Barberini and other Italian patrician families from the Renaissance onwards, but it was only

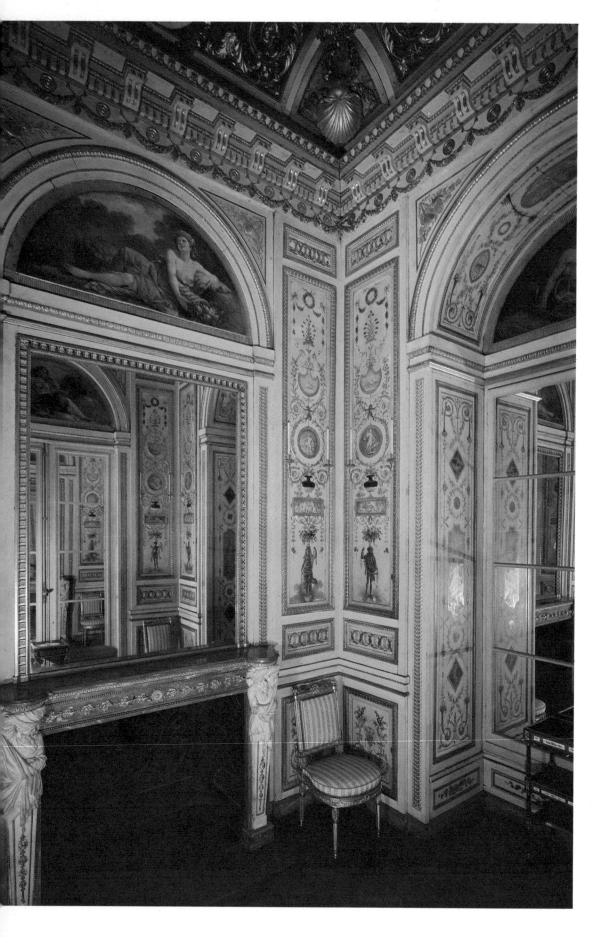

115 The Boudoir of Mme de Serilly, *late 1770s or 1780s*. London, Victoria and Albert Museum   Attributed to Ledoux, this is one of the finest early Neo-classical French interiors and contains work by the leading artists and craftsmen of the day. The wall decorations are by Jean-Simon Rousseau de la Rottière, the oil paintings by Jean-Jacques Lagrenée le Jeune and the chimney-piece by Clodion with mounts by Pierre Gouthière. Such a concentration of quality is not untypical of Parisian aspirations in the decade preceding the Revolution, when many bankruptcies occurred as a result of lavish expenditure on decoration. The mirrors originally had gilt festoons

116 *(right, above)* Boudoir of Queen Marie Antoinette, Fontainebleau, *c.* 1787 *The style étrusque reaches its apogee in France with this room, whose painted panels are probably by the brothers Rousseau. Of particular interest is the painted 'sky' on the ceiling*

117 *(right, below)* Section of the Drawing Room, Northumberland House, London. *Design for end wall by Robert Adam. Watercolour, pen and ink, pencil. London, Sir John Soane Museum   Adam's eclecticism and inventiveness reached its zenith in this extraordinary interior, a technical* tour de force, *part of which survives in the Victoria and Albert Museum. The Corinthian pilasters framing the eight large pier-glasses had central panels painted moss green on the reverse and flecked with shredded, gilt copper against varnished cloth to simulate highly polished porphyry. The glass had overlays of what Chambers disparagingly called 'filigrane toy work' – gilt-stamped copper palmettes with hanging husks. Above the doors and mirrors were further glass and foil panels simulating red Egyptian porphyry with gilt-lead framed oval and circular oil paintings. The ceiling decoration repeats the carpet pattern, giving the room a sense of unity, an effect also achieved in the Drawing Room at Osterley Park and the Music Room at Harewood House*

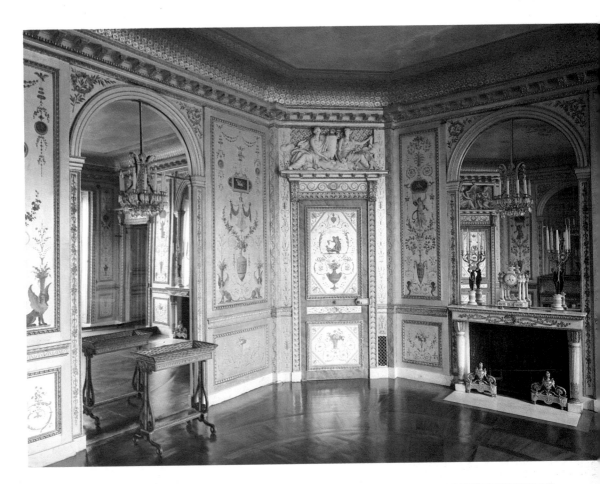

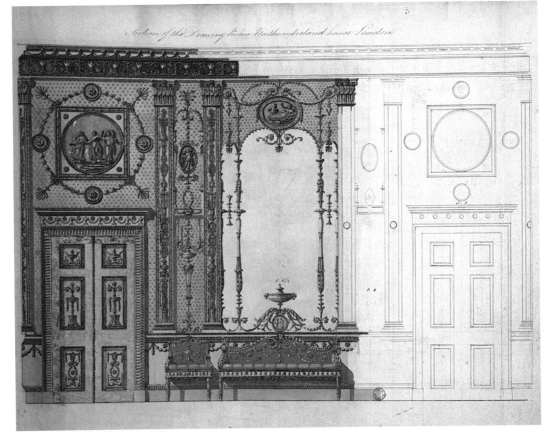

in the mid-eighteenth century that systematic excavations were seriously undertaken. It was the recovery of the movable works of art from the Vesuvian cities of Pompeii and Herculaneum which led to their excavation from the 1750s, with immense consequences for domestic interior design ensuing from the revelation of entire houses and villas with decoration intact.

Winckelmann settled in Rome in 1755, becoming adviser to Cardinal Albani and publishing his *Reflections on the Imitation of Greek Art in Painting and Sculpture* (1755) and the *History of Ancient Art amongst the Greeks* (1764). Through these works, he gave the Greeks (whose art he championed at the expense of the Romans) a new status in European eyes, and brought about a novel awareness of style. His most fervent opponent, the Venetian Giovanni Battista Piranesi (1720–78), was also resident in Rome, and championed Roman art. His large engravings series include the *Vedute di Roma* (1748–78), the more archaeological four-volume *Antichità romane* (1756), and *Della magnificenza ed architettura de' Romani*, which reveals his involvement in the Graeco-Roman controversy of the 1760s. Among his other works, more directly connected with interior decoration, were *Vasi, candelabri, cippi, Diverse maniere d'adornare i camini* (*Various Ways of Decorating Fireplaces*) and the drawings he made at Herculaneum, Pompeii and Hadrian's Villa, later engraved by his son Francesco. To the 'noble simplicity and calm grandeur' so admired by Winckelmann in the antique, Piranesi opposed a much more romantic ideal composed of magnificent scale, variety and decorative richness.

Stuart and Revett's *Antiquities* had been preceded by Leroy's series of engravings *Ruines des plus beaux monumens de la Grèce*, published in 1758. Ever since Vitruvius, Greek supremacy over Rome had been argued, and now the dispute became more intense, especially in France and Britain. It was on the side of the Greeks that German Neo-classicism finally settled. Piranesi's Roman bias influenced many foreign visitors to that city including Robert Adam, the French painter Hubert Robert, and Jacques Louis Clérisseau, with whom Adam went to Spalato (Split) in 1754 to survey Diocletian's Palace. A series of architectural treatises resulted from French contacts with Roman Neo-classical thought. Among the most important were Jean-François Neufforge's eight-volume *Recueil élémentaire d'architecture* (1757), Jean-François Blondel's *De la distribution des maisons de plaisance* (1737) and *Architecture française* (1752), and the witty writings of the Abbé Laugier.

It was in France that the richest and most sustained development of Neo-classical architecture and interior decoration occurred, and from there ideas spread to western Germany and Scandinavia. It is easy to form a picture of the Rococo sweeping all before it, but many architects and intellectuals were already formulating and publishing attacks on the style as early as the 1730s – contemporary with the quintessential Parisian Rococo

interior, the Salon de la Princesse in the Hôtel de Soubise (Plate 96). Voltaire, in his *The Temple of Taste* of 1773, writes of 'Everything panelled, varnished, whitened, gilded and straightaway admired by gapers', and in the *Maisons de plaisance* Blondel ridicules the 'jumble of shells, dragons, reeds, palm-trees and plants which is the sum total of interior decoration nowadays'. The amateur archaeologist the Comte de Caylus attacks 'the bad taste and paltriness of the decoration of houses these days'; Meissonier, Pineau and Lajou among others are described as 'mad', 'ridiculous' and 'depraved', and a series of newspaper articles by the engraver Cochin criticizes cornices bursting with vegetation, curves, octagonal rooms and the entire *style rocaille*. The message could hardly have been clearer, and the way was open for a complete change of direction.

Nostalgia for the 'Century of Louis XIV' was not confined to Voltaire (who wrote a book with that title), but affected artists in general and many elements of the French Neo-classical repertory derived from the preceding century. Even in otherwise distinctly Rococo houses, interiors using the Orders are recorded, for example the Hôtel du Contrôleur-Général with frescoes by the Brunetti brothers. The first French interior in the Neo-classical style was the study, or writing room, of the collector Lalive de Jully, made in around 1756 by de Chetdeville and others, including Le Lorrain. (Le Lorrain had recently designed the dining room of Count Carl Gustav Tessin in Sweden, and it was Tessin who played a crucial role in introducing the new style into Scandinavia.) Lalive de Jully's study has vanished, but its extant furniture probably reflects many of the features which made the room so revolutionary – thick garlands (*cordes à puits*), deeply fluted straight surfaces, meanders and ribbon decoration. This early Neo-classical style in Paris became known as the *goût grec*. Diderot wrote: '... everything is now made in the Greek manner ... the taste has passed from architecture into our milliners' shops ... our dandies would think it a disgrace to be seen with a snuff-box not in the Greek style.' Joseph Vien's famous painting of 1767, *Greek Girl at the Bath* (Ponce, Museum), shows how insipidly fashionable the style could be.

In 1765, M.-J. Peyre published his *Oeuvres d'architecture* which featured Roman buildings like the Baths of Diocletian and the Pantheon alongside suites of French interiors. Its influence was immediately felt in the application of Roman details like niches, coffered ceilings and unframed windows cut directly into walls – the *frisson* created by such simplifications after Rococo excesses is easily imagined. An important figure in French Neo-classicism in the 1750s was that of Pierre Contant d'Ivry (1698–1777). Like his near-contemporary, Jacques Germain Soufflot (1713–80), Contant tried to unite the structural vitality of Gothic architecture with the monumental qualities of the Classical Orders. His oval staircase of the Palais Royal (1766–8) is a transitional work, but the

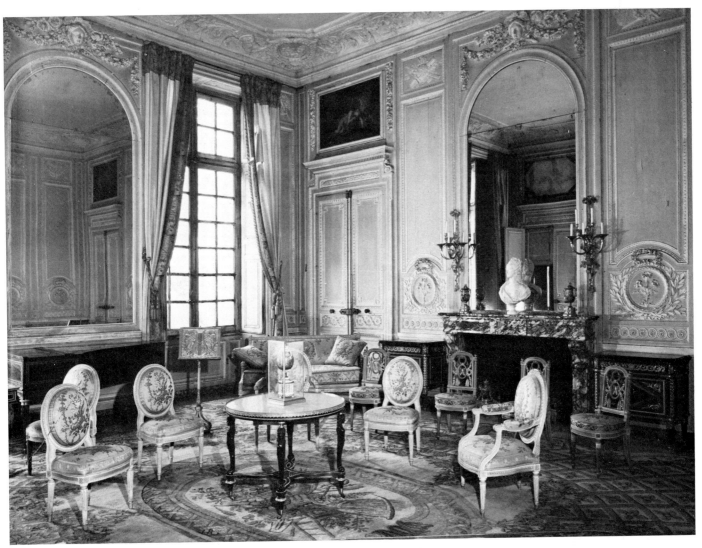

118 Salon de la Reine in the Petit Trianon, *Versailles*

severity of its stonework contrasting with a heavy wrought-iron handrail looks forward to later, more 'correct' Neo-classical staircases. Contant's style broke new ground by striking a balance between the heavy opulence of the *style Louis XIV* and the elegance of the Rococo.

The leading architect of early Neo-classicism in France was Ange-Jacques Gabriel (1698–1782), who studied architecture with his father and succeeded him as First Architect to the King in 1741. Louis XV gave him considerable support, and his major public buildings, such as the Place Louis XV (now Place de la Concorde), the Ecole Militaire and the Château de Compiègne, show his allegiance to the classicism of Louis XIV. Gabriel was also an interior designer of great talent, but his first major independent work in this sphere, the apartments of the Dauphin and Dauphine of 1744 at Versailles, is lost. Most of his early interiors for the Crown at Versailles and Fontainebleau are still Rococo (see Chapter 5), although rectilinear elements creep in to herald his shift to Neo-classical forms which occurs in his Pavillon Français,

between the Grand and the Petit Trianon, in 1749. Its use of the Corinthian Order conforms perfectly to Blondel's observation that architectural treatments are always superior to 'chimerical ornament', in interiors as on exteriors. In his work leading up to the Petit Trianon – where one side of early French Neo-classicism culminates – Gabriel must have rid his designs of almost all Rococo features. The Petit Château at Choisy (1754) had coffered window arches, rectangular doors with a frieze and cornice which was also used around the mirrors, a full entablature with consoles in the octagonal salon, and so on. At Saint-Hubert, the large circular salon too must have been completely classical, but as at Choisy, nothing survives.

Although the scale of the Petit Trianon is small, both its interiors and exteriors represent the early Neo-classical style at its most civilized and refined. Externally deriving from the British Palladian villa type which Gabriel would have known from, for example, Campbell's *Vitruvius Britannicus*, the rooms together form one of the most

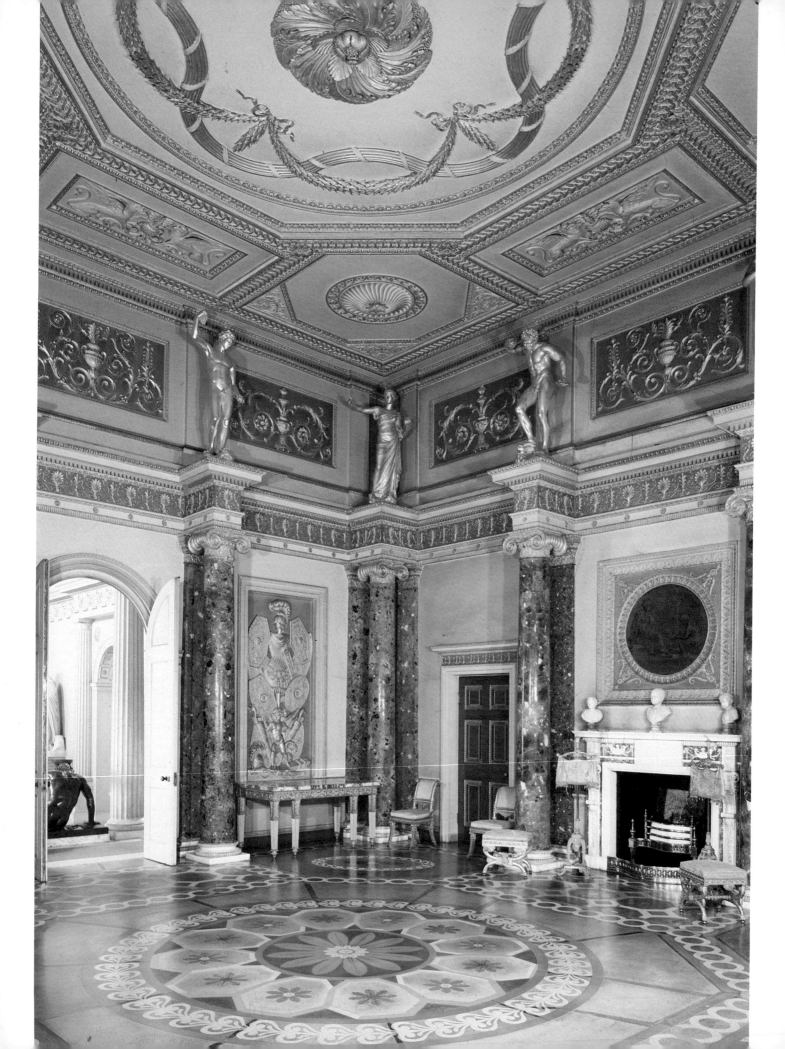

119 (left) The Ante-room
at Syon House, *by Robert
Adam In 1761, Adam
was commissioned by
the first Duke of
Northumberland to
remodel Syon House in
the antique style. This
richly coloured and
patterned room follows
on directly from the pale
grey and white Entrance
Hall. Twelve verde antico
columns with gilt Ionic
capitals and blue and gold
entablatures are offset
against the polished
scagliola floor, pale green
walls and mahogany and
gilt doors. Among Adam's
most 'Roman' interiors,
it shows one of his most
original uses of the
Classical Orders, with
unexpected features such
as the gilt statuary and
magnificent military
trophies*

120 (right) The Star
Chamber, Carlton House.
Watercolour. London,
William Drummond
Collection

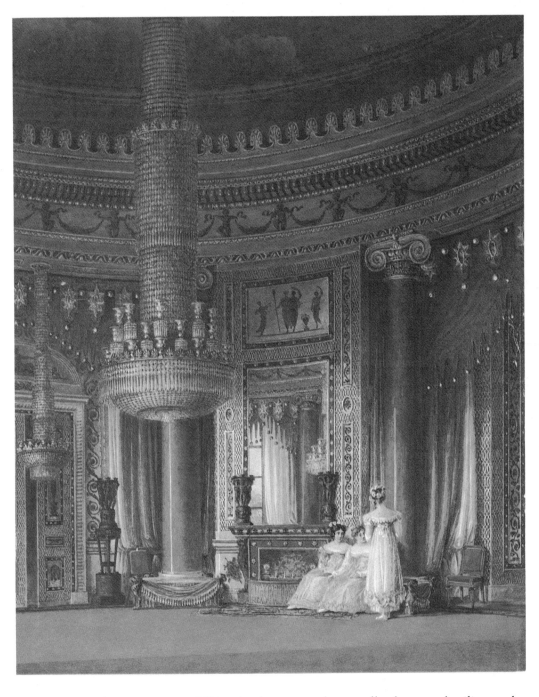

harmonious interiors in France (Plate 118). Built in 1762–8, all of the major rooms are rectangular, and decorated in soft tones of grey, white and other pale colours. Throughout, the wall-panelling and mirror-frames are rectilinear or arched, and the profiles of the mouldings and architraves strictly classical. A limited vocabulary of wreaths, swags, laurels, acanthus and trophies is sustained everywhere. Overdoors are strictly rectangular too, but because of Gabriel's immaculate sense of proportion and the use of decoration, the general atmosphere remains elegant rather than grand. From 1768–72 dates the Galerie Dorée in what is now the Ministry of Marine in Paris, where Gabriel makes greater use of a modified version of the *style Louis*

XIV, using heavy panels on walls, doors and ceilings – the contrast with the undecorated ceilings of the Petit Trianon could not be greater; Gabriel also uses the style in Louis XVI's library of 1774 at Versailles. No other European country reverted to a seventeenth-century style as inspiration in this way during the Neo-classical period, and Le Brun's modifications of Pietro da Cortona's Baroque style provided the starting point for many of the more solemn interiors of the period. Gabriel, for example, was able to refine Le Brun's style by making it more classical on the ceiling of the Queen's bedroom at Versailles.

Pierre Patte, who completed Blondel's *Cours d'architecture*, summed up these borrowings and the evolution of the new style when he discussed his own period's 'return to good taste':

To the good form of the last century's decorations we have added less severity, more delicacy, more variety in the shapes … in adopting rectangular forms, one may nonetheless, depending on the circumstances, adapt them to less serious contours more capable of producing agreeable interiors and less uniformity in the layout of apartments. The most admired ornaments of antiquity have been added to the decoration of interiors, such as acanthus leaves, laurel, festoons, *guilloches*, medallions, &c, to the extent that Architecture has resumed her rights over Sculpture.

Gabriel's main work as First Architect to Louis XV at Versailles was to create rooms of *commodité*, that is, small rooms which would provide greater comfort and intimacy than the *grands appartements*. Cochin noted that 'The more elevated socially the person, the smaller his apartment', a paradox borne out not only by the Petit Trianon, but also by Louis XV's *petits appartements* at Versailles. The fashion for small rooms began at the top of society and spread, and the *style Gabriel* suited their decoration to perfection – simple wall-panels, door-cases and cornices of classical restraint, offset by clean-cut chimney-pieces in fine marble surmounted by large, simple mirrors. With their wall surfaces painted grey, white or pale green, their ceilings plain white, these rooms created the classic French norm for elegant living: 'one lives in a comfort unknown to our parents and not yet attained by other nations', commented Voltaire. An interesting insight into decorative method is provided in a report on the King's chamber at Versailles by the decorator Peyrotte, who brought 'M. Gabriel a panel [drawn] on paper of the actual size of *boiserie* in the chamber, in the middle of which he proposes a trophy in the same style as the rest of the room'. This was obviously a cartoon or full-scale working drawing from which craftsmen could execute plasterwork or panelling.

Gabriel retired from royal service in 1775, one year after the death of Louis XV, but his architecture and interior decoration were widely imitated. The architect who learned most wisely from his style was Claude-Nicolas Ledoux (1736–1806). It now seems astonishing that Ledoux, later a leading Revolutionary architect, was initially one of the most sought-after of fashionable *hôtel* designers; and it was the *hôtels* in eighteenth-century Paris which led the way. In this way, they were the equivalent of the British country house and the Italian *palazzo*.

Ledoux's career was launched in 1762 with the interior of the Café Militaire in the Palais-Royal, now in the Musée Carnavalet. Its playful military *chic* is achieved by dividing large floor-length mirrors from panels bearing trophies of carved and gilded arms by long lictors' *fasces* supporting plumed helmets. The Café's success led to Ledoux's designing the Hôtel d'Uzès, in whose salon – also in the Carnavalet – he again used Roman military reliefs on the doors, with full-length wall-panels sculpted in exquisite low relief showing laurel trees supporting torches, medallions, lyres and other devices. While the simple gold and white of these rooms evokes the purity of Classicism, their glamorous effect is wholly of their period. Robert Adam admitted: 'To understand thoroughly the art of living, it is necessary, perhaps, to have passed some time among the French.'

In his designs of 1766 for the Hôtel d'Hallwyl, Ledoux can be seen developing the *style Gabriel*, and by the early 1770s his own intensely personal idiom is apparent in his salon design for the Hôtel de Montmorency. Slender rectangular panels frame elegant, elongated figures on circular bases with twisted fluting, which support garlands, festoons, flowers and torches extending to ceiling height; and from the simple arched overmantel mirrors hang a long tassel and two garlands looped up at either side. For the celebrated dancer Mlle Guimard, Ledoux designed the Hôtel Guimard, site of her notorious parties, and in the same year – 1770 – Mme du Barry's Pavilion at Louveciennes. The former was destroyed, and the Louveciennes interiors largely removed, but the pavilion's decoration is recorded in a watercolour by Moreau le Jeune, which shows rich coffered vaults, strictly applied Orders and rigidly rectangular door and window openings, often unrelieved by mouldings. Its elegant furnishings, also very advanced, included bronzes by the *ciseleur-fondeur* Pierre Gouthière (1732–1812/14), whose elaborately chased and gilded *bronzes d'ameublement* were said to have cost Mme du Barry more than a million livres, and the latest straight-legged chairs from the workshop of Louis Delanoise (1731–92), the leading Parisian chair-maker.

The elegant precision of Ledoux's interior style, and the sumptuous effects he obtained with the Classical vocabulary can be seen in the tiny boudoir he designed for Mme de Serilly, now in the Victoria and Albert Museum (Plate 115). Here he used another favourite device of the period – grotesques, which as we have seen were revived in the early Cinquecento in Italy by Raphael and Giovanni da Udine (see Plates 53 and 54). The grotesques in Raphael's Vatican Loggie were extensively imitated and copied by later artists, providing inspiration for much seventeenth-century French interior decoration and for the beginnings of Rococo arabesques. In 1765, Jombert's suite of engravings of the Loggie decorations appeared, and in the same year the projects for the decoration of the Hotel d'Uzès reflect their influence. The revival of grotesque decoration is largely due in this period to the mysterious Charles-Louis Clérisseau (1720–1820), painter (see Plate 132), architect, *cicerone* and decorator, who was deeply admired by contemporaries as different as Jefferson and Catherine the Great. Clérisseau used grotesques in his interiors at the Hôtel Grimrod de la Reynière of the mid-1770s and made their classically correct application instantly fashionable; with the general availability in Paris of Piranesi's *Various Ways of Decorating Fireplaces* after

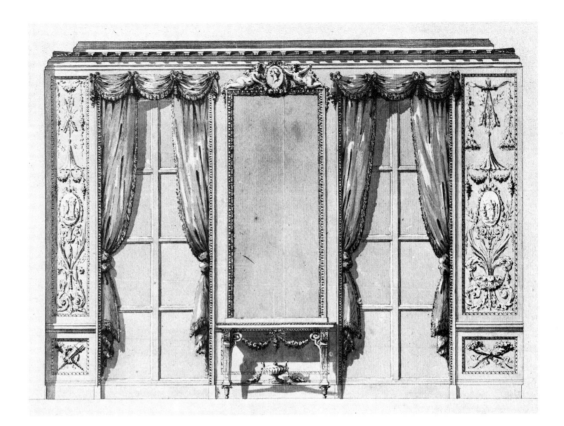

121 Project for a Salon de Compagnie, *1781, by Jean-François Thérèse Chalgrin (1739–1811). Paris, Musée des Arts Décoratifs*

1769, Etruscan and Egyptian details could be added to the Classical repertoire. A superb example of the fully evolved 'Etruscan style' in France is the Boudoir of Marie Antoinette at Fontainebleau (Plate 116), where the lavish detail, overdoor sculpture by Dauphin de Beauvais, and cloud-painted ceiling are far removed from the purity of Adam's Etruscan Room (Plate 127) at Osterley Park (1761–80).

Other French decorators of the early Neo-classical phase who require mention are Louis-Joseph Le Lorrain (1715–59), Jean-Charles Delafosse (1734–91) and Pierre-Louis Moreau-Desproux (1737–93). Le Lorrain's designs for festivals made during his stay in Rome in the 1740s pre-figure many developments in Paris in the following two decades. His interior designs for the castle of Åkerö in Sweden of 1754 use bulky columns, niches, statuary and festoons, and are possibly the first Neo-classical interiors of the century. Unlike Le Lorrain, Delafosse was trained as an architect, although his fastidious furniture designs have few rivals. His series of engravings, the *Nouvelle iconologie historique* of 1768, provided a corpus of illustrated Classical ornament without precedent. They place emphasis on heavy architectural forms such as swags, garlands and deeply fluted surfaces, and carry symbolic intent previously absent from Neo-classical motifs. Themes later used in Revolutionary decorations first appear in his designs, such as the arts, virtues, history, sciences or the occupations of man. In this respect his influence on crafts-men was considerable: his work as a decorator is exemplified by such interiors as the Hôtels Delbarre and Giox in Paris, where his feeling for contrasts of richly carved

detail (occasionally of an exuberance recalling Piranesi) with plain surfaces is highly developed.

Moreau-Desproux, who met his death at the guillotine, was another architect-designer of ability. His master-piece of interior decoration is the room from the Hôtel de Luynes now in the Louvre. In the Gabriel tradition, fluted Ionic pilasters with a rich carved cornice separate large arched mirrors and overdoor panels framing beribboned antique vases – all the detail being sumptuously gilded against a white background. His pupil, Jean-François Chalgrin (1739–1811), best known as the architect of the Arc de Triomphe, also designed many interiors, and one of these is of particular interest as it shows the type of curtains intended for a room with abundant grotesque decoration (Plate 121). Almost nothing survives of the delightful work of François-Joseph Bélanger (1745–1818), architect to Louis XVI's brother, the Comte d'Artois, for whom he designed the Pavilion of La Bagatelle in the Bois de Boulogne in 1777. Among the many well-preserved and meticulously prepared drawings by Bélanger is one for the Comte's bedroom, in the form of a classical tent with striped walls and lictors' *fasces*. Bélanger provides a link with the work of Adam and Sir William Chambers in Britain.

One French architect whose uniquely spectacular style of interior decoration has been seriously underestimated is Charles de Wailly (1729–98). In Rome, he was involved in archaeological excavations with Moreau-Desproux and others, and this, combined with his great knowledge of Italian Renaissance and Baroque architecture and stage-

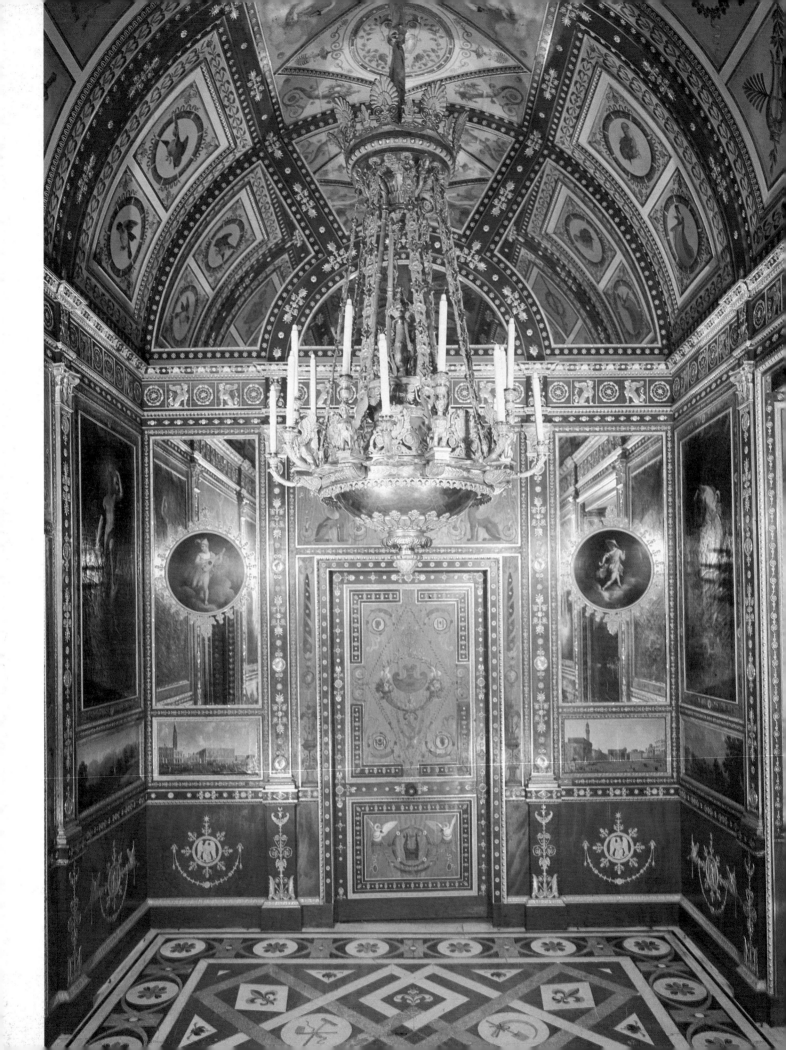

design (of which he was himself a master), resulted in a style more dramatic and large-scaled than that of his contemporaries. Unfortunately, his own house in Paris, the Hôtel d'Argenson (with opulent giant caryatids framing view-multiplying mirrors and supporting ceilings of Baroque profusion, recorded in the drawings of William Chambers), and his masterpiece, the Palazzo Spinola in Genoa, have all disappeared. De Wailly's own breathtaking drawings, together with engravings, record the impressive appearance of the great saloon at Palazzo Spinola, carried out in 1771–3 (Plate 123). Baroque in concept, its superb detail was Neo-classical, and was used with none of the timidity which might have spoiled its bravura effect. Although outside the mainstream of Neoclassical domestic interior decoration, it was to exercise considerable influence on French architects of the following century such as Charles Garnier – whose eclecticism it prefigures (see page 175).

In many ways, the British were the best prepared of any European nation for the advent of Neo-classicism: the anti-Baroque reforms of Lord Burlington, William Kent and the Palladian School had accustomed patrons to 'Romanized' interiors. The Palladian feature most important for the growth of Neo-classicism was the variety of room shapes, which, based on Palladio's reconstructions of Roman baths, filled great houses with suites of oblong, square, octagonal or circular rooms. Thus, a major English Neo-classical ground-plan like that of Adam's Syon House had an immediate predecessor in Lord Burlington's villa at Chiswick. Since the Rococo never gained much ground in Britain as a style of interior decoration, the way was open for the reforms which Adam instituted on his return from Italy in 1758, and his public were already receptive to many of his ideas on Classicism, if not on all aspects of interior decoration. It was Adam who dominated British architecture along with Sir William Chambers from about 1760 to 1790, and with James Wyatt and Henry Holland, they were the architects whose styles also led the way in interior decoration.

Of the four, Sir William Chambers (1723–92) and Henry Holland (1745–1806) were most influenced by French taste, the former through direct experience in Paris, the latter through assimilation of the *style Louis XVI* and the employment of a French leading assistant, J. P. T. Trécourt. Chambers was born in Sweden, and as a cadet in the Swedish East India Company he travelled extensively in the Far East and Europe. Unlike Adam, he first experienced early Neo-classicism in Paris, where he studied with Jacques-François Blondel and knew many leading architects and decorators, including de Wailly. He went to Italy in 1750, returning to England via Paris in 1755. His

experience of the Orient stood him in good stead, and his *Designs of Chinese Buildings*, published in 1757, was to remain a prime source for British designers seeking Chinese detail among his engravings of architecture, furniture and costumes. It is accuracy based on personal experience of his sources which distinguishes Chambers' book from others such as William Halfpenny's *New Designs for Chinese Temples* of 1750. The Chinese taste was already well-established for interior decoration in England, when Mrs Montagu in around 1752 decorated her Mayfair house in the 'barbarous gaudy goût of the Chinese' with the aid of John Linnell, who also designed the Chinese Room at Badminton House (1754). In 1759, Chambers, now working for some of Britain's most important patrons, produced the first edition of his *Treatise on Civil Architecture*, later (1791) more correctly entitled *A Treatise on the Decorative Part of Civil Architecture*. Like Adam, he was eclectic, and the fireplaces, doors, windows and ceilings in his book reveal sources as widely different as Peruzzi, Ammanati, Bernini and Pietro da Cortona.

In his own interiors, however, French taste influenced Chambers to produce restrained designs of great personal distinction, as at Peper Harrow in Surrey (begun 1765) for the 3rd Viscount Midleton, where he adopts many early Neo-classical French details – garlands, acanthus, sphinxes and lyres. One of his major contributions to interior decoration, the staircase of Carrington House, Whitehall (demolished in 1886), combined the double loggia type derived from Longhena's monumental staircase at S. Giorgio Maggiore in Venice with huge plaster wall decorations of distinctly French inspiration. Chambers' interiors in his major public building, Somerset House, London, give an idea of the understated style he preferred, but he was at his best on a small scale.

Chambers was essentially an architect who also designed interiors. Robert Adam (1728–92), however, was essentially an interior designer who also created architecture, although his interior style often took over on his exteriors: he saw decoration in flat two-dimensional terms, naturally suited to linear ornament. Not surprisingly, he regarded the ceiling – usually flat in his interiors – as the key to the room as a whole. At his best, Adam may be ranked among the finest decorators of any country or period, and he is unique in this field in having his own style named after him. The ingredients of that style are many, and might easily lead to his being categorized as much as a Romantic as a Neo-classicist, were not his interiors capable of an extraordinary purity (Plate 117). The second son of the distinguished Scottish architect William Adam, Robert travelled in France and Italy in 1754, where he befriended Clérisseau. During Adam's two-year stay in Rome, Clérisseau formed his taste for every aspect of antique architecture and ornament, which he mastered with astonishing facility.

From Clérisseau, Adam must have learned how to

122 Sala di Platino in the Casita del Labrador, *Aranjuez, near Madrid, Spain*

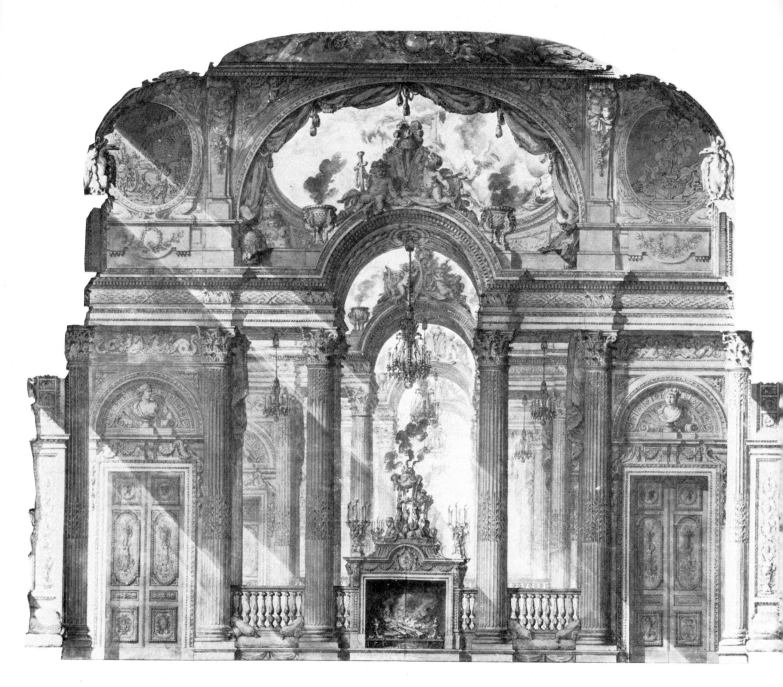

123 Longitudinal section of the saloon in the Palazzo Spinola, Genoa, *1771–3, by Charles de Wailly (1729–98). Pen and brown wash (133 × 161 cm). Paris, Musée des Arts Décoratifs A painter, architect and decorator, De Wailly was also active as a theatre designer, and in his designs for this vast saloon he exploited dramatic lighting effects to heighten the lavish profusion of decorative detail. The oval ceiling was painted by Antoine François Callet, and the gilt stucco ceiling caryatids and large bas-reliefs are by Philippe de Beauvais. Much of the detail is Louis XIV in origin, but the proportions and application are, on an inflated scale, wholly Louis XVI in effect. The chimney-piece, with its smoking tripod supported on sphinxes reflected endlessly in huge mirrors, recalls Piranesi's* Diverse maniere d'adornare i camini, *which, like this entire ensemble, has its roots in the profusion of the Baroque*

refine antique forms, notably the grotesque ornament which the Frenchman had made so popular in Paris, and which was also practised with such success there by the Rousseau brothers. Like Chambers, Adam too studied the architecture and decoration of the Italians, in particular Michelangelo, Raphael, Giulio Romano, Giovanni da Udine, Domenichino and Algardi, but his designs (Plate 124) lack the vigour which distinguished these artists' work and he is occasionally somewhat effete in his application of their ideas. Although he never visited Greece, he borrowed from the engraved works of Robert Wood, Le Roy, and Stuart and Revett. Nonetheless, he remained 'Bob the Roman', following faithfully in Piranesi's footsteps in his championship of Roman and later of 'Etruscan' decoration. His borrowings are always endowed with a new relevance in their updated settings: from Wood's *Ruins of Palmyra* came inspiration for ceilings like that of the Dining Room at Osterley, the frieze from Trajan's Column appears in the gallery at Croome Court, the gallery carpet at Syon is derived from a mosaic at Ostia and the trophies in the Syon ante-room from those of Augustus (Plate 119).

Adam's visit to Spalato (Split) resulted in his great folio, the *Ruins of the Palace of the Emperor Diocletian*, published in 1764, six years after his return to London. This confirmed his reputation as an antiquarian, and it cannot be doubted that he had a greater knowledge of Roman decorative detail than any contemporary British architect; his avid assimilation of 'antique cornices, friezes, figures, bas reliefs, vases, altars' in the form of originals, drawings and engravings provided him with an incomparably vast source for use on his return to Britain where he and his brother James soon established a flourishing practice.

Although his exterior architecture was fundamentally Palladian in its approach to proportion and outline, Adam was opposed from the outset to Palladian heaviness. He aimed to replace 'the massive entablature, the pon-

derous compartment ceiling, the tabernacle frame' with a 'beautiful variety of light mouldings gracefully formed and delicately enriched ... in the beautiful spirit of antiquity'. In the preface to the *Works in Architecture of Robert and James Adam* (1773–9) the brothers claim that their designs had 'brought about, in this country, a kind of revolution in the whole system of this elegant and useful art', and this was scarcely an exaggeration (see Plate 125). Instead of the massive forms and individualized emphases on door-case, ceiling and chimney-piece, Adam preferred to unify all his surfaces with one style of ornament, using wherever possible a flat ceiling with no coving. This approach lent itself admirably to the task of fitting his interiors into existing shells, as in three of the greatest houses with which he was involved, and which reveal his talent at its most brilliant – Syon House, Kedleston Hall and Osterley Park. In these interiors, which were begun during the 1760s along with Kenwood House, Harewood House and others, Adam's liberation from the tentative, somewhat heavy style of Hatchlands (1759) is rapidly completed. Not only do they contain superb examples of his grotesque, or grotesque-derived, style at its best – using

124 Design for Ceiling of the Drawing Room, Northumberland House, *London, by Robert Adam. Sir John Soane Museum*

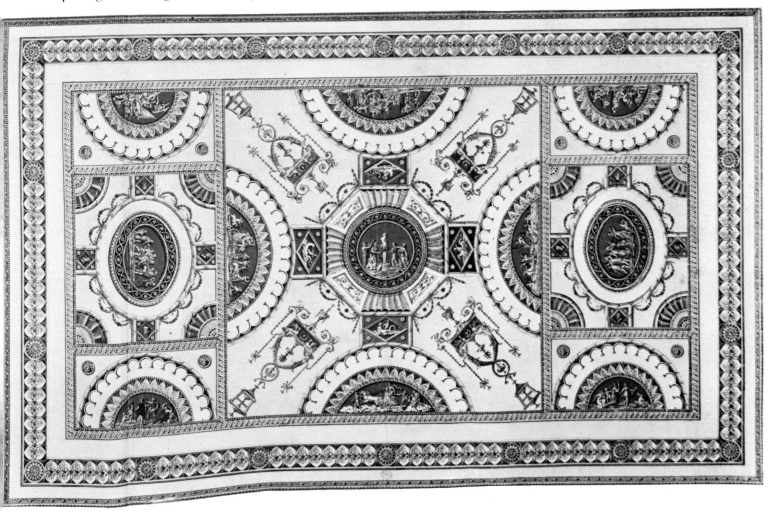

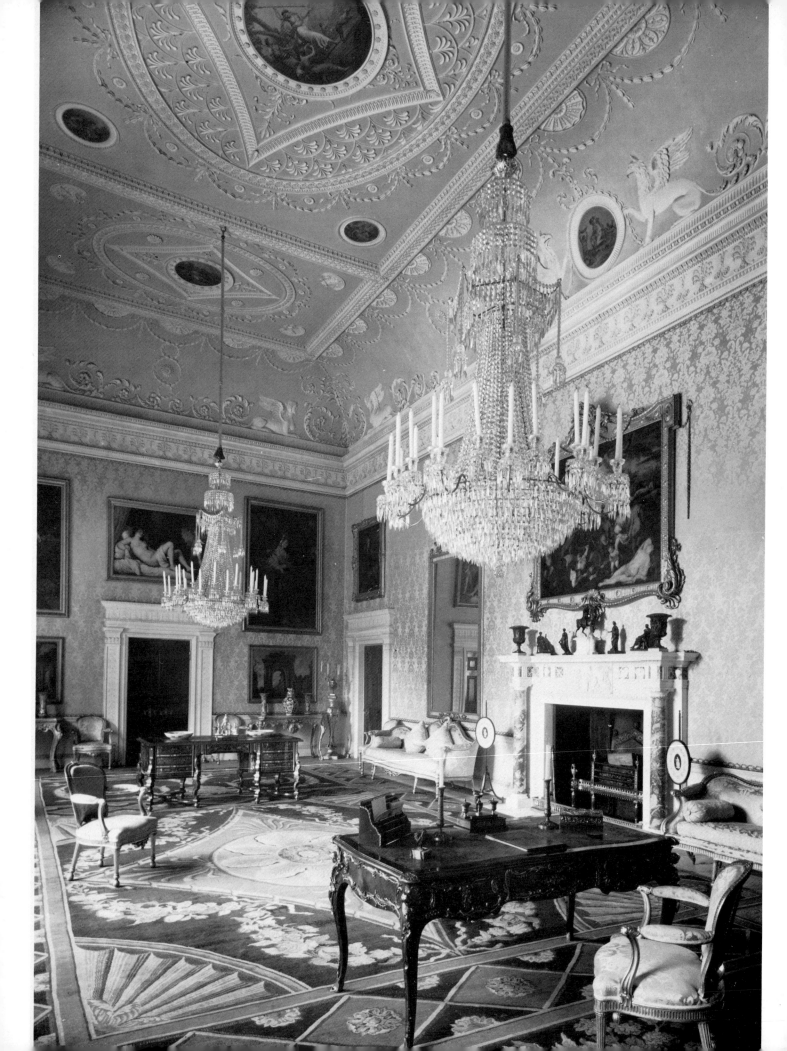

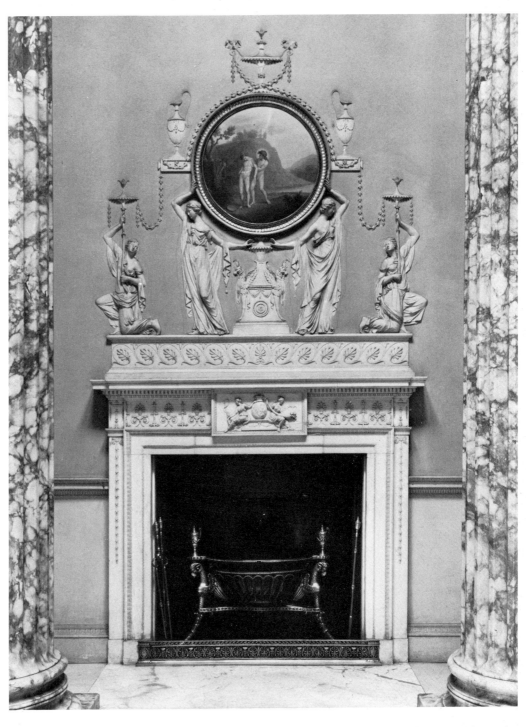

125 *(left)* The Saloon, Saltram House, *Devon, by Robert Adam   Adam's designs for Saltram's interior decoration are dated 1768, and the Saloon is one of the most complete examples of his style at its most refined, since much of the furniture, metalwork and carpets are by him. Its pale blue silk-hung walls are offset by the Renaissance-inspired door-cases and chimney-piece and the festive plasterwork of the magnificent coved ceiling with its swags, palmettes, sphinxes, griffins and inset oil paintings. Despite its grandeur, the first impression is one of aristocratic restraint, emphasized by the delicacy of all the ornament*

126 *(right)* Marble Hall fireplace, Kedleston Hall, *Derbyshire, 1759–65*

his favourite pale green, blue, pink or other backgrounds, relieved by small inset paintings – they also have interiors in his other 'manners'. At Kedleston, in Derbyshire, the magnificent hall has elaborate Corinthian columns offset by plain walls and two superbly delicate chimney-pieces (Plate 126), while Syon boasts the remarkable ante-room, also in a more monumental style using scagliola columns supposedly dredged from the Tiber. The 'movement' (expressing 'the rise and fall, the advance and recess ... [which] add greatly to the picturesque of the composition'), which Adam prized so highly in architec-

ture, is felt in the contrast experienced in moving from the lofty Syon entrance hall with its Cinquecento detailing painted grey and white, through this vividly coloured ante-room to the paler dining room, the sumptuous silk-hung drawing room into the minutely detailed long gallery.

At Osterley is the best surviving example (apart from Home House in Portman Square, London) of the style confusingly called 'Etruscan' by Adam. In the *Works*, the Etruscan style is presented as a novelty: 'It is ... remarkable, that neither in Adrian's Villa [*sic*], where so much attention was paid to elegance and variety ... nor in any part of Herculaneum or Pompeii, has any fragment been yet produced of interior decoration, executed in the taste now before us.' This is scarcely surprising, since the style was derived from Greek red- and black-figure vases, then thought to be Etruscan in origin, and collected with ever-increasing avidity by connoisseurs. Another Adam Etruscan interior was Lady Derby's dressing room in Derby House in Grosvenor Square, London, demolished in 1862. Like Home House (1775–7), Derby House contained rooms with a remarkable variety of shapes and decoration within a comparatively small space, and a 'third drawing room' with a segmental cross-vault possibly deriving from the Villa Madama loggia (Plate 54) and anticipating some of Soane's ceilings.

During the period of Adam's dominance of the country house practice (1759–75) few large new houses had been initiated, and so his talent as a decorator found its outlet in pre-existing buildings. In the 1760s he had created 'Gothick' interiors for the Duke of Northumberland at Alnwick Castle, but his interiors within his own 'castellated' Culzean Castle, Ayrshire, of 1775–90 are stubbornly, superbly Classical. By 1780 the novelty of his style began to wear thin, and he was attacked for what Chambers called his 'filigrane toy-work'. The way was now open for Henry Holland and James Wyatt, who chronologically and temperamentally span the transitional period from Neo-classicism to early Romanticism: Wyatt was to build that epitome of Romanticism, Fonthill Abbey.

Holland assisted the landscape gardener 'Capability' Brown, and married his daughter. Because of his associations with the Whig aristocracy, he was entrusted with the reconstruction of the Prince of Wales's town residence, Carlton House, which must certainly have been his masterpiece and one of the most delightful interiors of the period (Plate 120). No single interior survives, although the Chinese Drawing Room appears in Thomas Sheraton's *Cabinet-maker and Upholsterer's Drawing Book* and in Pyne's *Royal Residences*. Unlike Adam, Holland seems to have had little real feeling for *ensembles*, and many of his surviving interiors have a somewhat blank appearance, relieved, however, by the superb detail of which he was a master.

In 1787, Dominique Daguerre was importing 'the mirrors, beds, ormolu, bronzes and quantities of other furnishings' for Holland at Carlton House. French imports were no novelty (Adam's use of Boucher's Gobelins tapestries at Osterley in 1775 being a prime example), but Holland deliberately set out to evoke the latest French interiors for his strongly Francophile patrons, using French craftsmen and assistants. While unavoidably influenced by Adam, Holland's version of the Louis XVI style is recognizably personal, as in his interiors at Southill where the splendid library with its concave-cornered fitted bookcases beneath tall pier-glasses and Etruscan-cum-Louis XVI Boudoir with a ceiling by Delabrière show his style at its best. Of particular beauty are his chimney-pieces, such as the one in

the Yellow Drawing Room at Althorpe in Northamptonshire and the one from Carlton House's Chinese Drawing Room, now in Buckingham Palace. At Southill, the drawing room chimney-piece has a favourite Holland device, carved figures recessed at either side, while at the centre of the gilded pelmet-boxes eagles support the draperies. Holland's attention to detail even extended to heated window seats.

James Wyatt (1746–1813), one of a distinguished dynasty of architects, was in every sense larger than life, and can be said to have squandered a brilliant talent through persistent debauchery and irresponsibility. Catherine the Great invited him to be her architect (but eventually appointed Charles Cameron in his stead). With the success of his Pantheon in London (1770–2) his popularity rivalled that of the Adams. He returned from his Italian studies with a love of Raphael and Palladio, but his work in 'restoring' many English cathedrals earned him the title of 'Wyatt the Destroyer' from Pugin. He built two huge Gothic houses, Fonthill Abbey in Wiltshire and Ashridge in Hertfordshire: the surviving interiors at Ashridge are somewhat grim. His view of the many styles becoming popular in the 1770s was that of a convinced Classicist: 'Grecian must be Grecian – but fancies – such as Gothic, Moorish, Chinese Etc. might be imitated – some of them [are] capable of being reduced to rules.' Wyatt's own house had interiors in various styles, and he could turn his hand to almost anything – his remodellings at Windsor Castle included revived Baroque complete with 'Grinling Gibbons' carving and painted ceilings in the manner of the originals there. From the outset, he worked in various styles, ranging from papery Gothick at Lee Priory (1782) and Sheffield Park, Sussex (1776–7), through the serene classical perfection of Heveningham Hall, Suffolk, of around 1780–4, to the cathedral scale of Fonthill Abbey (Plate 145). Keeping patrons angrily waiting throughout the country, Wyatt capriciously went his own way, but succeeded nevertheless in creating some of the most elegant interiors of his age.

To a certain extent, he suffered from the same complaint as Holland – an inability to wholly integrate decorative detail into his all-over designs. This is evident in the famous Cupola Room of 1772 at Heaton Hall, Lancashire. Decorated by Biagio Rebecca to Wyatt's designs, the sum total of grotesque pilaster panels, sphinxes, mirrors, inset paintings and domed ceiling is wanting in unity; and in the Drawing Room at Bowden Park, Wiltshire (1796), Classical figures in low relief roundels, ovals and oblongs sit somewhat uncomfortably in large, otherwise unrelieved empty spaces. The interiors at Heveningham represent his greatest success, and although he had returned from Italy to find taste 'corrupted by the Adams', he was not above abstracting from their work features which he

127 The Etruscan Room, Osterley Park House, *c. 1775–9*

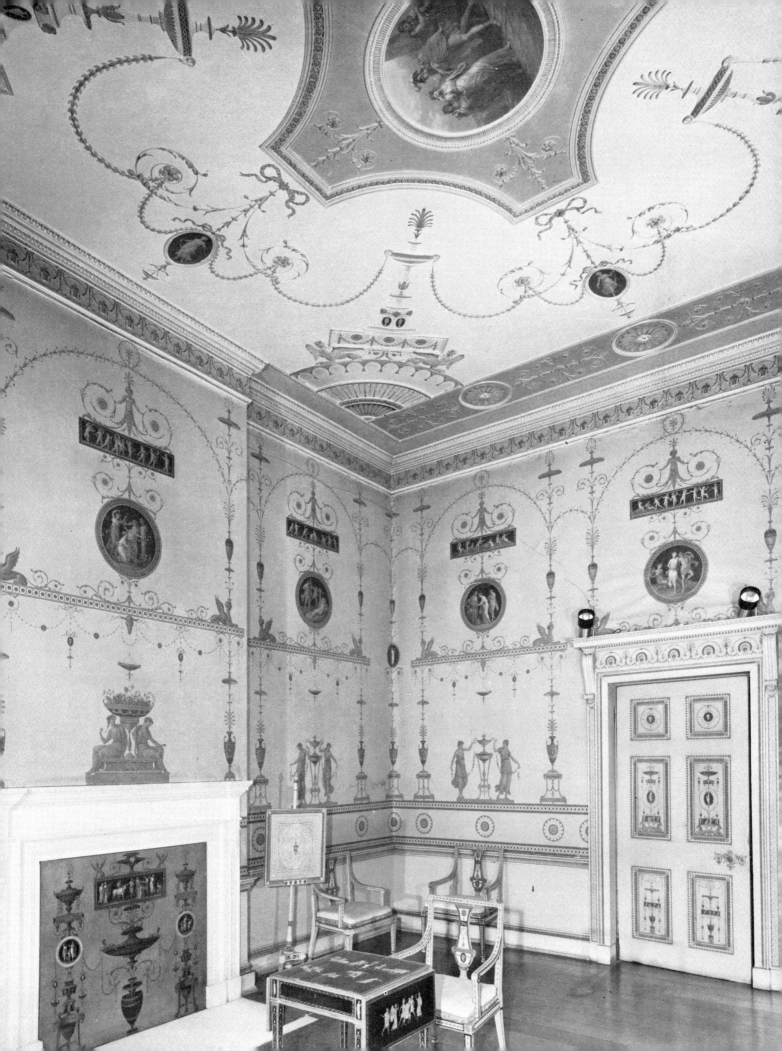

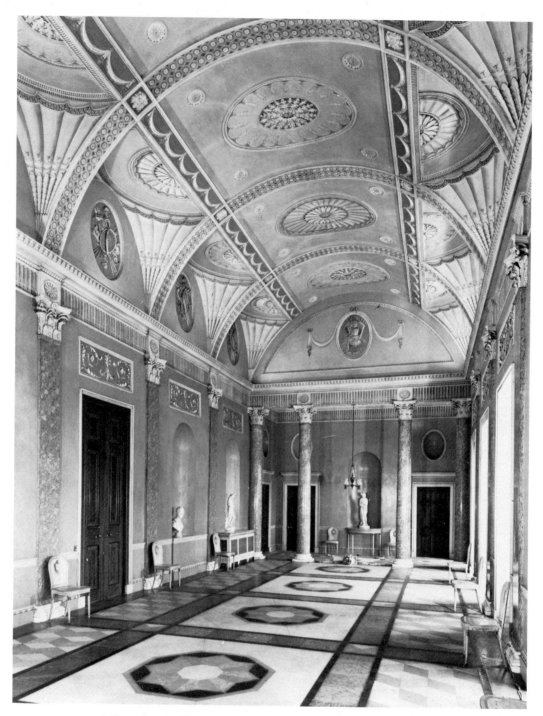

128 Entrance Hall, Heveningham Hall, Suffolk, *by James Wyatt, 1781–4*

admired. The Entrance Hall (Plate 128) is perhaps more 'masculine' than anything by Adam, the effectively plain wall surfaces articulated mainly by 'architectural' features – doors, windows, niches, pilasters. The combination of the richly inventive vault with the lower zone is one of the master touches of Neo-classicism.

The transition from the eighteenth to the nineteenth century in Britain was marked by one striking difference from the situation in Europe – Napoleon did not succeed in extending his Empire across the English Channel. This

was of fundamental importance for the differing evolutions of the two contemporary styles which distinguish the period from around 1800 to 1820, the Empire style in France and the Regency style in Britain. Through the various Napoleonic courts established as widely apart as Florence, Kassel and Aranjuez, the Directory, Consulate and Empire styles spread rapidly throughout Europe, aided by prefabrication in the form of such rooms as Percier and Fontaine's Sala di Platino in the Casita del Labrador at Aranjuez (Plate 122). The Bavarian cities of

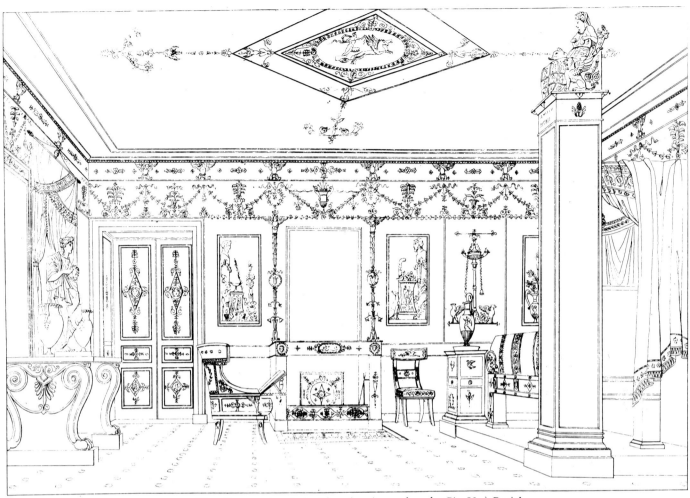

129 'Vue Perspective de la Chambre à coucher du Cit. V. à Paris'.
Plate 13 of Recueil des décorations intérieurs *by Percier and Fontaine, Paris, 1812*

Munich and Würzburg eagerly adopted the Empire style, and some of the most beautiful but least-known interiors in the latest Parisian manner by Grandjean de Montigny survive in Schloss Wilhelmshöhe at Kassel.

In Russia a pure and somewhat severe classical style came to dominate the new capital of St Petersburg, reflecting the presence of French and Italian architects and the mainly French staff at the recently founded (1757) Academy of Fine Arts. Jean-Baptiste Vallin de la Mothe (1729–1800), Charles-Louis Clérisseau (see page 142) and Giacomo Quarenghi (1744–1817) all worked here, the first being responsible for the Old Hermitage of the late 1760s. Clérisseau's pupil Charles Cameron (*c.* 1740–1812) extended Catherine II's palace at Tsarskoe Selo: he decorated the private rooms in the Pompeian style, while favouring milky glass, elaborate plasterwork, mirrors and columns with bronze bases and capitals for the reception rooms. In his famous Agate Pavilion, intricate inlaid patterns of agate and malachite are the outstanding feature.

The social changes which affected all Europe were reflected in interior decoration and furnishing. Whereas Adam, Wyatt and Chambers had directed their attentions to the upper echelons of British society, the aim of many early nineteenth-century designers was to reach a wider audience. This they achieved through their publications. Of these, the most important were the *Recueil de décorations intérieures* by Charles Percier and Pierre François Léonard Fontaine, published from 1801 in instalments and in a single volume in 1812, Thomas Hope's *Household Furniture and Interior Decoration* of 1807, and its immediate offspring, George Smith's *A Collection of Designs for Household Furniture and Decoration* of 1808.

The *Recueil* is by far the most original work and contains a stimulating introduction, and superb line engravings showing a wide variety of interiors (Plate 129) and details of their ornament and furnishings. Ceilings, chimney-pieces, furniture and metalwork are all represented, forming a record of most of Percier and Fontaine's major designs up to that date. In some ways, the book and its authors' attitude signal the birth of the twentieth century's 'designer cult' since they leave the reader in no doubt as to the meaning of 'taste'. It was of the essence in their designs that every element had its predestined – and often fixed – position in a room. Some of their interiors were designed around the immense carved beds, for both night and day use, which constitute such an important part of the *Recueil*'s plates.

Percier and Fontaine were particularly well-equipped to launch a revolution in interior decoration having spent the years 1787 to 1790 in Rome. In 1798, they published their *Palais, maisons ... à Rome*, which demonstrates that, like Robert Adam, their decorative vocabulary derived from a wide variety of sources, by no means all Classical. In his *Monuments de Paris*, Percier says:

It should be recognized that the beauty and perfection of the works of the fifteenth century are more applicable to our needs than those of the Greeks and Romans ... The majority are remarkable ... for the delicacy and happy choice of their ornament, for the pleasing variety of the materials of which they are composed and, above all, for the harmony of their rich effects and by their outstanding taste ... the true perfection of art consists less in the discovery of unknown things than in the judicious use of those elements already sanctioned by custom and taste.

Thus, Percier and Fontaine concentrated on the work of the Renaissance architects Bramante, Peruzzi and Antonio da Sangallo, rather in the way their contemporary Ingres studied Raphael. By grafting their decorative innovations onto the antique, they achieved a style of the utmost refinement, which also, incidentally, conformed to the French academic tradition of allegiance to the best Italian models.

Their designs found immediate followers and copyists throughout Europe, among them Hope, Pietro Ruga in Italy and the 'Russian' Thomas de Thomon. (The Tsar Alexander ordered watercolours of their interiors at the Tuileries in 1809–15.) Their first joint official commission was the preparation of designs for the furnishings of the Salle de la Convention at the Tuileries, and during the Consulate they were entrusted with the restoration of the former royal palaces which still bear the imprint of their talent for reshaping existing interiors. It was the more elaborate Empire style which dominated the decoration of Fontainebleau, Compiègne and Rambouillet. At the Elysée Palace their Murat Room of 1805–6 survives in part and its delicate columns and pilasters recall earlier Neoclassicism, while the bedroom of the Empress Marie-Louise at Compiègne is closer to Italian Quattrocento and Cinquecento models. They began the remodelling of the interiors at the Château de Malmaison outside Paris while Napoleon was First Consul and these rooms chart the development from the Consulate style of the Council Chamber – which adopted the form of a tent supported by 'pikes, *fasces* and insignia, between which are suspended trophies of arms recalling the most celebrated warring nations of the globe' – to the more developed decoration of the Music Room and the Bedroom of the Empress Josephine. The elegant simplicity of the Music Room (Plate 136) (whose panelling and slender paired columns reflect the Library in the Château) is far removed from the full-blown Empire style, as is the Empress's famous Bedroom

with its painted 'open' sky above a Roman Imperial tent of crimson cashmere supported on delicate gilded columns framing a gilded swan-decorated bed by Jacob-Desmalter.

Although they were architects, Percier and Fontaine's principal interest was always decoration and furniture. They believed that 'furniture is too much a part of interior decoration for the architect to remain indifferent to it', and the precision and sophistication of many of their interiors, using elaborately ornamented surfaces of many materials, exactly parallels the somewhat architectural furniture designed to be placed in them. They also worked in close collaboration with the finest cabinet-makers of the day such as Georges Jacob (1739–1814) whose work forms a bridge between the Louis XVI and Empire styles. His business was passed on to his sons Georges II and François-Honoré Georges, who took the name Jacob-Desmalter.

Possibly one of the most exciting groups of interiors to survive largely intact from the period is at the Hôtel de Beauharnais in Paris, which belonged to Napoleon's stepson, Eugène de Beauharnais, and his sister Hortense, Queen of Holland. The designers and craftsmen responsible for the Hôtel's interiors remain anonymous, but the lofty Music Room, brilliantly painted in the manner of Prud'hon and Girodet with large figures and Pompeian and Assyrian motifs, reflects a taste for the most intense of colours in decorative detail. Not surprisingly, Napoleon balked at the immense bill of one and a half million francs for this pleasure palace, but the degree of lavishness achieved fully justifies the expense, in retrospect at least. The Turkish boudoir (with a painted frieze of almost *kitsch* pseudo-Orientalism), the silk-hung Pompeian-ceilinged bedroom of Queen Hortense complete with immense columned bed and swan furniture, and the spectacular bathroom, whose skilfully placed mirrors multiply myriad reflections, typify the Empire interior at its most sybaritic. The Salon of the Seasons too retains all of its original decoration (Plate 137). Queen Hortense's Boudoir in her *hôtel* in the rue Cerutti provides an insight into the reaction to the ideal of antique correctness which, ironically, lies at the core of many of the finest Neoclassical interiors, shortly to burgeon into Historicism under the impact of the early Romantic movement.

In their emphasis on military ornament interiors of the Empire period reflected historical events of the time (the Council Chamber and the Empress's Bedroom at Malmaison, for example), and Napoleon's Egyptian Campaign of 1798–9 created a new vogue throughout Europe. Dominique Vivant, Baron Denon (1754–1825), had been one of the many scholars who accompanied the campaign, and his *Voyage dans la Basse et Haute Egypte*, first published in Paris in 1802, had appeared in English, Italian and German editions by 1808. Although Piranesi had introduced Egyptian detail in his designs for ornament (see pages 142–3), it was Denon's engravings of Egyptian architecture and detail which created the fashion called *Retour d'Egypte*.

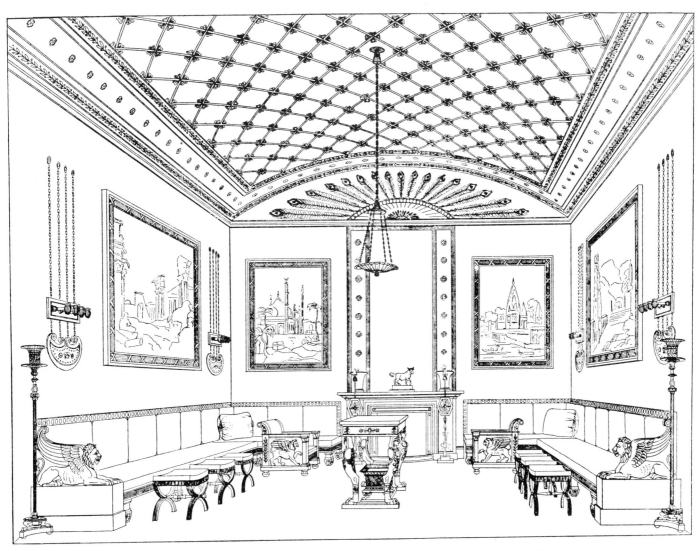

130 The Indian Room. *Plate VI of* Household Furniture and Interior Decoration *by Thomas Hope, 1807*

One other French designer of this time deserves attention. He was the eccentric Pierre de la Mésangère (1761–1831), whose fashionable journal, the *Collection des meubles et objets de goût*, appeared between 1802 and 1835. Its total of almost four hundred plates offered the public accessible versions of the more elaborate designs made for the Imperial family, and its continuing popularity throughout Europe shows how the Empire style lingered on to merge into the *style Charles X* in France and the Biedermeier style in Germany and Austria. Other pattern books of the period include Duguers de Montrosier's *Recueil* of 1806 and the collection of 72 plates engraved by Mme Soyer after Santi's designs (published in 1828). The latter is a fascinating record of the elaborate draperies of all kinds applied to windows and beds in this period and increasingly extended for use in every part of the room as the century advanced.

In England, Thomas Hope evolved a personal style from these Continental prototypes. He loathed 'the degraded French school of the middle of the last century' and wanted to create 'a deviation from the prevailing style'. His London house so pleased him that he issued tickets of admission to Royal Academy members to view it! In a sense, his approach was more Romantic, since there were interiors in Egyptian, Greek, Roman, Turkish, Chinese and even Hindu styles, while at The Deepdene, his country house in Surrey, one room – 'the only eccentric room' – was 'decorated in a heavy Egyptian style, with a quantity of dull red paint'. The constituent elements of Hope's style were essentially those of Percier and Fontaine, comprising, in his words, '... that prodigious variety of details and of embellishments ... of instruments and of trophies, of terms, caryatids, griffins, chimaeras, scenic masks, sacrificial implements, civil and military emblems ...' Hope, like Pelagio Palagi, was a distinguished collector, and assembled a large group of antique sculpture and vases, Italian paintings, and works by the leading Neoclassical sculptors Flaxman, Thorvaldsen and Canova. In 1790 he commissioned Flaxman to sculpt a group of *Cephalus and Aurora*, and at Duchess Street constructed

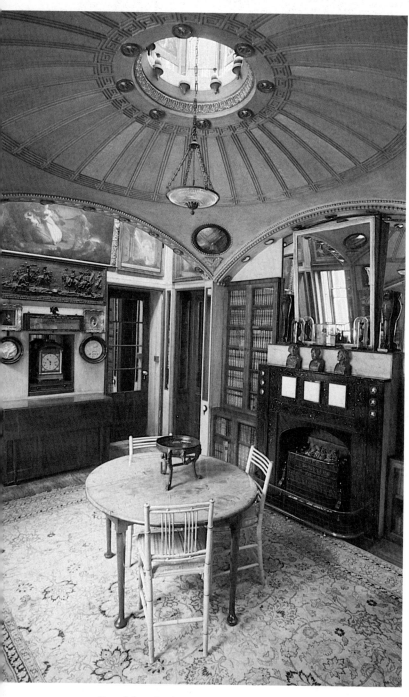

131 Breakfast Parlour, No. 13 Lincoln's Inn Fields *(Soane Museum), 1812, by Sir John Soane   This interior encapsulates the finest features of Soane's picturesque approach to interior design – his use of wide depressed arches springing from fragile supports, his love for incised 'Greek' decoration and his exploitation of surprising effects. Although light falls from the dome lantern, the concealed lighting on the far wall is stronger, thereby separating the wall visually from the domed area. Above the chimney-piece, a mirror is set at an angle in front of others, while the ceiling is punctuated by circular convex mirrors. Nothing is left to chance, and the proportions and finish of the bookcases are meticulously calculated; a certain heaviness prefigures Victorian interiors*

the remarkable 'Flaxman or Star Room' to house them which must have been breathtaking in its effect. Hope's express wish was to 'contribute my mite not only towards remotely giving new food to the industry of the poor, but new decorum to the expenditure of the rich'.

Hope's Indian Room (Plate 130) was designed to display four large paintings of buildings in India by Thomas Daniell, and was fitted with 'a low sofa, after the eastern fashion ... [a] ceiling, imitated from those panels in Turkish palaces ... [and] a canopy of trellis work, or reeds tied together with ribbons'. The room's colours were 'everywhere very vivid, and very strongly contrasted' – deep crimson, sky blue, pale yellow, azure, sea-green and gold of various shades. Although Hope had travelled in the East, there was nothing remotely Indian about the shape or proportions of this room, which retained a rigorously Neo-classical air: gone were the *chinoiseries* and *turqueries* of the eighteenth century. It was left to the Prince Regent to create the archetypal exotic interior of the period at the Brighton Pavilion, a group of rooms unrivalled in early nineteenth-century Europe for their fantasy and daring (Plate 142). An interesting extension of the Indian idea, however, is found in the Otaheitisches Kabinett in the Castle of Pfaueninsel at Berlin, where the decorator Burnat transformed a circular domed room into a *trompe-l'oeil* bamboo cabin framing 'views' of Eastern landscape by P. L. Lütke. A further example of the assimilation of heterogeneous elements from Egypt, Pompeii and Cinquecento Italy into a fine group of interiors was George Dance II's Stratton Park in Hampshire, of which only the portico survives.

Apart from Hope, the most interesting innovator of the early nineteenth century was perhaps Sir John Soane (1753–1837), a pupil of George Dance. Many of Soane's ambitions were thwarted and his masterpiece, the Bank of England, has been demolished. His few years in Italy (1776–9) profoundly influenced his thought, and under the direct impact of Piranesi he retained a feeling not only for megalomaniac scale, but also for encrustations of decorative detail derived from a wide variety of often unexpected sources. French Neo-classicism also influenced his early period. During the 1780s he worked on various country houses under the influence of Holland and Wyatt, but the years 1791 to 1806, when he created superb interiors at Wimpole, Buckingham House and Tyringham, were his most fertile. At Bentley Priory, Middlesex (1789–99), the entrance hall typifies his approach to the Neo-classical vocabulary inherited from his immediate predecessors: above a chaste application of fluted Doric columns springs a vault painted with vigorous Grecian ornament centred on a large central circle of Greek-key motif. From the same years dates the magnificent staircase at Buckingham House, Pall Mall, with Ionic scagliola columns and impressive caryatids above.

Soane's talent for interior decoration found its full Romantic realization in his own house at Lincoln's Inn

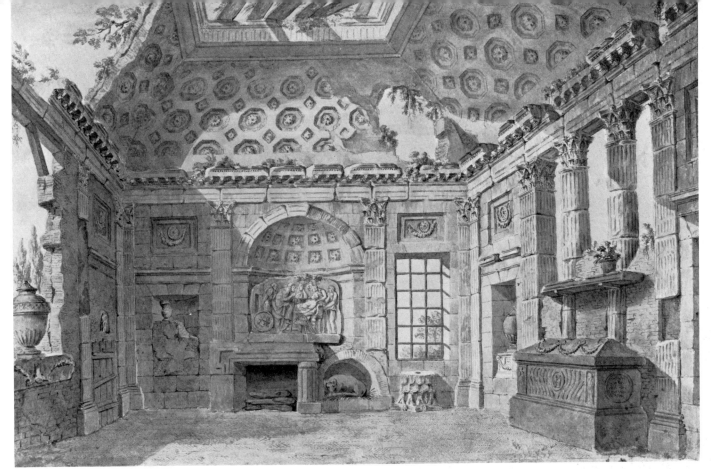

132 Design for the Ruin Room, *by Charles-Louis Clérisseau (1720–1820). S. Trinità dei Monti, Rome. Before 1767* This trompe-l'oeil *room was painted by Clérisseau for the mathematician Père le Sueur and his associate in the convent of S. Trinità dei Monti, and is one of the fullest expressions of the passion for the antique. Clérisseau's brother-in-law described its original appearance: 'On entering one imagined that one was seeing the cella of a temple, enriched with antique fragments that had survived the ravages of time …*

To enhance this effect even further, all the furniture was in keeping: the bed was a richly decorated basin, the fireplace a combination of various fragments, the desk a damaged antique sarcophagus, the table and seats, a fragment of a cornice and inverted capitals respectively. Even the dog, the faithful guardian of this style of furniture, was housed in the remains of a vase.' The room, which survives without its furnishings, was a source of inspiration to Adam, Piranesi and others

Fields, London, and Pitzhanger Manor, Ealing, of 1800–2. Vanbrugh, creator of Blenheim Palace (1705), was Soane's hero in English architecture, and Soane derived the love of 'movement' from him. Many of Soane's domestic interiors reflect the advances made in his architecture. The picturesque use of top-lighting, introduced in the Bank interiors, became a feature of many of his rooms, and creates highly unexpected effects at Lincoln's Inn Fields. The wealth of invention displayed throughout this house baffles brief description: a wall-painting borrowed from Angelo Campanella's engravings of the Villa Negroni at Rome is turned into a real wall surface, quasi-Gothic hanging arches are used on a miniature scale for the dining room, convex mirrors are set into ceilings (Plate 131); there are deceptive views from one room to another, changes in room level and, most extraordinary of all, the Monk's Parlour with its massed archaeological fragments.

Many of the most distinguished British Classical interiors of the Regency and early Victorian periods show a tendency to an increasingly heavy use of the Orders and a pronounced diminution in the surface ornamentation of wall surfaces. This was in keeping with the spirit of the Greek Revival, which gained ground considerably in Britain between 1803 and 1809, when the style ceased to be merely picturesque and triumphed as the 'official' style for both public and private architecture. In exteriors, heavy Doric columns, fluted or unfluted, proliferated, and many architects turned their domestic interiors into Greek temple variants. Staircase halls were the obvious setting for such monumental aspirations, and among the more spectacular were George Dance the Younger's Stratton Park, Hampshire (1803–6) and Ashburnham Place, Sussex (1813–17) (both destroyed), Thomas Hopper's Leigh Court, Somerset (1814), C. R. Cockerell's Oakley Park, Shropshire (c. 1820), and Belsay Hall, Northumberland, by various architects including John Dobson. In Scotland, Edinburgh became known as 'the Athens of the North' as much on account of its large number of severe Grecian buildings as for its intellectual climate. Several architects designed superb Greek interiors as well, including James Playfair and Archibald Simpson, whose Strathcathro House, Angus, of 1827 is one of the last outstanding interiors of the style. Victorian pedantry and inaccuracy subsequently tolled the death-knell of the best of the Neo-classical style in British interior decoration.

The situation in Italy was somewhat different from what might be expected in the country which provided so much original inspiration for others. Although Rome was the inspirational centre of European Neo-classicism, the movement's prime movers were at first either foreigners – Clérisseau, Adam, Winckelmann – or non-Roman, as in the case of Piranesi. Until more is known of Clérisseau's activities, his achievements as a decorator cannot be defined; his immense enthusiasm, however, must have been important in transmitting many of his ideas. Undoubtedly, one of his most personal interiors is the Ruin Room in the Trinità dei Monti in Rome (Plate 132). Its conception is still that of a Baroque *trompe l'oeil*, despite the rigorous antique detail, and the same is true of other Italian building of this period, such as the Palazzo Strozzi di Mantova, Florence, by Niccolò Contestabile (1759–1824).

The Baroque had implanted itself so firmly in the Italian decorative vocabulary that it was with regret that many designers abandoned the later manifestations of the style. We have seen the effect Genoese Baroque architecture had on Charles de Wailly. Interiors of immaculate classical strictness appear in paintings by David and Mengs (again, both of them foreigners working in Rome), but it is interesting to observe that the background of Mengs's *Augustus and Cleopatra* (formerly Czernin Collection, Vienna) resembles a fashionable French interior of the 1770s. In Italy, as in other parts of Europe, the eight volumes of the *Antichità di Ercolano esposte* had a considerable influence on decorators. They were issued by the Accademia Ercolanense between 1757 and 1792, but as the Academy was firmly under the control of its founder, King Charles III, copies initially went only to selected recipients. However, the figures from the plates soon began to appear in countless decorative schemes, and the combination of black background with vividly coloured draperies – regarded by the ancient Romans as the most glamorous of combinations – set a new vogue. Dubois, the Parisian publisher of *Peintures de vases antiques, vulgairement appelés étrusques*, which appeared in two volumes from 1808, declared that its 150 hand-coloured plates could be removed, varnished for their protection and used '*pour décorer les appartements*'. Such a practice conformed to the eighteenth-century fashion for covering entire interiors with unframed prints. English examples survive at Woodhall Park, Hertfordshire, Uppark in Sussex and The Vyne in Hampshire.

It seems incredible that Rome, source of inspiration to so many artists, should herself have failed to produce a single important Neo-classical building to compare with those of other Italian and foreign cities. Major interiors of the period too are scarce, possibly because most of the great Roman families were content simply to furnish their existing palaces in the new fashion; the age of large-scale domestic rebuilding had ended in the early eighteenth century. Typical of the decorative schemes of the period when, intellectually, the Neo-classical movement was at its most active in Rome, are the rooms at the Palazzo Barberini. Although these were begun in 1750, they are still Rococo in concept, and it is only in the later rooms in the palace that the new style makes a tentative appearance. The delicious Salottino dei Ritratti, despite its pink and white classical friezes, its grotesque panels and Piranesian furniture, has mirrored Rococo doors, while the Palazzo Doria's Mirror Room is fully Rococo. In Northern Italy, the Rococo lingered much longer than it did in Rome: the court at Turin remained faithful to the style perfected there by Juvarra (see Plate 98), and as late as 1760–70 the gallery of the Palazzo dell'Accademia Filarmonica was decorated in the most exuberant Rococo manner by Benedetto Allieri and G. B. Borra.

Under Piranesi's influence, Classical or Egyptian details often crept into earlier interiors which remained otherwise unchanged, for example Penna's magnificent white marble chimney-piece ornamented with a frieze and caryatids in red Egyptian porphyry in the Villa Borghese, in Rome. Interiors such as the painter Felice Giani's at the Palace of the Spanish Embassy, and various rooms in Etruscan, Pompeian or Egyptian style, in the Quirinal, Braschi and Altieri palaces, and elsewhere, cannot equal the great complexes found in other European countries at the time.

One room which shows the transition – precocious when compared with others in Rome – to a fuller Neo-classicism is the Salone d'Oro in the Palazzo Chigi (Plate 139). This remarkable interior at first appears to reflect French or English ideas, but its date (1765–7) precludes much foreign influence. It shows the predominantly architectural emphasis of so much Italian Neo-classical interior decoration, a feature which came particularly to the fore during the Empire period. Giovanni Stern's treatment of the Salone d'Oro is also somewhat unusual for Italy, and the more common type of wall and ceiling articulation adopted there is best seen in the Romulus Room of the Palazzo Altieri, decorated in 1791 by Stefano Tofanelli and Vincenzo Pacetti. Walls and ceiling are rigidly compartmentalized, with alternating grotesque panels, pier glasses, reliefs and a large painted ceiling. Although a style comparable in intention with the Adam style is found in Italy, no designer of Adam's stature appeared during the eighteenth century. A comparison of such a room as the Mirror Room in the Palazzo Rocca-Saporiti, Milan, with its elaborate plaster grotesques, small relief panels and shallow coved ceiling with tomb-derived motifs, with any Adam interior shows the immense superiority of Adam's organization of decorated surfaces.

In 1809, Rome became the 'second city of the Empire'.

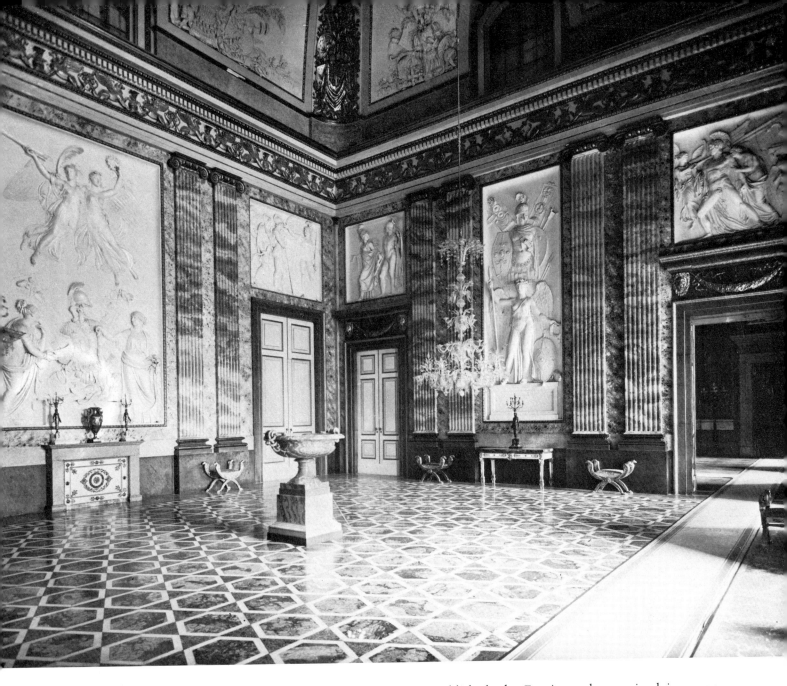

133 The Room of Mars, Royal Palace, Caserta, *near Naples Forming part of the New Apartment of the Palace, this Italian Empire room is decorated by twelve bas-reliefs illustrating scenes from the* Iliad *by Valerio Villareale, Claudio Monti and Domenico Masucci; the vault frescoes show the* Death of Hector *and the* Triumph of Achilles *by Raffaelle Calliano (1815). The other rooms in the Apartment are the Throne Room and the Room of Astrea; the whole suite dates from 1807–45. The extensive use of marble is typical of later Italian Neo-classicism*

Although massive projects were envisaged (such as Raffaele Stern's plan for a grandiose Villa Imperiale, transforming Rome into a garden city for Napoleon) precious little was realized there, and the finest interiors in the Empire style appeared in Naples (Plate 133) and Tuscany.

Once established, the Empire style remained in vogue much longer in Italy than it did in France. The lavish interiors of the Casino Borghese in Florence (notably the large vaulted and domed gallery) were decorated in a full-blown version of the style in the early 1820s, and as late as 1835–8 Salvatore Giusti could produce an Empire ballroom in the Palazzo di Capodimonte at Naples. A direct line runs almost unbroken from Italian Neo-classicism to the *Stile Liberty* – Italian Art Nouveau – and despite the strong influence of Romanticism, to the type of ceiling found in Biagio Accolti Gil's book *Soffitti della fantasia*.

As in the Rococo period, Italian Neo-classical decorators continued to favour large areas of wall and ceiling fresco, and many palaces were completely covered internally with such paintings. Felice Giani (1758–1823) was one of the most successful Neo-classical frescoists, and

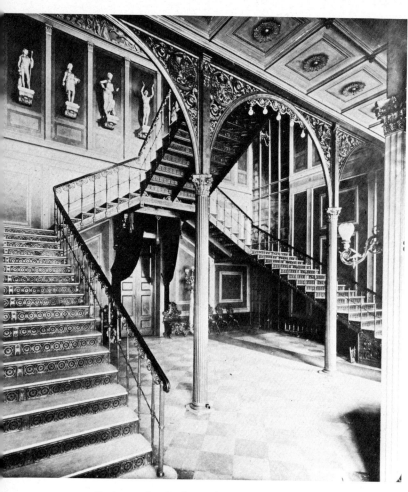

134 Staircase by Karl Friedrich Schinkel, *Palace of Prince Albert, Berlin (now destroyed)*

among the decorative cycles with which he was involved is the Gallery of the Palazzo Zacchia-Laderchi at Faenza (with the *Story of Psyche*) – a high point of Italian Neo-classicism. Other notable painters who carried out extensive domestic decoration in fresco and other media were Andrea Appiani (1754–1813), who, like Giani, worked throughout the Italian peninsula, and Vincenzo Bonomini, called Il Borromino (1756–1839), who worked mainly in Bergamo. His frescoes in the Palazzo Maffeis-De Beni are among the most enchanting of the period, and include extensive landscapes with exotic birds. Luigi Sabatelli (1772–1850) practised a more grandiose style (as in his famous ceiling fresco of the *Council of the Gods* in Palazzo Pitti, Florence), while Giuseppe Velasco (1750–1826) was the foremost frescoist in southern Italy and Sicily, decorating many palaces and villas in and around his native Palermo. The Neo-classical tradition of large decorative paintings and frescoes blends imperceptibly into the Romantic period's continued use of fresco in Italy.

No account of the period in Italy would be complete without a mention of Pelagio Palagi (1775–1860), a Bolognese architect, designer and painter – he practised all three professions with equal talent in Rome, Milan and Turin – and a sensitive collector of all types of object from medieval miniatures to Greek and Egyptian sculpture and Islamic art. His designs are equally wide-ranging, and his career spanned the transition from Neo-classicism to full Romanticism. The Biblioteca dell'Archiginnasio in Bologna houses a large group of his drawings, which show that, like many other Italian designers, his early style was formed by the study of the rich repertoire of ornament in Piranesi's *Diverse maniere*. His contact with Felice Giani, and his own Roman stay of 1806–15, resulted in the rich and refined style which gained him the patronage of King Carlo Alberto of Savoy. For the King, he created the sumptuous interiors at the Castello di Racconigi, ranging from the chaste bathroom and highly original Etruscan Room to the Apollo Cabinet with its foretaste of the style of Franz von Stuck. Like Percier and Fontaine, Palagi was concerned with the design of every detail of his interiors, and the resulting unity is always striking – even in monumental rooms such as those in the Royal Palace at Turin. Copiously carved and gilded decoration using heavy consoles and large caryatids pre-figures the eclectic style beloved of King Vittorio Emanuele and links the last manifestations of Neo-classicism in Italy with Historicism.

While other European countries wavered between Rome or Greece, Germany quickly gave its allegiance to Greece, almost, it might be imagined, in contrition for its long-lasting devotion to the Rococo. The severity and monumentality of Greek architecture rapidly gained ground, but unlike the situation in Britain, were mainly confined to public buildings. In Berlin, Friedrich Gilly (1772–1800) played an important part in interpreting French Revolutionary ideas for architects like Leo von Klenze (1784–1864) and Karl Friedrich Schinkel (1781–1841). Schinkel, the greatest architect of his period in Germany, was also a painter, stage designer and interior designer of equal stature. Like Palagi, he was fascinated by medieval architecture, and adopted its structural clarity in his classical architecture: the result was a unity between his exteriors and interiors (Plate 134) as well as a degree of originality almost unparalleled among Neo-classical architects. Similar principles guided his designs for a Royal Palace on the Athenian Acropolis, from which, however, the Italian Quattrocento elements which enliven earlier interiors are excluded.

Schinkel worked almost exclusively in Berlin, perfecting his 'Prussian Hellenism' without ever seeing Greece. Klenze was the only major architect of the group to go there, in 1834. He succeeded Karl von Fischer (1782–1820) as Munich's leading Neo-classical architect, and while Fischer's style had been based on Palladianism (as in his palace of Abbé Salabert, now the Prinz Carl Palais, of 1802), Klenze's achieved a pure, often chilly classicism. Crown Prince Ludwig of Bavaria, whom he met in 1814, encouraged his passion for antiquity, and on Ludwig's accession to the throne Klenze was able to transform Munich into an impressively Classical city. The King commissioned him to build the Königsbau of the Munich Residenz (1827–35), and within an Italian Renaissance shell Klenze designed large simplified rooms which provided the settings for vast paintings of the *Nibelungenlied* by Schnorr von Carolsfeld and others. No greater contrast with the elegance of the eighteenth-century rooms of the Residenz can be imagined. At this point, the way divides in the German and Austrian interior, with a search for grandeur in aristocratic Austrian architecture contrasting strongly with the bourgeois escape into comfort in the Biedermeier style.

Among the principal American architects and designers working at this period (in addition to Thomas Jefferson, see Chapter 5), Asher Benjamin (1773–1845) published several books whose popularity and influence were considerable; they included *The Country Builder's Assistant* of 1797 and *The American Builder's Companion* of 1806. Benjamin's pupil Ithiel Town (1784–1844), in partnership with Martin E. Thompson and, later, Alexander Jackson Davis, designed a number of fine houses in the 'Greek Revival' style in New York (such as the Coster house, 539 Broadway, of 1834) and throughout New England. One of the most distinctive changes in interior architecture at about this time was in the treatment of the staircase. In the period before the colonies gained independence, stairs had been rather heavy, with straight lines and solidly carved balusters. In the Adam-style houses that were now being built up and down the eastern seaboard the staircase took on a new lightness, curving in beautiful shapes – oval, circular or a combination of the two – and with slender and insubstantial stair-rails. The effect is one of extraordinary grace and elegance. A fine example is in the Octagon House in Washington DC, designed by William Thornton (*c.* 1800).

The turn of the nineteenth century saw many changes in American interior decoration. Painted, papered or fabric-covered walls replaced wooden panelling, with plaster cornices and elaborate wooden or marble chimney-pieces in the European taste. In Salem, Massachusetts, Samuel McIntyre (see also Chapter 5) produced much beautiful carving for the mantels and doors of the numerous houses he designed, employing a style derived from the Adam brothers; the rich detail includes festoons and swags, baskets of fruit and – reflecting the surge of national pride after the achievement of independence – the American eagle. Around 1800 European block-printed papers with allover patterns or scenic views (see page 172) became fashionable. Woodwork was usually white or cream, but was often offset by vibrant red, green, blue or yellow wall surfaces – the perfect foil for furniture of mahogany or similar woods, gilded mirror frames and detail; the result was generally a more frugal version of the Empire or Regency styles.

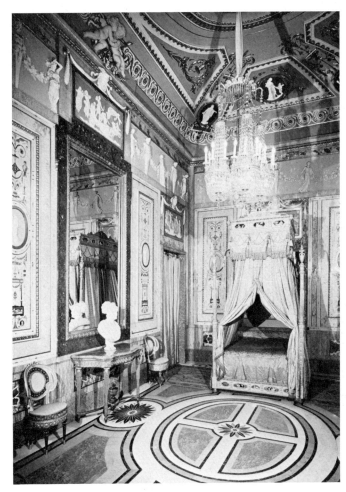

135 Bedroom of Queen Maria Luisa of Parma, *Royal Palace, Madrid Dating from the last years of the eighteenth century, this room uses combined relief and style étrusque decorations set in a framework of marble sheeting*

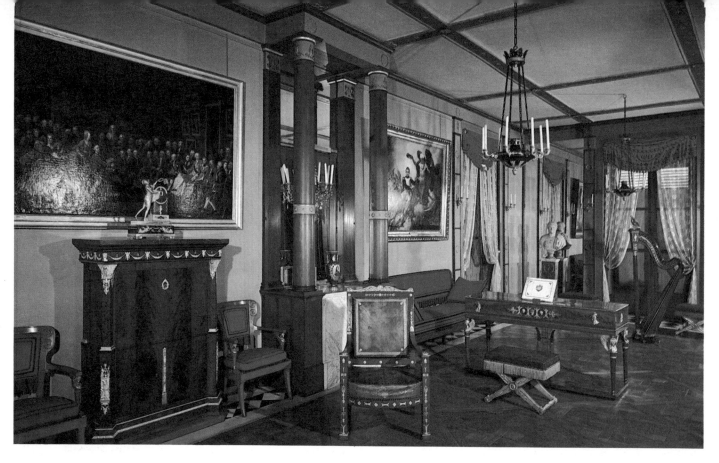

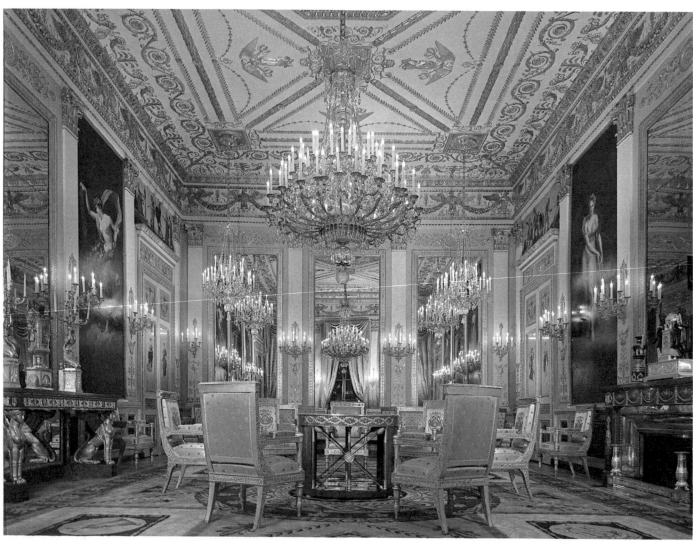

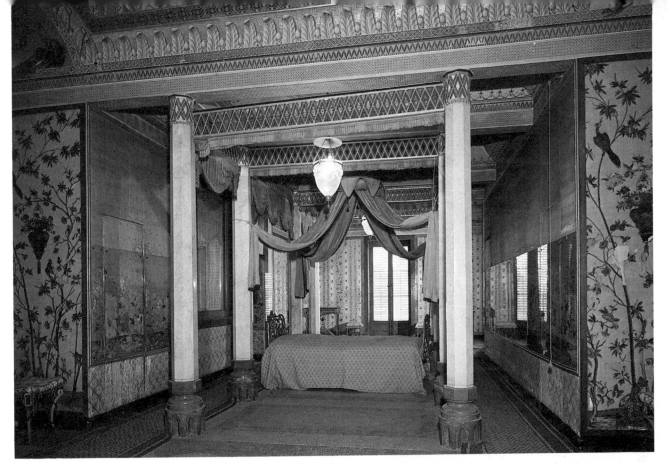

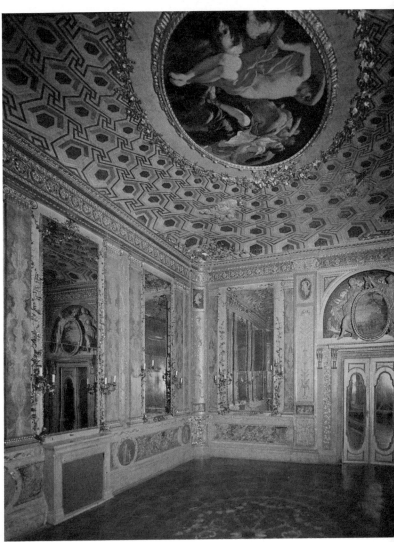

136 *(left, above)* The Music Room, *Château de Malmaison*

137 *(left, below)* Salon des Saisons, *Hôtel de Beauharnais, Paris, 1804–6* *Napoleon I's stepson, Eugène de Beauharnais, took possession of this hôtel in 1803, and by 1806 it was described as 'the smartest in Paris'; it had cost one and a half million francs. It was mainly used by Eugène's sister Hortense, and its dazzling Empire rooms reflect her taste. This room has two large paintings by the school of Prud'hon and a wealth of Classical and 'Pompeian' detail; like other interiors here (such as the sumptuous bedroom and bathroom of Queen Hortense) it retains some of the finest furniture of the period*

138 *(above)* The King's Bedroom, Palazzina Cinese, *Palermo, Sicily* *This delightful villa was built by Venanzio Marvuglia in 1799 for Ferdinando II Bourbon, and mixes Chinese, Turkish and Pompeian styles indiscriminately; Ferdinando insisted that the 'Pompeian' murals have 'damp' marks to give an appearance of age*

139 *(right)* Salone d'Oro, Palazzo Chigi, *Rome, 1765–7, by Giovanni Stern* *Decorated for the marriage of Don Sigismondo Chigi and Maria Flaminia Odescalchi, the room is one of the most individual Neo-classical interiors in Italy. On the ceiling is a painting of Diana and Endymion by Baciccio (1639–1709), framed in a trompe l'oeil of marble coffering; the elegant female figures in the overdoor are by the sculptor Tommaso Righi. The plasterwork grotesques, griffins and gilded cornice rosettes suggest the fully evolved Louis XVI style, as do the ribbons and garlands throughout the room. Although the fine original furniture has gone, the superb parquet, echoing the ceiling pattern, survives intact*

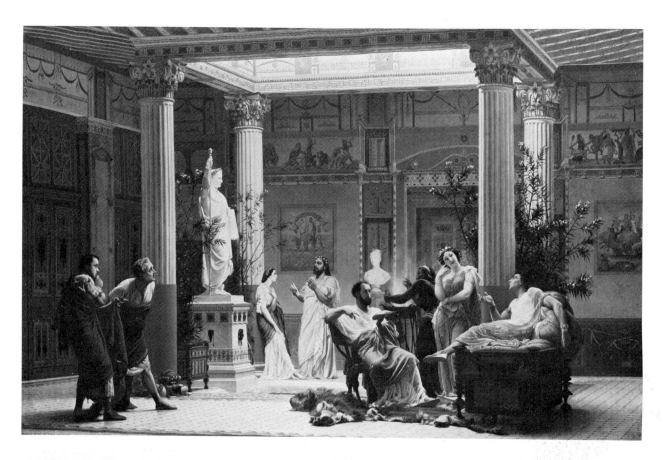

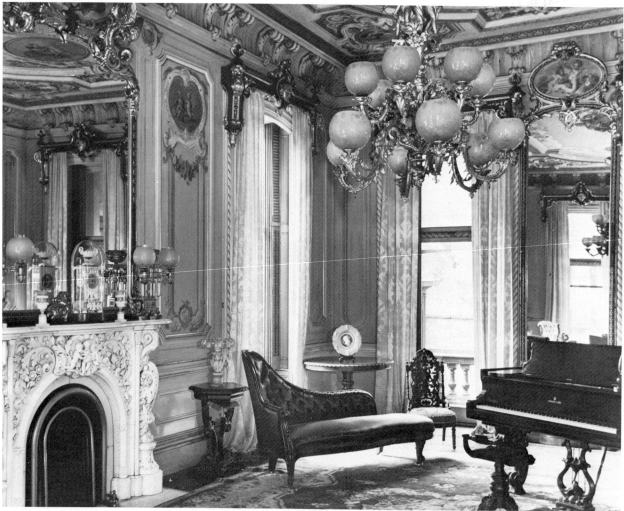

7

The Age of Revivals

Each style of architecture has its
character, each epoch its beauties

Charles Garnier

Ever since the Renaissance, architects and designers had been trying to re-create past styles, mainly those of ancient Greece and Rome. The Renaissance itself developed from the premise that the artist could use the incomparable achievements of the antique as the basis for a new art; the Baroque and Neo-classicism built on Renaissance ideas, the Rococo being the only intervening style largely to reject them. Although, as we have seen, there are isolated examples of revived non-Classical styles before the nineteenth century, the vastly increased historical

140 (left, above) Gustave Boulanger: Performances of 'The Flute Player' and 'The Wife of Diomedes' in Prince Napoleon's Maison Pompéienne, 1861. Oil on canvas (0.83 × 1.30 m). Versailles, Musée National du Château
This painting shows the reading of works by Gautier and Augier on 2 February 1860 in the presence of the Emperor and Empress to inaugurate the new house built by Alfred-Nicolas Normand (1822–1909) in the Pompeian style. Normand modelled the entire villa loosely on several Pompeian originals, including the villas of Diomedes and Pansa, and the interiors were decorated in the Third Style of Pompeian painting; this scene is set in the atrium, the villa's most important room. The walls were painted with allegories of the Elements by Cornu, who also worked elsewhere in the villa, with decorative backgrounds of great delicacy by Chauvin. The refined atmosphere – typical of the gatherings of a select, intellectual group of aristocrats – recalls Ingres's famous painting Antiochus and Stratonice of 1840 (Chantilly, Musée Condé), one of the first signs of an accurate Pompeian revival in France. Although the Maison Pompéienne was demolished in 1891, Normand's superb coloured drawings for the interior decoration survive in the Musée des Arts Décoratifs in Paris, together with an album of photographs of the villa. Many houses in the Gothic, Renaissance and Moorish styles were built for members of the Parisian aristocracy in the last century; most of these, including the Greek house built in 1812 in imitation of the Erechtheion for the Comte de Choiseul-Gouffier, have been demolished

141 (left, below) Music Room, Victoria Mansion, Portland, Maine

awareness of the Age of Reason and the dissemination of information resulting from ever-widening travel led to interest in styles other than Greek and Roman. But it should be noted that much of the nineteenth century's passion for these 'revived' styles in architecture and interior decoration originated from elements in Neo-classicism. The desire to evoke the atmosphere of the Classical world often resulted in a highly romantic vision of the past, notably in the work of artists like Piranesi. This combination of nostalgia and fantasy, together with the desire to copy earlier styles, is one of the mainsprings of nineteenth-century Historicism (see Plate 144).

Historicism as a movement resulted in many of the most characteristic works of art of the century, and in general we still think of the typical Victorian interior as a mixture of elements drawn from different periods. From the most humble room, where even the few mass-produced artefacts in evidence would be in one or other of the 'styles', to the megalomaniac interiors of King Ludwig II of Bavaria (Plates 150 and 152) Historicism carried the day. A self-explanatory term, it is nevertheless sometimes difficult to distinguish it from Romanticism, whose interpretative freedom it frequently shares. More than a style, Historicism might best be defined as an *attitude*, which pervaded all of the arts. Medieval, Renaissance, Baroque and even Oriental history were all plundered for their colourful potential, often with inaccurate results alarming to modern conceptions of historical fidelities. But one of the direct results of Historicism was a new internationalism in the arts, whether in Schiller's choice of Mary Stuart and Joan of Arc as heroines, or Queen Victoria's and Prince Albert's decision to build their Isle of Wight retreat, Osborne House, as a gigantic Tuscan villa.

If the confusing strands of nineteenth-century revivals are disentangled, three broad categories emerge which have direct reflections in interior decoration: Historicism, Romanticism and Eclecticism. The first is generally the most accurate, seeking to re-create past styles through observation, measurement, and careful, even archaeo-

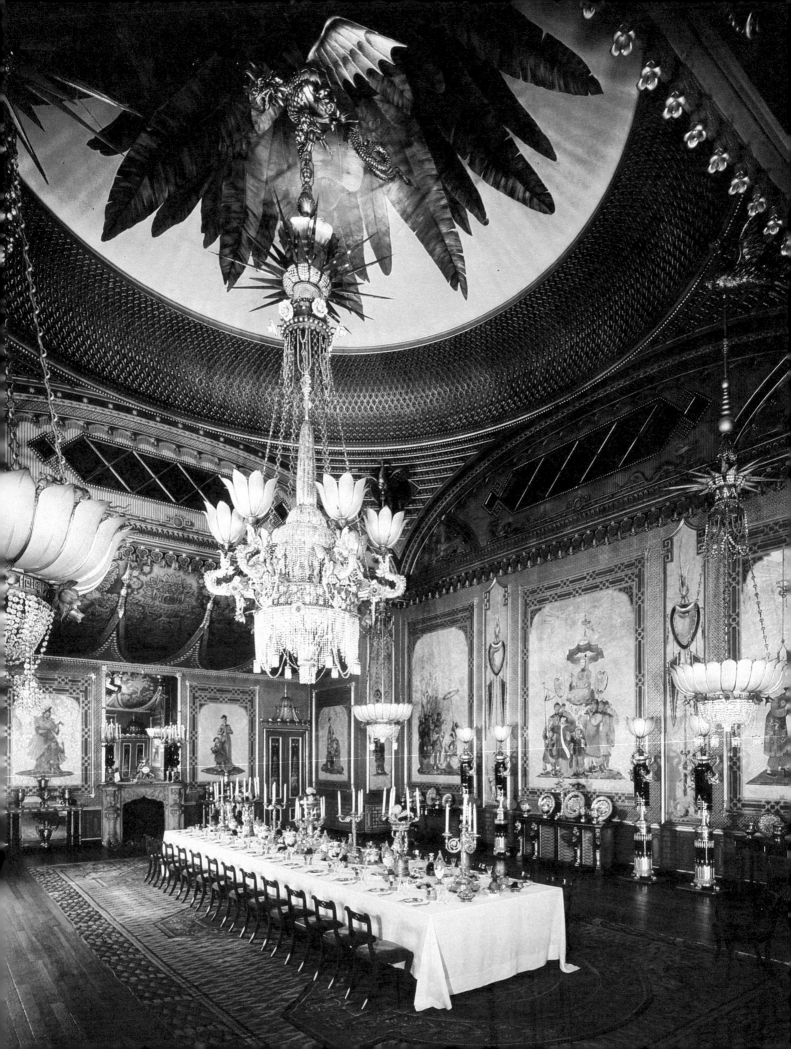

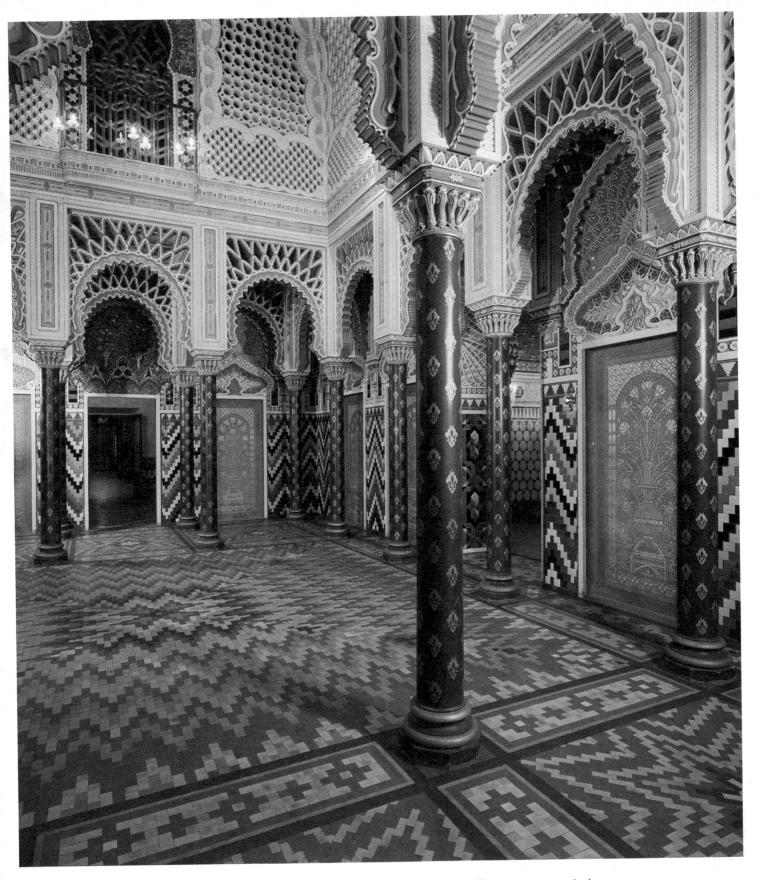

142 *(left)* The Banqueting Room, The Royal Pavilion, Brighton, *1815–22*

143 *(above)* Hall at Sammezano, *Italy*

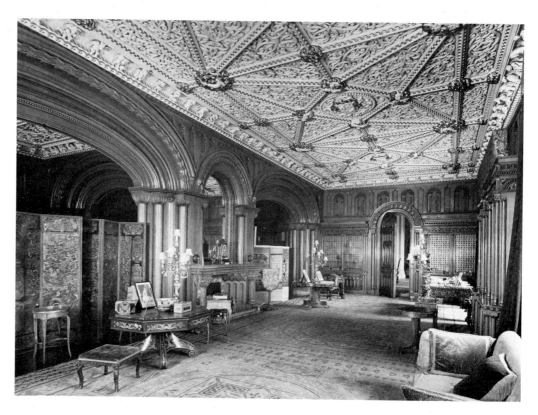

144 The Norman Drawing Room, Penrhyn Castle, *Carnarvonshire, North Wales, 1827–46?, by Thomas Hopper This extraordinary castle, built with the proceeds of a fortune made from slate quarries (and containing slate furniture), represents the peak of the European 'Norman' revival. The heaviness of the style, which has been called 'the Baroque of romantic revival architecture', and the fact that it was almost exclusively confined to large ecclesiastical buildings, made its use comparatively rare. The style did not lend itself easily to furnishings, and the massive doors, immense plate-glass mirrors, and totally un-Norman candelabra strike discordant notes*

logical, observation of the originals. Romanticism used past styles to stir particular emotions in the beholder by an associative approach, evoking medieval chivalry and pageant through the Gothic style, scholarship through the Renaissance, and so on. Eclecticism united elements of both, taking stylistic features from any and every historical period. Because this approach offered the greatest freedom, it gained the widest approval, and was responsible for the chaotic mixtures characterizing most nineteenth-century domestic interiors after 1830.

Perhaps more than in any other period, it was important for architects and designers in the nineteenth century to be able to distinguish the best from the second-rate, since the mediocre and the thoroughly bad proliferated as the result of ignorance, misinformation and increasing mass-production. In interior decoration, precise quotations from famous sources (such as Versailles) carried with them connotations of wealth or status, and particular styles came to have precise associations. The French eighteenth-century styles evoked aristocratic taste and immense wealth, while the Gothic style carried overtones of willingly enjoyed gloom, remote antecedents, and respectability. For the vast majority, however, content with a cast-iron stove, a wall-clock or a chair in a debased version of one of the 'styles', such associations meant nothing.

It is wellnigh impossible to chart with accuracy the various shifts of emphasis in nineteenth-century interior decoration after the decline of Neo-classicism and before the appearance of new styles breaking with Historicism, that is to say between the early 1830s and the 1880s. This is principally because after the Napoleonic period many different styles co-existed in fashionable esteem – the Classical, the Gothic, the Oriental and, from the 1820s as a tentative novelty in domestic interiors in both France and England, the Rococo. 'New' styles could spring to the forefront with rapidity, as when Sir Walter Scott (a key figure in reviving the past with his *Waverley Novels*) gave what amounted to official sanction to the Scottish Baronial style in the interiors of his house at Abbotsford after 1819. That style's near relations, the Elizabethan and the French *style Henri III* with their obvious nationalistic appeal, gained immensely in popularity at that time. The decision to build Gothic rather than Classical Houses of Parliament in London further strengthened the hold of the more romantic vision. By the middle years of the century it was taken for granted that the same patron would naturally select different historical styles for each of his or her residences. This is amply borne out by Queen Victoria's Balmoral (Scottish Baronial) and Osborne (Tuscan Renaissance), by Napoleon III's Pierrefonds (Gothic) and Louvre interiors (Baroque), and by Ludwig II's Neuschwanstein (Gothic, Byzantine etc.), Herrenchiemsee (Baroque) and Linderhof (Rococo).

Because of the unprecedented wealth of building and interior decoration carried out during the nineteenth century this chapter can deal only with the main trends. Ideas expressed in the houses of the rich were rapidly conveyed to a much wider market than in preceding periods, and were almost inevitably debased in the process. The role played by the great international exhibitions in London and Paris in showing not only the artefacts, but also the latest means of reproducing them, was considerable. Almost any historical detail, from Gothic crockets and tracery to Rococo shellwork, Baroque caryatids and Moorish vaulting (Plate 143), could now be reproduced with the aid of 'industrial art' as it was misleadingly called. England led the way in this mass-production, as was made painfully obvious by the Great Exhibition of 1851 in London, in many ways the apotheosis of Historicism.

One of the principal differences between the eighteenth and nineteenth centuries in the revival of styles like the Gothic was that while the earlier period constantly emphasized the frivolity of non-Classical styles, the nineteenth century took them seriously. Only when Gothic architecture became associated in people's minds with religious or moral revivals, and was no longer seen as John Evelyn had perceived Henry VII's Chapel at Westminster as 'Lace and other cut work, and Crinkle-Crankle', did it assume a serious character.

The domestic interior's history during the Gothic Revival is largely unwritten, but two extraordinary buildings clearly mark its beginnings in England, Horace Walpole's Strawberry Hill (Plate 112) and William Beckford's Fonthill Abbey (Plate 145). While Strawberry Hill (see page 134) is a product of the Picturesque movement, Fonthill attempted to re-create something of the grandeur of medieval monastic buildings both externally and internally. A *unicum* in the history of art and taste, its apartments of immense height and length expressed its creator's own excesses. Beckford, 'England's Wealthiest Son', had had his tastes for exoticism fostered in his childhood in the fantastic Egyptian Hall of his father's Wiltshire mansion, Fonthill Splendens. 'The solid Egyptian Hall', Beckford later wrote,

looked as if hewn out of a living rock – the line of apartments and apparently endless passages leading from it on either side were all vaulted – an interminable staircase, which when you looked down it – appeared as deep as the well in the pyramid – and when you looked up – was lost in vapour, led to suites of stately apartments gleaming with marble pavements as polished as glass – and gawdy ceilings – painted by Casali with all the profligacy of pencil ...

Fonthill Abbey was built by James Wyatt from 1796 to 1818; by then Wyatt had already experimented with Gothic at Lee Priory in Kent (1782–90) whose toy-like Strawberry Room is now in the Victoria and Albert Museum, and he was later to build Ashridge in Hertfordshire in the same vein as Fonthill. But nothing can recapture the lavish interiors of the Abbey, demolished some time after the collapse of its almost three-hundred-foot tower in 1825. John Rutter's book, *Delineations of Fonthill and its Abbey*, of 1823, at least shows and describes some of them. Beckford's opulent taste is reflected in Rutter's description of details like the 'curtains of scarlet and deep blue, bordered with the royal tressure, partially concealing the long lines of splendid ebony and gold, which contain within them, or bear on their marble slabs,

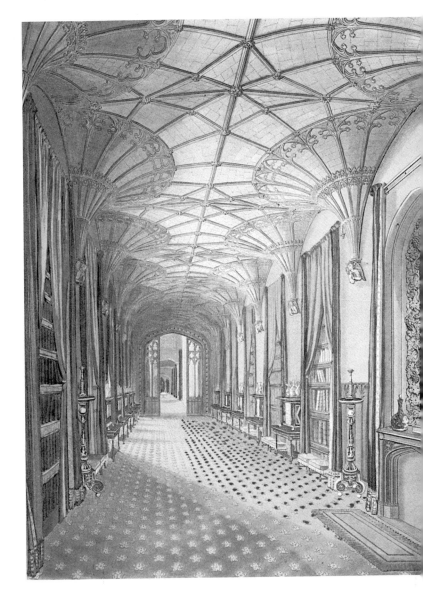

145 St Michael's Gallery, Fonthill Abbey, Wiltshire, *from John Rutter's* Delineations of Fonthill *This gallery was some 127 feet long and 13 feet wide, and was probably the most convincing interior of the Abbey. Its walls were tinted with the pink which Beckford unaccountably selected for many surfaces in the Abbey's interior. Thanks to the window arrangement, the Gallery received direct lighting throughout the day. The windows contained armorial bearings and historical figures in stained or tinted glass, and were echoed opposite by similarly shaped bookshelf openings; all were hung with double curtains, the inner scarlet, the outer purple. The carpet was crimson, patterned with the cinquefoils of the Hamilton family, and most of the furnishings were of ebony, while silver sconces held candles for illumination at night. A writer in 1812 described the effect of light elsewhere in the Abbey as 'a most enchanting play of colours, and the effect produced by the sombre hue of twilight, contrasted with the vivid appearance at different hours of the day, is indescribably pleasing and grand'*

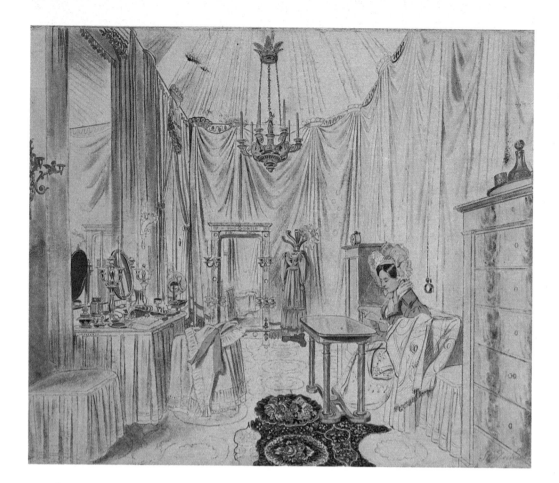

the most precious specimens of virtu'. In one room the ceiling beams were 'carried at their ends by carved and gilt corbels, and the hangings are of garter-blue silk damask, embellished with gold mouldings'.

The essence of Beckford's taste was eclecticism, and his imaginative use of dramatic spatial effects with brilliantly contrived lighting and colour distinguished his interiors from those of his contemporaries with the possible exception of Soane (see page 156). Although curtains and other draperies were widely used in many Regency interiors, Beckford outshone all rivals with his 'purple curtains fifty feet long' in Fonthill's Octagon. 'I wonder architects and fitters-up of apartments do not avail themselves more frequently of the powers of drapery', he wrote, and accordingly incorporated an entire wall of scarlet drapery in his house in Lansdown Crescent in Bath. He hoped in the future to indulge himself in 'every variety of plait and fold that can possibly be invented'. In many of his interiors, he used curtains to shut off breathtaking vistas of further rooms, or, at Bath, where space was limited, to create the illusion of greater space in conjunction with mirrors and carefully controlled light.

Despite the Gothic decoration of Fonthill, Beckford mixed furniture, paintings and objects of every period with a capriciousness which has no precedent in the history of interior decoration. His *mélanges* were remarkable for the superb quality of their components and for the genius

with which they were juxtaposed, often in conjunction with the flower arrangements for which he was famous. Paintings such as Raphael's *St Catherine* and Bellini's *Agony in the Garden* (both now in the National Gallery in London) were seen alongside such distinguished furniture as Riesener's Bureau of King Stanislas (now in the Wallace Collection). Beckford's esteem for French furniture of the Ancien Régime did not extend to whole interiors, and while he was among the first to seek out the masterpieces of eighteenth-century French furniture dispersed by the Revolution, it was left to others to recreate its original settings.

In some ways, Fonthill prefigured many aspects of the Victorian interior, not least in its often confusing lack of clear stylistic direction. Apart from the Gothic rooms (if interiors such as the huge Octagon can be called a room), anomalies like a 'Chintz Boudoir' must have struck alien notes in an 'abbey', and the Grand Drawing Room was already in the early Victorian taste. Pale wood fittings, large blank areas of wall space punctuated by solitary pictures, and isolated pieces of heavy, classicizing furniture recall elements of the Empire and Regency interior but lack its cohesion. This was the style used by Beckford in his remarkable Lansdown Tower at Bath, built and decorated for him by Henry Goodridge, one of the pioneers in England of a style based on Italian Renaissance and Greek sources. English's *Views of Lansdown Tower* record

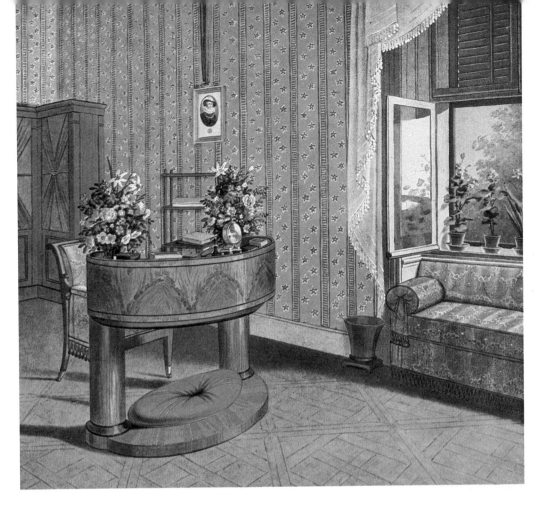

147 Drawing Room of the Archduchess Sophie in Laxenburg, *from Herman Schmitz:* Vor hundert Jahren. Festräume und Wohnzimmer des Deutschen Klassizismus und Biedermeier, *Berlin, 1920*

these somewhat claustrophobic interiors, similar to those in Goodridge's own Bath home, Montebello (a typically evocative name), and other villas in the area.

Fonthill's scale and internal magnificence proved the exception of the early Gothic Revival. Elsewhere the vogue continued much in the 'Gothick' manner of Strawberry Hill, purveyed by architects who, like Wyatt, turned to the medieval manner when need arose but retained their Classical allegiances. Perhaps because of the comparative lack of archaeologically accurate studies of medieval architecture and decoration at this time, interiors in the Gothic taste tend to play down the architectural element in favour of an array of individual motifs selected from specific sources. A particularly fine example of this is Sir John Soane's Gothic Library at Stowe, Buckinghamshire, which marries details derived from Henry VII's Chapel at Westminster to an interior of Georgian proportions. Thus, in the 'Gothick' tradition of Strawberry Hill the over-mantel (housing a mirror in totally unmedieval fashion) is based on a fretted tomb canopy. The glazed bookcases, which were designed to hold the Marquess of Buckingham's 'Saxon Manuscripts', have traceried windows, and the ceiling is a flattened version of the Chapel's famous fan vaulting. As with many interiors of its type, the effect is rather one of Augustan repose than of Gothic gloom, and the elaborate plasterwork belongs entirely to the eighteenth-century tradition. The other great Gothick

house of the first quarter of the century, Eaton Hall in Cheshire by William Porden, boasted huge plate glass Gothic overmantel mirrors and positively theatrical window curtains. It is interesting to note that Porden saw the Gothic style as 'preserving that distinction to Rank and Fortune, which it is the habit of the age to diminish ...'

It was, however, in Britain that some of the most significant advances towards accurate re-creations of the medieval domestic interior were made. Europe, in general, was lagging behind, as is shown by a comparison of the Hall at Blithfield, Staffordshire, for example, reconstructed in 1822 by J. Buckler and F. Bernasconi, which is convincingly Gothic in scale, and has full vaulting and striking detail, with the papery detailing of interiors in the almost contemporary neo-Gothic rooms in the Castle of Pfaueninsel near Berlin. In Italy, too, an architect of the calibre of Pelagio Palagi – capable of designing the brilliant Classical interiors discussed in Chapter 6 – still found the Gothic style taxing as late as the 1830s.

The key figure in the change which overtook attitudes to medieval architecture in the later 1820s was Augustus Welby Pugin (1812–52); it is surprising, however, that his devotion to instilling seriousness of purpose into revived Gothic should have failed to produce many domestic interiors of note. Those he designed for Sir Charles Barry's Houses of Parliament remain unrivalled for their richness and imaginative re-creation of an earlier style, but were never repeated in a private house. Pugin himself observed, 'I have passed my life in thinking of fine things, designing fine things and realizing very poor ones.' Nonetheless, the influence of his exquisite drawings and the training he gave his craftsmen was considerable in Britain. Many pages of his *Ecclesiastical Architecture* deal with interior decoration and arrangement, and his passion for ecclesiastical terminology shows that he belongs to the Romantic movement as much as Sir Walter Scott. He realized that the 'soul' of Gothic art was 'lamentably deficient' in most modern replicas, and noted that 'A man who remains any length of time in a modern Gothic room and escapes without being wounded by some of its minutiae, may consider himself extremely fortunate.' It was Pugin's work at Alton Towers in Staffordshire and Scarisbrick Hall in Lancashire which led Barry to offer him his greatest challenge at the Houses of Parliament.

Like Beckford and Walpole, Scott too realized many of his literary dreams through his home, although it is perhaps fortunate that unlike Fonthill and Strawberry Hill, Abbotsford was never the subject of an illustrated book, since it had internal oddities like tartan wallpaper and poor-quality detailing. The immense and incalculable influence on European taste of the *Waverley Novels* was bolstered by the mistaken impression that their author lived in a Gothic house. Scott's writings were instrumental in creating the Troubadour Style in France, where as a result of this association all things Scottish carried an aura of romance.

The Troubadour Style offers an approximate parallel to the Gothic Revival, but extends to virtually all of the arts in addition to architecture and interior decoration: even the great Ingres painted *style troubadour* pictures. The Duchesse de Berry made the style particularly fashionable and it gained great impetus in France in the 1820s. In 1827, the celebrated producer of 'scenic wallpaper', Jean Zuber (fl. 1793–1850?), introduced one of his most ambitious *ensembles*, a wallpaper panorama entitled *Vues d'Ecosse ou La dame du lac*, loosely based on Scott and incorporating patently unScottish scenic backgrounds along with special Gothic wainscoting paper to match – an instant Troubadour interior.

It was Zuber who made the greatest advances in wallpaper design during this period, and he was the first to conceive of 'endless' paper which would remove the need for elaborate sticking of separate sheets. The choice of styles open to the decorator using Zuber's scenic wallpapers is indicated by some of his titles marketed between 1813 and 1836 – *Vues d'Italie, Jardins français* (significantly altered to *Jardins espagnols* in 1849, when Spain was attracting increasing attention!), *Vues de la Grèce moderne* and *Le décor chinois*. Such wallpapers provided a continuous scene around the walls of a room, usually above dado level, their rich and often exotic colours forming the perfect foil to the simplified, highly polished furniture of the post-Empire period.

The bourgeois domestic interior in Austria and to a lesser extent in Germany from 1815 to the mid-century is characterized by the twentieth-century name given to the period as a whole – *Biedermeier*. This was a style which, while evolving from the forms of French Empire decoration, depended less on architectural or other fixed wall or ceiling treatment for its effect. On the one hand, its emphasis on comfort was characteristic of the second quarter of the century throughout Europe and America, but on the other its practicality looked forward to the modern period – which in Austria depended to a surprising degree on Biedermeier ideas. Simplicity and domesticity are the keynotes of the style; Adalbert Stifter's novel *Der Nachsommer* (1857) emphasizes 'pure family life . . . the greatest happiness', and an atmosphere of relaxation pervades many of the countless watercolours which record middle-class homes of the period. Even in the tallest rooms, furniture and furnishings rarely rise higher than eye-level and in preference to the large pictures in heavy, elaborately carved and gilded frames so popular in many nineteenth-century interiors, smaller, more intimate oils, watercolours and prints in simple mouldings were hung in rows. Walls were painted in clear, bright colours and ceilings in white or grey; despite comfortable chairs and no lack of other small pieces of furniture, Biedermeier rooms can seem austere even by twentieth-century standards. This austerity was further accentuated by simple parquet flooring or even bare boards with rugs, or, in the finer interiors, a type of fitted carpeting.

As a background to the smaller scale of Biedermeier furniture in mahogany, cherrywood, pearwood, maplewood, ashwood or walnut, some rooms had their walls covered with wallpaper or fabric in fine stripes or small flowered patterns. Curtains and draperies in white or in pale colours were generally suspended on brass rods, and roller blinds were also common, fitted close to the window frame. A hangover from the Empire period was the popularity of walls (and occasionally ceilings) draped with fabric gathered in folds and bunches and held back to reveal large mirrors (Plate 146). How pervasive through all social levels Biedermeier influence became is shown by the decoration and furnishing of the Archduchess Sophie's Drawing Room in Laxenburg near Vienna (Plate 147), of the later 1820s, but they are far removed from the fashionable interiors found elsewhere in Europe at that time.

The reign of Louis-Philippe in France saw not only the acceptance of the Troubadour Style, reinforced by the success of Victor Hugo's historical novel *Notre-Dame de Paris* (1831), which led to the sudden popularity among decorators of the 'French Renaissance' style, but also a new awareness of the French eighteenth century. The picturesque disorder of the Musée de Cluny, then being arranged by Alexandre du Sommerand, was also influential; its haphazard grouping of many genuine pieces of medieval furniture, panelling and architectural fragments struck a romantic chord in many minds; its influence is best reflected in the delightful interior of Princess Marie d'Orléans's oratory in the Tuileries as recorded in de Montaut's delicate drawing of 1848 (Plate 148). This is *troubadour* at its richest and most bastard. Gothic screens jostle Renaissance cabinets and Louis XIII chairs, heavy figured curtains hang beneath Henri IV valances and Fontainebleau plasterwork. The progress from Aimé Chenevard's well-known design for a Gothic *salon* of c. 1830 (also in the Musée des Arts Décoratifs, Paris) with its elaborately carved hammer-beam ceiling, ornate tri-partite arches and fully armed figure sculptures, into romantic eclecticism is complete.

The breadth of Louis-Philippe's interests is shown by the Room of the Crusades at Versailles, by his restoration of Fontainebleau, which included new suites of 'Renais-sance' furniture from Guillaume Grohé, and by his love of the furniture of André-Charles Boulle. Romanticism established direct connections between the arts as in no preceding period and the fullest and most immediate ex-pression of this is in the interiors of the middle and upper classes. Alexandre Dumas's dramas, such as *Henri III et sa cour* (1829), popularized that style, while *Les Trois Mousquetaires* (1844) revived the Louis XIII style. Parisian theatre- and opera-goers of the 1830s became accustomed to the intricately historicizing stage sets of Luc-Charles Cicéri (some in a precociously neo-Baroque style) and with the aid of industry were soon able to reproduce their effects in their homes – with varying degrees of success. Contemporary developments in pictorial reproduction such as chromo-lithography enabled both patrons and decorators to obtain colour plates of historical styles and detail.

In every field of the decorative arts, advances in mass-production made available to an ever larger public a wide variety of materials reproducing every known style. Charles Blanc noted the contemporary advance in the age-old Italian technique of painting plaster to resemble metals in his fascinating *Grammaire des arts décoratifs* of 1882. This use of galvanized plaster to simulate the gilded bronze previously the prerogative of the very rich, together with mass-produced *papier mâché* decorative detail in any 'style', brought even complicated historical styles within the purchasing power of the middle classes.

The lowering of quality arising from public acceptance of anything bearing a historical label is perfectly illustrated by an English manual entitled *The House Decorator and Painter's Guide, containing a series of Designs for decorat-ing apartments ...* by H. W. and A. Arrowsmith, 'Decora-tors to Her Majesty', published in 1840. The improvements outlined are illustrated with coloured drawings of hideous crudity, and include '*Greek, Roman, Arabesque, Pom-peian, Gothic, Cinque Cento (sic), François Premier, Elizabethan, and the more modern French ...*' In fact, the 'Greek' consists of a collision between Mannerist strap-work and Rococo, with a vaguely Greek cornice, while the 'Louis Quatorze Style' is patently Louis XV, and so on. That such gross inaccuracies could find their way into print is indicative of the spirit of the age.

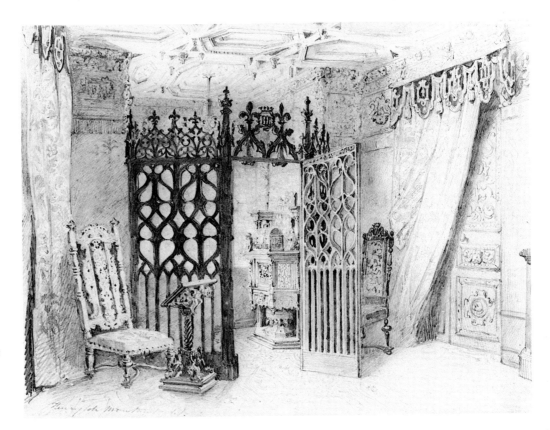

148 The Oratory of the Princess Marie d'Orléans in the Pavillon de Marsan of the Louvre, *1848. Water-colour by Henri de Montaut. Paris, Musée des Arts Décoratifs The picturesque disarray of this mixture of Flamboyant Gothic screen, François I ceiling and other details in a variety of styles reflects the often promiscuous evocation of an imprecise past sought by the Troubadour designers. The romantic softness created by the watercolour was, unfortunately, rarely achieved in reality; the interiors of the Château de Chantilly, for example, show how hard and insensitive the style could be under the impact of mechanical reproduction*

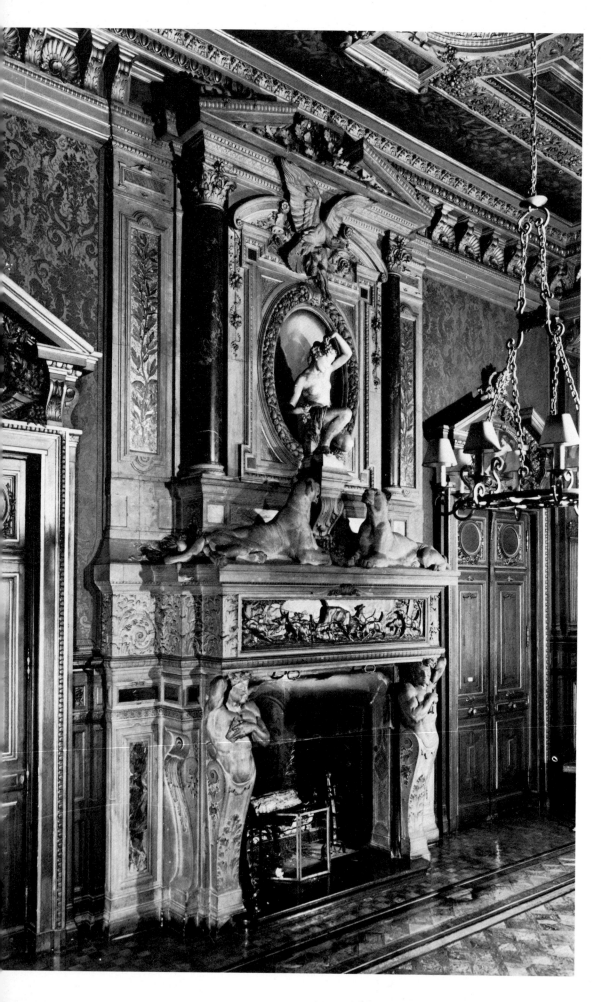

149 Chimney from a salon in the Hôtel de Païva, *Avenue des Champs Elysées, Paris, 1850s* Built for the *Polish adventuress Thérèse Lachmann, by marriage the Marquise de Païva, this* hôtel, *now the Travellers' Club, is one of the finest surviving examples of the Second Empire style in interior decoration. Leading decorators of the day, such as Paul Baudry, Carrier-Belleuse and Jules Delou, created interiors of spectacular lavishness. The language of decorative forms borrows from the Renaissance, Baroque and Rococo, creating a style which, as the architect of the* hôtel, *Charles Garnier, hoped, was not merely imitative, but new*

A distinct reaction to this vulgarization in interior decoration was almost immediate among the rich bourgeois and upper classes throughout Europe. Since the 'historical' interior with its attendant furnishings was now relatively widely available – often as little more than a conglomeration of parts – the very rich sought a wholly new solution to interior decoration; they bought the actual interiors from their original settings, thereby paving the way to a concept fundamental to many modern museums. Entire rooms could be dismantled and later reassembled in almost any setting, however distant from the original location. Such rooms provided not only atmosphere but also the added *cachet* of provenance. In certain cases the latter carried with it precise connotations for the new owner; by setting themselves among the finest interiors of the Ancien Régime, whether at Waddesdon Manor in Buckinghamshire or in France at Ferrières, the Rothschilds instantly bought themselves a pedigree.

Such a pedigree was not necessary for the Empress Eugénie in France. She instigated a cult of Marie Antoinette, seeking out her furniture from the Royal *garde-meuble* and even commissioning copies of favourite pieces for her various residences. Romanticism's impact can be seen in the increased naturalism of details in the versions and copies made for the Empress, of furniture, *boiseries* and other decorations from the eighteenth century. In de Fournier's watercolour of her bedroom at St-Cloud, the initial impression of Neo-classical correctness is soon dispelled by the discovery of too much upholstery, too much buttoned-down silk and, most surprising of all, the heavy 'Transitional' bed whose proportions and detail destroy the effect of the whole room. The Empress's real taste was best seen in the three *salons* which Hector Martin Lefuel (1810–80) decorated for her in the Louvre. A *salon* 'of a lively green, the colour of young shoots' was followed by a pink room which included red poppies in its decoration, and by the blue *salon* decorated with Winterhalter's and Dubuffe's portraits of the Court's ladies of honour. All Lefuel's projects for these rooms were gathered together in a large album, which provides many insights into the Empress's choice or rejection of elements in her decorative schemes.

The triumph in France of the *style Louis XVI* was signalled by the pavilion furnished for the Empress by Perron in the gardens of the 1867 Exhibition. This set the official seal of approval on the style in France, and guaranteed its continuing success there and elsewhere until the First World War. Apart from its adoption for the interiors of the Ritz Hotel (thus giving the later manifestations of the style the name *Le goût Ritz*), it became the accepted grand manner for the interiors of important public and private rooms of the rich from Vienna to New York (see below).

When the Empress Eugénie was shown the sketches for the new Paris Opéra she asked the architect, Charles Garnier (1825–98), 'But what on earth *is* its style?' With perfect presence of mind Garnier replied 'Le style Napoléon III, Ma'am', and thus encapsulated the next really progressive phase of French architecture and interior decoration. While Historicism had used specific styles or combinations of styles, Garnier consciously sought to evolve a new mode.

As symbols of their wealth, such families as the Rothschilds and the Demidoffs employed French eighteenth-century furnishings and pictures to evoke a light-hearted, sociable and visibly aristocratic atmosphere, but dark tapestries, heavy bronzes, Dutch paintings and ebony to suggest a sombre one – in effect an imitation of theatrical devices. In *Le style actuel* of 1869, Garnier admits, 'Of course archaeology is a useful science, and in its pursuit there can be no exclusion of any age or style ... each style of architecture has its character, each epoch its beauties ... everything which is true, everything which is beautiful, must speak to the soul ... one must be eclectic in order to admire eclecticism.' He had the courage to admire the architecture of every period and to learn from it: a proof of his ability to utilize his sources – ranging from Greek temples to the Baroque – is the extraordinary stylistic richness of the Opéra's interiors. The sources of his one still intact domestic interior, the Hôtel de Païva (Plate 149) (now the Travellers' Club), lay as far afield as the interiors of Charles de Wailly (see page 143), whose famous saloon in Palazzo Spinola in Genoa of 1772–3 together with Venetian sixteenth- and seventeenth-century interiors provided him with inspiration. Like all great Second Empire houses in Paris, the Hôtel de Païva was designed principally for use at night, the paintings of artists like Paul Baudry and the sculpture by Carrier-Belleuse combining with the lavish use of marbles (as on the onyx staircase) and bronze, mirrors and superb textiles to create the *mondain* atmosphere of the younger Dumas's *La dame aux camélias*.

The loss of many such interiors must be lamented, although some issues of the journal *La vie parisienne* capture the reckless magnificence of similar houses, such as that of the chocolate manufacturer Menier in an area particularly well-endowed with Second Empire architectural splendours, near the Parc Monceau. One of the very few surviving *hôtels particuliers* in the area to preserve its interiors and furnishings remarkably intact, it is probably also the work of Garnier. Inset into vibrant orange-pink and turquoise woodwork are painted panels combining grotesques and vases of flowers. The coved and consoled ceiling is decorated with similar painting in geometric patterns, while the dark-brown marble chimney-piece and black and gold furniture strike a sombre note. The style is similar to that of the new Louvre rooms decorated for the Imperial couple.

As in contemporary furniture, where heavily upholstered comfort prevailed in pieces of predominantly rounded outline, entire interiors were decorated with layers of decorative drapery. Mme de Girardin has left an enthusiastic account of such enveloping hangings:

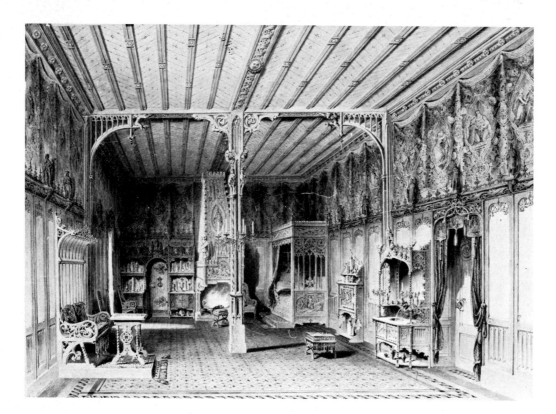

150 Design for the King's bedroom at Neuschwanstein, 1869, by Peter Herwegen. Munich, Ludwig II Museum The exceptionally fine detail in this room, and the attempt to incorporate the furnishings (such as the bed, cupboards and settle) into the Gothic panelling, make it a remarkably accurate evocation of a medieval interior. Devoid of the over-furnishing which character-ized so much earlier Gothic Revival design, it suggests a discipline rare even among Ludwig II's interior designers

The fireplaces have *housses* of gold-fringed velvet, the chairs are covered in lace, wooden wall-panelling is hidden beneath marvellous worked stuffs overlaid or woven with gold … curtains are fabulously beautiful: they use them double, even triple, and they curtain everywhere. The door conceals itself behind a curtain; the book-case often covers itself with a curtain; there are sometimes as many as eight or nine areas of curtaining in one room.

Just as interiors like Garnier's upset the delicate balance between the components of an eighteenth-century room and asserted the dominance of the decoration, so the *papiers peints* by the large Parisian firm of Jules Desfossé (such as *Le jardin d'Armide* of 1854) replaced the elegant restraint of First Empire papers with succulent forms and saturated colours. The Second Empire style was almost matched in its excesses and in its variety (Plate 140) by High Victorian interiors in Britain and was exported to all parts of the world.

Viollet-le-Duc's restoration of Pierrefonds – Louis d'Orléans's fourteenth-century château – in 1859 was the major tribute of Napoleon III's Court to the Gothic Revival style; the interior was totally renovated, and in every sense re-invented. Although the decoration was never completed, it represents the height of Second Empire Romanticism, its scale rivalled only by Ludwig II's Neuschwanstein. Pierrefonds's interiors are important in the French Gothic Revival in spite of their present appearance of hard insensitivity. In place of the medieval pastiches still in vogue in the aftermath of the Louis-Philippe style, Viollet-le-Duc substituted '… the play of a free imagina-tion, comparable with that of a Gustave Doré or a Gran-

ville' (Louis-Grodecki) and provided the ideal backdrop for the Court's medieval costume balls there. The spirit in which Viollet-le-Duc approached his medieval theme is seen both in his inclusion of portrait sculptures of the Empress and her ladies-in-waiting in the armoury and in his mixture of fictive painted curtains with carved panels by Cordon and Zoëgger, which prefigure the vegetal elements of French Art Nouveau. Of all the interiors, the Empress's bedroom is the most impressive, with its immense painted vault, elaborately carved brackets and massive chimney-piece, surmounted by a stylized painted 'tree' containing busts of the Knights of the Round Table. The architect's atmospheric watercolours show these interiors complete with their original furnishings, and convey very well the rich and sumptuous effect which he intended.

Miraculously, the nineteenth century's supreme achieve-ments in reviving historical interiors – the three Bavarian castles of King Ludwig II – survive exactly as Ludwig left them at his death, complete to the last detail of decoration and furnishings. These remarkable buildings, Neuschwan-stein (Plate 150), Herrenchiemsee (Plate 152) and Linderhof, represent the three styles most favoured by European re-vivalist designers – Romanesque-Gothic, French Baroque and Rococo. While Neuschwanstein's style is arguably native to its setting, Linderhof's and Herrenchiemsee's are not and belong to a romantic tradition of setting great houses in totally alien surroundings. One of the most striking examples of this is Baron Ferdinand de Roths-child's Waddesdon Manor, built from 1874 in the French Renaissance style but containing a mixture of real and

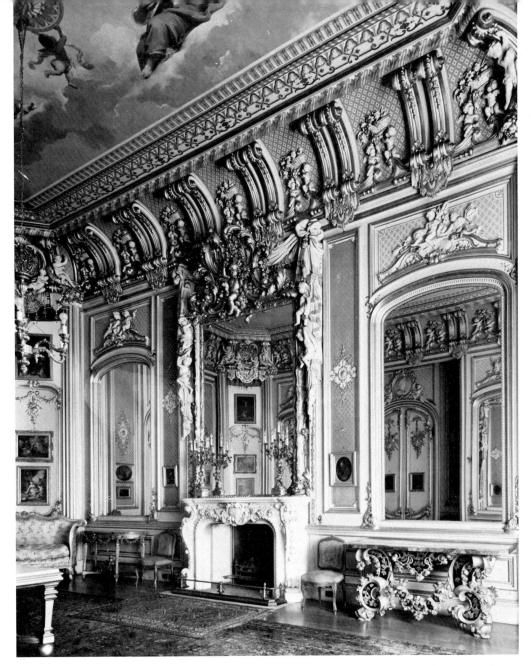

151 The Music Room,
Harlaxton Manor,
*Lincolnshire, c. 1850,
by William Burn   Burn,
generally associated with
Scottish Baronial
architecture, here achieved
an impressive synthesis of
decorative elements drawn
from Continental
(principally Austrian), late
Baroque and Rococo styles.
While the conjunction of
chimney-piece, pier-glass
overmantel and exuberant
ceiling cove are convincing
in terms of design and
historical evocation, the
depressed-arch side mirrors
have a blank quality
characteristic of such large-
scale Victorian wall filling*

imitation French eighteenth-century interiors.

Ludwig II's Rococo interiors follow another tradition initiated by the English, however, that of constructing new interiors largely or wholly without incorporating genuine fragments. The earliest example of this was Benjamin Dean Wyatt and Mathew Cotes Wyatt's Elizabeth Saloon at Belvoir Castle, made for the fifth Duchess of Rutland around 1825 and containing pieces from a 'Château of Mme de Maintenon'. This was closely followed by the magnificent interiors at York (now Lancaster) House in London and by the celebrated Waterloo Gallery of 1828 in Apsley House, which by contrast with the others already appears 'Victorian' in its arbitrary application of Rococo detail. At Wrest Park in Bedfordshire, Lord de Grey, who had made a special study of French eighteenth-century interiors in the late 1820s, created in the following decade a series of rooms whose coarsely modelled detail has none

of the quality or feeling of their prototypes. A fine example of the 'Louis Revival' style is the splendidly remodelled Ballroom of Norfolk House, London (1842–5), while the culmination of the revived Rococo in Britain in the mid-century is William Burn's (1789–1870) South Gallery at Harlaxton Manor, Lincolnshire. Like the same architect's fantastic neo-Baroque staircase, this room is derived from Austrian rather than French sources (Plate 151). The style spread rapidly through Europe, and between 1836 and 1848 Vienna saw the main rooms of one of its principal palaces, the Palais Liechtenstein, transformed in the *Zweites Rokoko* or 'Second Rococo' style with unrivalled splendour by Carl Leistler, profiting from the wealth of genuine ornament of the Rococo period closer at hand than in England.

Ludwig II's inspiration for Linderhof and Herrenchiemsee seems to have stemmed from his visit to Versailles and

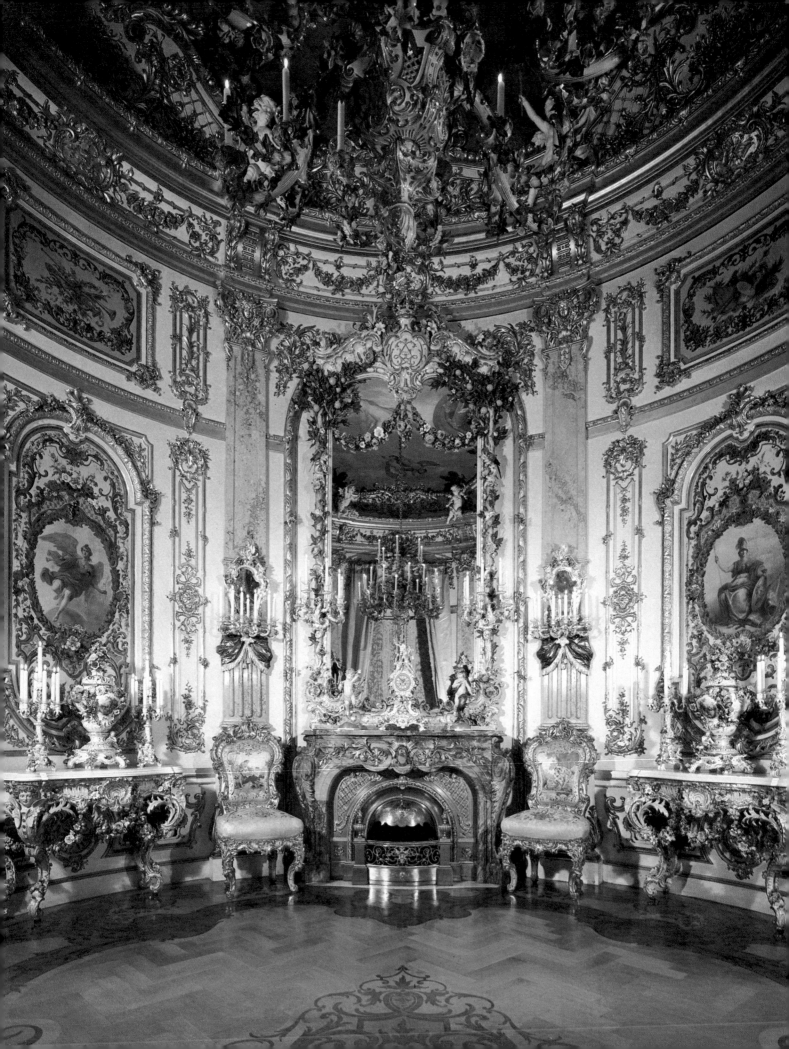

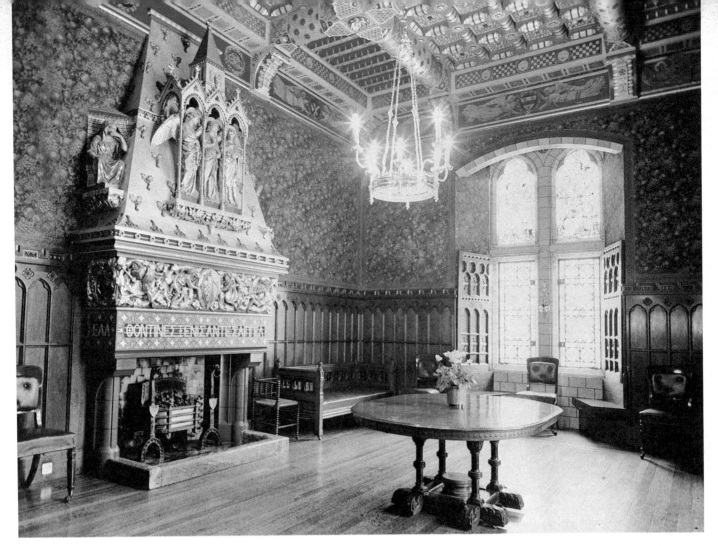

152 *(left)* The Porzellankabinett, Schloss Herrenchiemsee, *Bavaria*

153 *(above)* The Dining Room, Cardiff Castle, *by William Burges, c. 1870–75*

Paris in 1867, where he found what might be termed an 'Ancien Régime revival' in full swing under the Second Empire. His visit to Pierrefonds was also important for the development of Neuschwanstein. Between 1865 and 1869, the stage designer and Director of the Munich Court Theatre, Franz Seitz, remodelled the King's rooms in the Munich Residenz in a variety of styles ranging from *Louis XIV* to *Louis XVI*, thereby setting two precedents for the future interiors at the King's castles – the use of designers trained in the theatre and the conscious adoption of 'Bourbon' styles. The first royal castle was Neuschwanstein, begun in 1869 by Eduard Riedel (1813–85). The inspiration for much of the interior decoration came from the King's passion for the operas of Richard Wagner, and the identification of the Throne Hall (begun in 1880 by Julius Hofmann) with *Parsifal*'s Hall of the Grail resulted from the original plan to hold that opera's première there. This was the only Byzantine interior realized for Ludwig and it is one of the largest and costliest, faced throughout with marbles and mosaics. Other interiors there were decorated with murals illustrating the *Nibelungenlied*, and, as on the elaborate staircase, with

somewhat oppressive all-over decorative patterns of the type generally adopted in Gothic Revival interiors, where large wall areas had to be treated economically.

At Linderhof, originally conceived in its lonely valley as a copy of Versailles (realized at Herrenchiemsee), the prevailing style of decoration is Rococo, but of a strain unmatched for fantasy and exuberance. Even in its earliest phase, this style had been envisaged for Linderhof by Seitz and Jank (who produced Rococo stage sets for the King's private performances), but it appears that the final elevations were the work of the building's architect Georg Dollmann. It is centred like Versailles around the King's bedchamber, and every detail, from the breathtaking plasterwork to such furnishings as the great blue glass night-light on its gilt *torchère* and the monstrous lace-draped washstand, shows a nightmarish devotion to the Rococo at its most excessive and bizarre.

Borrowing elements from real eighteenth-century interiors such as François Cuvilliés's mirror rooms at the Munich Residenz and the Amalienburg (Plate 101), Ludwig's designer multiplied their already profuse forms, heaping scroll on shellwork, palm-frond on festoon and adding colours of totally un-Rococo intensity, notably pink and blue. It is a mistake to regard these hallucinatory interiors as no more than tasteless excesses, since their designers had the fullest command of their subject, and had craftsmen of a skill unrivalled in Europe at their disposal. Deliberately setting out to heighten the sensations and associations inherent for their patron in the original Rococo style, the result is an assault on the senses as overwhelming as the heady orchestration of the Wagner operas so beloved of the King; it is hardly surprising that Ludwig spent more time at Linderhof than in any of the other castles. The many parallels with stage sets made for Ludwig underline his fundamental opposition to the sterile re-creation of exact replicas or importation of original rooms, both of which would have cost him considerably less money.

Herrenchiemsee, the largest and most expensive of the three, was conceived as an *improvement* on Versailles, for Ludwig planned here not one, but two Escaliers des Ambassadeurs, reconstructing the great destroyed main staircase of Louis XIV's original château from engravings and descriptions; the last major copy was in the Palais Talleyrand, Paris, dating from the final years of the nineteenth century, while a little-known but interesting copy of the Escalier de la Reine from Versailles was made by Paris Singer in his 'mini-Versailles' for Isadora Duncan at Paignton, in Devon. In all of the interiors at Linderhof and Herrenchiemsee, the presiding genius Georg Dollmann appears to have been profoundly influenced by Léon Feuchère's pioneering work, *L'art industriel*, published in Paris in 1842. Feuchère's inclusion of all types of decorative accessory in his engraved interior elevations in every style – *Pompadour* being the blanket term in France for most aspects of the Rococo! – was a considerable aid to designers unversed in combining the various elements to form a satisfactory whole. The later Liechtenstein interiors in Vienna were probably also traceable to Feuchère, and they in turn provided inspiration for Ludwig's craftsmen. Perhaps the most remote appearance of the revived

Rococo in interior decoration was the Emperor Maximilian's Palace of Chapultepec in Mexico, which was enlarged in 1863–4.

Although the Third Republic in France was perhaps more forward-looking artistically, the lavish expenditure which produced such opulence during the Second Empire prompted a need for economies, notably on the part of the Parisian moneyed classes. Emphasis shifted sharply to London, which during the 1870s assumed a leading role in the adoption of historicizing decorative styles – but also in the reaction against them (see Chapter 8). In spite of the new attitudes to design introduced by William Morris and others, wealthy British patrons continued to favour the French eighteenth-century styles in their homes; the fascinating photographs of H. Bedford Lemere fully document late Victorian and Edwardian interiors in their complete – and replete – opulence. Baron Ferdinand de Rothschild summed up all the virtues of French eighteenth-century interior decoration:

it is not classical, it is not heroic, but does it not combine, as no previous art did, artistic quality with practical usefulness? ... French eighteenth-century art became popular and sought-for, because of that adaptability which more ancient art lacks ... Fashions will fluctuate, but French eighteenth-century art seems destined to maintain its spell on society ...

The Rococo remained the domain of the very rich by virtue of its intricacy, while the late Victorian 'Empire' style (whose delicacy was paralleled by the revival of the Sheraton-Hepplewhite style in furniture and is perfectly encapsulated in some of Sir William Orchardson's paintings) was preferred, along with the simpler Louis XVI style, by the less affluent. Although the First World War dispersed the *beau-monde* able to create such interiors on any scale, the *chic* element of much Edwardian interior decoration survived into the best Art Déco, often thinly disguised to give it superficial conformity with the new style, in which many elements of eighteenth-century interior design lived on.

8

Arts and Crafts

Chambres garnies pour belles âmes . . .

Julius Meier-Graefe

By the mid-nineteenth century, the well-to-do domestic interior was invariably over-decorated and over-furnished, whether in Britain, in Europe or in America. Commerce and industry conspired to instil into the Victorian mind the notion that 'more *is* more' (to paraphrase Mies van der Rohe), and this philosophy was nowhere more in evidence than in the home. In decoration, the battle of the styles outlined in the last chapter had faded to an acceptance of the potential inherent in all styles, from Gothic to Moorish. Against a background of increasingly elaborate and stylistically uncertain wallpapers, fabrics and carpeting, was set an indiscriminate selection of furniture, ceramics, metalwork and *bric-à-brac* of all descriptions. This *horror vacui* was accepted by the Victorians as synonymous with comfort, respectability and taste. As Nikolaus Pevsner has noted,

A stodgy and complacent optimism was the frame of mind prevailing in England about 1850. Here was England, thanks to the enterprise of manufacturers and merchants, wealthier than ever, the workshop of the world and the paradise of a successful *bourgeoisie*, governed by a *bourgeoise* queen and an efficient prince consort.

The horrors of the taste which naturally found favour in such an atmosphere inspired Henry James to write some of his most vitriolic lines in his description of the interiors at Waterbath in *The Spoils of Poynton*:

They had smothered it with trumpery ornament and scrap-book art, with strange excrescences and bunchy draperies, with gimcracks that might have been keepsakes for maid-servants and nondescript conveniences that might have been prizes for the blind. They had gone wildly astray over carpets and curtains, they had an infallible instinct for gross deviation . . . the worst horror was the acres of varnish, something advertised and smelly, with which everything was smeared . . .

Where craftsmen had made individual statements in interior decoration, the machine now generalized, driving through the morass of ill-understood motifs and forms inherited from the past. The result was a vulgarity without

precedent, and its impact was made even worse by mass-production. Industrial expansion, so evident notably in England from the later eighteenth century on, created a vicious circle in the Victorian age. As population expanded, so demand grew for mass-production, and this resulted not in the provision of better quality for all, but in generally poorer standards for the many. The only class capable of resisting mass-production were the wealthy, who could still afford to employ the finest craftsmen and furnish their homes with individually made pieces; it was not solely for reasons of novelty or exclusivity that rich collectors sought out French eighteenth-century furniture, but also because no contemporary furniture of such quality existed.

In spite of the stand taken by writers such as John Ruskin and by practising architects such as Augustus Welby Pugin in favour of Gothic as the only 'true' style, their victory was never complete. One of their underlying principles, however, found increasing support from architects and designers who questioned the merits of slavishly imitating past styles. This was the demand for honesty in architecture and design and for truth to materials – the loss of which had been a major side-effect of mass-production. While Gothic seemed to many to be the only acceptable style in this context on account of the role of the craftsman in the Middle Ages, few were able to evolve new styles based on the principles of medieval art. Ruskin and Pugin did not, while Viollet-le-Duc in France succeeded in doing so in his architectural projects using cast-iron. It was in the realm of design other than architectural that Britain suddenly gave birth to a group of artists whose work and theory were eventually to lead to the break with Historicism which signals the beginning of the modern period.

These artists were not working exclusively in reaction against that eclectic borrowing of earlier styles which characterized Victorian design, since they too – inevitably – learned many of their most important lessons from the past, and from the Orient. Some were already creating their new styles at the same time that Historicism was reaching its first flush of international popularity, not subsequently.

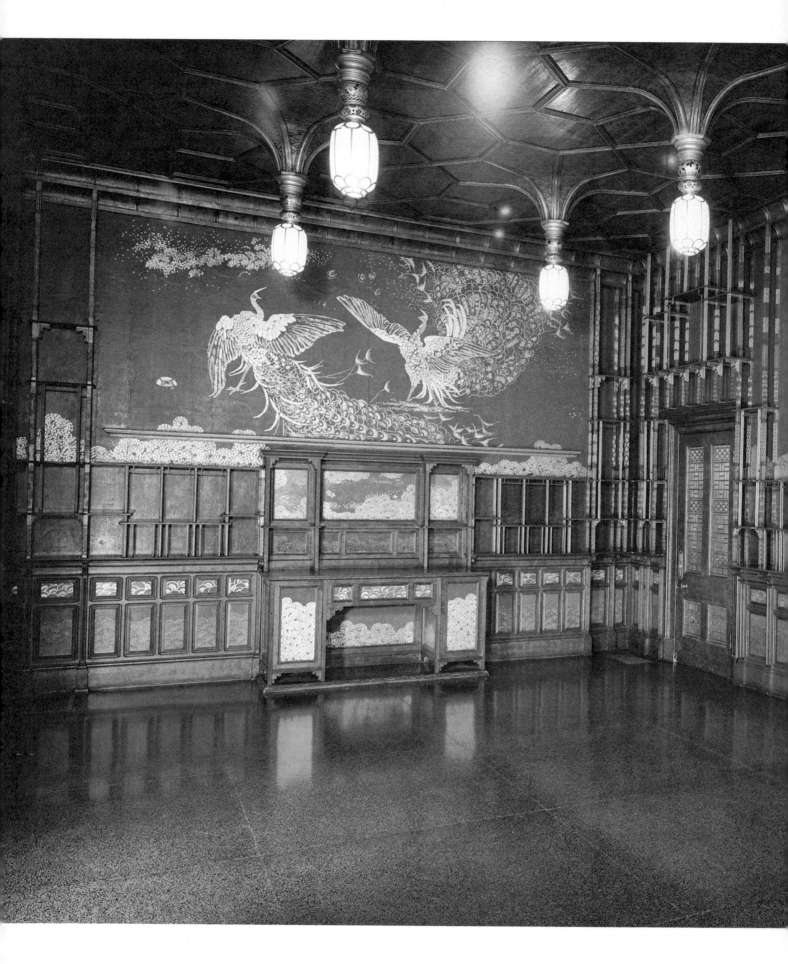

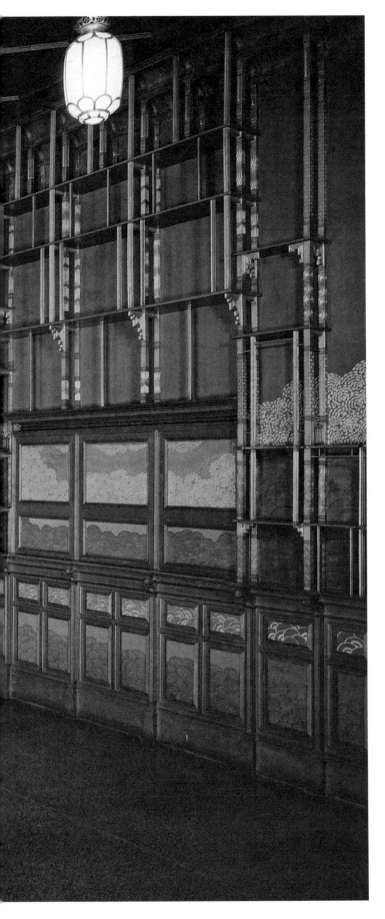

Even before the Great Exhibition of 1851 in London, which may be regarded as the high-water mark of Victorian mass-production, Owen Jones (1809–74) and Henry Cole (1808–82), two of the prime movers in design reform, were actively engaged in the struggle for what Pugin calls the 'true principles' of design. Cole was primarily a reformer, and was one of those most deeply involved in the Great Exhibition, which was conceived as a means of uniting all aspects of the applied arts of the period under one roof, that of the famous Crystal Palace. Significantly, he became the first head of the South Kensington (now Victoria and Albert) Museum, subsequently so important in the formation of many young designers. In 1849 Jones launched the *Journal of Design and Manufactures*, in which were propagated ideas fundamental to modern design concepts, but at that time alien to design practice: 'Ornament ... must be secondary to the thing decorated', while flat interior surfaces such as carpets or wallpaper should have no decoration 'suggestive of anything but a level or plain'. This was wholly at variance with the prevailing tendency to fill rooms with as much three-dimensional pattern as possible. It was Cole who conceived the idea of the 'appropriate' in decorating and furnishing an interior which has played so important a role in the modern age.

More directly involved in production was Cole's friend Owen Jones, who was conversant with all the historical styles, as is clear from his book, *The Grammar of Ornament*. Jones's un-Victorian ideals are encapsulated in his description of one of his chintz designs as 'quite unobtrusive', and its colours – deep purple and black on a white ground – were also novel in their striking simplicity. But the outstanding feature of his fabric and wallpaper designs was their two-dimensional appearance, respecting the flat surface. Neither Cole nor Jones can properly be called a decorator, but their approach was indicative of the direction which interior decoration was subsequently to take; in designing, producing and making generally available wallpapers, fabrics and certain types of furniture, they made it possible to decorate a room from individually selected items. This had of course been an accepted method of decorating less important interiors since the eighteenth century, but it now became increasingly the norm for rooms which were not conceived in any of the 'styles'. It is perhaps difficult today to appreciate how great a breakthrough this represented.

Their natural successor was William Morris (1834–96), poet, designer and theorist, for whose important reforms Cole and Jones had paved the way. Although Cole had tried to alter the pattern of mass-production somewhat by using the designs of painters and sculptors, both he and Jones saw the future of design only in machine-made

154 The Peacock Room, 1876–77, by James McNeill Whistler. *Oil colour and gold on leather and wood. Washington DC, Smithsonian Institution, Freer Gallery of Art*

objects; this was where Morris stepped in (Plate 155). At his death it was said of him that he had 'revolutionized the public taste in domestic art'. In 1861 he founded the firm of Morris, Marshall, Faulkner and Co. (later Morris & Co.), and in the following year they exhibited their furniture and embroidered textiles at the Manchester Exhibition, to wide acclaim. The painter Rossetti noted that their productions were 'intensely medieval', but from the first there was a dichotomy between Morris's Socialist theory and his practice. 'What business have we with art at all unless we can share it?' he asked, determined to bring fine design and craftsmanship within the grasp of the man in the street; ironically, his best interiors were made for the rich.

The influence of Cole and Jones was paramount on the early work of Morris, and is best seen in the interiors of his own house, the Red House at Bexleyheath. With its unrelieved wood and simplified design throughout, it presents a very different image from Morris's later, more luxurious styles, but its break with purely imitative Historicism is very important. The Red House was designed for Morris and his wife in 1859 by a young architect friend, Philip Webb (1831–1915), and it was due to Webb rather than to Morris that many of the internal features were so different from prevailing taste. The exposed brick chimney-pieces may recall the medieval hooded variety in form, but their novelty lies in their simplicity and their lack of 'period' detailing. Throughout the house, Webb rejected the inevitable symmetry of the classically proportioned domestic interior which had dominated European architecture since the Renaissance. For it he substituted asymmetry, which results in a feeling of comfort rather than elegance, and the detailing deliberately avoids the high finish characteristic of the Classical repertoire. Returning for inspiration to the native building tradition which had nothing to do with Greece or Rome, Webb established the pattern for the classic English country or suburban home (Plate 156). It was over this unpretentious framework that Morris was able to lay his own designs for wallpaper and textiles. Indeed, the clear colours and deceptively simple patterns of many of his fabrics and wallpapers (such as the 'Daisy' wallpaper of 1861) introduced a new, lighter inspiration both in form and in colour. Like the paintings of his friends the Pre-Raphaelites, they were a reaction against the stodginess and academicism of mid-Victorian art. But, like these painters too, Morris later tended towards heavier, darker forms of increased complexity, as in the famous 'Honeysuckle' chintz of 1883 with its dependence on late Renaissance prototypes.

Morris was not the only important figure responding to the new consciousness of a need for design reform in the 1860s. In 1867 the first edition of Charles Eastlake's *Hints on Household Taste* appeared, soon to be followed by a further four English editions and six in the United States. It appears that this was the first occasion on which the term 'art furniture' appeared in print, and the word 'aesthetic' also was widely used to describe the newly emerging taste for lighter, less eclectic styles of decoration and furnishing. Two elements dominate in the emergence of the 'Aesthetic Movement' in England – Japanese art, and the 'Queen Anne Style', whose chief exponents were Richard Norman Shaw (1831–1912) and Eden Nesfield (1835–88); 'Art Decoration' and the Aesthetic Movement are inextricably linked. Eastlake, like Morris, insisted on the supremacy of the traditional craftsman individually manufacturing everything by hand, and this philosophy became associated in many minds with the growing opposition to the hated philistinism of mass-production; if an object was hand-made, it was therefore 'aesthetic' and not 'philistine'. It was Oscar Wilde who alerted public consciousness (particularly in America through his lectures there) to the full horror of being 'philistine' and stimulated the enthusiasm for the several movements then in formation in England which were intent upon design reform.

The 'Battle of the Styles' also affected America, and by 1850, residual Empire Classicism jostled all the styles in the interiors of the great houses of New York, Detroit and other rapidly expanding cities. Under Eastlake's influence, Gothic retained its popularity, often in a rather flimsy form as in the Library of the D. S. Kennedy house, 41 Fifth Avenue, New York; also in this house is an ornate drawing room in the 'Second Rococo' style, which, along with Baroque, was particularly popular with the *nouveaux riches*. The last decades saw the Italian Renaissance style gain ground, either entirely recreated, as in the magnificent salon of the Barney house, 67 Park Avenue, New York (c. 1895) by Stanford White (1853–1906), or compiled from parts of actual European interiors, as at the Isabella Stewart Gardner house in Boston. It was against the background of such historicizing profusion that the vigorous and simplified new style of H. H. Richardson (1838–1886) evolved in the 1880s.

In England there now appeared the first of a spate of books and periodicals dealing with interior decoration and furnishings of all kinds. Their general tone is different from that of the great manuals of the past, such as Percier and Fontaine's *Recueil*. Instead of presenting outstanding examples of interior decoration as works of art in their own right, they offer advice (usually in a somewhat patronizing tone) on 'how to' decorate rooms of every description from *The Dining Room* (Mrs Loftie, 1878) to *The Bedroom and the Boudoir* (by Lady Baker, of the same year). Readers could select as little or as much as they wanted from such books, which meant that interior decoration would no longer be exclusive to the rich, or at least to the informed few. Although the rich still called in leading decorators (such as Morris became), it was now possible to piece together a room in the most fashionable style without their aid. This increasingly widespread habit flourished in the late Victorian atmosphere of home comfort and self-improvement.

In spite of the changes introduced by Morris and others, the actual transition from the interior which we normally

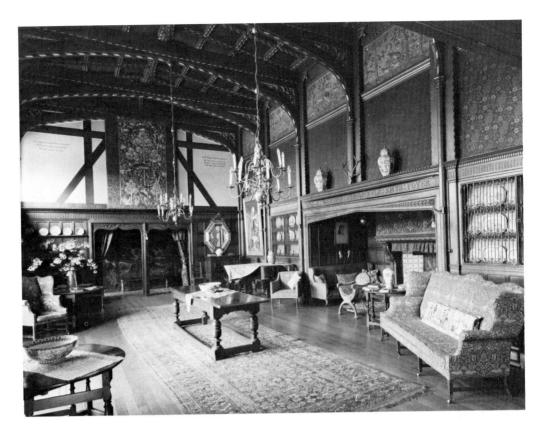

155 (right) The Great
Parlour, *by William Morris.
Wightwick Manor,
Shropshire, 1887–93*

156 (below) The Drawing
Room at Clouds, *by
Philip Webb. East Knoyle,
Wiltshire, 1879–91*

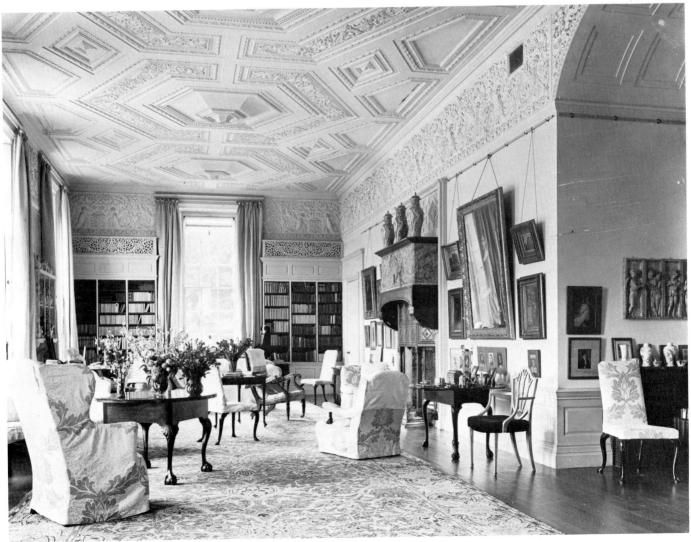

regard as 'Victorian' to the average 'art' interior is sometimes difficult to define. The dividing line between historicist styles such as Queen Anne or that most favoured for many interiors, the so-called 'bracket-and-overmantel' or 'Free Renaissance' style, is often unclear. In the frontispiece to *Furniture and Decoration of Town Houses* of 1880 by Robert Edis, for example, we see a massive chimney-piece consisting of a Perpendicular Gothic fireplace opening, surmounted by Wren-like flower garlands, over which rises an Italian Renaissance-cum-Jacobean-cum-Queen Anne structure of display shelves, mirror and pedimented finial. At each side, above the wooden wainscoting, the walls are covered in a heavy Tudor rose-patterned wallpaper. The effect, however, is not as heavy as might be expected, and the twisted brackets, delicate supporting consoles and low-relief carvings could easily be translated into the new 'art' styles with their Japanese-influenced forms and generally lighter decoration.

One of the most distinctive features of the 'art' interior was its individual use of colour. A particular shade of dull green, introduced by the Pre-Raphaelite painter Ford Madox Brown around 1860 for staining Morris firm furniture, caught the imagination of interior decorators, and in conjunction with the new flat-patterned wallpapers and textiles created the mood of many interiors of the 1860s and the following two decades. Such greens replaced the varnished mahogany or oak (either real or simulated) which were used for skirting-boards, chair-rails, door-frames and other mural articulation, and provided the perfect foil for the secondary or tertiary colours of fashionable wallpapers by Morris, Lewis F. Day (1845–1910) and Bruce J. Talbert (1838–81). All of these designers, it may be noted, were first and foremost concerned with furniture and only subsequently turned their hands to textiles and papers. Among the first major schemes carried out by Morris and Company was the Armoury Room in St James's Palace in London, decorated around 1866 in just such colour combinations; the Green Dining Room in the Victoria and Albert Museum was in similar vein, and was particularly important since it was seen by many young designers, such as Edward W. Godwin (1833–86), who derived their ideas from it.

It had now become usual to subdivide the walls into several horizontal zones – a 'dado' between skirting-board and chair-rail (common from the eighteenth century onwards to protect the wall from the chair back), surmounted by the largest area of wall surface, and a frieze between this and the plaster cornice around the room at ceiling level. Each zone could carry a different type of paper and the upper frieze was sometimes decorated with a continuous low plaster relief or with the lightly embossed and gilt Japanese imitation-leather paper which first appears in Britain in the 1870s. The wooden picture-rail, which defined this upper frieze, could be deepened at will to form a support for the Oriental plates, fans, and blue and white porcelain rapidly coming into vogue. Gone were the

heavy draperies over doorways, chimney-pieces and even furniture, gone the massive gilded picture- and mirror-frames and the overcrowded rooms loaded with *bric-à-brac*, and in their place the 'enlightened' house owner substituted fewer pieces of lighter, sometimes painted furniture, and drawings or Japanese prints in slight frames. The general preference was still, however, for dark tones:

a room with a deep-blue ceiling and walls of Vandyck brown and similar dark colours may have doors black or deep sage-green; a room whose walls and ceiling are chiefly coloured with tertiary citrine (a mixture of orange and green, a yellowish colour) may have doors of a very dull green or brownish purple; a room papered with scarlet deeply indented to break the monotony of that tint may have black or sage-green doors and wainscoting.

The passion for ceramics often extended to framing fireplace surrounds with tiles (Plate 158), a practice already common in the seventeenth century.

An important part of the Aesthetic Movement and later of Art Nouveau was the taste for all things Japanese, which appears to have originated at the International Exhibition of 1862 in London, where the collection of the first British Minister in Japan, Sir Rutherford Alcock, was shown. Surprisingly, the neo-medieval architect William Burges (1827–81), creator of one of the most intensely personal monuments of his age (Plate 153), was also a prime mover in the rediscovery and reassessment of Japanese art. Arthur Lasenby Liberty (1843–1917), Oriental Manager for a London firm until he opened his own soon-to-be-famous shop in Regent Street, also played an important part in bringing Japanese goods to Britain; many others followed his example, but the quality of their imports rapidly declined as demand outweighed supply. The Japanese style was given the highest recognition at the Paris Exhibition of 1878, when the Prince of Wales's morning room had 'Anglo-Japanese' furniture designed by Godwin and decorated by James A. M. Whistler (1834–1903). It is easy to understand the fascination exerted on Victorian taste by Japanese art, which seemed to offer so many of the features praised by thinking designers – simplicity, clean lines, and decoration deriving from natural forms. The Japanese domestic interior, inasmuch as it was known in Europe, was the antithesis of mid-nineteenth-century clutter.

The Godwin-Whistler partnership resulted in some of the most beautiful rooms of the period. Godwin's passion for things Japanese (which led him to dress the children of his mistress, the actress Ellen Terry, in small kimonos) resulted in a refinement rare at the period, and it was undoubtedly his taste which inspired Whistler's. As early as 1862, he had decorated his own house in Bristol in a strikingly simple manner. Plain painted walls and bare

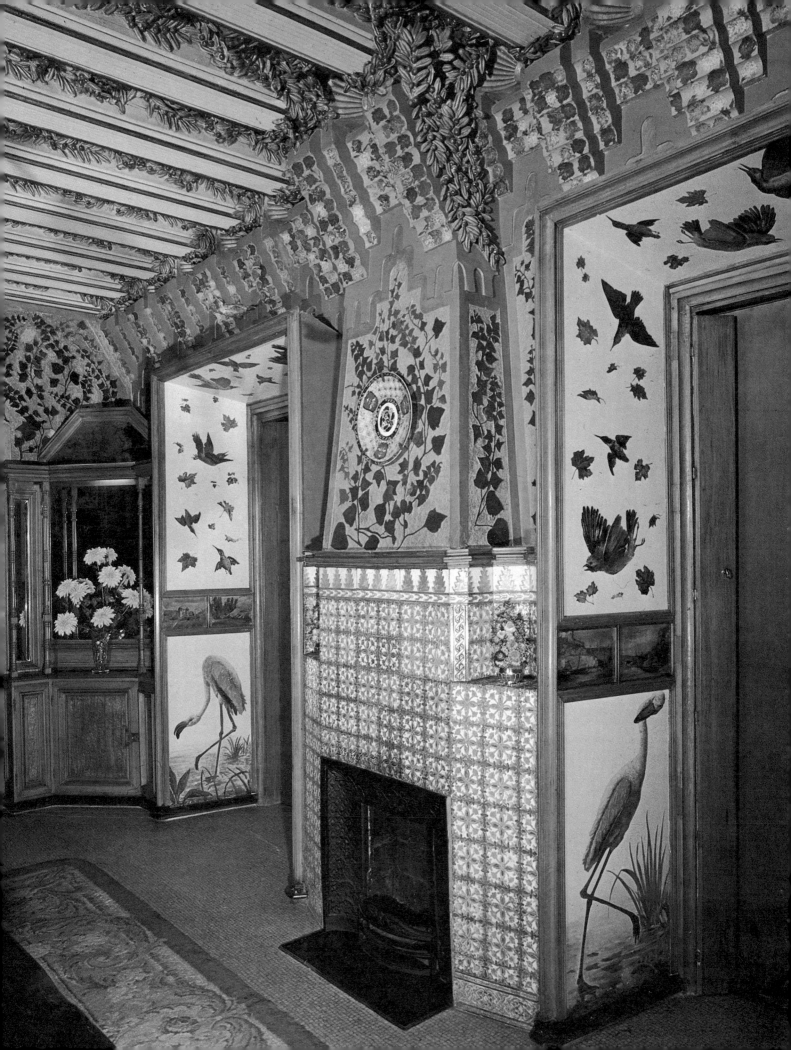

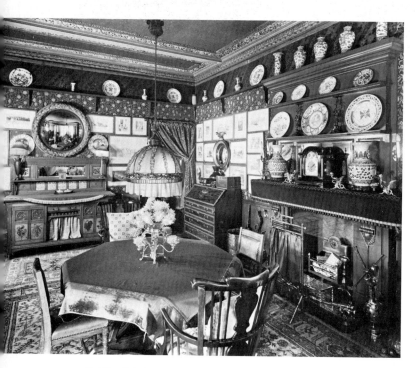

158 The Dining Room, Linley Sambourne House, 18 Stafford Terrace, *London, 1890s*

boards were offset by Persian rugs, Japanese prints and a minimum of fine furniture. In 1878, he built and decorated Whistler's house in Tite Street, Chelsea, providing the perfect setting for the painter's subtly tonal oil paintings. Godwin was the first English designer to make skilful use of carefully balanced schemes of colours, usually pale, such as the room for Oscar Wilde decorated in 1884 in various tones of white – unthinkable to other designers of the period. The care which he took in obtaining precisely the right colour balance is more typical of eighteenth- or twentieth-century than of mid-Victorian interiors: 'The whole of the woodwork to be painted in enamel white and grey to a height of five feet six inches. The rest of the walls to be finished in lime white with a slight addition of black to give a greyish tone.' Godwin was a prolific designer of wallpapers and textiles, which were manufactured by the firms of Warners and Jeffery for the many interiors which he decorated.

The less-known architect Thomas Jeckyll (1827–81) also produced 'Japanese' interiors, notably in the 1870s; his most famous creation, The Peacock Room now in the Freer Gallery, Washington, is usually associated with Whistler (Plate 154). That enlightened patrons were ready to adopt the Japanese manner is evident from the well-known collector Alexander Ionides' shift from the Morris style to Jeckyll's in his London house at 1 Holland Park; in the billiard room, Jeckyll inset Japanese lacquer trays, coloured prints and paintings on silk in a framework of oak dividing the walls and ceiling into many small panels, and in the sitting room he used carved coral-coloured lacquer in the overmantel to show porcelain to advantage.

After the 1868 Japanese revolution, the market was flooded with Japanese objects, and the taste retained its hold on interior decoration at every level until the First World War, although few designers attained the same degree of refinement as Godwin in interpreting the lessons of Japanese design.

It is worth noting at this point the effect of Oscar Wilde's lecture tour of the United States of America in 1882, since it was he who conveyed in watered-down and often preposterous form the ideas first proposed by Morris in his lectures on 'The Decorative Arts' begun in 1877. From the latter Wilde derived the principle: 'Have nothing in your houses which you do not know to be useful or believe to be beautiful' – an attitude partly introduced into America by Eastlake's *Household Taste*, which paved the way for the Aesthetic Movement's success there. Wilde did not hesitate to lecture on 'The English Renaissance' and on 'House Decoration', although he often had as little idea as his hapless audience about the true nature of his subject, having jumped on the 'art' bandwagon at just the right moment.

The Aesthetic Movement and its various offshoots was exclusively a British phenomenon, and one whose most obvious manifestations were in the decoration of domestic interiors. It was this field which was often attacked and parodied, as in a poem called *The Downfall of the Dado* published in *Punch* in 1881. Gilbert and Sullivan's operetta *Patience* of the same year parodied the 'sentimental passion of vegetable fashion' so characteristic of the 'aesthetes'. It was, however, precisely this 'vegetable fashion' which gave rise to the next important phase of design to affect the domestic interior on an international scale – Art Nouveau.

Art Nouveau's wide diffusion is evinced by the many names by which it was known: *Jugendstil* in Germany, *Sezessionstil* in Austria, *Stile Liberty* or *Floreale* in Italy and *Art Nouveau* in France. While the various national manifestations are different, they all share some common features, the more florid varieties being generally conspicuous in the Latin countries. The style's sources can be traced in many preceding movements, going back as far as the asymmetry of the Rococo in the early eighteenth century, but the real impetus was given by Arthur H. Mackmurdo's famous cover for his book on Wren's City Churches published in 1883. Its sinuously weaving forms, as of plants moving under water, prefigure aspects of Art Nouveau design in all the decorative arts – furniture, ceramics, textiles and metalwork – just as its extraordinary cohesiveness was to become one of the main characteristics of the Art Nouveau interior.

If the Arts and Crafts and the Aesthetic Movements in Britain signalled the end of Historicism and in some ways represent a transitional period, Art Nouveau is linked firmly with the 1890s, and with a new escapist mood in the arts epitomizing the closing years of a momentous century. Art Nouveau's life was brief, its appearance, development

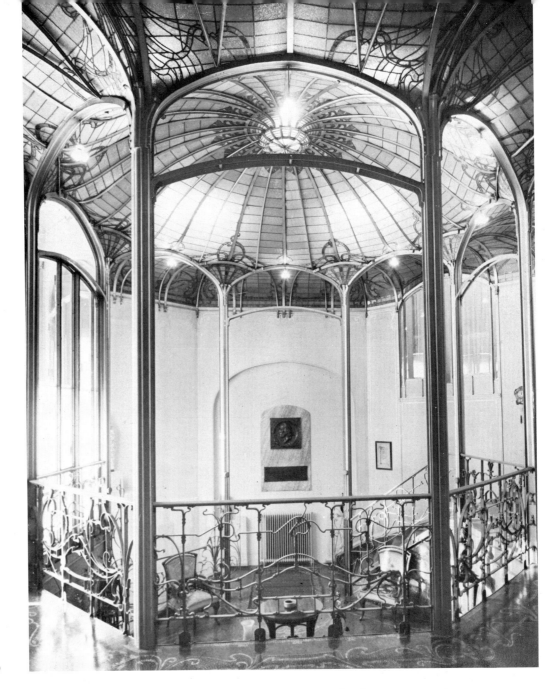

159 Salon of the Van
Eetvelde House, *by Victor
Horta, Brussels, 1897–1900*

and demise spanning little more than a decade.

The first architect to create fully evolved Art Nouveau domestic interiors was the Belgian Victor Horta (1861–1947). It is significant that he combined architecture with internal decoration in a way which makes him much more than just a decorator, and links him to the other great designers of his period, Mackintosh and Gaudí. As with the Rococo, it is of the essence of Art Nouveau at its finest to synthesize architecture and decoration in an indivisible unity. From Viollet-le-Duc's two-volume treatise *Entretiens sur l'architecture*, published in Boston in 1875–81, came Horta's interest in the structural and expressive possibilities of iron architecture, and it was Viollet-le-Duc's idea of a light-weight armature or skeleton in iron which inspired the finest of Horta's interiors (Plate 159). His first house, the Tassel Residence at No. 6 rue Paul-

Emile Janson in Brussels of 1892–3, was also in many ways his best, and its famous staircase prefigured all his subsequent work. Ironwork is exposed throughout in columns and girders which curve and twist into tendril-like forms. These are echoed in the painting on walls and ceilings, and in the mosaic floor patterns, which Horta used in several houses. Precisely this love of sinuous line is seen in the contemporary paintings of the Dutch painter Jan Toorop.

'The realization of any and every undertaking', wrote Horta, 'involves the empirical execution of a programme which is technically appropriate to the purpose in hand'; he was also a planner of great skill, substituting vestibules at different levels in his houses for the long corridors common to most Victorian homes. He also designed every part of an interior himself, from the door-handles to the stained glass, which he used not only in window and door

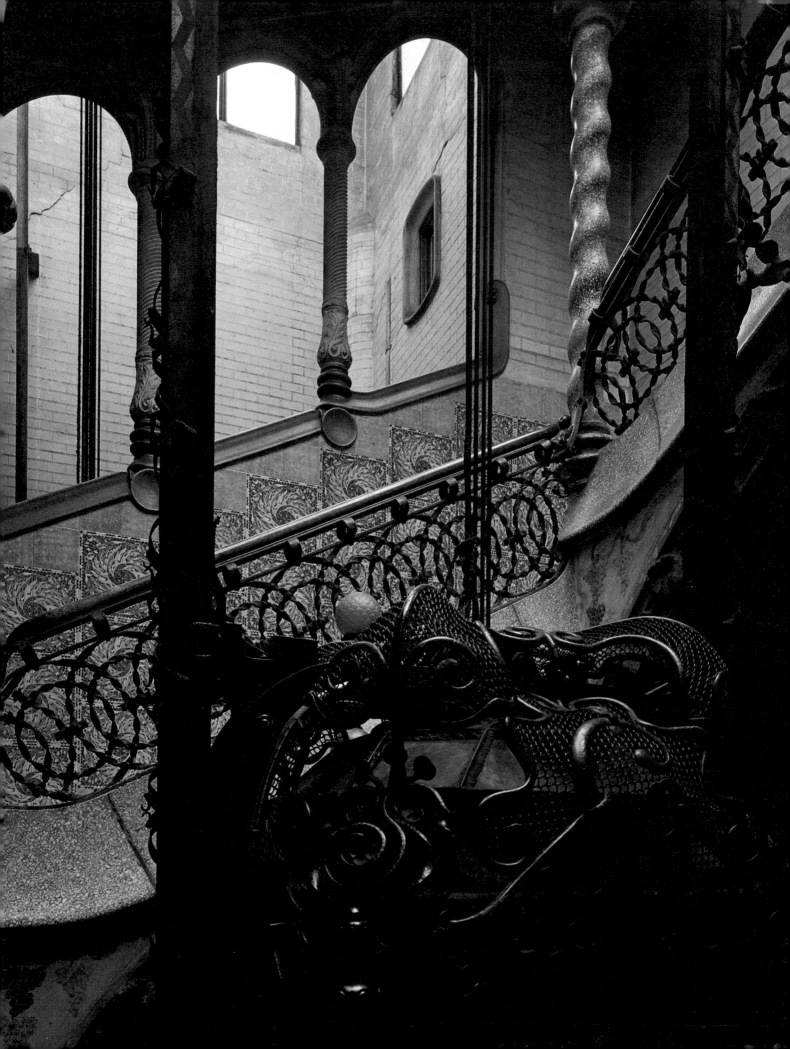

panels, but also for whole internal ceilings, as in the Hôtel Van Eetvelde (completed in 1895). Horta's love of iron-work took very different forms from those of other de-signers, as in the remarkable balustrade of the Solvay Residence in Brussels of 1895–1900, where the complex writhing forms made up of jointed sections make great play on their exposed structural bolts. The contrast with the average *Beaux-Arts*-influenced ironwork of the im-mediately preceding period with its weighty neo-Baroque complexity could not be greater. Horta was only one of many Art Nouveau designers such as Gaudí and Mack-intosh who realized the possibilities of ironwork for abstraction and for the strength it could give to even the flimsiest of forms.

Like many architect-designers, notably in France, Horta could not remain oblivious to the unified effect obtained in the eighteenth-century Rococo interior, where flowing line linked wall panelling, plasterwork and furnishings. One of the finest examples in his work of this influence is the magnificent dining room in the Hôtel Solvay. A quasi-organic sense of growth linking each form distinguishes this room, where, although strong verticals predominate, chimney-piece, large overmantel mirror and fitted, glazed cabinets at either side seem to belong to the same structural and decorative unit; this aspect of Horta's interiors looks forward to the best twentieth-century design and dis-tinguishes him as one of the most sensitive decorators of the period. His wall treatment suggests a fine web of lines, into which he inserts stained glass, mirrors and windows with great delicacy; to modern eyes his work combines the best of the European tradition with a forward-looking approach, and it was said that the shock of seeing the Tassel Residence reduced Horta's former master Alphonse Balat to tears.

Two other architect-designers in the Low Countries developed variants of Art Nouveau in somewhat different directions from Horta's. These were H. P. Berlage (1856–1934) and Henry van de Velde (1863–1957). Berlage, whose furniture designs were realized in the Amsterdam studio known as *Het Binnenhuis* ('The Interior'), belongs partly to a trend which played an important role in certain countries' development of Art Nouveau – the concern with folk art and native building and decorative traditions. His interest in the exposed brick characteristic of much Dutch architecture, both external and internal, led him to use this in his domestic interiors to a somewhat chilly effect, as in the prison-like staircase of his house at 42–4 Oude Scheveningsche Weg in The Hague of 1898. Its deliberate harshness is contrasted with the luxuriousness of many Art Nouveau interiors, and predates similar Expressionist experiments by more than twenty years. Van de Velde too had a more functionalist approach to decoration. 'It is dangerous', he said, 'to pursue beauty for beauty's sake', and in his own house, Bloemenwerf, at

160 Casa Calvet, Barcelona, *by Antoni Gaudí, 1898–1904*

Uccle near Brussels he pursued a policy of eradicating decoration throughout wherever possible. This ruthless modernism gained him the patronage of the Grand Duke of Saxony, the Hamburg dealer based in Paris Samuel Bing, and the art critic Julius Meier-Graefe among others, as well as the devotion of a large group of artists who were deeply influenced by his style. In 1899, he moved to Ger-many, and his ideas, based on the theory of Morris, were fundamental in the period leading up to the foundation of the Bauhaus. One of the most enterprising interior decora-tors was Gerritt W. Dijsselhof, who developed his style from medieval precedents, as is seen in the superb room now in the Gemeentemuseum, The Hague, with its delicate tapestries inset into pale, polished wooden panelling.

Perhaps the greatest interior decorator of the period, however, was Charles Rennie Mackintosh (1868–1928), a precociously gifted Scottish architect whose influence was international within his lifetime. He toured Italy on a scholarship in 1890 and on his return to his native Glasgow married Margaret Macdonald; his friend Herbert Mac-Nair married her sister, Frances, thus creating an *équipe* known as The Four, whose work already caused a stir when shown at the 1902 Turin Exhibition. Mackintosh's interiors, fabrics, posters and furniture were soon hailed by leading artistic and intellectual circles in Vienna, Munich and Darmstadt, where his unique style, combining a certain puritanism with an underlying sensuousness, struck a sympathetic chord. His first Glasgow work, the Glasgow School of Art (1896–9), contains the germs of his subsequent development. His imaginative spatial relation-ships, showing an understanding of internal space almost entirely lacking in his Continental contemporaries, give his rooms an individuality and an air of distinction, accentuated by the decorative devices which he and his wife made particularly their own. It was probably she who originated the elongated, ascetic forms, whether human or floral, which people the interiors in the form of flat, two-dimensional patterns of stiff vertical lines with infills in lilac, pink and white. The style's apogee came in the Cranston Tearooms, in Sauchiehall Street, Glasgow (sub-sequently senselessly destroyed), where painted caryatid-like hieratic female figures enmeshed in a cage of stylized flowers processed in a frieze round the walls above the level of the chair-rail, their intense verticality emphasized by tall ladder-back chairs beneath. Regrettably, few of Mackintosh's interiors survive (Plate 1) in the degree of completeness which he envisaged.

Utterly different from the Rococo-inspired 'movement' of Horta, Mackintosh's aristocratic style drew its inspira-tion from a variety of sources such as Celtic art (whose carved stylizations Mackintosh regularly adopted) and the Scottish Baronial tradition of architecture. From C. F. A. Voysey's furniture came the predilection for combining attenuated vertical shafts with almost non-existent cor-nices forming paper-thin ledges around a wall, which Mackintosh used frequently in his interiors. Like his contemporary M. H. Baillie Scott (1865–1945), Mackintosh integrated built-in furniture and traditional ingle-nooks into his wall patterns, unified as in Baillie Scott's work by colour schemes of great delicacy, with pastel shades predominating. This combination of remarkable restraint with the 'intoxicating exaggerations' of Art Nouveau results in a deliberately self-conscious style very different from the homespun Arts and Crafts interior. The unnerving predominance of straight lines suddenly offset by an elongated tense curve culminating in stylized roses or abstracted oval forms, and his exquisite designs – which record his intentions – where even the flower arrangements follow the same nervous linear patterns, suggest that the ideal occupants of Mackintosh's interiors should be 'slim gilt souls'. To a lesser extent, the same is true of Baillie Scott's interiors, such as those he designed for *The House of an Art Lover* and those featured in *The Studio* magazine between 1894 and 1902. Never did Baillie Scott indulge in the fantasies which led the work of The Four to be called the 'spook school'.

No other talent comparable with Mackintosh's appeared in Britain, but an important development there around 1900 was the growth in the number of commercial furniture firms which offered their clients Arts and Crafts-influenced designs; of these the most famous was Heal and Son. Together with others such as Wylie and Lockhead, Heal was responsible for the acceptance by an ever-increasing number of people of the simplified interiors with only a few well-designed pieces of furniture which had found favour with the élite for close on twenty years. Throughout the nineteenth century catalogues of furniture had increased the buying public's awareness of progressive trends, and Heal continued and developed this tradition, incidentally providing an interesting record of the shifting nuances of taste. With London at the centre of the furnishing trade, these catalogues made it possible for purchasers to select the latest fashionable pieces at any distance from the capital, and throughout Britain furniture-makers copied Heal's innovations. As with the 'art' styles when first introduced, most of Heal's pieces could be placed in any moderately simple setting without difficulty, with the result that the average English house around 1900 often combined half-timbered or panelled rooms in the Tudor and Jacobean tradition, pieces of Japanese-influenced furniture, highly polished mahogany and miscellaneous pieces of Oriental porcelain – in fact, the comfortable, undemanding style generally associated with the Edwardian period.

In France, the Art Nouveau (which is, after all, a French term deriving from Bing's shop of that name in the rue de Provence in Paris) was, generally speaking, much more elaborate than elsewhere in Europe, notably in furniture and interior decoration. To a lesser extent than in Britain, there had been a reaction against Historicism on the part of enlightened thinkers like Viollet-le-Duc and the Comte Léon de Laborde, whose two-volume *De l'union des arts et de l'industrie*, published in 1856, advocated the return to craftsmanship. 1866 saw the publication of Ruprich-Robert's *Flore ornementale*, whose interest in natural forms was one of the leading influences on French Art Nouveau. More than any other country except perhaps Italy, France looked back with nostalgia to the Rococo, and this, combined with the new interest in natural forms, resulted in the most characteristic manifestations of Art Nouveau. There were two main centres, Paris, and Nancy where the Ecole de Nancy's many craftsmen produced a highly elaborate local style. The Union Centrale des Arts Décoratifs was so named in 1877, and set out to bridge the gap between designer and industry. In 1891, the *Revue Blanche* was founded in Paris, and, like the English *Studio* which began to appear two years later, this propagated the latest ideas germane to the spread of Art Nouveau. In 1898 came *L'Art Décoratif*, and in the same year Meier-Graefe opened his shop La Maison Moderne. Bing's shop L'Art Nouveau was the centre of remarkable productivity on the part of his group of artists and craftsmen, including Georges de Feure, Eugène Colonna, Eugène Gaillard and the work of the American modernist Louis Comfort Tiffany. As with the Arts and Crafts movement in England, it was from the goods purchased in such shops that most Art Nouveau interiors were composed, but there were also many designers who conceived whole decorative schemes, the foremost of whom was Hector Guimard.

Guimard (1867–1942) is rightly best remembered for his superb ironwork Métro stations in Paris, which encapsulate the joyfully sinuous vegetal style in which he excelled. Between 1894 and 1898 he built the apartment block known as the Castel Béranger at No. 14 rue La Fontaine in Passy, whose remarkable interiors have an abstraction matched only by the work of Gaudí in Spain. Like the glass vases of Tiffany and Gallé, Guimard's room shapes follow their own laws, based on the wayward growth patterns of plants. In this he was diametrically opposed to the rationalism of Mackintosh and the Viennese. Features such as wall-mirrors and door-cases seem to grow out of the structure containing them, suggesting a fantastic element which led one writer to describe Guimard's highly eccentric Castel Henriette at Sèvres of 1903 as 'the dwelling of Mélisande' – the ill-fated wistful heroine of Maurice Maeterlinck's Symbolist fairytale *Pelléas et Mélisande*. Guimard described himself as an *'architect d'art'*, and continued to create interiors in his full Art Nouveau style long after it was *démodé* in France (Plate 161).

Although furniture was often fitted and much of the decoration tended to be fixed in the form of panelling or other wooden decoration, interiors by the leading designers of the period are still fascinating without their original contents. Nevertheless, the Art Nouveau room is best understood when full of furniture and objects in the same style. Notably in France we can see the cumulative effect of glass by Gallé (he described some of his pieces as a 'miniature floral anthology'), furniture writhing with carved plant forms by Louis Majorelle or Alexandre Charpentier or painted with exquisite lightness of touch by Georges de Feure, and wallpaper, silver or ceramics to the design of Alphonse Mucha. Mucha (1860–1939) is perhaps the artist most representative of the triumph of Art Nouveau in Paris around 1900, when it received official sanction at the Exposition Universelle; his three books, which appeared in the next few years, codified the style for the French – *Combinaisons ornementales*, *Figures décoratives* and *Documents décoratifs*. His interior decoration was conceived on a luxurious basis, using sumptuous materials and colours, as in his famous printed velvet showing the type of languorous women who appear in his posters framed in dense floral patterns in autumnal colours

161 Staircase of Maison Guimard, *by Hector Guimard, Paris, 1900*

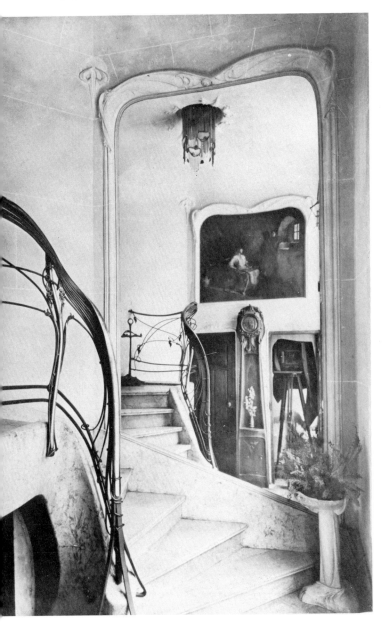

against a black background. In France, Colonna and De Feure designed carpets equivalent to those by Voysey and Frank Brangwyn in England, and tapestry enjoyed a revival in France at this time.

Art Nouveau at its most fantastic, inventive and abstract is found in the work of Antoni Gaudí (1852–1926), who worked almost entirely in and around Barcelona. Like Mackintosh, Gaudí derived many elements from local traditions – in his case Gothic and Moorish – and evolved a style which is sometimes capricious, often nightmarish, and always original. He was intensely religious (he was mourned almost as a saint in Barcelona after his death) and a fanatical element carries all his buildings, externally and internally, to the point of obsessive, proto-Expressionist elaboration. The closest comparison is with Guimard, and like him Gaudí designed blocks of flats (such as the Casa Batlló and Casa Milá of 1905–7 and 1905–10 respectively). The ground-plans of his flats, however, look like the hives of crazed bees, with virtually no right angles in any room and internal walls which follow the same apparently total lack of logic as the exteriors. Because Gaudí is renowned above all for his astonishing buildings, such as the Sagrada Familia Cathedral and the Colonia Güell, his interiors are much less well known than they deserve to be.

His first major private house was the Casa Vicens of 1878–80, some of whose interiors reflect the Arts and Crafts Movement (Plate 157). Walls are articulated by fitted furniture (including picture frames) in clear wood with simple mouldings. In the remaining space are painted birds and ivy, which appears to grow from behind the woodwork. A disturbing note is introduced by the ceilings, where realistically painted foliage clusters between fluted beams, occasionally descending over the walls. Throughout the house, modified Moorish elements appear, culminating in the *fumoir* with its ceiling pendants, Islamic lamps and beaded window-screen. In the entrance hall of the Palacio Güell, built in 1885–9 for his most important patron, Eusibio Güell, Islamic and Gothic elements combine with flat brick ceilings of great beauty and massive, twisted internal window bars in wrought iron to create an impression of capricious originality. The vigour of Gaudí's interiors distinguishes them from all contemporary developments elsewhere in Europe, rendering somewhat effete the pallid rooms of Mackintosh and the writhings of Horta's decorations.

His sense for the integrity of architecture and decoration is best seen in the remarkable interiors of the block of flats called the Casa Calvet (Plate 160), whose conventional exterior belies the barbaric splendour within. Twisted granite columns, columns with bulging bases reminiscent of Garnier's Second Empire details in the Paris Opéra, blue-and-white-tile-covered walls contrasting with large unrelieved brick areas, smoothly moulded inset windows and doors, highly polished dark wooden panelling and fantastic ironwork all place these rooms in a unique category of inventiveness both in form and in the use of

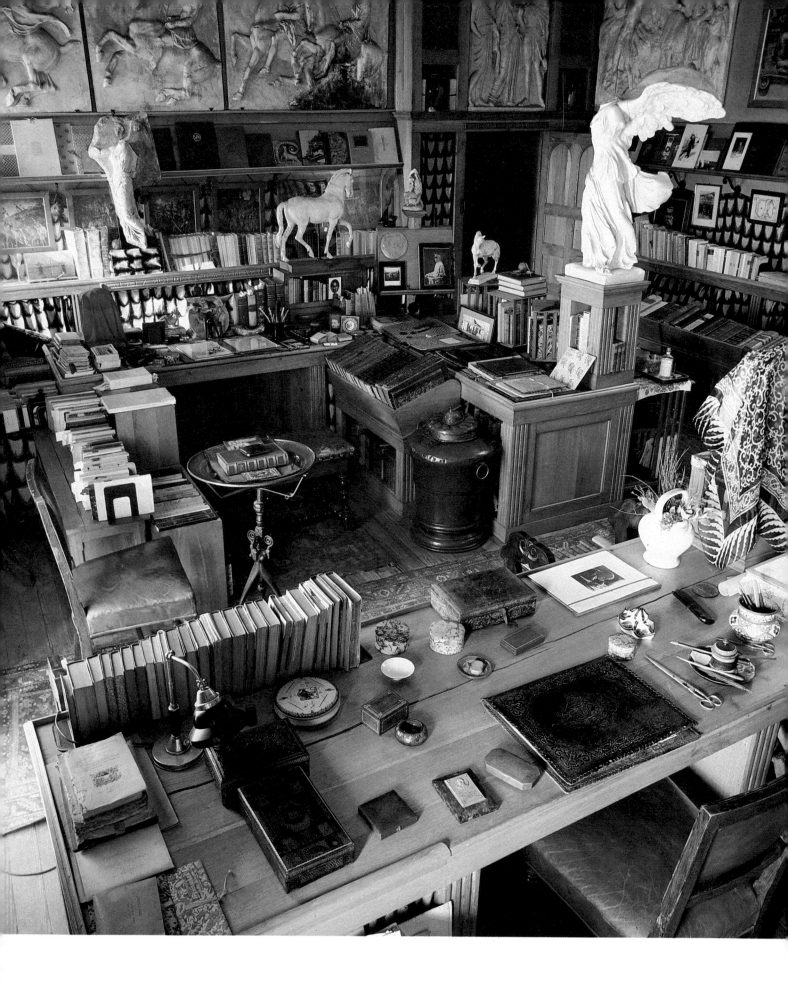

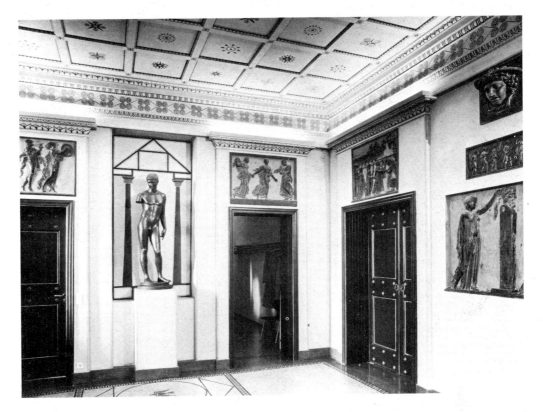

162 *(left)* The Study of
Gabriele d'Annunzio. *From*
La dimora di D'Annunzio.
Il Vittoriale, *Palermo,
Edizioni Novecento*

163 *(right)* Entrance Hall to
Villa Stuck, *Munich, 1897*

materials. As Pevsner has noted, how 'remote from the conditions of London, Paris or Brussels the conditions were in which Gaudí could develop this intransigent brand of Art Nouveau'.

By contrast, the work of the German and Austrian designers derived much of its inspiration from British innovations. Munich and Dresden saw exhibitions in 1897 which included examples of foreign Art Nouveau, and the influential magazine *Jugend* had been started the previous year as a mouthpiece of the new art. The Münchener Vereinigte Werkstätte workshops were important in developing the style in Southern Germany. In Munich, in spite of outrageous exceptions (Plate 164), Neo-classicism continued to exercise a strong influence, notably in the work of Franz von Stuck, whose aristocratically refined interiors 'quote' antiquity as Gaudí had quoted Islamic art, albeit in a much less virile tone (Plate 163).

The three architects who created the Viennese version of Art Nouveau – the Sezession – were Otto Wagner (1841–1918), Joseph Maria Olbrich (1867–1908) and Joseph Hoffmann (1870–1955). Here, Mackintosh's influence in interior decoration was paramount because the Viennese designers disliked the more languid vegetable inspirations of the Belgians and French. Since their great success at the Turin exhibition of 1902, Mackintosh and his wife had become increasingly well known throughout Europe, and it was their combination of functionalism with distinctive stylishness which appealed to the Viennese. The Sezession was founded in 1897 to create a new style breaking with the conservatism of art in the Austrian capital, and its determination not to depend on earlier styles links it more

firmly with modernism than most other manifestations of Art Nouveau.

Known to the Sezession probably from as early as 1897, when some of his designs appeared in *The Studio*, Mackintosh was invited to Vienna in 1900. Ahlers-Hestermann has left a description of the Music Room designed by Mackintosh for Fritz Wärndorfer, who gave the money for the foundation in 1903 of the Wiener Werkstätte, with Hoffmann as one of its leading figures:

... the oddest mixture of puritanically severe forms designed for use, with a truly lyrical evaporation of all interest in usefulness. These rooms were like dreams, narrow panels, grey silk, very very slender wooden shafts – verticals everywhere. Little cupboards of rectangular shape and with far projecting top cornices, smooth, not of visible frame and panel construction; straight, white and serious-looking, as if they were young girls ready to go to their first Holy Communion – and yet not really; for somewhere there was a piece of decoration like a gem, never interfering with the contour, lines of hesitant elegance, like a faint distant echo of Van de Velde. The fascination of these proportions, the aristocratically effortless certainty with which an ornament of enamel, coloured glass, semi-precious stone, beaten metal was placed, fascinated the artists of Vienna who were already a little bored with the eternal solid goodness of English interiors ... As against the former overcrowding, there was hardly anything in these rooms...

The ingredients of the Sezession interior thus arrived ready-made in Vienna.

The Sezession architect-designers studied Mackintosh with care. His peculiar mixture of austerity and elegance,

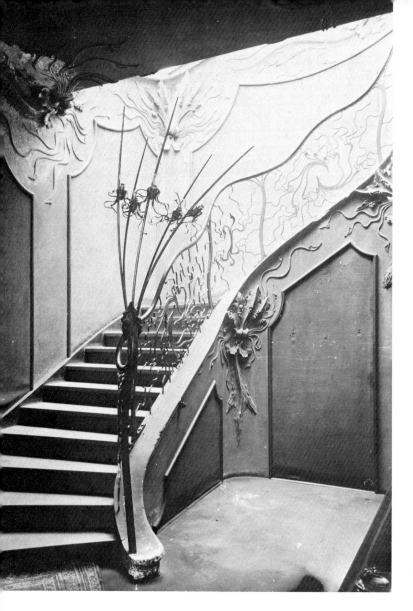

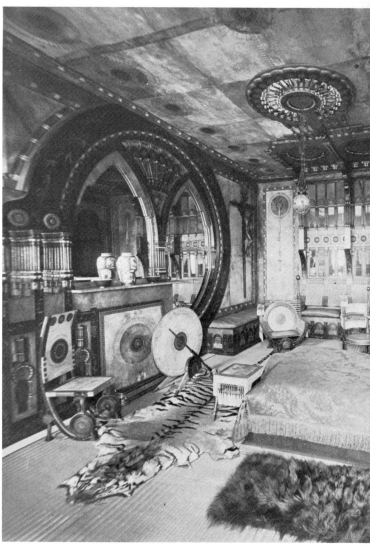

164 *(above)* Staircase
of Atelier Elvira, Munich
(destroyed 1895)

166 *(right)* Dining Room of
the Palais Stoclet, *Brussels,
by Josef Hoffmann, with
mosaics by Gustav Klimt*

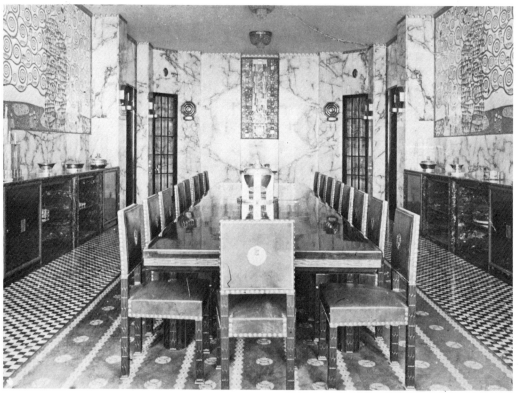

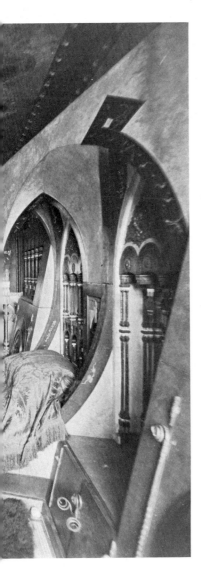

165 Bedroom, *by Carlo Bugatti   This was probably the room designed by Bugatti (1856–1940) for Lord Battersea at his London house at 7 Marble Arch. Manufactured in Milan, it was sent to London with a team of workmen who installed it around 1903. Bugatti had won the Diploma of Honour at the 1902 Turin Exhibition for his Snail Room, whose surfaces were covered with vellum and decorated with Bugatti's dragonfly motif. It is a short step from this style, with its part Oriental, part machine-inspired motifs, to Art Déco*

In Italy, 'Il Liberty' or 'Lo Stile Floreale' enjoyed an immense vogue, not only in major cities such as Milan, where many new apartment blocks of the 1890s were decorated internally in modified Art Nouveau forms, but also in unexpected places such as Pesaro. Many of the best examples of 'Il Liberty' remain – surprisingly, in view of their quality – anonymous; the two most famous architects were Raimondo d'Aronco (1857–1932) and Giuseppe Sommaruga (1867–1917). Both reflected the essentially eclectic nature of Italian Art Nouveau, drawing on French and Austrian precedents. Following tradition, many Italian interiors paid lip-service to Art Nouveau decoration in the form of walls patterned with linear designs in rooms whose shapes remained essentially unchanged.

Among the leading decorators in the style were Fausto Codenotti (1875–1963) and Costantino Grondona (b. 1891), who, like most of their Italian contemporaries, were deeply influenced by the Glasgow School. To Mackintosh's primarily vertical and rectilinear emphases, they added 'Lo Stile Floreale's' vegetable excesses in their wall-paintings, panels, textiles and stained glass. Grondona's *Modelli di arte decorativa*, published in 1908, provided many decorative schemes which prefigure Art Déco, and Giovanni Battista Gianotti's review *Per l'Arte*, founded in 1909, spread the influence of Viennese and Darmstadt *Sezessionstil*. Galileo and Chino Chini were brilliant creators of Floreale pavements, and Umberto Bellotto's (1882–1936) ironwork and glass were much admired by D'Annunzio, whose astonishing eclecticism ranged from Classical and Byzantine interior detail to the latest styles (Plate 162). In Sicily, Ernesto Basile (1857–1932) created many of the most outrageous Floreale interiors, where creeping forms cover every part of the walls, ceiling and floor.

The spread of Art Nouveau in America was fostered by, among others, Louis Comfort Tiffany (1848–1933). Stained-glass windows in gorgeous colours are among the most dazzling features of his elaborate interiors, which were created by his firm for rich patrons such as H. O. Havemeyer (the Havemeyer House, New York).

Art Nouveau and its various offshoots (see Plate 165) provided a romantic finale to the most eclectic of centuries, and its *fin-de-siècle* refinement and worldliness are strangely at variance with the youthful freshness attributed to the style. The French version of the style represents the conclusion of several traditions, while Mackintosh and the Viennese look forward to the twentieth century's more original developments. Perhaps its most important contribution to interior decoration was its strong emphasis on *stylishness* and on the unity of the domestic interior. Its widespread diffusion – furthered by major exhibitions and periodicals – was also to be an important factor in the rapid spread of modernism, and the creation of a truly international style.

utility and decoration, proved irresistible. The two features of his style which most affected the Viennese were his strong vertical emphases, and the sparse application of his highly idiosyncratic decorative vocabulary. His love of dividing wall surfaces into separate panelled zones, often creating a frieze-like area immediately beneath ceiling level (an echo of the 'Aesthetic' interior in England) profoundly affected the way in which the Viennese articulated space. The most famous interior executed under the impact of Sezession developments was that of the Palais Stoclet in Brussels (Plate 166), where preference for luxuriant materials, colours and textures was typical not only of Viennese interior decoration in this period, but also of painting, notably the work of Gustav Klimt (1862–1918); Klimt's glittering, jewel-like paintings are the essence of the sophistication aimed at in the affluent home of his Viennese bourgeois patrons. From Van de Velde onwards, many designers of the Art Nouveau period were involved with commercial interiors and those of yachts and trains.

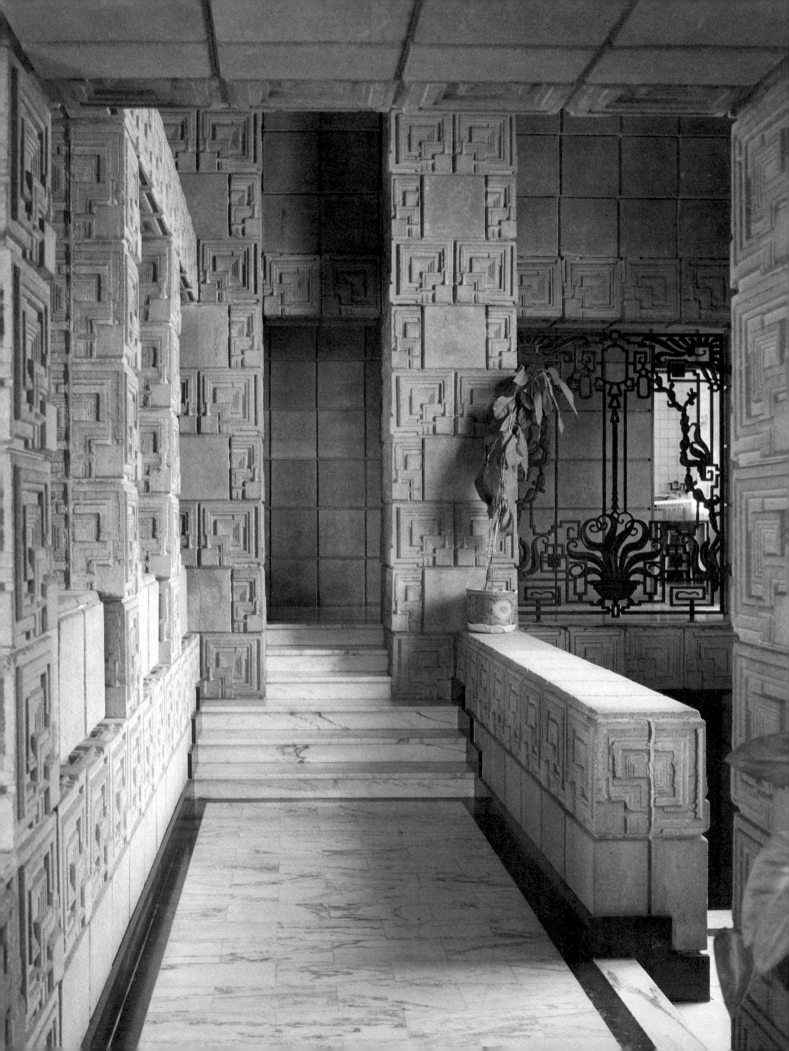

9

The Twentieth Century

The complete building is the final aim of the visual arts. Their noblest function was once the decoration of buildings. Today they exist in isolation, from which they can be rescued only through the conscious, cooperative effort of all craftsmen. Architects, painters and sculptors must recognize anew the composite character of a building as an entity. Only then will their work be imbued with the architectural spirit which it has lost as 'salon art'.

From the First Proclamation of the Weimar Bauhaus

This book appears at a time when it seems safe to say that most of the major architectural advances of the twentieth century have already taken place; a comparison with the same decade in any century since the Renaissance would seem to bear this out. By the 1580s the Renaissance had fully run its course, while a century later the Baroque was completely evolved and was spreading from its country of origin, Italy. In 1780, Neo-classicism was already a European movement which had largely killed the Rococo style of the earlier part of the eighteenth century, and by the 1880s the new movements which were to sweep Historicism away were already growing fast. Consequently, the 1980s are perhaps a good time at which to look back over the twentieth century and attempt to assess – however superficially – the main trends in interior design and decoration.

In his book *Inscape, the Design of Interiors*, published in 1968, Sir Hugh Casson wrote:

Broadly speaking, for the interior designer there will be two approaches: the first is the 'integrated' where the interior is indivisible from the structure and where pattern, form, texture and lighting are part of the architecture, and qualities of permanence and monumentality are sought. The second, which may be termed the 'superimposed', is where the interior is required to be more flexible, and easily modified or even transformed without mutilating the architecture in which it is temporarily contained.

Although to a limited extent this has always been true of the domestic interior, the division between the two

types has been accentuated in the twentieth century and the term 'interior decoration' always applied to the latter, while the former is generally described as 'architectural'. Thus, taking a random selection of interiors reproduced in this book, those in Plates 22 and 119 are 'architectural' while those in Plates 101 and 156 conform more closely to what we now think of as 'decoration'. In this context, Casson continues, 'Many architects refuse to believe that

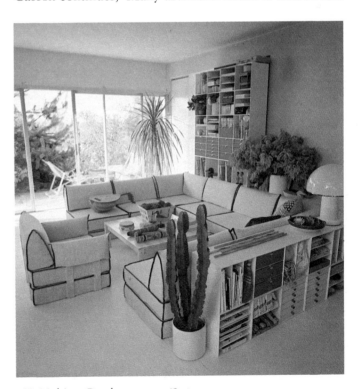

168 Habitat Catalogue 1977/8, *page 23*

167 *(left)* Ennis House, Los Angeles, *by Frank Lloyd Wright, 1924*

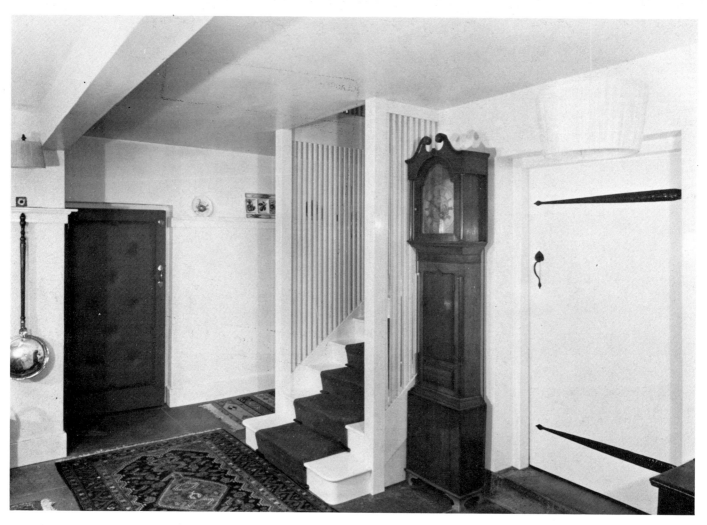

169 The Orchard, Chorleywood, *Hertfordshire, by C. F. A. Voysey, 1900–1*

interior design exists at all', which is the point at which the stigma attached by some architects to the term 'interior decorator' arises.

The gap between domestic architecture and its interior decoration is a particularly twentieth-century phenomenon, and one which is related to the changed nature of important building commissions in the present century. In the nineteenth century, the balance between industrial and commercial building on the one hand and domestic building on the other still existed, with the result that while money and attention might be lavished on commercial buildings, houses were still being built on a magnificent scale. Today this magnificence is almost entirely confined to banks, offices and other public buildings, where the type of decoration formerly found on palaces and ecclesiastical architecture now – albeit sporadically – appears. Where a rich family in the eighteenth century might have built a vast country mansion, in the twentieth century a small house designed by Mies van der Rohe or Le Corbusier is the equivalent status symbol. Nevertheless, the rich of today continue to spend lavishly on domestic interior decoration, as is witnessed by the proliferation of decorators since the Second World War and the growth industry in glossy periodicals, which purvey fashionable interiors to an ever-growing audience.

But the rift between architect and decorator in the twentieth century is a reality. As we have seen, from ancient times on, many fine interiors were the result of collaboration between architects and the leading painters or sculptors of the day. The emphasis was on *collaboration*, since architects like Bramante, Le Vau and Robert Adam depended on the ability of craftsmen of all kinds to realize their ideas. This was often particularly apparent in interiors which might be classified as more strictly architectural, notably important staircases, halls and public reception rooms. In the twentieth century, the greatly increased emphasis placed by architects on function, even in the domestic interior, has naturally diminished the importance of all fixed decoration extraneous to the structure. Thus, in houses designed from the ground up by one architect, there is rarely any need for an interior decorator, as in most of such interiors the internal architecture provides the spatial articulation and treat-

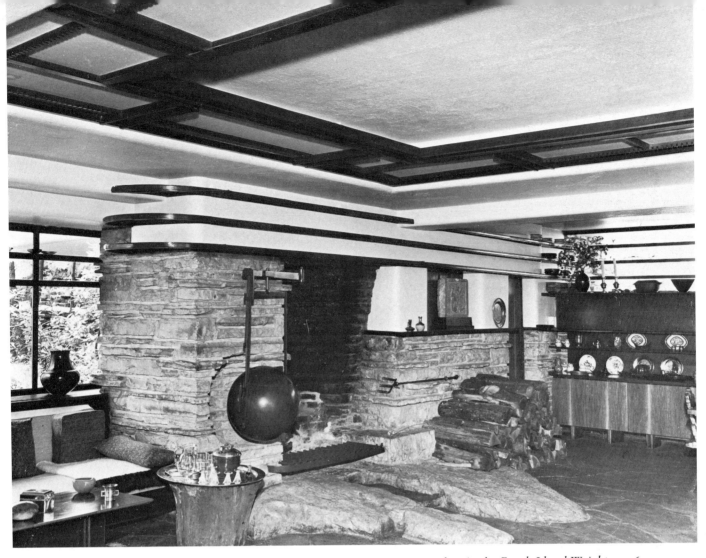

170 Falling Water, the Edgar J. Kaufmann House, Bear Run, Pennsylvania, *by Frank Lloyd Wright, 1936*

ment of exposed surfaces formerly given over to painted, carved, panelled or other decoration.

The first signs of such integration appear in the latter part of the nineteenth century in the work of architect-designers like Charles Annesley Voysey (1857–1941), who wrote of 'discarding the mass of useless ornaments'. He designed with equal facility houses, wallpaper and household utensils, but was, unlike Morris and his kind, primarily an architect. It is his considerable ability to turn functional features in his interiors to decorative effect which links him firmly with the modern movement. This is seen in interiors like the hall in The Orchard at Chorleywood in Hertfordshire (Plate 169) of 1900, where, in spite of nostalgic sideways glances at the traditional English cottage, the treatment of such elements as the staircase are novel and inventive. Also important is the close stylistic relationship between Voysey's exterior architecture and his restful, simplified interiors. The deceptive simplicity of his work did not lend itself easily to imitation; nevertheless the appearance of English suburbia with its semi-detached, timbered and gabled houses owes its inspiration to his originals. Another important English figure whose life

spanned the transition from the Victorian to the modern era was Sir Ambrose Heal (1872–1959). Around the turn of the century he abandoned Victorian furniture types in his London shop in favour of lighter woods with little and carefully integrated decoration, which parallels Voysey's experiments. Heal's illustrated catalogues were widely circulated throughout Britain and helped create the new vogue for simpler interiors.

At the same time that Voysey was creating his masterpieces around the turn of the century, America suddenly came to the fore in architecture with the work of Frank Lloyd Wright (1869–1959). Wright had studied under Louis Sullivan (1856–1924), who advocated buildings which were 'well-formed and comely in the nude', and was also influenced by the architecture of Henry Hobson Richardson (1838–86), whose open-plan interiors had a considerable effect on his own. Wright wanted his architecture to develop 'from within outwards in harmony with the conditions of its being'. His 'prairie houses' around Chicago developed out of conditions which made them very different from anything in Europe: their particularly American character stamps them as the beginning of a real

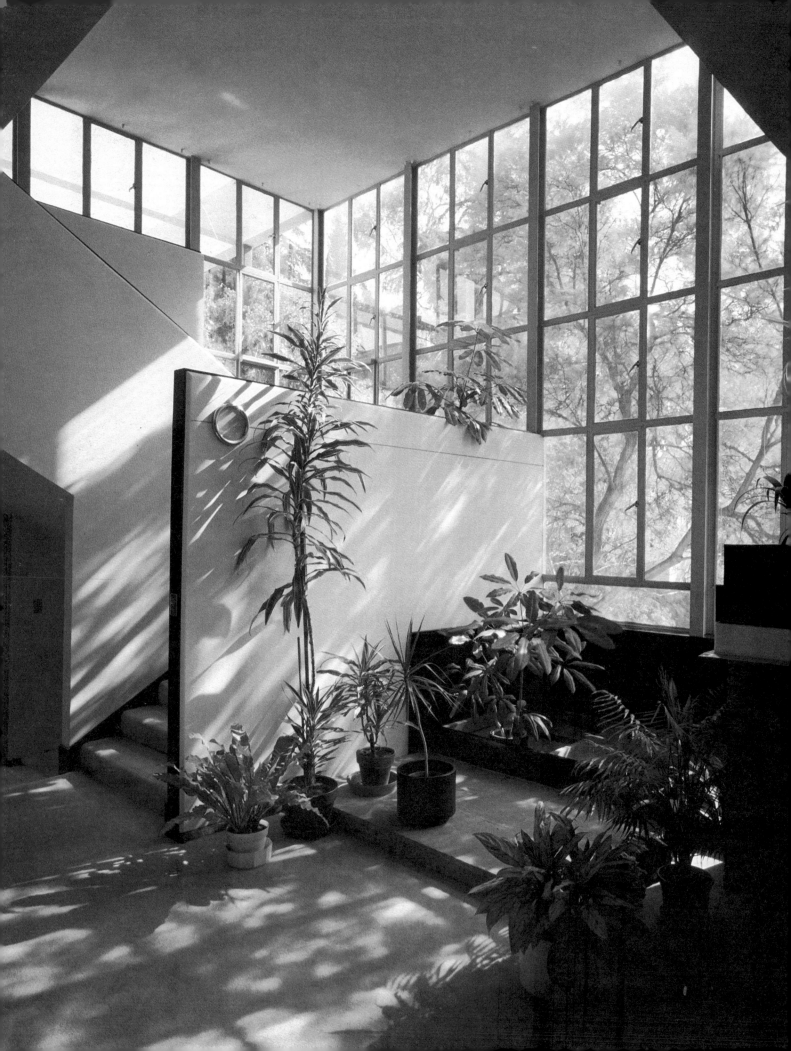

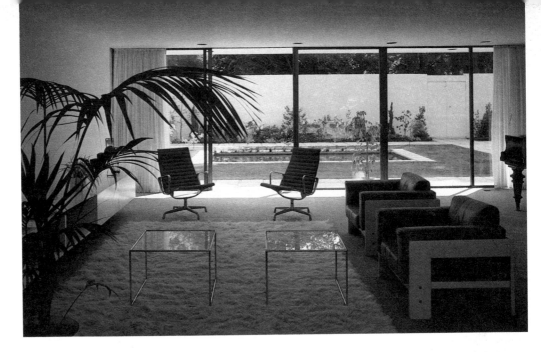

171 (left) Lovell House, Los Angeles, *by Richard J. Neutra, late 1920s*

172 (right) House by Richard Horden for his parents, *Poole, 1976*

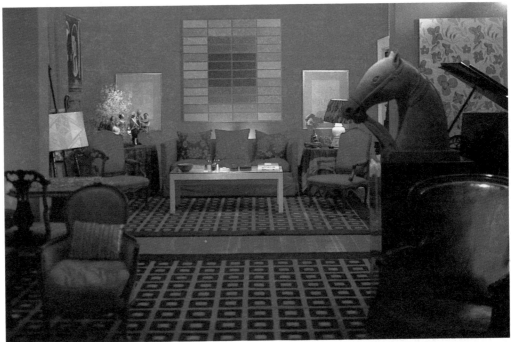

173 (right) Sitting-room of a house in Oxfordshire, *designed in the 1970s by David Hicks*

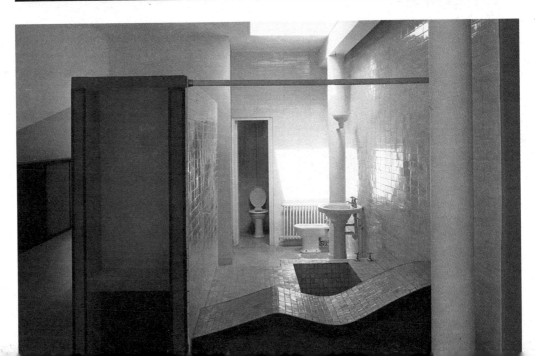

174 (right) Villa Savoye, Poissy, *by Le Corbusier, 1928–30*

architectural independence. By comparison with the average Victorian interior in America (see Plate 141), Wright's were startlingly bare, boldly exposing internal brickwork and using this in conjunction with carefully selected woods to obtain an effect at once welcoming and uncluttered. In a number of the houses of all sizes which he designed in the 1890s such as the Winslow House at River Forest, Illinois, he also used sheeted windows, whose patterns dominate the interiors and break up the image of nature beyond. The relationship of Wright's interiors to their surroundings is unique, and one of the most striking features in many of his houses is the prominence (symbolic as well as functional for him) given to the fireplaces. It seems unimaginable that any architect born in the Victorian age could think as Wright did of setting a fireplace on a bed-rock which is allowed to rise into the interior of the house, further emphasizing his preference for breaking down divisions between exterior and interior.

Occasionally, the sharp angularity of some of the features Wright employed approaches brutalism, but the effect when seen in predominantly low, spreading rooms, whose shapes and interrelationship are sometimes deliberately unclear, is relaxing. It is a tribute to his patrons that they were able to accept his advanced ideas. His concern for his clients is particularly well-documented in the case of the Hanna House at Stanford in California, where an entire archive of correspondence allows one to follow the growth of each part of the house to the satisfaction of both architect and owner. Apart from certain details, Wright's interiors of the first decade of this century already appear strikingly modern (Plate 170), and indeed his particular combinations of textures have retained their appeal until the present day without being superseded by the more overtly luxurious interiors of Mies van der Rohe. It was Wright who popularized brick chimney-breasts which run the full height of a room or (as at the Coonley House, Riverside, Illinois, of 1908) to a narrow ledge running the full length of the wall. Although highly idiosyncratic, few of his fully evolved interiors resort to decorative mannerisms like the eccentric patterning in oblongs around the edge of the wood-panelled ceiling at the Coonley House; the more virile aspects of his style were widely transmitted through his school at Taliesin, Arizona. Wright created for himself an unassailed position as the father of American Modernism by his refusal to compromise with passing trends such as Art Déco (which his 'Mayan Temple' style in poured concrete at the Hollyhock and Ennis Houses in Los Angeles of the 1920s (Plate 167) helped to create), although he remained alert to other architects' innovations as in the Mies-influenced interiors at Rosenbaum House at Florence, Alabama, and the Winkler House in Okemos, Michigan.

In Europe, the Dutch were particularly receptive to Wright's masculine, unaffected interior architecture, perhaps because of their own brick-building traditions, and the work of proto-Expressionist architects like Berlage

(see page 191). But it was Germany which saw the major moves towards real Modernism as early as the 1890s, producing artist-theoreticians whose concepts spread rapidly as far afield as America. The degree to which the Germans were capable of rejecting all links with past styles even at the height of the Art Nouveau period is shown by a remarkable apartment designed for Alfred Walter von Heymel by his cousin, the decorator-poet Rudolf A. Schröder (1878–1962), in Berlin in 1899. This astonishing *unicum* had a degree of stylistic simplicity and unity setting it apart from anything else of its date. Its simple geometric decoration prefigures by several years certain works by Josef Hoffmann (1870–1956) (Plate 166) and the Austrian architect Adolf Loos (1870–1933), who transformed it in his Steiner House in Vienna in 1910 into a starkly simple style virtually indistinguishable from the Modernism of two decades later. The spirit of good design for all was already in the air in Germany, and in the Dresden exhibition of industrial art held in 1899–1900 a whole apartment consisting of two living rooms, kitchen and bedroom, which could be manufactured at an unprecedentedly low price, was shown. Apart from England, it was Germany which showed the greatest interest in making available the components from which simple interiors could be formed, and in 1909 Walter Gropius (1883–1969) produced a programme for the mass-production of small houses using standardized parts.

In 1907, the Deutscher Werkbund was formed by a group of far-seeing manufacturers, officials, architects, artists and writers whose aim was to encourage the practical application of good design and sound craftsmanship to create 'an organic whole'. The need to unite the arts had already been felt in nineteenth-century Germany, where the ideal of the medieval *Bauhütte*, or society of artist-craftsmen, with the great cathedrals as their focal point, was studied; this and ideologies like Wagner's *Gesamtkunstwerk* or total art work paved the way to the Bauhaus, founded in 1919 under the direction of Gropius.

The Staatliches Bauhaus came into being as a result of Gropius's reorganization of the Weimar Art School for the Grand Duke of Saxe-Weimar, and remained the focus of forward-looking design in all its aspects until Gropius resigned in 1928. In its first programme, Gropius spoke of the 'desire for a universal style of design stemming from and expressive of an integral society and culture'. This linked the social context to Frank Lloyd Wright's ideal of 'One thing instead of many things; a great thing instead of a collection of small ones'. 'In organic architecture', Wright goes on, 'it is quite impossible to consider the building as one thing, its furnishings another.' Nonetheless, it was in some ways with the Bauhaus that the growing concept of interiors as extensions of external architecture gained ground; in the catalogue of the 1914 Cologne exhibition, where the Werkbund triumphed, there is only one illustration of a domestic interior, and it is an advertisement showing a distinctly old-fashioned room.

This increasingly architectural thinking about interiors was linked with the emphasis on machine manufacture (however carefully controlled) in the Werkbund, although the Bauhaus's programme emphasized a balanced education in stoneworking, carpentry, metalwork, textile weaving, construction technique, theory of space, colour and design, and so on. When the Bauhaus moved from Weimar to Dessau in 1925, a new generation of teachers had already been trained, and from that year many of the now familiar productions of the school were in circulation, including furniture, textiles and metalwork, all of which were to change the appearance of interiors of every kind.

Gropius came from a family of architects and entered the office of Peter Behrens in 1907 after studying in Berlin and Munich; it is significant that two other leading architects of the Modern Movement also spent some time with Behrens – Mies van der Rohe and Le Corbusier. Before 1914, Gropius's interiors were rather conservative and showed little indication of the direction he later took. In *The New Architecture and the Bauhaus* (1935) Gropius writes, '... I became obsessed by the conviction that modern constructional technique could not be denied expression in architecture and that that expression demanded the use of unprecedented forms.' Although for Gropius these forms found their fullest outlet in his industrial building, where steel and glass construction 'etherealized' architecture (Wright), he seemed less able to apply it to his domestic designs. Whereas the Model Factory at the 1914 Cologne exhibition incorporated the famous external glazed spiral staircase, he later veered

between the Expressionism of the interiors at the Sommerfeld House, Berlin (Plate 175), and the strikingly modern interiors of the Bauhaus itself, finished two years later in 1923. The Director's Room shows the early Bauhaus style with its unrelieved wall surfaces, prominent light fittings of tubular bulbs wired through thin aluminium tubes, and wall hangings by Guntha Sharon-Stölz using yellow, grey, brown, violet and white in cotton, wool and rayon. While the emphasis there was emphatically on the display of crafts, a quite different style distinguished his office in the new building at Dessau: less emphasis on individual craft pieces and general streamlining of surfaces and detail, with the addition of fitted furniture, gave the room a more dateless appearance, and one which other contemporary architects preferred to emulate.

Mention should be made of another group, called *de Stijl*, dedicated like the Bauhaus to creating forward-looking design and to rejecting any links with past styles. The leading member of this Dutch group was Gerrit Rietveld (1888–1964), who, as a constructivist, based his design on abstract, rectangular forms in the primary colours of red, yellow and blue. *De Stijl* took its name from the magazine of that title, and believed in the philosophical and spiritual properties of these forms and colours; the famous 'red-blue chair' made by Rietveld in 1917 with its severely simple slab-like seat and back looks forward to similar uses of plain surface and strong colour during the 1950s. From 1924 dates Rietveld's architectural masterpiece, the Schröder House in Utrecht, whose interiors are virtually interchangeable with its exteriors:

175 Sommerfeld House, Berlin, *by Walter Gropius, Adolf Meyer and Joost Schmidt, 1921–2*

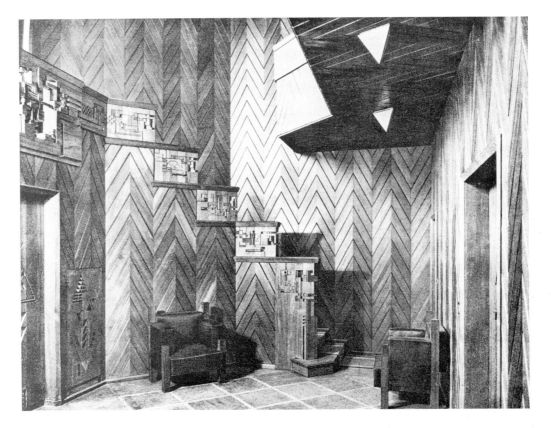

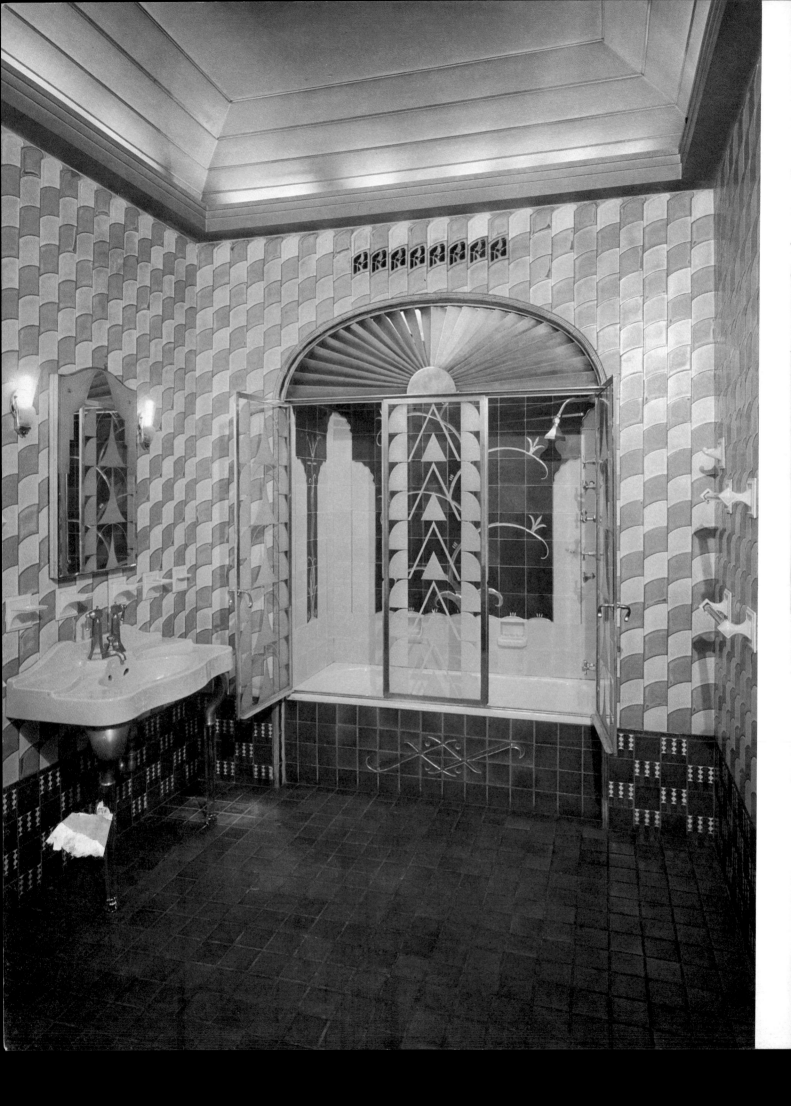

176 *(left)* Bathroom in the Executive Suite, The Chanin
Building, New York, *1929   Designed by Jacques Delamarre
under the supervision of I. S. Chanin, this is one of American
Deco's more lavish interiors; gold-plating is used extensively,
on the basin and shower taps, and on the edges of the
engraved glass shower-doors. The gold is offset by the cream
and gold tiles. The small frieze of ceramic bird tiles over the
bath conceals the ventilating duct. Metalwork and
deliberately brash devices were extensively used in public
interiors of the period in American cities, but this room sums
up the best aspects of American Modernism and shows that
opulence could be contained within the limits of the
functional requirements of a room*

177 *(below)* Schreiber House, Hampstead, *London, by
James Gowan, 1965*

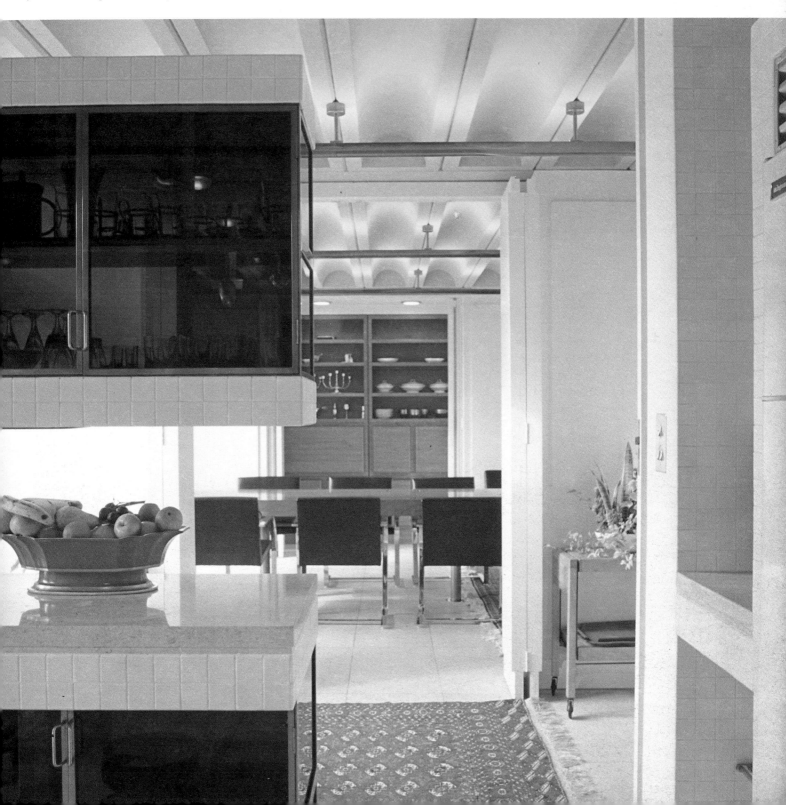

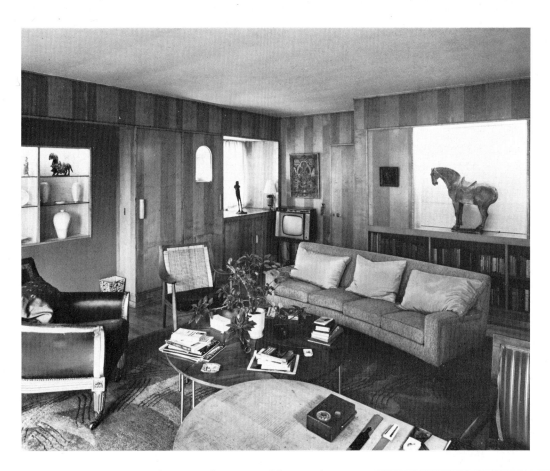

178 (left) No. 64 Old
Church Street, Chelsea,
London, by Erich
Mendelsohn and Serge
Chermayeff, 1936

179 (below) Entrance Hall
and Staircase, by Mario
Faravelli, c. 1930. From
L'arredamento moderno,
Milan, 1934 Roberto Aloi's
L'arredamento moderno is
one of the best contemporary
records of top European
interiors and furnishings of
the later 1920s and early
1930s, including both Art
Déco and the International
Style. This interior, in
diaspro di Sicilia marble, is
typical of many by Faravelli
in the Neo-classical style
which came to be identified
with Italian and German
Fascism in the 1930s. The
Neo-classical columns,
coffered ceilings and overdoor relief panels are offset
by strikingly Art Déco
metalwork

clean-cut, slab-like surfaces without mouldings of any
kind form both walls and ceilings, while metal-framed
windows in continuous horizontal strips run right up to
ceiling level. The whole effect is one of clean line without
austerity, and Wright's ideal of the total interchangeability
of interior with exterior is fully realized with the barest
minimum of means. In the Schröder House, Rietveld not
only prefigures Bauhaus ideas but also the International
Style, as it came to be called in America.

Before examining the interiors of the two greatest
architects of the modern period, Mies van der Rohe and
Le Corbusier, a group of architects who brought the
International Style to the fore should be mentioned. Erich
Mendelsohn (1887–1953) became noted for his curving
façades with window bands which follow the curve round
corners; in 1929 he designed one of the most significant
houses of its date, in the Grünwald forest on the east slope
of the Havel Lake. The importance of its interiors lay in
the extensive fitted furniture of all kinds, from music
cabinets to built-in radios, telephones and gramophones.
Another interesting house is the one he designed in Chelsea
with Serge Chermayeff (Plate 178). Peter Behrens (1868–
1940) in his house in the Taunus mountains carries
luxurious simplicity to a fine art.

In Italy, although the official Neo-classicism associated
with Fascism (Plate 179) produced some stunning interiors
where marble, glass bricks, elaborate and often very
beautiful metalwork and lavish wooden veneers dominate,

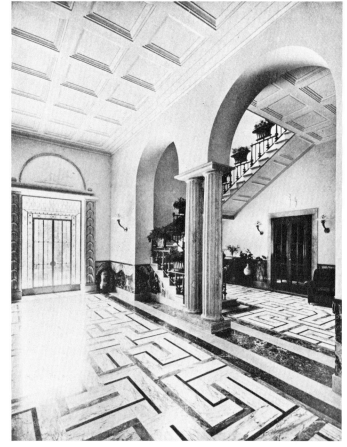

the International Style gained ground in the work of the Gruppo 7 of Milan. Its most gifted member was Giuseppe Terragni (1904–42), whose Villa Bianca at Seveso near Milan and Villa Bianchi at Rebbio near Como show Le Corbusier's influence. The most exciting Milanese Art Déco designer was Mario Faravelli (Plate 179), who introduced fantastic elements into his interiors such as floors and ceilings decorated with the signs of the zodiac; Michele Mavelli, another Milanese architect-designer, even used musical scales or individual notes on certain of his ceilings. After the Second World War, it looked as if Italy might lead the way in architecture and design, with the work of architects like Pier Luigi Nervi (1891–1979), Gio Ponti (1891–1979), and others, but this period was short-lived.

In England, architecture was given impetus by the arrival of several Germans, including Mendelsohn, Gropius and Marcel Breuer, and the Tecton group was founded by the Russian architect Berthold Lubetkin with Anthony Chitty and Denys Lasdun. Others such as Raymond McGrath and Godfrey Samuel also contributed to the International Style in Britain. The Britain Can Make It exhibition arranged by Sir Basil Spence at the Victoria and Albert Museum, and the 1951 Festival of Britain Exhibition organized by Sir Hugh Casson, both gave considerable impetus to British design and encouraged the post-war British to revitalize their homes in the light of the new styles of decoration and furnishings. The 'see-through' interior came into vogue, not made of glass, but (in the tradition of Frank Lloyd Wright's interiors) consisting of room divisions made by low bookcases or cupboards, bookcases which frame open spaces and fireplaces whose flues rise at one side leaving the overmantel space open with a clear view to the room or space beyond. Such breaking up of the traditional wall spaces and other divisions of an interior went hand in hand with the development of fitted furniture designed specifically for adjustment to every size and shape of room; Bauhaus designers had experimented with such furniture (adjustable shelving, for example), which has subsequently come to play such an important part in every kind of modern interior (see Plate 168).

The International Style interior at its best is a finely designed shell where proportion plays a more important part than decoration, which is generally limited to movable features. Into this shell could be inserted any type of furniture, painting or other object without altering the intrinsic quality of the interior space. Such simplicity is deceptive, and in the hands of a mediocre architect can be merely banal: in the hands of a very few architects of genius, however, some of the finest artistic achievements of any age have emerged. One of these architects is Ludwig Mies van der Rohe (1886–1969).

Mies's often-quoted 'simplicity is not simple' and 'less is more' provide a key to the brilliance and great beauty of his architecture, which, probably more than any other twentieth-century architect's, is wholly interchangeable with his interiors in terms of structure and design. In addition to being 'classic', Mies's work is also 'classical', possessing the finality of the best Greek or Roman architecture where nothing can be altered without detriment to the whole. Interestingly, one of his earliest designs (for a house for Mrs Kröller-Müller of 1912) has the massing, relationship to its surroundings, coupled-column loggia reflected in water, and even the rustication of antique villas as interpreted by German Neo-classicists like Schinkel; the latter's buildings exercised a profound influence on the young Mies after his arrival in Berlin in 1905 from his native Aachen, and his Perls and Urbig Houses in Berlin-Zehlendorf and Neubabelsberg (1911 and 1914) are still heavily Neo-classical with festoons and other fully Classical detail. The First World War changed all this, and the steel and glass architecture which had once been acceptable only for factories or other commercial buildings now began to appear in domestic use. Mies's involvement with the Bauhaus, of which he became Director in 1930, helped him eradicate all traces of Classical detailing from his designs, and his collaboration with Lilly Reich during the 1920s confirmed his love of functionalist materials and restrained colour; at the 1927 Werkbund Exhibition at Stuttgart he introduced black and white linoleum flooring and etched clear, opaque and grey glass partitions. He first demonstrated the flexibility of a metal skeleton structure for domestic housing in his apartment blocks, such as the Weissenhofsiedlung of 1927 in Stuttgart. Having established his basic prototype for apartment interiors, he continued to refine on it until the end of his life: in the Lafayette Towers at Lafayette Park, Detroit, the walls are composed entirely of window except for the continuous area beneath, which houses heating-pipes and optional air conditioning.

In 1929, Mies created the prototype for luxurious International Style interiors with his German Pavilion at the Barcelona International Exhibition (Plate 180). Here for the first time structural and space-defining elements were separated, and a total synthesis achieved between exterior and interior space. Arthur Drexler wrote:

The Barcelona Pavilion was without practical purpose . . . [it] consisted of walls and columns arranged on a low travertine marble podium . . . it channelled space between separate vertical and horizontal planes . . . the flow of space was held within clamp-like walls at each end of the podium. Between these walls the building 'happened' like a slow dance on a stage.

A miracle of simplicity, the interiors depended entirely on their superb proportions and on the dazzling beauty of their materials – travertine, grey glass and green marble. The steel columns supporting the roof were sheathed in chrome and the two reflecting pools were lined with black glass. The only piece of 'decorative' art was a Georg Kolbe sculpture. The pavilion housed the type of chairs designed by Mies which became known as 'the Barcelona chair' and which he used throughout his subsequent interiors. What

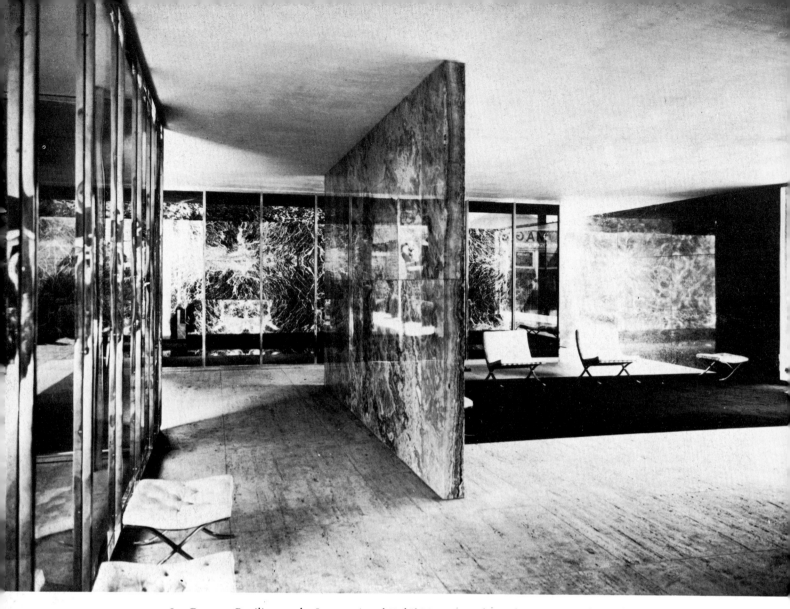

180 German Pavilion at the International Exhibition, Barcelona, *by Mies van der Rohe, 1929*

was revolutionary about the Barcelona Pavilion was its luxurious atmosphere created with a minimum of materials and component parts, all within the restrictions of functional design. Another superb example of Mies's internal open planning is the Tugendhat House at Brno in Czechoslovakia of 1928–30 where there are cruciform chromium columns, onyx walls and a curved space-divider of stripes of black and pale-brown macassar ebony. Specially designed furniture and raw silk curtains completed the *ensemble*.

In 1937 Mies moved to the United States, where he created some of the most important public and private buildings of this century. One of his most beautiful houses is the Farnsworth House at Fox River, Illinois, of 1945–50 (Plate 181), which goes almost as far as is possible in breaking down the division between interior and surroundings. Although not an easy house to live in, it has countless imitations throughout the world, but none can rival its spectacular self-confidence. Mies's range was by

no means limited to the steel and glass structure, and in his McCormick House at Elmhurst, Illinois, of 1952 he used unrelieved brick for the internal walls of the living room. It is interesting to compare this house with one designed by Frank Lloyd Wright in the same year, the Mossberg House, South Bend, Indiana, whose interior is much more romantic, with frequent changes in level, soaring ceilings of varied shape and exposed brick walls advancing and receding in a way very different from Mies's classicism.

The International Style was already being practised in the United States before Mies's arrival by an Austrian architect, Richard Neutra (1892–1970), whose Health and Lovell Houses (Plate 171) of 1927–9 broke completely with the Wright traditions. Other architects of international reputation who continued the style into the post-war period include Philip Johnson, Charles Eames and Eero Saarinen. Although it is obvious that every 'style' imposes certain restraints on architects and designers, the International Style left little room for personal expression ex-

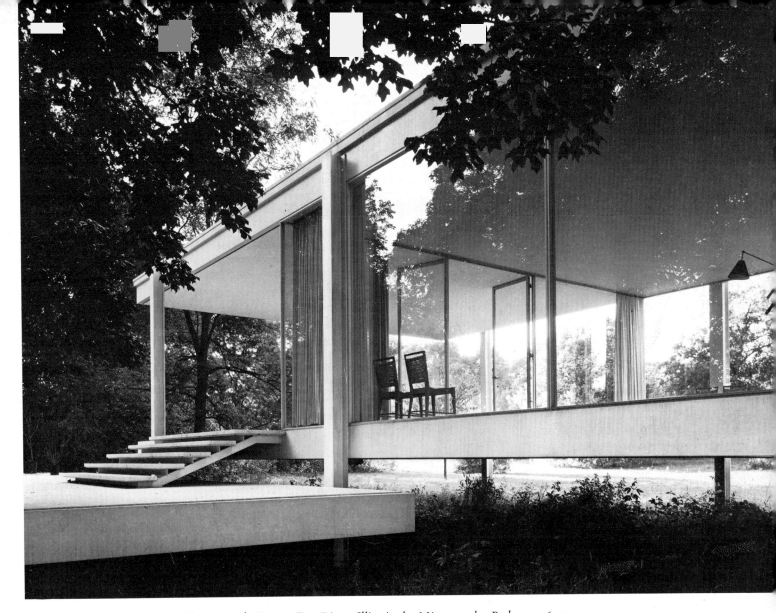

181 Farnsworth House, Fox River, Illinois, *by Mies van der Rohe, 1946–50*

cept on the part of the very gifted (see Plates 172 and 182), and a reaction set in soon after the Second World War. The owner of the Farnsworth House dismissed his house as 'glib sophistication' in *House Beautiful*, and one critic described Mies's works as 'elegant monuments of nothingness … [with] no relation to site, climate, insulation, function, or internal activity'. The reaction – Post-Modernism – opened the way for strong self-expression in the work of architects like Robert Venturi (b. 1925) in America, Aldo Rossi (b. 1931) in Italy, the Spaniard Ricardo Bofill (b. 1939) and the Japanese Arata Isozaki (b. 1931). While retaining the simplicity of the International Style interior, these architects increasingly permit themselves the licence to introduce unexpected elements into their room shapes, such as the irregular placing of windows.

Charles Edouard Jeanneret (1887–1965), known by his pseudonym Le Corbusier, remains to some extent outside the conventional currents of the International Style in his treatment of interiors. During his early travels he met Josef Hoffmann in Vienna and in Paris studied with one of the first architects to realize the potential of concrete architecture, Auguste Perret (1874–1954). In 1910–11 he was in Germany, mainly with Peter Behrens, and participated in the Deutscher Werkbund exhibition before travelling in the Balkans and Asia Minor in 1911 and settling in Paris in 1917. Le Corbusier defined the house as 'a machine for living in' and already in his Dom-Ino house of 1914 revealed the clarity of his planning principles. His main contribution to house design came between the two wars; during the 1920s he was mainly occupied with private houses, eighteen of his twenty-six buildings erected between 1922 and 1932 being domestic. The exact opposite of Mies, who had no formal training and whose personality remained enigmatic to the end of his life, Corbusier's open and forceful character is felt throughout his interiors. In his 1922 house at Vaucresson all of his subsequent ideas are revealed in embryo – the use of concrete with large horizontal windows to catch the sun,

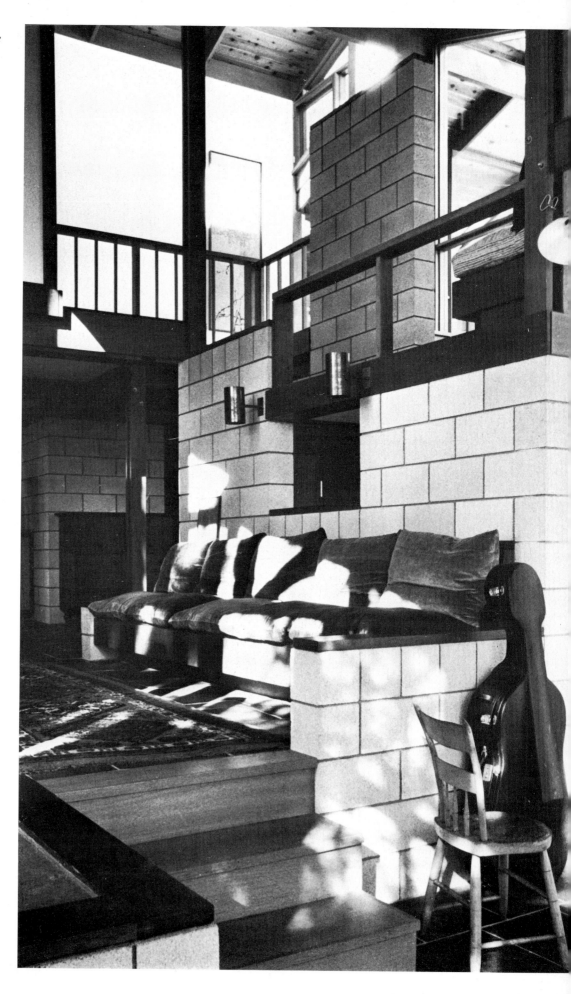

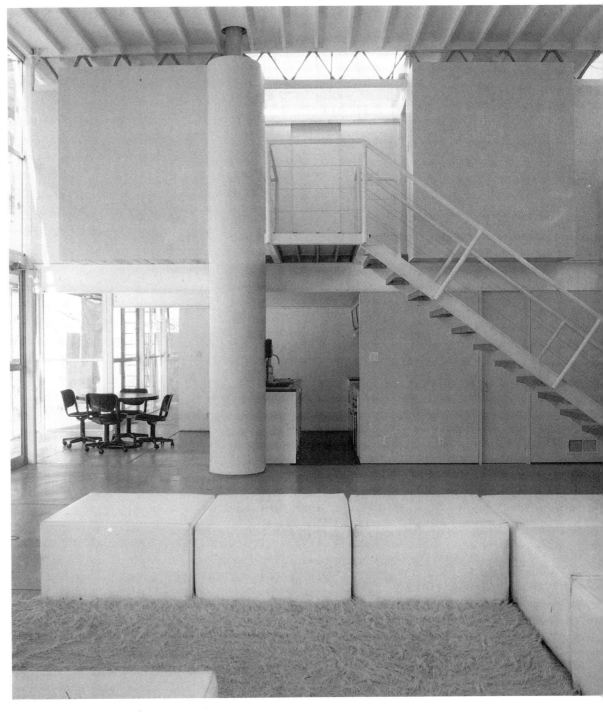

183 'High-tech' house in Los Angeles, *California, 1960s This is a good example of how industrial components, originally utilized as a method of saving money, can create surprising effects*

and an open internal plan with a movable partition for dividing living- and dining-spaces. For Le Corbusier the window was a fundamental part of interior and exterior:

Reinforced concrete has brought about a revolution in the history of the window. Windows can now run from one edge of the façade to the other. The window is a repeatable, serviceable element of the house, for all town-houses, workers' houses, and apartment houses ... exterior walls are no longer load-bearing, and can be opened up or closed, with windows or insulating elements at will to satisfy aesthetic or functional requirements.

Structural elements are incorporated into Le Corbusier's interiors too, as in the massive columns running through houses like Garches near Paris, where space is divided in an almost abstract way which completely departs from traditional room shapes and conventions of size and inter-relationship. Almost obsessed with the need to adapt such innovations to large-scale dwellings, he conceived his massive apartment blocks (*unité d'habitation*) as upward extensions of his house types. Coupled with his interest in reforming interior furnishings in collaboration with his cousin Pierre Jeanneret and Charlotte Perriand from 1925,

Le Corbusier's designs had perhaps greater immediate effect than Mies's, as much in America as in Europe. In the *Unité d'habitation* shown at the Salon d'Automne des Artistes Décorateurs in Paris in 1929, their combined efforts produced a design which has scarcely dated except perhaps in detail; all the ingredients of the 'modern interior' are seen already fully developed, including fitted shelving and cupboards, laminated surfaces and concealed lighting, all in conjunction with chromium-plated steel-tube furniture (see also Plate 174).

Although in retrospect it appears that Modernism swept all before it immediately after the First World War, with the result that any style which did not conform to its rigorous demands was essentially backward-looking, it should be remembered that the other side of the modern coin was Art Déco, which evolved at precisely the same time as Le Corbusier was making a complete break with the 'styles' in his domestic architecture of the 1920s.

As in most European countries, the First World War was of crucial importance in determining the direction taken by French architecture and interior decoration. In spite of Art Nouveau and the subsequent modernism of Perret and Garnier, the preferred style for many French interiors during the first two decades of this century was a diluted 'Louis XVI'. This encompassed elements from the Directoire and Empire periods – a mixture which continues to dominate traditionalist French interior decorators' work. A hangover from the '*goût Ritz*', this safe, almost official French style remains for many the essence of *chic*. The French seemed to feel that they could not improve on the upright rectangular emphasis, classically inspired detail and simple mouldings of late eighteenth-century interiors, much as the English revere the 'Georgian' style. Associated with this taste in France was the painter Paul Helleu, who, like his contemporaries, the society painters Giovanni Boldini and John Singer Sargent, evoked his sitters' wealth and fashion by placing them against such backgrounds. Proust's characters too implicitly inhabit such a world, rather than starkly modernist interiors, thereby creating an atmosphere of modern, yet somehow timeless elegance. If the Great War disbanded forever the society which favoured the *goût Ritz*, the 1920s required all the more urgently a new style carrying with it the connotations of a luxury supposedly removed by the war; the result was Art Déco.

Art Déco is arguably the last completely 'new' style of the twentieth century which clearly demonstrates its stylistic roots in the past. In France, at least, it is the last child of Neo-classicism, combining influences from the antique, the eighteenth century, the Orientalism of the Ballets Russes and even, on occasion, primitive art. Although it shunned Art Nouveau, its immediate predecessors were the interiors of the Viennese Sezession and Munich's Stuck Villa (Plate 163), whose derivation from Classical prototypes is obvious. The difference was that Art Déco interiors tended to be the sum of their parts, being more groupings of individual elements than any Art Nouveau room – furniture, textiles, ceramics, glass and metalwork. From the Classical vocabulary came fluted columns, festoons, baskets of chunky, stylized fruit and flowers (deriving partly from Mackintosh's designs), inset relief panels often showing Classical or allegorical themes updated with Twenties' *chic*, and coffering and other sophisticated reworkings of earlier motifs. The dynamism of the motor-car age replaced the elegance of earlier Classical revivals with emphasis on speed, energy and power, whether in the form of natural elements such as water or the muscular human form, both male and female. Amazingly, some of the most advanced Art Déco interiors retain a framework which, when denuded of its contents, would be indistinguishable from the run-of-the-mill Neo-classicism of the early part of the century.

The high point of 1920s' design in France was the 1925 Exhibition of Decorative and Industrial Arts held in Paris. Originally conceived for 1915, this massive assembly of all the leading trends of the day included many specially erected pavilions containing room settings in the very latest styles; from photographs of these we can often gain a better image of Art Déco interior decoration than from surviving domestic examples. Jacques-Emile Ruhlmann (1879–1933) was the most distinguished designer exhibiting there. Like most of his contemporaries who were known as decorators, he was primarily a furniture designer, and as such was compared by many with the great *ébénistes* of the eighteenth century like Riesener and Roentgen. Ruhlmann certainly shared their taste for the use of luxury materials. Among these were tortoiseshell, ivory, lapis, shagreen and lizard skin, whose very unexpectedness gives some indication of the *recherché* nature of his work.

Ruhlmann's Pavillon d'un Collectionneur (Plate 184) at the Exhibition exemplified some of his magnificent ideas, best realized when he was untrammelled by problems of scale or budgeting. Its salon was vast, circular, and dominated by a massive crystal chandelier, whose form was echoed in similar, fountain-like cascades of crystal on the walls; the latter were covered with a repeat pattern in silk showing stylized flower vases, flowers and birds beneath a large frieze apparently executed in plaster. Above the brick chimney-piece (a concession to Modernism?) hung Jean Dupas's decorative panel *Les Perruches* showing a typically Art Déco group of pneumatically muscular ladies in a primarily decorative grouping. But while the general mood was clearly sumptuously Déco, the basic constituents were still those of many earlier rooms.

Like Ruhlmann, André Groult (1884–1967) became one of the most sought-after decorators in the 1920s. He set his rethinkings of eighteenth-century furniture in simplified Louis XVI interiors, with the addition of bold contemporary accents such as mural panels by Charles Martin in predominant tones of blue, pink and grey, wallpapers by Laboureur and Marie Laurencin – whose paintings 'began

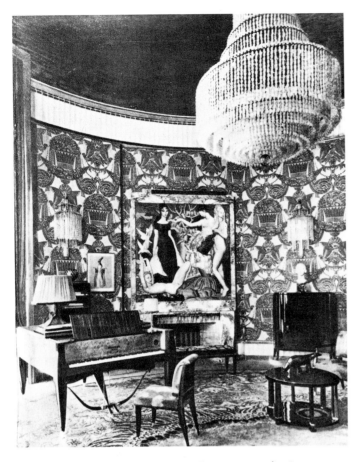

184 Salon of Le Pavillon d'un Collectionneur, *by Jacques Ruhlmann, Exposition Internationale des Arts Décoratifs et Industriels Modernes, Paris, 1925*

where music ended' and were much favoured by fashionable designers. Of considerable importance in the best Art Déco interiors was elaborately wrought ironwork, notably that of Edgar Brandt, who combined wrought iron with bronze, using a wide variety of motifs such as stylized birds, clouds, rays of light, fountains and clusters of abstracted flowers so favoured by 1920s designers. Among the other important metal workers in France were Raymond Subes, Paul Kiss, Gabriel Lacroix – 'the prince of metal' – Baguès and Jean Dunand (1877–1942), who worked in both metal and lacquer. He designed a smoking room for the 1925 Exhibition with red and silvered lacquer panels, and a ceiling decorated with silver leaf and touches of red lacquer applied to sheets at different depths, allowing concealed lighting to fall on highly polished black furniture and an off-white carpet. The English designer Eileen Gray (1878–1977) settled in Paris and was thought to have been the originator of the craze for lacquer in the 1920s; her refined taste for dark colours and large simplified forms prefigured elements of the International Style in the later part of the decade, and she collaborated on interior decoration with Jean Badovici. Another French designer of note was Armand Rateau (1882–1938), whose superb domed bathroom for the Madrid palace of the Duchess of Alba of 1926 had a single-block white marble sunken bath in a black-and-white marble floor with gold-lacquered walls showing animals of all kinds set amidst luxurious vegetation.

Art Déco blends at times imperceptibly into Modernism in France, partly under the impact of Cubism, which exercised considerable influence on interior decoration. The contemporary ideas of Le Corbusier, Jeanneret and Perriand gained ground and bred a reaction to the florid aspects of Déco. Many Déco interiors had depended for their effect on fairly simple basic forms, against which exuberant decoration could be offset, and it was these simple outlines which began to predominate towards the end of the 1920s. Among the most important designers in this respect was Jean Michel Frank, who used muted colour, skilfully contrasted textures and very simple, if luxurious, furniture. His natural-coloured silk curtains hung simply from ceiling to floor, and he often covered his walls with parchment or undyed leather, using concealed lighting to further soften his effects. Robert Mallet-Stevens (1886–1945) and Pierre Chareau (1883–1950) also enjoyed considerable success with their variants of luxurious Modernism, the latter 'replacing the tarnished and dusty shades with fresh harmonies of royal blue and grey, lemon-yellow and grey or the tones of pearl, rose and blue . . .' René Lalique (1860–1945), famous for his glass, created a dining room for 'Le Pavillon de la Manufacture Nationale de Sèvres' at the Paris Exhibition of 1925 with incised grey-veined beige marble walls inlaid with silver or white composition, and an Italianate ceiling with glass beams and coffers containing concealed lighting. The variations were endless, and the style found great favour in the United States, where designers such as John Wellborn Root and Ralph Walker translated European ideas into American terms, often favouring contrasting woods and less flamboyant elements in domestic interiors.

The early twentieth century saw the birth of the interior decorator as distinct from the architect, and many society ladies turned their hand to decoration. In England, these included Syrie Maugham (whose white-walled and pickled-and-waxed panelled White House in Chelsea set a vogue), Lady Colefax, Mrs Mann and the Marchesa Malacreda; in America, the redoubtable Elsie de Wolfe headed the band of Marian Hall, Elsie Cobb Wilson and Rose Cumming with Ronald Fleming in their wake. The Second World War suspended both their activity and that of architect-designers and abruptly ended the boom in interior decoration which had lasted since the 1920s.

In the gloomy period after the war, wallpaper in Britain enjoyed a revival since it offered a cheap method of brightening dull interiors, and 1950 saw the publication of *Wallpapers for the Small Home*. Most Fifties' wallpapers tended to be variations on stripes, dots or star-designs, although by the middle of the decade a new boldness of colour and scale appeared. In 1951, John Line's influential *Limited Editions 1951*, a collection of handprinted papers, set a new standard. Commissioned from leading artists such as Lucienne Day, John Minton and Jacqueline Groag, it was probably the first British screen-printed collection. During the 1960s, wallpaper began to assume a more important role in interior decoration, and to be seriously considered even for the most expensive rooms. Technical advances led to the development of new ranges, including Chinese grass-paper, various weaves (hessian being a favourite), silk of every kind from watered to damask, marble, wood, brick and stone. The importance of designers is attested to by the firm of Arthur Sanderson & Sons' decision to celebrate their centenary by launching a special collection of papers and fabrics which included Gio Ponti's *Eclipse* and Frank Lloyd Wright's *Design 706*. Imperial Chemical Industries' increasing involvement with design in the Sixties is shown by their pioneering of paper-backed vinyl wall coverings in 1962; washable and steam-resistant papers soon radically altered the appearance of the average bathroom or kitchen. This was only one of the features which contributed to making the bathroom, in John Prizeman's words, 'a space in which to relax, think, listen to music, look at pictures, read, dream, drink, eat grapes, exercise and sing'.

The end of the 'Swinging Sixties' in Britain brought a strong element of nostalgia to youthful thinking on interiors, and together with the revival of interest in 1930s and 1940s cinema, which had many side-effects on furnishing, William Morris, Art Nouveau and Art Déco were 'rediscovered' along with Victoriana. Sandersons again were instrumental in reviving wallpapers from designs of these periods. Parallel to such revivals, there was a rebirth of interest in natural materials such as pine, which was cheap enough to cover whole walls if necessary, together with cork, or fabrics like jute stuck to paper.

All aspects of design – not least that for interiors – were given a fillip by the 1951 exhibition for the Festival of Britain. This gave many designers during the following decade the necessary confidence to break with the austerity of the immediate post-war period and move forward to make Modernism part of everyday life in a much more pronounced way than it had been in the pre-war period. The 1950s saw many of the basic changes which were to be fundamental in shaping interior decoration and furniture design for the next two decades. Almost everyone at every level of society accepted the need to live not only in smaller homes, but also in more restricted space, with the result that many of the space-saving ideas of the pioneers of modern architecture in the first thirty years of the century now filtered through society as a matter of necessity. The multi-purpose room for living, eating, entertaining and study gained in popularity, while the status of the kitchen rose immeasurably although it still lagged considerably behind American advances.

The concept of more manageable, more beautiful homes for many more people crystallized in the Ideal Home Exhibitions, with their strong accent on 'do-it-yourself'.

In the 1956 exhibition, for example, the 'House of the Future' was shown as having a mass-produced body like a car's, features such as tables rising from the floor and self-rinsing, thermostatically controlled baths which filled from the bottom. In Britain, the New Brutalism was particularly associated with James Stirling, James Gowan (Plate 177), and Alison and Peter Smithson, who designed the 'House of the Future'. It was the great age of 'how to' and in their 'How to furnish your home' of 1953, G. Russel and A. Jarvis advised their readers:

Not too many colours in one room
Not too many bright colours in one room
Not too much of a single colour in one room
Not too much pattern in one room
Not too many different kinds of pattern in one room

This advice was perhaps a little premature since the colour range was limited by post-war restrictions on dye stuffs and resins. It was only at the end of the 1950s that oil emulsions were developed to replace water-borne distemper for house painting, but this did not prevent one of the more regrettable yet characteristic features of the early Fifties' interior – having one plain wall offset by three or more which were patterned. From the 1960s, 'mini-mosaics' gained a certain popularity, usually in blue: these came ready-fixed to paper-rolls to facilitate hanging.

The 'how to' approach formed part of a determined campaign to raise standards in decoration, most notable in the pronounced didacticism of many periodicals of the time. This was accompanied by a desire to draw attention to the work of the best designers of the day, who included John Fowler, David Hicks, Anthony Denney, Felix Harbord and Jon Bannenberg; theirs were the names most bandied about in fashionable decorating circles, but significantly they were the decorators with the strongest links with the past. John Fowler was renowned for his careful study of the 'correct' fabrics and colour schemes he was called in to restore or redesign in many important country houses, and it was he who established standards of accuracy in every detail of a restored interior. David Hicks on the other hand gained a reputation for his bold mixing of old and new furniture and objects, often offset by colour schemes of startling juxtapositions. In his *David Hicks on Decoration* of 1966 – one of a series of books in which Hicks describes his interiors as they appear in glossy photographs alongside the text – he calls interior decoration 'the art of achieving the maximum with the minimum'. 'Good period and modern interiors have one thing in common' – he notes – 'style'. Indeed, it is the quest for stylishness which dominates most twentieth-century decorators' approach to the domestic interior. It is defined rather nebulously by the editor of *Architectural Digest of International Interiors* as 'really a way of seeing and living creatively in the world'.

Interestingly, most interior decorators dislike what might legitimately be regarded as the most genuine expression of recent technological developments, the so-called 'high-tech' which uses in effect spare parts to create its environments and has found particular favour in the United States (Plate 183). 'It's fantastic when you walk into it,' observed the German designer Eric Jacobsen, 'it excites the eye. But it's so demanding of the people who live in it. You can't just sit there. You have to be colourful and "designed" yourself' – a reaction which might equally well apply to the most decorated interiors. High-tech lacks the glamour now attached to international design and decoration, and architects who hope to build their practice through social contact would not wish to play down their ability in these fields.

During the 1930s there had been radical changes in the way in which decorator/designers saw their profession. Previously, they had been content to work with pre-existing architectural shells, but the new technologies and materials made them conscious of the need to think structurally as much as decoratively. The inter-relationship of architecture and interior space in the work of the century's leading architects up to that point now led decorators to re-examine their precise rôle in the visual arts, and to conceive it in a larger context than had previously been the case. Technical knowledge became as important to them as aesthetic judgement, and the decorators of the inter-war period such as Sybil Colefax, Elsie de Wolfe and Ruby Ross Wood declared war on amateurism.

Their successors have continued this tradition of steely professionalism, and since the Second World War interior design has become a major profession which, at its highest level, is organized in the same way as any other business concern to cater for a demanding clientèle prepared to pay for the best design using the best craftsmanship and materials. While the idea of entrusting the decoration of one's home to a designer is often questioned as if it were a novelty of the twentieth century, in fact the practice has its roots in all aspects of design in the past: the principal difference is that contemporary designers are prepared and able to create every single aspect of a given interior. This is a source of the eclecticism of so much modern interior design, which can unashamedly bring together elements of many different periods, creating a style which does not however have any of the evocative intentions of nineteenth-century historicism. Forward-looking designers of the nineteenth century or early twentieth century would have regarded the practice with horror, and might perhaps have suggested that it indicated the fundamental uncertainty of direction underlying such an approach. In many respects, such a criticism would be well founded.

While it is difficult to select a representative group of designers from the post-war period whose work gives a clear idea of the range of recent achievements, a few names are outstanding internationally – since the measure of contemporary success in the field is to obtain a more than local clientèle. The United States have made an unprece-

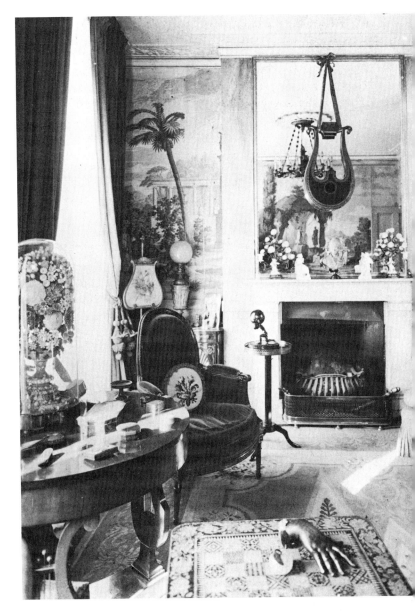

185 'Madame Andrée Bessire's former sitting-room in Paultons Square, Chelsea'. *From the House and Garden Book of Interiors, 1962 With its 'French narrative wallpaper drawn by Bader and painted by Dufour in 1826 conspiring to create an almost subaqueous sense of tranquillity . . .' this interior typifies the sense of elegant well-being sought during the later 1950s and 1960s. Many examples are illustrated in* The House and Garden Book. *Ranging from ultra-modern kitchens to the interiors of the Castle of May, the emphasis is on achieving efficiency and comfort. Surprisingly, some of the outstanding examples of the period included in the book – such as Mrs Nancy Lancaster's splendid gold drawing room – have remained classics; like the room illustrated here, their essence is an eclectic mixture of the most elegant constituents from past styles, giving the impression that they were always designed to be seen together. The predominant tendency was to prefer light interiors, often with chintzes, a reaction perhaps to the gloomy colour schemes of the Second World War period*

dented impact in this respect. Mrs Henry Parish II ('Sister' Parish) and her partner Albert Hadley span the pre- and post-war generations; their proven system of planning furniture layout before all else is shared by many other designers, who like them turn to colour and the use of fabric as the next most important stages. Like most major interior designers today, their range is impressively wide, from chintz-and-wicker country style to dazzlingly colourful interiors bursting with pictures, objects and furniture. Above all, their flair for using furnishings as the key to a room's appeal is unique. In the same classic tradition is the internationally renowned firm of McMillen Inc, founded in 1924 by Eleanor McMillen Brown, to which many leading American designers have at some time been affiliated. McMillen Inc now consists of six decorators, a president and two vice-presidents and operates like any American business concern offering the highest quality in decoration for great houses and apartments for many distinguished clients. Their hallmark is an assurance devoid of any aggression, which unfailingly creates the right atmosphere for the interior architecture involved, whether modernistic or traditional; nowhere in evidence is the conspicuous 'expensiveness' so disfiguring to much modern interior design. The restrained sumptuousness of their style is shared by other top American designers such as Mario Buatta, who was influenced by Palladio's interior spaces, and Georgina Fairholme (who has been continuing the John Fowler tradition of period accuracy in the United States for almost a decade). A parallel is found in the style of Tom Parr and Ian Lieber in Britain. Their most characteristic contribution to the contemporary interior is to create diversity out of traditional motifs and methods, in interiors preserving the best of the past in conjunction with modern detail. In spite of this, some designers dislike being labelled traditionalists: Mario Buatta says, 'I think in terms of decorating in the traditional way for people who are living in the 1980s. My work ... is practical and realistic for the way we live today. It is not a study of the past.'

Different as individual interiors in this traditionally-based style may be, the basic components remain largely the same. To classify them as 'tasteful' may seem demeaning, but apart from the occasional flight of fancy, the elements involved are generally chosen for their ability to integrate completely with one another. Walls are generally painted in one of a wide range of pale colours, cream, green, grey, coffee or beige, often with panelling or mouldings picked out in white. This provides a discreet foil for contrasting curtains – sumptuous glazed chintz still holds its own as a firm favourite, with parquet flooring or predominantly pale monotonal fitted carpeting being the perfect background for oriental rugs (still the test of a well-heeled home). Whether in use or not, a carved marble or wood chimneypiece often provides the focus in such schemes, surmounted as in the past by a painting, groups of prints or drawings or a mirror. For window-curtains, tie-backs are de rigueur unless sophisticatedly simple hangings from a wooden or metal pole are used, and draped valances of varying depth are common. 'Festooned' window hangings have regained the popularity they enjoyed in the eighteenth century.

Unless the owner has a particular taste in paintings, the general rule for decorators of this type seems to be to use wherever possible undemanding, decorative pictures: eighteenth- and nineteenth-century portraits, still-life and landscape predominate, on rare occasions providing the colour-accent most evident throughout the room. In Italy and France in particular, the traditional love of and understanding for subject-pictures is often a distinguishing factor, while in the Anglo-Saxon countries it is rare to find religious or mythological paintings in any other than the older collections. This radically alters the significance of the rôle played in a room by paintings, since a painting chosen for its neutrality remains essentially decoration.

Sadly, few decorators have been able to make a name for creating interiors using furnishings which do not conform to certain unwritten laws of what is and what is not acceptable. Acceptable is most notably French eighteenth-century furniture, especially *fauteuils* and *canapés* of the Louis XV period, or imitations of these. This and French Empire or English Regency furniture provide the stock-in-trade of a large preponderance of designers in preference to Baroque or earlier furnishings, by reason of their comparative simplicity and remarkable adaptability to a wide variety of interiors. Designers such as Hicks now manufacture simplified versions of such furniture, indicating its hold on the market. In a certain type of interior, regardless of its modernity, a Louis XV *console* or *commode* is invariably regarded as in keeping, suggesting that objects of quality from any and every period can be mixed without clashing. An extension of this approach is the use of strikingly modern furniture in a meticulously preserved older interior: Eric Jacobsen is particularly good at this, as are many contemporary Italian designers. The nature of the Italian laws on the preservation of the architectural heritage has led many Italian designers to adapt their go-ahead modern ideas on architecture and furniture to existing shells, achieving a balance rarely found elsewhere between architectural detailing often of great beauty and rigorously modern furnishing and lighting.

Italian designers like Carla Venosta or Gae Aulenti are particularly adept at using strikingly modern features such as differing floor levels with continuous fitted carpeting dissolving the transitions from one area to another (originally an American innovation), within very old buildings whose pronounced architectural features such as vaulting or open loggias require sensitive treatment. Given that the centres of most Italian cities are composed in their entirety of medieval or Renaissance/Baroque buildings, completely modern architecture and interiors are rarely found together – with the outstanding exception of country or seaside villas. Some Italian designers such as

Stefano Mantovani are able to continue the grand manner of the great Italian palazzi in smaller and less sumptuous interiors; the strong reds of Italian Baroque silk damasks are reflected in painted walls of similar colours; the dominant presence of large, gilt-framed oil paintings is allowed to create its own atmosphere along with coloured marbles, dark bronzes and deep-toned furniture. A fear of opulent effects which inhibits many Anglo-Saxon designers is absent from many Latin designers' work, whose natural setting is spacious, triumphantly frescoed interiors with large doorways, floor-to-ceiling windows and magnificent vaulted and arched ceilings. The work of John Stefanidis is unique in uniting Mediterranean feeling for light with Italian design sense and English restraint; Stefanidis is a Greek who lives in England after spending his childhood in Egypt and studying in Milan.

In direct opposition to designers who have made their names adopting traditionalism to varying degrees are those who disassociate themselves from any connections with historical styles and create interiors based as much as possible on modern precepts of architecture and design. To a great extent, these are all inevitably followers of the major innovators of the first half of this century, notably Le Corbusier and Mies van der Rohe: the individualistic elements in their work are refinements on that tradition, where pure forms, generally accentuated by being painted white, are offset by glass and all forms of lighting. The many innovations in direct and concealed lighting in the post-war period have contributed enormously to the effect of such interiors. For such designers, structure and space are genuinely of much more importance than for traditionalists, and the connections between much of their work and contemporary industrial design are obviously strong. After the seeds of certain aspects of modernism had been sown in the United States by European refugees, America became the continent most ready to adopt whole-heartedly modern interiors, from Texas (as in the work of Beverly Jacomini, Katrine Tolleson and Richard Holley) to the peculiarly New York style of Earl Burns Combs, Joseph Paul d'Urso or Juan Montoya. One of the most striking characteristics of most such designers is that they avoid surface patterns in the same degree that their traditionalist colleagues deliberately seek to create much of their effect with them. The structural quality of walls is accentuated even in window treatment, using vertical strip blinds or, in the case of one top designer working in France, François Catroux, polished brass or metal grids.

There are some similarities between many of today's best interiors of this type and non-domestic interiors such as offices and museums, to which the same criteria of functional clarity, maximum use of space and lighting apply. The subtle display of individual works of art plays perhaps a more important rôle in these rooms than in the traditionalist interior; Mies's Barcelona Pavilion set the tone for the careful placing of sculpture offset against superb materials (see page 209): from similar sources comes the modern museum's tendency to isolate exhibits as opposed to crowding them together. As in offices, even the domestic interior seeks to use ready-made, built-in storage and working furniture, now the mainstay of many chain-stores such as Habitat in Britain. The resulting improvement in the general standard of interior decoration at all financial levels has been considerable.

One major question remains to be asked: what *is* the true style of the late twentieth-century interior, if such a thing exists? If it does not, it is the first time in the history of decoration that the style of the period cannot be defined with some degree of certainty. Individually delightful as decorators' interiors may be, with their eclecticism, their sophistication (even when creating 'unsophisticated' rooms) and their highly self-conscious use of certain acceptable formulae, it seems undeniable that in the main they represent the end of a tradition rather than a recognizably major step forward. Our unprecedented awareness of the past, and the astonishing facility with which we can find out about almost any aspect of the arts, has perhaps made eclecticism inevitable. If it is necessary to select a particular style which best represents advance rather than the consolidations of previous advances, then unquestionably high-tech and the use of prefabricated internal architecture must be regarded as the most representative style of the later twentieth century. Anything less may be seen as backward-looking, but the apparently overwhelming preference for comfort, fashion and even, to some extent, conformity may already have spelled the doom of the revolutions of the early part of the century.

If certainty was the keynote of the Modernist Movement, that of today is *laissez-faire*; it is clear that the way is now open for every type of development during the last years of this century. One of the virtues of the greatly increased awareness of the importance of design in all its aspects is that it widens the choices available, and this seems to be the healthiest pointer to the future.

Acknowledgements

John Calmann and Cooper Ltd wish to thank the institutions and individuals who have kindly provided photographic material for use in this book. Museums and galleries are given in the captions; other sources are listed below.

Actualit, Brussels: 159
Alinari, Florence: 3; 5; 9; 10; 41; 50; 51; 52; 58; 60; 76; 80; 133
Alinari/Mansell Collection, London: 46
Anderson, Florence: 4; 61; 79
Wayne Andrews, Grosse Pointe, Michigan: 141; 170
Arch. Phot. Paris/SPADEM: 23; 31
Banco Popolare di Vicenza: 59
Banque de France, Paris: 97
Bauhaus Archiv, Berlin: 175
Bavaria Verlag, Gauting, Munich: 67
Bayerische Verwaltung der Staatlichen Schlösser, Gärten und Seen, Munich: 150
Bayerisches Nationalmuseum, Munich: 99
Raffaello Bencini, Florence: 157; 160
John Bethell, St Albans: 29; 66; 107; 110; 113; 126
Bibliotheca Hertziana, Rome: 57
Bibliothèque et Universitaire, Geneva: 36
Bildarchiv Foto Marburg: 32; 91; 164
Bildarchiv Preussischer Kulturbesitz, Berlin: 134
Osvaldo Böhm, Venice: 55; 74
Bridgeman Art Library, London: 18
Brogi, Florence: 48; 49
Cardiff City Council: 153
Trustees of the Chatsworth Settlement: 71

Condé Nast Publications Ltd, London: 185
Connaissance des Arts, Paris/Roger Guillemot: 137
The Connoisseur, London/Arigo Coppitz: 143
Country Life, London: 69; 151; 155; 156
De Antonis, Rome: 54; 77; 139
John Donat, London: 172; 174; 177; 178; 182
Edizioni Novecento, Palermo: 162
Fitzwilliam Museum, Cambridge: 132
Fratelli Fabbri Editori, Milan: 72; 138
Freer Gallery of Art, Washington DC: 154
Giraudon, Paris: 22; 83; 84; 100; 116; 149
Habitat, London: 168
David Hicks, London: 173
Hedrich-Blessing, Chicago: 181
Historisches Museum der Stadt Wien: 146
Michael Holford, Loughton, Essex: 12; 47
Angelo Hornak, London: 70; 101; 131; 176
A. F. Kersting, London: 21; 30; 68; 87; 88; 89; 105; 108; 112; 119; 125; 127; 128; 144; 158; 163; 169
MAS, Barcelona: 38
Metropolitan Museum of Art, New York: 11; 24; 78; 111; 114
Derry Moore, London: 167; 171; 183
Musée des Arts Décoratifs, Paris: 121; 123; 148
The Museum of Modern Art, New York: 161; 180
National Monuments Record, London: 109

Netherlands Information Service, Gravenhage: 86
Werner Neumeister, Munich: 152
Oronoz, Madrid: 122; 135
Österreichische Nationalbibliothek Bild-Archiv und Porträt-Sammlung, Vienna: 166
Österreichisches Museum für zugewandte Kunst, Vienna: 147
Prado, Madrid: 27
Publifoto, Palermo: 37
Réunion des Musées Nationaux, Paris: 26; 62; 92; 118; 136; 140
Roger-Viollet, Paris: 93
Royal Commission on the Ancient & Historical Monuments of Scotland, Edinburgh: 1 (frontispiece)
Royal Pavilion, Brighton: 142
Scala, Florence: 6; 7; 13; 15; 16; 17; 19; 33; 39; 40; 43; 44; 53; 56; 82; 85; 95; 98; 102; 103; 106
Helga Schmidt-Glassner, Stuttgart: 28; 64
Ronald Sheridan's Photo-Library, Harrow-on-the-Hill: 2; 8
Edwin Smith, Saffron Walden: 45; 104
Trustees of the Sir John Soane Museum: 117; 124; 131 (photographer Angelo Hornak)
Wim Swaan, London: 34
Swiss National Museum, Zurich: 90
Agence Top, Paris/Charbonnier: 81
Agence Top, Paris/J. Guillot: 96
Vatican Museums & Galleries: 14
Villa di Maser, Treviso: 42
Westfälisches Landesmuseum für Kunst und Kulturgeschichte, Munster: 65
Christopher Wood Gallery, London: 165

Bibliography

Acton, Harold: *Tuscan Villas*, 1973
Aloi, Roberto: *L'arredamento moderno*, 1934, 1947
– *Esempi di arredamento moderno di tutto il mondo*, 1950–3
Anthony, E. W.: *A History of Mosaics*, 1935
Arcangeli, F.: *Le Tarsie*, 1943
Architectural Digest magazine, Los Angeles, 1978–
Aslin, E.: *The Aesthetic Movement: Prelude to Art Nouveau*, 1981
Babelon, J. P.: *Demeures Parisiennes sous Henri IV et Louis XIII*, 1965
Bankart, G.: *The Art of the Plasterer*, 1909
Baraiti, E.: *L'Italia Liberty*, 1973
Battersby, Martin: *The Decorative Twenties*, 1969
– *The Decorative Thirties*, 1971
Beard, Geoffrey: *Craftsmen and Interior Decoration in England 1660–1820*, 1971
– *Decorative Plasterwork in Great Britain*, 1975
– *Georgian Craftsmen and their Work*, 1966
– *Stucco in Europe*, 1983
Bérain, Jean: *Desseins de cheminées dediez à Monsieur Jules Hardouin Mansart*, 1699
– *Nouvelles Cheminées . . .* 1690s
Beyen, H. G.: *Pompejanisches Wanddekoration vom zweiten bis zum vierten Stil*, I–II; 1938–60
Birrell, Verla: *The Textile Arts*, 1973
Blondel, Jacques-François: *De la Distribution des Maisons de Plaisance et de la Décoration des Edefices en general*, 2 vols, 1737–8
Blunt, A.: *Art and Architecture in France 1500–1700*, 1953, 1973
– *Baroque and Rococo Architecture and Decoration*, 1978
– *Sicilian Baroque*, 1968
Boethius, A.: *The Golden House of Nero*, 1960
Boethius, Axel, and Ward-Perkins, J. B.: *Etruscan and Roman Architecture*, 1970
Bolton, A. T.: *The Architecture of Robert and James Adam*, 2 vols, 1922
Borsi, F.: *Bruxelles – Art Nouveau*, 1971
– *Paris 1900*, 1976
Borsook, Eve: *The Mural Painters of Tuscany*, 1981
Bossaglia, R.: *Il Déco Italiano*, 1975
Boucher, François the Younger: *Recueil de décorations intérieures*, 1775
Brosio, V.: *Ambienti italiani dell'ottocento*, 1963
Brown, Erica: *Interior Views*, 1980
Brunhammer, Yvonne: *Le Style 1925*, 1975
Busch, H.: *Gothic Europe*, 1959
Camesasca, E.: *History of the House*, 1971
Casson, Hugh: *Inscape, the design of interiors*, 1968
Chadenet, Sylvie: *Les Styles Empire et Restauration*, 1976

Chamberlain, S.: *Salem Interiors: Two Centuries of New England Interiors*, 1980
Chierici, G.: *Il Palazzo italiano*, 1964
Chiesa, G.: *Il Seicento: mobili, arti decorative, costume*, 1973
Cirici Pellicer, A.: *1900 en Barcelona*, 1967
Colosanti, A.: *Case e Palazzi Barocchi di Roma*, 1934
– *Volte e Soffitti italiani*, 1915
Colvin, H. M.: *A Biographical Dictionary of English Architects 1660–1840*, 1954
Cooper, Nicholas: *The Opulent Eye: late Victorian and Edwardian taste in interior design*, 1976
Cornforth, John: *English Interiors 1790–1848: the Quest for Comfort*, 1978
Country Life magazine: *English Country Houses*, 1955–70
Cremona, Italo: *Il tempo dell'art nouveau*, n.d.
Cresti, Carlo: *Le Corbusier*, 1970
Croft-Murray, E.: *Decorative Painting in England*, 1962
Cuvilliés, Jean François de: *L'Oeuvre*, 1738–68
Daubourg, E.: *L'Architecture intérieure*, 1876
Décor, *Le décor de la maison*, 1949
Del Puglia, Raffaelle: *Mobili e ambienti italiani del gótico al floreale*, 2 vols, 1963
Destailleur, F. H.: *Recueil d'estampes relatives à l'ornamentation des appartements au XVIme, XVIIme et XVIIIme siècles*, 1863
Deutsche Werkbund catalogue, 1914
Deville: *Dictionnaire de tapisserie*, 1878–80
Domus magazine, 1928–
Dongerkery, Kamela S.: *Interior Decoration in India, past and present*, 1973
Eastlake, Sir Charles Lock: *Hints on Household Taste in Furniture . . .* 3rd edn, 1872
Ebersoldt, Jean: *Le Grand Palais de Constantin*, 1910
Entwisle, E. A.: *The Book of Wallpaper*, 1970
Eriksen, Svend: *Early Neo-Classicism in France*, 1974
Fayet, M. de: *Renaissance espagnole*, 1961
Ferriday, P.: *Victorian Architecture*, 1963
Fowler, J., and Cornforth, J.: *English Decoration in the 18th Century*, 1974
Franciscono, M.: *Walter Gropius*, 1971
Frankl, Paul: *Gothic Architecture*, 1962
Garland, Madge: *The Indecisive Decade*, 1968
Geymuller, H. von: *Die Baukunst der Renaissance*, 1898–1901
Gill, Brendan: *The Dream Come True: great houses of Los Angeles*, 1980
Girouard, Mark: *Life in the English Country House: A Social and Architectural History*, 1978

– *Sweetness and Light: the 'Queen Anne' movement, 1860–1900*, 1977
Glasgow School of Art: *Mackintosh and the Modern Interior*, 1961
Gonzales-Palacios, Alvar: *Il mobile nei secoli*, n.d.
Grandjean, René: *Décoration égyptienne*, 1910
Grant, Ian: *Great Interiors 1650–1960*, 1967
Grodecki, Louis: *Au seuil de l'art roman, l'architecture ottonienne*, 1958
Gropius, Walter: *Bauhausbauten, Dessau*, 1930
Guenther, Sonja: *Interieurs um 1900*, 1971
Gusman, *L'Art décoratif de Rome*, 1908
Hammacher, A. M.: *Le Monde de H. van de Velde*, 1967
Harvey, J. H.: *The Medieval Architect*, 1972
– *The Gothic World 1100–1600*, 1950
Hautecoeur, L.: *Histoire de l'architecture classique en France*, n.d.
Hayward, Helena (ed.): *World Furniture*, 1965
Hempel, Eberhard: *Baroque Art and Architecture in Central Europe*, 1965
Heydenreich, L. H.: *Architecture in Italy 1400–1600*, 1974
Hicks, David: *On Living – with Taste*, 1968
– *David Hicks on Decoration*, 1972
Hirth, Georg: *Das deutsche Zimmer*, 1886–
Hitchcock, Henry-Russell: *Architecture Nineteenth and Twentieth Centuries*, 1963
– *Rococo Architecture in Southern Germany*, 1968
Honour, Hugh: *Chinoiserie*, 1961
Honour, Hugh, and Fleming, John: *A World History of Art*, 1982
Hope, Thomas: *Household Furniture and Interior Decoration executed from Designs by Thomas Hope*, 1807
House and Garden magazine, 1947–
House and Garden *Book of Interiors*, 1962
Ishimoto, Tatsuo and Kiyoko: *The Japanese House: its interior and exterior*, 1963
Jahn, J.: *Deutsche Renaissance*, 1969
Jessen, P.: *Daniel Marot*, n.d.
Jordan, R. F.: *Le Corbusier*, 1972
Jourdain, Margaret: *English Decoration and Furniture of the Early Renaissance*, 1924
– *English Interior Decoration 1500–1830*, 1950
Jullian, Philippe: *Le Style second Empire*, 1975
– *Le Style Louis XVI*, 1977
Kalnein, Graf Wend, and Levey, Michael: *Art and Architecture of the Eighteenth Century in France*, 1972
Kettell, Russell Hawes: *Early American Rooms*, 1926
Kimball, Fiske: *The Creation of the Rococo*, 1943
Kitzinger, E.: *Byzantine Art in the Making*, 1977

Knight, Arthur: *The Hollywood Style*, 1969

Korf, Dingeman: *Dutch Tiles*, 1963

Kreisel, Heinrich: *Deutsche Spiegelkabinette*, 1953

Lloyd, Nathaniel: *History of the English House*, 1971

Lotz, Wolfgang: *Architecture in Italy 1400–1600*, 1974

Mackay, A. G.: *Roman Houses, Villas and Palaces*, 1975

Magnani, Franco: *Room for the Seventies*, 1971

Maiuri, A.: *Roman Paintings*, 1953

Mariacher, Giovanni: *Ambienti italiani del trecento e quattrocento*, 1963

Marie, Alfred: *Naissance de Versailles*, 1968

Masson, Georgina: *Italian Villas and Palaces*, 1959

Mayhew, E. de N. and Myers, M.: *A Documentary History of American Interiors*, 1980

Mazzotti, G.: *Le Ville Venete*, 1954

Meiss, Millard: *The Great Age of Fresco*, 1970

Mordaunt Crook, J.: *William Burges*, 1981

– *The Greek Revival*

Moussinac, Léon: *Intérieures*, 2 vols, 1924

Mumford, Lewis: *The Culture of Cities*, 1938

Munich Residenz: *König Ludwig II und die Kunst*, 1968

Musée des Arts décoratifs, Paris: *Le décor de la vie à l'époque romantique 1820–1848*, 1930

Museum of Modern Art, New York: *Italy: the new domestic landscape*, 1973

Muthesius, Hermann: *Das englische Haus*, 1904–5; trans. J. Seligman, *The English House*, 1979

Nogara, B.: *I Musaici antichi dei Musei Vaticani*, 1910

Parsons, Frank A.: *Interior Decoration*, 1916

Pedrini, Augusto: *L'ambiente, il mobilio e le decorazioni del Rinascimento in Italia*, 1925; 1948

Percier, C. and Fontaine, P. F. L.: *Recueil de Décorations Intérieures comprenant tout ce qui a rapport à l'ameublement*, 1812

Percival, J.: *The Roman Villa*, 1976

Peterson, Harold L.: *American Interiors from Colonial Times to the late Victorians. A pictorial source book of American domestic interiors*, 1971

Pevsner, Nikolaus: *An outline of European Architecture*, 1948

Plaisirs de France, Edns, *La décoration, du moyen âge au modern style*, 1965

Platt, Frederick: *America's gilded age: its architecture and decoration*, 1976

Pliny: *Natural History*, 10 vols, Eng. edn 1958–67

– *Chapters on the history of Art*, 1968

Plumb, B.: *Houses Architects Live In*, 1977

– *Young Designs in Living*, 1961

Praz, Mario: *An illustrated history of interior decoration from Pompeii to art nouveau*, 1964

Rense, Paige (ed.): *Architectural Digest International Interiors*, 1979

Répertoire du Goût Moderne, 5 vols, 1928–9

Rheims, Maurice: *L'Art 1900*, 1965

Richter, Gisela: *The Furniture of the Greeks and Romans*, 1966

Roche, Serge: *Miroirs, Galeries et Cabinets de glaces…*, 1956

Rosenau, Helen: *Design and Medieval Architecture*, 1934

Rosenberg, J., Slive, S., and Ter Kuile, E. H.: *Dutch Art and Architecture 1600–1800*, 1966

Royal College of Art, London: *Bugatti*, catalogue 1979

Savage, George: *French Decorative Art*, 1969

Schmützler, R.: *Art Nouveau*, 1964

Schwartz, M. D.: *American Interiors 1675–1885: a guide to the American period rooms in the Brooklyn Museum*, 1968

Serlio, Sebastiano: *Tutte l'Opere*, new edn 1964

Service, A.: *Edwardian Interiors*, 1982

Smith, E. Baldwin: *Architectural Symbolism of Imperial Rome*, 1956

Smith, George: *A collection of designs for household furniture and interior decoration*, 1808

Stechow, Wolfgang: *Northern Renaissance Architecture 1400–1600*, 1966

Summerson, John: *Architecture in Britain 1530–1830*, 1963, 1969

– *Sir John Soane*, 1952

Susinno, Stefano and di Majo, Elena: *Le Stanze della Memoria, Vedute di ambienti, ritratti in interni e scene di conversazione della Collezione Praz, 1776–1870*, 1987

Swann, Wim: *The Late Middle Ages*, 1977

Thornton, Peter: *Seventeenth-Century Interior Decoration in England, France and Holland*, 1978

Timmers, M. W.: *The Way We Live Now, designs for interiors 1950 to the present day*, V&A catalogue, 1978–9

Tipping, H. A.: *English Homes: Norman and Plantagenet 1066–1485*, 1921

– *English Homes: Early Renaissance*, 1912

– *English Homes: Early Tudor*, 1924

– *English Homes: Late Tudor, Early Stuart*, 2 vols, 1922, 1927

Verlet, Pierre: *French furniture and interior decoration of the 18th century*, 1967

– *Styles, Meubles, Décors, du Moyen Age à nos jours*, 2 vols, 1972

– *Versailles*, 1961

Veronese, G.: *Lo stile 1925*, 1967

Vitruvius: *De architettura libri X*, trans. M. H. Morgan, 1910

Waterer, J. W.: *Spanish Leather*, 1971

Weigert, R. A. (intro.): *Louis XIV: faste et décors*, Musée des Arts décoratifs catalogue, 1960

Whiffen, M., and Koeper, F.: *American Architecture 1607–1976*, 1980

Wilckens, Leonie von: *Deutsche Raumkunst*, 1964

Williams, Henry L. and Ottalia K.: *America's small houses and city apartments: the personal homes of designers and collectors*, 1964

– *Great Houses of America*, 1967

Wood, Margaret: *The English Medieval House*, 1965

Zweig, Marianne: *Zweites Rokoko: Inneräume und Hausrat in Wien um 1830–1860*, 1924

Index

Aachen, 33–4
Adam, Robert, 28, 63, 131, 134, 135, 138, 142, 143, 145–50, 152, 153, 158, 161, 200; *Pls. 117, 119, 124, 125*
Aesthetic Movement, 184, 186, 188, 197
Alberti, L. B., 10, 57, 58–63, 68, 80, 135
Alessi, Galeazzo, 71
Amalienburg, 125, 179; *Pl. 101*
Amboise, 79
Antwerp, Rubens House, *Pl. 82*
Aranjuez, 112; *Pl. 95*; Casita del Labrador, 152; *Pl. 122*
Arcetri, Villa La Gallina, 74
Art Déco, 180, 204, 214–15, 216
Art Nouveau, 159, 176, 180–97, 204, 214, 216
Arts and Crafts Movement, 181–6, 192, 193
Aubert, Jean, 120; *Pl. 100*
Audley End, Essex, 104
Audran, Claude, 112, 113, 116
Augustusburg Castle, *Pl. 91*
Avignon, Palais des Papes, 44–6; *Pl. 31*

Baillie Scott, M. H., 192
Bambini, Niccolo, *Pl. 74*
Barcelona, Casa Calvet, 193–5; *Pl. 160*; Casa Vicens, 193; *Pl. 157*
Bauhaus, 191, 204–5, 208, 209
Beckford, William, 169–71, 172
Behrens, Peter, 205, 208, 211
Bélanger, François-Joseph, 143
Bentley Priory, Middx, 156
Bérain, Jean, 101, 103, 112, 120
Berlage, H. P., 191, 204
Berlin, Palace of Prince Albert, *Pl. 134*; Schloss, 109; Sommerfeld House, 205; *Pl. 175*
Bernini, Gianlorenzo, 88, 90, 93–5, 96, 109, 121, 145
Biedermeier, 161, 172
Boffrand, Germain, 121, 124; *Pl. 96*
Borromini, Francesco, 88, 93, 96, 109, 116, 121; *Pl. 75*
Boscoreale, 20–1; *Pl. 11*
Botticelli, Sandro, 74–5, 76
Boulanger, Gustave, *Pl. 140*
Boulle, A.-C., 101, 102, 111, 173
Bourges, Coeur House, 36; *Pl. 23*
Bramante, 55, 63, 97, 154, 200
Brighton Pavilion, 156; *Pl. 142*
Brunelleschi, 55, 57, 58–9, 65, 76
Brussels, Hôtel Solvay, 191; Hôtel Van Eetvelde, 191; *Pl. 159*; Palais Stoclet, 197; *Pl. 166*
Burges, William, 186; *Pl. 153*
Burlington, Lord, 108, 128, 145
Burn, William, 177; *Pl. 151*

Cameron, Charles, 153
Campbell, Colen, 108, 128, 139
Caprarola, Villa Farnese, 69, 76
Cardiff Castle, *Pl. 153*

Carpaccio, 77; *Pl. 61*
Carpi, Scibec de, 79, 80
Carracci, Annibale, 69, 88, 89
Caserta, Royal Palace, *Pl. 133*
Castel Sant'Angelo, 71, 72, 73
Castle Howard, Yorks, 108
Cervetri, 14; *Pl. 3*
Chalgrin, J.-F., 143; *Pl. 121*
Chambers, Sir W., 143, 145, 146, 150, 153
Chantilly, Petit Château, 112, 120; *Pl. 100*
Charlemagne, Emperor, 33–4
Chatsworth, Derbys, 85, 108; *Pl. 71*
Chermayeff, Serge, 208; *Pl. 178*
Chevening, Kent, 106
chimney-pieces, 65–8, 95–6, 102, 112, 116, 117
chinoiserie, 112, 124, 131, 134
Clarendon Palace, Wilts, 33, 37, 40, 42, 44, 48
Classicism, 9, 10, 104, 135, 145
Claydon House, Bucks, 131; *Pls. 109, 110*
Clérisseau, C. L., 142, 145–6, 153, 158; *Pl. 132*
Cole, Henry, 183–4
Coleshill, Berks, 106
Constantinople, 29–32, 51, 54
Contant d'Ivry, Pierre, 138–9
Le Corbusier, 200, 205, 208, 209, 211–14, 215, 219; *Pl. 174*
Corleone, Simone di, 65; *Pl. 48*
Cortona, Pietro da, 73, 88, 89, 90–3, 96, 98, 108, 141, 145; *Pl. 73*
Cuvilliés, François du, 125, 179; *Pl. 99*

D'Annunzio, Gabriele, 197; *Pl. 162*
de Stijl, 205–8
Del Tasso brothers, 65; *Pl. 49*
Delafosse, Jean-Charles, 143
Delamarre, Jacques, *Pl. 176*
della Robbia, Luca, 68–9
Deutscher Werkbund, 204–5, 211
Dollmann, Georg, 179, 180
Dossi, Dosso, 75
Dresden, Zwinger Palace, 125
du Cerceau, Jacques Androuet, 80, 101
Dunand, Jean, 215

Eastlake, Charles, 184, 188
Eclecticism, 165–8
Effner, Joseph, 124
Empire style, 152–5, 159, 161
Escorial, 80
Etruscans, 14, 20, 149–50

Falling Water (Pa), *Pl. 170*
Faravelli, Mario, 209; *Pl. 179*
Farnsworth House, 210, 211; *Pl. 181*
Ferrara, Palazzo Schifanoia, 69, 74; *Pl. 51*
Ferrari, Gregorio de, 93
Ferri, Ciro, 93; *Pls. 73, 77*
Feuchère, Léon, 180

Fischer von Erlach, J. B., 109
Florence, 55–7, 76, 152; Accademia, 65; Palazzo Davanzati, 42, 44, 57; *Pl. 33*; Palazzo Gondi, 65–8; Palazzo Medici-Riccardi, 59, 76, 88, 93, 96, 99; *Pl. 80*; Palazzo Pitti, 93, 96, 98, 160; *Pl. 73*; Palazzo Vecchio, 65, 76; *Pls. 39, 40, 49*; Villa Lammi, 74–5
Foligno, Palazzo Trinci, 74
Fontaine, P. F. L., 135, 152, 153–4, 155, 160, 184; *Pl. 129*
Fontainebleau, 79, 80, 97, 101, 102, 121, 139, 143, 154; *Pls. 47, 62, 116*
Fonthill Abbey, 150, 169–72; *Pl. 145*
Francesco di Giorgio, 62, 76
Frank, Jean Michel, 215
Frascati, Villa Falconieri, *Pl. 77*
fresco, 73–6, 88–93

Gabriel, J.-A., 121, 139–42, 143
Garnier, Charles, 145, 175–6, 193
Gaudí, Antoni, 189, 191, 192, 193–5; *Pls. 157, 160*
Genga, Girolamo, 75
Genoa, Palazzo Doria, 71; Palazzo Rosso, 93, 96; Palazzo Spinola, 145, 175; *Pl. 123*
Ghiberti, Lorenzo, 51
Giani, Felice, 159–60
Gibbons, Grinling, 107, 108, 150; *Pl. 89*
Giordano, Luca, 93, 109; *Pl. 80*
Giovanni da Udine, 28, 71, 72, 73, 112, 142, 146; *Pls. 43, 55*
Giuliano da Maiano, 76, 81
Giulio Romano, 72, 73, 75, 79, 146
Gobelins, 96, 98, 100, 150
Godwin, Edward W., 186–8
Goslar, Town Hall, *Pl. 28*
Gothic, 33, 78–9, 80
Gothic Revival, 134, 168–72, 176, 179, 181, 184
Gothick, 131–4, 150, 171
Gowan, James, *Pl. 177*
Granada, Alhambra, 51–4, 80; *Pl. 38*
Gray, Eileen, 215
Greek Revival, 157–8, 161
Grimaldi, G. F., 97; *Pl. 77*
Gropius, Walter, 204, 209; *Pl. 175*
grotesques, 27–8, 69–72, 79, 80, 101, 112, 128, 142, 147–9
Groulet, André, 214–15
Gruppo 7, 209
Guercino, il, 89
Guimard, Hector, 192, 193; *Pl. 161*

Habitat, 219; *Pl. 168*
Haddon Hall, Derbys, *Pl. 69*
Hague, The, Binnenhof, 103; *Pl. 86*
Ham House, Surrey, 104, 107; *Pl. 88*
Hampton Court, 81, 103
Hardwick Hall, Derbys, 84; *Pl. 70*
Harlaxton Manor, Lincs, 177; *Pl. 151*
Heal and Son, 192, 201
Heaton Hall, Lancs, 150
Herculaneum, 9, 11, 14, 15, 18,

23–4, 135, 138; *Pl. 13*
Herland, Hugh, 35
Herrenchiemsee, 176, 177–9, 180; *Pl. 152*
Hesdin, Château de, 43
Heveningham Hall, Suffolk, 150–2; *Pl. 128*
Hicks, David, 216, 218; *Pl. 173*
Hildebrandt, J. L. von, 109
Historicism, 165–9, 175, 181, 184, 188, 192, 199
Hoffmann, Joseph, 195, 204, 211; *Pl. 166*
Hohensalzburg Castle, 48; *Pl. 32*
Holkham Hall, Norfolk, 128, 131
Holland, Henry, 145, 150, 156
Hope, Thomas, 153, 154, 155–6; *Pl. 130*
Hopper, Thomas, *Pl. 144*
Horden, Richard, *Pl. 172*
Horta, Victor, 189–91, 193; *Pl. 159*
Houghton, Norfolk, 128

intarsie, 76, 102
International Style, 208–11, 215

Jeckyll, Thomas, 188
Jefferson, Thomas, 134, 142, 161
Jones, Inigo, 84, 104, 106, 128, 134
Jones, Owen 183–4
Juvarra, Filippo, 88, 158; *Pl. 98*

Karlstein, 51
Kedleston Hall, Derbys, 147, 149; *Pl. 126*
Kent, William, 128, 145
Kimbolton Castle, Hunts, 108
Klenze, Leo von, 160–1
Knole, Kent, *Pl. 66*

Laguerre, Louis, 108
La Mésangère, Pierre de, 155
Landshut, Stadtresidenz, *Pl. 64*
Lanfranco, Giovanni, 89–90
Lanhydrock House, Cornwall, *Pl. 68*
Laurana, Luciano, 62
Laxenburg, 172; *Pl. 147*
Le Blond, J. B. A., 109, 115
Le Brun, Charles, 96, 98, 101, 108, 141
Ledoux, C.-N., 142; *Pl. 115*
Le Lorrain, Louis-Joseph, 143
Lendinara, Cristoforo da, 76
Leonardo da Vinci, 55, 75, 79
Le Pautre, Jean, 95, 101, 102
Le Pautre, Pierre, 111, 112, 113
Lescot, Pierre, 80
Le Vau, Louis, 96, 98, 101, 111, 200
Linderhof, 168, 176, 179–80
Little Moreton Hall, Cheshire, *Pl. 30*
Liudprand, Bishop of Cremona, 29
London, 180; Ashburnham House, 106; Banqueting House, 104; 44 Berkeley Square, 128; Carlton House, 150; *Pl. 120*; Chiswick House, 128, 145; *Pl. 107*; Derby

House, 150; 13 Lincoln's Inn Fields, 156–7; *Pl. 131*; Linley Sambourne House, *Pl. 158*; Northumberland House, *Pls. 117, 124*; 64 Old Church Street, 208; *Pl. 178*; Queen's House, Greenwich, 104; St James's Palace, 81, 186; Schreiber House, *Pl. 177*; Somerset House, 104, 145; Westminster Hall, 35, 36; Westminster Palace, 37, 42
Longthorpe Tower, Northants, 42; *Pl. 29*
Lorenzetti, Pietro, 44
L'Orme, Philibert de, 79, 80, 102
Los Angeles, Ennis House, 204; *Pl. 167*; Lovell House, 210; *Pl. 171*

Mackintosh, C. R., 189, 191–3, 195–7, 214; *Pl. 1*
McMillen Inc., 218
Madrid, Royal Palace, 93, 120; *Pls. 103, 135*
Maisons Laffitte, 97, 99; *Pl. 83*
Malmaison, Château de, 154; *Pl. 136*
Mannerism, 55, 72–3, 79, 84, 88, 96, 104
Mansart, F., 96, 97–8, 100, 111; *Pl. 83*
Mansart, J.-H., 98, 102, 111–12, 113, 120, 121
Mantegna, Andrea, 55, 75; *Pl. 44*
Mantua, Palazzo del Te, 73, 75, 79; Palazzo Ducale, 55, 65, 71, 74, 75; *Pl. 44*
marble, 17, 30, 93–5, 117
Marmion (Va), *Pl. 111*
Marot, Daniel, 102–4, 112; *Pl. 86*
Maser, Villa Barbaro, 55; *Pl. 42*
Meissonier, J. A., 120–1, 131, 138
Melk, Monastery of, *Pl. 102*
La Ménagerie, Château de, 113
Mendelsohn, Erich, 208, 209; *Pl. 178*
Meyer, Adolf, *Pl. 175*
Mies van der Rohe, Ludwig, 181, 200, 204, 205, 208, 209–11, 214, 219; *Pls. 180, 181*
Milan, Castello Sforzesco, 75
mirrors, 99, 112, 113, 116–17, 125
Modernism, 204, 205, 214, 215, 219
Moreau-Desproux, P.-L., 143
Morris, William, 180, 183–6, 188, 191, 201, 216; *Pl. 155*
mosaics, 11–12, 15, 17–20, 29, 32, 68
Munich, 153; Atelier Elvire, *Pl. 164*; Residenz, 109, 125, 161, 179; *Pl. 104*; Villa Stuck, 214; *Pl. 163*

Naranco, 34–5
Naro, Cecco di, 65; *Pl. 48*
Nero, Emperor, 22, 24–7
Neuschwanstein, 168, 176, 179; *Pl. 150*
Neutra, R. J., 210; *Pl. 171*
New York, Chanin Building, *Pl. 176*
Nonesuch Palace, 81
Nostell Priory, Yorks, *Pl. 108*

Odo the Goldsmith, 42, 43–4
Oppenordt, G.-M., 116, 120, 121, 124
Orchard, The, Chorleywood, 201; *Pl. 169*

Osterley Park House, Middx, 143, 147, 149, 150; *Pl. 127*
Ostia, House of Cupid and Psyche, *Pl. 15*
Palagi, Pelagio, 160, 171
Palazzina di Caccia, Stupinigi, *Pl. 98*
Palermo, Palace of La Zisa, 51; *Pl. 34*; Palazzina Cinese, *Pl. 138*; Palazzo Chiaramonte, 65; *Pl. 48*; Royal Palace, 51; *Pl. 37*
Palladianism, 104, 106, 120, 126–31, 134, 135, 145, 147, 160
Palladio, Andrea, 10, 58, 59, 63, 75, 80, 104, 128, 135, 145, 150, 218; *Pl. 60*
Paris, 96–7, 116; Hôtel de Beauharnais, 154; *Pl. 137*; Hôtel Lambert, 98, 101; Hôtel de Lassay, 120; Hôtel Lauzun, *Pl. 81*; Hôtel de Maisons, 121; Hôtel de Païva, 175; *Pl. 149*; Hôtel de Soubise, 116, 121, 138; *Pl. 96*; Hôtel de Toulouse, 116; *Pl. 97*; Hôtel d'Uzès, 142; Louvre, 80, 98, 106, 168, 175; Opéra, 175, 193
Pella, 11; *Pl. 2*
Pellegrini, G. A., 108, 131
Penrhyn Castle, *Pl. 144*
Penshurst Place, Kent, 35, 36; *Pl. 21*
Percier, Charles, 135, 152, 153–4, 155, 160, 184; *Pl. 129*
Perugia, Collegio del Cambio, 70; *Pl. 52*
Perugino, 70; *Pl. 52*
Peruzzi, Baldassare, 71, 75, 145, 154; *Pl. 57*
Pesaro, Palazzo della Prefettura, 71; Villa Imperiale, 71, 75
Piero della Francesca, 62, 76
Pierrefonds, 168, 176, 179
Pineau, Nicolas, 120, 121, 138
Piranesi, G. B., 138, 142–3, 146, 154, 156, 158, 160, 165
plasterwork, 106–7, 125
Plateresque style, 80
Pliny the Elder, 10–15, 17, 21, 22, 23, 24, 25
Poggio a Caiano, Villa Medicea, 55; *Pl. 41*
Poitiers, Palais des Contes, 35, 37; *Pl. 22*
Pollaiuolo, Antonio, 74
Pompeii, 9, 11, 13, 14–15, 18–24, 135, 138; *Pls. 5, 7, 10, 17*
Porden, William, 171
Portland, Victoria Mansion, *Pl. 141*
Post-Modernism, 211
Pozzo, Andrea, 93
Prague, Vladislav Hall, 35–6
Pratt, Sir Roger, 104–6, 107, 108
Preti, Mattia, 93
Primaticcio, Francesco, 79, 101; *Pls. 47, 62*
Pugin, A. W., 171–2, 181, 183

Queen Anne Style, 184, 186

Rambouillet, 121
Raphael, 55, 69, 70, 71, 75, 77, 100, 101, 112, 142, 146, 150, 154, 170; *Pls. 53, 54*

Rastrelli, Bartolomeo, 109
Red House, Bexleyheath, 184
Ricci, Sebastiano, 93, 111, 131
Ridolfi, Bartolomeo, *Pl. 59*
Rietveld, Gerrit, 205–8
Ring, Hermann Tom, *Pl. 65*
Romanticism, 150, 159, 165–8, 173, 175–6
Rome, 57, 88, 158–9; Cancellaria Palace, 71, 75, 88; *Pl. 58*; Casino Ludovisi, 89; Farnese Gallery, 69; Golden House of Nero, 15, 17, 18, 23, 24–7, 29, 30, 71; *Pl. 6*; Palazzo Barberini, 93, 96, 158; Palazzo Chigi, 158; *Pl. 139*; Palazzo Colonna, 93, 95, 99; *Pl. 79*; Palazzo Falconieri, *Pl. 75*; Palazzo Farnese, 88; *Pl. 76*; Palazzo Mattei, 96; Palazzo Ricci Sacchetti, 75–6, 89; Palazzo Spada, 79; *Pl. 56*; Quirinal Palace, 93, 96, 158; Tomb of the Pancrazi, 28; *Pl. 16*; Trinità dei Monti, 158; *Pl. 132*; Vatican, 69, 70, 71, 72, 73, 75, 79, 89, 142; *Pls. 43, 53*; Villa Borghese, 90, 158; Villa di Papa Giulio, 73; Villa Farnesina, 21, 27, 71, 75; *Pl. 57*; Villa Madama, 70, 71, 72, 150; *Pl. 54*
Rosso Fiorentino, 79; *Pl. 62*
Rousham House, Oxon, 128
Ruhlmann, Jacques-Emile, 214; *Pl. 184*

Sabatelli, Luigi, 160
St Petersburg, 109, 153
St-Pôl, Château de, 43
Saltram House, Devon, *Pl. 125*
Salviati, Francesco, 75–6; *Pl. 55*
Sammezano, *Pl. 143*
San Gallo, Giuliano da, 65–8; *Pl. 41*
Schinkel, K. F., 160, 209; *Pl. 134*
Schloss Brühl, 125; *Pl. 104*
Schloss Nymphenburg, 124–5
Schloss Pommersfelden, *Pl. 106*
Schlüter, Andreas, 109
Schmidt, Joost, *Pl. 175*
Schröder, Rudolf A., 204
Scott, Sir Walter, 168, 172
Second Empire style, 175–6, 179, 180
Serlio, Sebastiano, 79–80, 102, 104; *Pl. 63*
Serpotta, Giovanni, 96
Settignano, Desiderio da, 68
Sezession, 195–7, 214
Smith, Maurice, *Pl. 182*
Soane, Sir John, 156–7, 170, 171
Soffiano, Villa Carducci, 74
Stowe, Bucks, 171
strapwork, 79, 80, 81, 104
Strawberry Hill, Twickenham, 134, 169, 171, 172; *Pls. 112, 113*
stucco, 27–8, 88, 96, 125
Sudbury Hall, Derbys, 107; *Pl. 89*
Syon House, Middx, 145, 147, 149; *Pl. 119*

tapestries, 46–8, 93, 100–1
Tattenbach Palace, *Pl. 99*
Terragni, Giuseppe, 209
Tiepolo, G. B., 75, 93

Tiffany, Louis Comfort, 192, 197
tiles, 39–40, 68–9
Tivoli, Hadrian's Villa, 18, 25, 27, 28, 31, 138, 149
Toro, Jean Bernard, 116, 121
Torrigiano, Pietro, 81
Tressini, Domenico, 109
Troubadour Style, 172–3
Turin, Palazzo Reale, *Pls. 72, 94*

Uccello, Paolo, 65, 76; *Pl. 50*
Urbino, Ducal Palace, 58, 62–5, 70, 74, 76; *Pls. 45, 46*
Utrecht, Schröder House, 205–8

Val de Recel, Château de, 43
Van de Velde, Henry, 191
Van Rensselaer Manor House, Albany, *Pl. 114*
Vasari, Giorgio, 51, 68–9, 71, 73–4, 75, 76, 79; *Pl. 39*
Vaux-le-Vicomte, 98, 112
Venice, 29, 65, 74, 76, 88, 99; Palazzo Albrizzi, 96; Palazzo Ducale, 76; *Pl. 60*; Palazzo Foscari, 77; Palazzo Grimani, 72; *Pl. 55*; Palazzo Pesaro, *Pl. 74*; Palazzo Sagredo, 96; *Pl. 78*; Scuolo di San Rocco, 76
Verbeckt, Jacques, 121
Versailles, 80, 85, 95, 96, 98–101, 102, 109, 111–12, 113, 116, 117, 121, 125, 139–42, 168, 173, 177–9, 180; *Pls. 84, 85, 93, 118*
Vicenza, Palazzo Thiene, *Pl. 59*; Villa Valmarana, 75
Vienna, Palais Liechtenstein, 177
Vignola, G. B. da, 73, 80
Villa Savoye, *Pl. 174*
Viollet-le-Duc, E., 176, 181, 189, 192
Vitruvius, 10–15, 18, 21, 22, 59, 62, 63, 79–80, 128, 138
Voysey, C. F. A., 191, 193, 201; *Pl. 169*
Vranov Castle, 109
Vredeman de Vries, Hans, 103, 104

Waddesdon Manor, Bucks, 175, 176–7
Wailly, Charles de, 143–5, 158, 175; *Pl. 123*
wall paintings, 20–2, 40–3, 44; *see also* fresco
Webb, John, 104, 106
Webb, Philip, 184; *Pl. 156*
Weikersheim, 67
Whistler, J. A. M., 186–8; *Pl. 154*
Wilton House, Wilts, 104, 107; *Pl. 87*
Winckelmann, J. J., 135, 138, 158
windows, 23, 37–8, 101
Windsor Castle, 36, 44, 107–8, 150
wood carving, 107
Wren, Christopher, 106, 108, 128
Wright, Frank Lloyd, 201–4, 208, 209, 210, 216; *Pls. 167, 170*
Würzburg, 153; Residenz, 125; *Pl. 105*
Wyatt, James, 134, 145, 150–2, 153, 156, 169, 171

Zuber, Jean, 172